PROFESSIONAL
SHAREPOINT® 2010 BRANDING AND
USER INTERFACE DESIGN

PROFESSIONAL

SharePoint® 2010 Branding and User Interface Design

Randy Drisgill
John Ross
Jacob J. Sanford
Paul Stubbs
Larry Riemann

WILEY

Wiley Publishing, Inc.

Professional SharePoint® 2010 Branding and User Interface Design

Published by
Wiley Publishing, Inc.
10475 Crosspoint Boulevard
Indianapolis, IN 46256
www.wiley.com

Published simultaneously in Canada

ISBN: 978-0-470-58464-4
ISBN: 978-1-118-01759-3 (ebk)
ISBN: 978-1-118-01843-9 (ebk)
ISBN: 978-1-118-01844-6 (ebk)

Manufactured in the United States of America

10 9 8 7 6 5 4 3 2

For general information on our other products and services please contact our Customer Care Department within the United States at (877) 762-2974, outside the United States at (317) 572-3993 or fax (317) 572-4002.

Wiley also publishes its books in a variety of electronic formats. Some content that appears in print may not be available in electronic books.

Library of Congress Control Number: 2010932458

Dedicated to waffles (thank you for being delicious) and to Jackie (the love of my life) for always being there to eat them with me.

— RANDY DRISGILL

To my dad, who was convinced that my dirty room as a child was a sign I'd become a deviant. I'm glad he had the chance to see my first book and wish he was still here to see this one, which was written in my dirty office. Thanks for always pushing me to be the best. Miss you, dad!

— JOHN ROSS

To my beautiful wife, Shannan, and my kids, Matt, Hayden, and Wendy. You guys are way too funny, and I would much rather play with you than work or write. So thank you for understanding and letting me get another book done.

— JACOB J. SANFORD

I dedicate this book to my son, Kevin, who has achieved more as a teenager than most people have in a lifetime.

— PAUL STUBBS

To Dina and Emily: I love you both very much.

— LARRY RIEMANN

CREDITS

ACQUISITIONS EDITOR
Paul Reese

PROJECT EDITOR
John Sleeva

TECHNICAL EDITORS
Ryan Keller
Heather Waterman

PRODUCTION EDITOR
Rebecca Anderson

COPY EDITOR
Luann Rouff

EDITORIAL DIRECTOR
Robyn B. Siesky

EDITORIAL MANAGER
Mary Beth Wakefield

FREELANCER EDITORIAL MANAGER
Rosemarie Graham

ASSOCIATE DIRECTOR OF MARKETING
David Mayhew

PRODUCTION MANAGER
Tim Tate

**VICE PRESIDENT AND
EXECUTIVE GROUP PUBLISHER**
Richard Swadley

**VICE PRESIDENT AND
EXECUTIVE PUBLISHER**
Barry Pruett

ASSOCIATE PUBLISHER
Jim Minatel

PROJECT COORDINATOR, COVER
Lynsey Stanford

COMPOSITOR
Jeff Lytle, Happenstance Type-O-Rama

PROOFREADER
Nancy Carrasco

INDEXER
Robert Swanson

COVER DESIGNER
Michael E. Trent

COVER IMAGE
© Martin Alfaro/istockphoto.com

ABOUT THE AUTHORS

 RANDY DRISGILL has been working with SharePoint911 as their branding and design lead since 2008. He has more than 10 years of experience developing, designing, and implementing web-based applications for clients ranging from small business to Fortune 500 companies. For the past three years, he has been working exclusively with SharePoint products and technologies and has worked on many large-scale internal and public-facing SharePoint 2007 and 2010 branding projects. Randy is an active member of the SharePoint community, having contributed to several articles and books on the topic, as well as being the co-founder / co-manager of the Orlando SharePoint User Group (OSPUG). In 2009, Microsoft recognized Randy as an authority on SharePoint branding by awarding him MVP status for SharePoint Server. Randy lives in Orlando, Florida with his wife and best friend, Jackie, their two cats, and their dog, Frito. You can find Randy online on Twitter as @Drisgill or at his blog, `http://blog.drisgill.com`.

 JOHN ROSS is a Sr. Consultant for SharePoint911 from Orlando, FL, with more than eight years of experience implementing solutions for clients ranging from small businesses to Fortune 500 companies, as well as governmental organizations. He has been involved with a wide range of SharePoint solutions, including public-facing Internet sites, corporate intranets, and extranets. Additionally, John is co-founder of the Orlando SharePoint User Group (`www.orlandosharepoint.com`). His blog can be found at `www.sharepoint911.com/blogs/john`.

 JACOB J. SANFORD is a senior consultant for Cornerstone Software Services in Tallahassee, FL. He has been working with web application development using Microsoft technologies for more than 10 years, specializing in .NET solutions since the 1.0/1.1 Framework. Jacob is a frequent speaker at local and regional .NET and SharePoint events and is the founder of the Tallahassee SharePoint Experts Exchange for Developers (SPEED), a SharePoint User Group in Tallahassee, FL. He has written three previous books for Wrox: *ASP.NET 2.0 Design* (September 2007), *Professional Microsoft SharePoint 2007 Design* (September 2008), and *Professional Microsoft SharePoint Server 2007 Reporting with SQL Server 2008 Reporting Services* (September 2009). With the media blitz on HTML5 and CSS3, Jacob has renewed his vigor for design and branding topics and loves talking to anyone he can about these topics. Lately, he mostly focuses on design standards and technologies and organizes sessions on these topics when he can. He currently lives in Tallahassee, FL with his wife, Shannan, and three kids, Matthew, Hayden, and Wendy.

PAUL STUBBS is a Microsoft Technical Evangelist for SharePoint and Office, where he focuses on the information worker development community around SharePoint and Office, Silverlight, and Web 2.0 social networking. He has authored three books on solution development using Microsoft Office, SharePoint, and Silverlight; several articles for *MSDN Magazine* and *SharePoint Pro Magazine*; and has also spoken at Microsoft Tech-Ed, PDC, SharePoint Conference, DevConnections and Tech-Ready conferences around the world. Paul has also worked as a Senior Program Manager with the Visual Studio Tools for Office (VSTO) team in Redmond, Washington. Paul is a Microsoft Certified Trainer (MCT) and has received Microsoft Certified Applications Developer (MCAD) and Microsoft Certified Solution Developer (MCSD) certifications. Paul also frequently participates in the developer community on the Microsoft forums. Paul also started a developer focused show on MSDN's Channel 9 site called the SharePoint Sideshow, where he teaches future SharePoint developers how to get started. Visit Paul's blog at blogs.msdn.com/pstubbs for a lot of deep SharePoint developer information.

LARRY RIEMANN has more than 16 years of experience architecting and creating business applications for some of the world's largest companies. Larry is an independent consultant who owns Indigo Integrations and does SharePoint consulting exclusively through SharePoint911. He writes articles for publication, is a contributing author on another book, and occasionally speaks at conferences. For the last several years, he has been focused on SharePoint, creating and extending functionality where SharePoint leaves off. In addition to working with SharePoint, Larry is an accomplished .NET Architect and has extensive expertise in systems integration, enterprise architecture and high availability solutions. You can find Larry on his blog, at http://lriemann.blogspot.com.

ABOUT THE TECHNICAL EDITORS

RYAN KELLER has been working with SharePoint technologies since 2007 and has worked as a consultant with SharePoint911 since 2009. Prior to joining the SharePoint911 team, he worked for Boulder Valley School District, where he got his first introduction to SharePoint. He has since worked with many companies and organizations troubleshooting issues and helping them plan successful SharePoint deployments. In addition, Ryan helped author and edit material related to SharePoint 2010 for Microsoft. He was a contributing author on *Professional SharePoint 2010 Administration*, and a technical editor for *Beginning SharePoint Designer 2010*. Ryan lives in Firestone, Colorado with his wife, Brittany, their two dogs and a cat. He and his wife are expecting their first child in April 2011.

HEATHER WATERMAN is the Director of the Visual Design Team at the Washington DC-based Synteractive, Inc. She is responsible for leading the designers and developers, with an emphasis on web design for SharePoint. She has more than 10 years of web design and development experience, the past four with a primary focus on SharePoint branding. With these skills, she has quickly become a leader in the SharePoint branding community. Her current SharePoint branding projects include Recovery.gov and Treasury.gov, among others. On each of these, she leveraged her expertise in SharePoint branding, design, and development to create unique and functional sites.

Prior to joining Synteractive, Heather was the President and CEO of the Waterman Design Group, during which time she developed website templates for resell and developed SharePoint designs for clients that include a major oil company, a major pharmaceutical company, and a leading appliance manufacturer. When not working on client projects, Heather actively contributes design and branding time to the community by developing blogs and sites for other community leaders. You can find her on Twitter as @hwaterman or via her blog at www.heatherwaterman.com.

ACKNOWLEDGMENTS

AS A READER of many technical books, I was never really aware of the amount of effort and long nights that go into making them. A few years ago, I worked on my first technical book and quickly realized that my dreams of retiring rich and famous after spending a few nights writing were nothing more than a fever dream. For this book, I experienced a whole new set of challenges trying to rapidly gather tons of information about SharePoint 2010 branding and putting that knowledge to the test on real-world projects before the author team could even start writing. Because of this, I have a lot of different people to thank for making the book a reality.

First, obviously, the writing team on this book really went the distance to make sure we created the best collection of SharePoint 2010 branding knowledge that we knew how to create, in what ended up being a fairly compressed schedule by the time the final bits for SharePoint 2010 were released to us. This includes Jacob J. Sanford, Paul Stubbs, Larry Riemann, and, of course, my partner in crime, John Ross. John Ross deserves a special shout out for being the inspiration for one of the major focuses for the book. His idea was to not only put out a book that would serve to help out people who need to do extremely custom SharePoint branding, but to also focus a good portion of the book on those that are new to these concepts and need to just add a little style to their SharePoint sites.

Along with the writing team, another obvious big thanks goes out to everyone at Wrox who helped us get this book to you. This includes Paul Reese, John Sleeva, David Mayhew, Rebecca Anderson, and probably several other people behind the scenes. They not only helped us sound intelligent but also put together a really great looking book. We also owe a great deal of thanks to our technical editors, Ryan Keller and Heather Waterman, for putting in the long hours to make sure all of our chapters were both technically sound and easy to follow.

I want to personally thank several folks who helped answer questions about new features in SharePoint 2010 at all hours of the night. Primarily, this job fell to the amazing Elisabeth Olson, who took a lot of time out of her work day (where she was actually building parts of SharePoint 2010) to help me understand everything I was doing wrong. Some of the other people who helped me either with understanding SharePoint 2010 or by allowing me to pick their brains and bounce questions off them include, in no particular order: Kevin Davis (AWESOME), Arpan Shah, Dallas Tester, Chris Johnson, Dave Pae, Greg Chan, Randall Isenhour, Rob Howard, Andrew Connell, Ted Pattison, Heather Solomon, Heather Waterman, all the SharePoint MVPs, and everyone on the SharePoint 2010 product team, for creating a truly great web content management system. Without the help of all these people, I'm sure the book would have been lacking in many ways.

A special thanks goes out to Shane and Nicola Young for creating SharePoint911 and not only employing me, but for allowing all their employees to take the time to truly understand SharePoint 2010 completely, to contribute actively to the SharePoint community, and, ultimately, to have the time to create books like this one. All my co-workers deserve heartfelt thanks for being an awesome team and for helping me in many ways with this book: Chris Caravajal, Jennifer Hammond, Jennifer Mason, John Ross, Larry Riemann, Laura Rogers, Ryan Keller, and Todd Klindt.

Lastly, I need to thank all my friends and family who put up with me working long hours through-out several months to put together this book. Most of them have no idea what I do for a living and will probably never read past this paragraph, but I couldn't have done it without all your friendship and support throughout the years. This includes my beautiful wife, Jackie Drisgill; my parents, Pat and Tom Drisgill; my in-laws, Debbie and Dave Auerbach; Adam McCard; Marcela Errazquin; Jenn and Mark Clemons; Vanessa and John Ross; Jason Montilla; Nik and Katy Molnar; Joshua Witter; Rachel Rappaport; and all my other past and present Orlando friends: You know who you are!

— RANDY DRISGILL

THIS BOOK WAS MADE possible through the hard work of many people. First, I'd like to thank the rest of the author team. This book originally was conceived before any of us had seen SharePoint 2010, which made for a huge challenge. All the authors worked tirelessly to compile the information for this book, even when the necessary details didn't yet exist. Great job, Randy, Jacob, Paul, and Larry! You guys are awesome.

To the technical editors, Heather Waterman and Ryan Keller, thanks for keeping us honest. In the end, your efforts have made this book better. We couldn't have picked two nicer folks to pore over these chapters and make sure we all sound smart. Thank you both!

Thanks to Elisabeth Olson and the rest of the SharePoint Team at Microsoft for answering our many questions throughout this process!

Thanks to the team at Wrox for giving us the opportunity to write this book and helping us get it out the door. To Paul Reese and John Sleeva, and the rest of the editing team, thanks for putting up with us through all the ups and downs.

To the entire SharePoint911 team, I couldn't ask for a better group of people to work with. I've never worked harder and had more fun doing it!

I would like to especially thank my wife, Vanessa, who thought I was crazy for wanting to write another book. You are the best. I love you! And to my kids, Ben and Julia, I love you both. I'm sure someday when you both grow up and look at this book that Daddy wrote, you'll be disappointed to learn it isn't about cool motorcycles. It is okay; just make sure to keep telling your friends it's a motorcycle book.

To my family and friends, I hope to be spending more time with you all now that this book is done. See, I wasn't just making it up when I said I couldn't do something because I had to write a book.

Finally, I'd like to say thanks to Randy Drisgill. This whole book was mostly your fault and likely hatched over a burrito at lunch. If this book makes us rich and famous, I think we should just buy a Chipotle franchise. You owe me about a billion dollars in gas money for picking you up every day. Seriously, though, thanks for making the dynamite go boom.

— JOHN ROSS

I WOULD LIKE TO FIRST acknowledge all the folks at Wrox for their dedication, persistence, and cooperation in the efforts to get this book out. There were times that each of us probably wondered if this book was going to actually make it to the shelf. Because of your endurance and help, we made it. I cannot thank you enough.

I would also like to thank all the folks who have helped me on my path in the last few years to get to where I am today. Marsha Ryan took a chance on hiring me and letting me start learning code on my own years ago, and I have never, and will never, forget that. David Drinkwine has helped me make the leap from local developer to a real consultant and has remained an amazing friend throughout. Keith Rowe helped me get back home when I got tired of the road and his consul, both professionally and personally, and he has meant more to me than he will ever know. While I only mention these three, if I have worked with you or for you, you are part of my success and I am forever grateful.

I would like to thank all my family. My father, for being the inspiration for my first book. He taught me how cool it was to be an author and provided the confidence (and hard headedness) to get through the first one. My mother, who has always been one of my best friends, when I needed that, and my mother, when I needed that. My brother and his family, for helping me understand what family means and for being there to help support me and my family. My wife and kids, for being the best things that ever happened to me, for being my constant inspiration in everything I do, and my eternal north star for where I need to be going.

Finally, I would like to thank my friends. Thanks for keeping me grounded and not letting me forget where I came from. You don't know how much I need that sometimes, and I'll always love you guys, even if we only get to hang out once a week or even once a month. Thank you.

— JACOB J. SANFORD

I WOULD LIKE TO THANK Randy Drisgill and John Ross at SharePoint 911 for giving me the opportunity to contribute to this book.

— PAUL STUBBS

IN MY BEST RICHMEISTER VOICE, Randy-y-y...Rando-o-o...Randomly selected for your listening pleasure...The Randinator. Thank you for getting me on this project and finding a way to keep me on it even though other obligations limited my contributions.

John, Jacob, and Paul, thank you for letting me help and contribute where I could. Also, thank you to all the folks at Wrox and to John Sleeva.

Mr. Shane Young, you are next; thank you for pulling me into the SharePoint world. I call him Mr. because admins like to feel important (it helps them get through the day). All kidding aside, I thank you; it has been a fun ride.

I would also like to thank my mom and dad for all of their love and support throughout my life. Dad, thank you for buying me my first several computers and showing me that a computer can be used for something other than playing games. (Remember the baseball stats program?)

I hear the music playing, so I better wrap this up. I saved the best for last. Dina and Emily, where would my life be without you? I love you (and any new possible additions) more than I will ever be able to tell you. Dina, thank you for all your love and support. Thank you for putting up with the late nights, the travel, and, at times, the uncertainty of what I do. I love you both very much.

— LARRY RIEMANN

CONTENTS

FOREWORD

Whenever I talk to people at a conference about SharePoint, invariably I am approached by someone — who has never worked with SharePoint before — and asked, "So, what is SharePoint? What does it do?" These questions tend to flummox me a little, because SharePoint is an extremely flexible tool that can do just about anything. Companies use SharePoint to put up small internal sites for specific projects, huge corporate intranets, extranets for those working at home or abroad, or even Internet-facing websites. In fact, if you're the average Internet user, I'd bet you've visited quite a few sites in just the last week without realizing that they were built on SharePoint.

Of course, it's no longer enough to be simply functional. Today, experiences must be eye-catching, clean, and designed specifically for their own purpose. It's vital that with a single glance, a user knows where they are and what they can do on the site. Providing that kind of experience involves at least a few elements of custom design.

While the new theming engine in SharePoint 2010 is quite powerful and allows you to pick any custom colors and fonts you'd like to use to theme your site, colors and fonts are often just a piece of the larger design. Custom images, layouts, navigation, site structure, and more are vital parts of a custom design, but using those with SharePoint can require specific knowledge of the way SharePoint works and how to fit branding into it.

If anyone knows about branding SharePoint 2010, it's Randy Drisgill and John Ross. As soon as we started the beta program for SharePoint 2010, the two of them immediately rolled up their sleeves and got to work. They both already had a store of knowledge about how to brand earlier versions of SharePoint, and they quickly caught on to the new features we'd added, as well as the old features we'd changed. I loved talking to them about what they were doing. My favorite part of the conversation was when they explained how cool something in the new product was, because I got to say, "Yeah, that was my feature."

John, Randy, and the top-notch author team that they've assembled for this book have put countless hours into exploring every piece of SharePoint 2010 and how each piece interacts with the others. They've distilled that knowledge into this book, which will enable you to brand your own SharePoint projects quickly and easily.

Specialized, gorgeous designs are rapidly becoming the norm, even on internal sites. The skills you'll gain from this book will be vital to creating a successful SharePoint 2010 site.

— Elisabeth Olson
SharePoint Program Manager
Microsoft Corporation

INTRODUCTION

WHEN IT COMES TO working with SharePoint, there always seems to be a gap between developers and designers. To make the SharePoint user interface really look nice requires a designer who is comfortable with design theory and traditional web technologies and has the ability to deal with topics that are traditionally handled by developers. When you first look at trying to brand a SharePoint site, it can often seem like an insurmountable task; designing for SharePoint is different from designing for your own website or your own custom code. Designing for SharePoint involves overriding and adjusting a design to fit within someone else's code — in this case, Microsoft's out-of-the-box SharePoint code. But don't be alarmed. This book aims to provide you with all the knowledge and techniques you need to bridge the gap.

Not everyone who picks up this book is looking to become the next Picasso of SharePoint. For those readers, a portion of the book is dedicated to understanding just enough about SharePoint branding to apply some custom style to their sites. Parts I and II of the book introduce SharePoint branding and provide simple techniques for making SharePoint look like something other than Microsoft's default user interface. Some of the other topics covered in the book include understanding what's new in SharePoint 2010, planning for branding projects, an overview of SharePoint Designer 2010, working with SharePoint navigation, Cascading Style Sheets (CSS), master pages, page layouts, Web Parts, and Extensible Stylesheet Language Transformation (XSLT), how to deploy branding to a production server, and even how to use JavaScript, jQuery, and Silverlight with SharePoint 2010.

WHO THIS BOOK IS FOR

One of the most common SharePoint branding requests you might hear is to make your site "not look like SharePoint." In many organizations, this request might be made to someone who wears many hats but isn't specifically a web designer. In other cases, the request might be made to a web designer or even a business user. To many of those users, SharePoint branding might simply mean that you want to change some colors and put your company header at the top of the page, while other users are looking to create a public-facing Internet site with a cutting-edge design. This book is intended for a wide range of readers and skill levels. Parts I and II cover introductory topics, including some simple branding techniques for SharePoint. If you are experienced with SharePoint branding, you can probably breeze through these chapters on the way to the more in-depth topics. However, the first two Parts contain a lot of information that is important to understand, so they are recommended reading for both beginners and advanced readers.

WHAT THIS BOOK COVERS

This book is focused on branding for both SharePoint Foundation 2010 and SharePoint Server 2010. Also, while many of the concepts have remained similar wherever possible, concepts that have changed from SharePoint 2007 have been highlighted. The book begins by discussing how to get started with SharePoint branding, followed by a discussion of what's new in SharePoint 2010 that affects branding. Next, you will learn how to properly plan for a SharePoint branding project and you will learn about some simple branding techniques as well as how to work with the SharePoint navigation. Each major technology involved in SharePoint branding gets its own chapter, including Cascading Style Sheets, master pages, page layouts, Web Parts, and deployment. Lastly, some advanced topics are covered, including working with the SharePoint 2010 ribbon, the client-side object model, jQuery, and Silverlight.

HOW THIS BOOK IS STRUCTURED

This book is divided into three primary sections. Part I covers the basics of SharePoint and SharePoint branding; Part II discusses more of the simple and intermediate SharePoint branding topics; Parts II and IV cover the more advanced topics. The primary goal is to provide a reference for the reader that would serve as a guide regardless of the reader's specific skill level. Although you can certainly use the book as a reference for specific topics, some of the examples throughout the book build on each other. By the end of the book, you will have learned how to work with all the technology needed to create a fully branded SharePoint site.

WHAT YOU NEED TO USE THIS BOOK

Having a SharePoint 2010 installation available to follow along with the examples will definitely make a big difference when reading this book. If you don't have access to a dedicated SharePoint 2010 server, you can install SharePoint 2010 on a virtual machine to try it out locally. You will also want to install SharePoint Designer 2010, which is a free download from Microsoft. Also, the last few chapters focus on advanced topics that require Visual Studio 2010. Furthermore, you may also need to have some traditional web-design programs, such as Adobe Dreamweaver, Adobe Photoshop, or Microsoft Expression Studio. The following list can get you started with software for following along with the book:

➤ **Download a pre-built Windows Server 2008 R2 Hyper-V virtual machine** — www.microsoft.com/downloads/details .aspx?FamilyID=751fa0d1-356c-4002-9c60-d539896c66ce&displaylang=en

➤ **Instructions for installing your own instance of SharePoint 2010** — msdn.microsoft .com/en-us/library/ee554869.aspx

➤ **SharePoint Designer 2010** — www.microsoft.com/downloads/details .aspx?FamilyID=d88a1505-849b-4587-b854-a7054ee28d66&displaylang=en

➤ **Visual Studio 2010** — www.microsoft.com/visualstudio/en-us

➤ **Adobe** — www.adobe.com

➤ **Microsoft Expression Studio** — www.microsoft.com/expression/

Having some knowledge of SharePoint 2007 or ASP.NET will also be helpful, but it is not required. Wherever possible, the SharePoint 2010 experience is compared to how things worked in SharePoint 2007 or in traditional ASP.NET applications.

CONVENTIONS

To help you get the most from the text and keep track of what's happening, we've used a number of conventions throughout the book.

 Boxes like this one hold important, not-to-be forgotten information that is directly relevant to the surrounding text.

 Notes, tips, hints, tricks, and asides to the current discussion are offset and placed in italics like this.

As for styles in the text:

➤ We *highlight* new terms and important words when we introduce them.

➤ We show keyboard strokes like this: Ctrl+A.

➤ We show file names, URLs, and code within the text like so: `persistence.properties`.

➤ We present code in two different ways:

```
We use a monofont type with no highlighting for most code examples.
We use bold highlighting to emphasize code that is of particular importance in the
present context.
```

SOURCE CODE

As you work through the examples in this book, you may choose either to type in all the code manually or to use the source code files that accompany the book. All of the source code used in this book is available for download at `www.wrox.com`. Once at the site, simply locate the book's title (either by using the Search box or by using one of the title lists) and click the Download Code link on the book's detail page to obtain all the source code for the book.

 Because many books have similar titles, you may find it easiest to search by ISBN; this book's ISBN is 978-0-470-58464-4.

Once you download the code, just decompress it with your favorite compression tool. Alternately, you can go to the main Wrox code download page at www.wrox.com/dynamic/books/download .aspx to see the code available for this book and all other Wrox books.

ERRATA

We make every effort to ensure that there are no errors in the text or in the code. However, no one is perfect, and mistakes do occur. If you find an error in one of our books, like a spelling mistake or faulty piece of code, we would be very grateful for your feedback. By sending in errata you may save another reader hours of frustration and at the same time you will be helping us provide even higher quality information.

To find the errata page for this book, go to www.wrox.com and locate the title using the Search box or one of the title lists. Then, on the book details page, click the Book Errata link. On this page you can view all errata that has been submitted for this book and posted by Wrox editors. A complete book list including links to each book's errata is also available at www.wrox.com/misc-pages/booklist.shtml.

If you don't spot "your" error on the Book Errata page, go to www.wrox.com/contact/ techsupport.shtml and complete the form there to send us the error you have found. We'll check the information and, if appropriate, post a message to the book's errata page and fix the problem in subsequent editions of the book.

P2P.WROX.COM

For author and peer discussion, join the P2P forums at p2p.wrox.com. The forums are a Web-based system for you to post messages relating to Wrox books and related technologies and interact with other readers and technology users. The forums offer a subscription feature to e-mail you topics of interest of your choosing when new posts are made to the forums. Wrox authors, editors, other industry experts, and your fellow readers are present on these forums.

At p2p.wrox.com you will find a number of different forums that will help you not only as you read this book, but also as you develop your own applications. To join the forums, just follow these steps:

1. Go to p2p.wrox.com and click the Register link.

2. Read the terms of use and click Agree.

3. Complete the required information to join as well as any optional information you wish to provide and click Submit.

4. You will receive an e-mail with information describing how to verify your account and complete the joining process.

You can read messages in the forums without joining P2P, but in order to post your own messages, you must join.

Once you join, you can post new messages and respond to messages other users post. You can read messages at any time on the Web. If you would like to have new messages from a particular forum e-mailed to you, click the Subscribe to this Forum icon by the forum name in the forum listing.

For more information about how to use the Wrox P2P, be sure to read the P2P FAQs for answers to questions about how the forum software works as well as many common questions specific to P2P and Wrox books. To read the FAQs, click the FAQ link on any P2P page.

PART I
Introduction to SharePoint Branding

What Is SharePoint Branding?

WHAT'S IN THIS CHAPTER?

➤ What is branding?

➤ Why brand SharePoint?

➤ How branding works in SharePoint

If you have picked up a copy of this book, you probably already have the desire to take control of the way your SharePoint sites look. Maybe this means that you want to make your SharePoint portal look more like your legacy corporate Internet site. Or maybe you want to make your new SharePoint site look cutting edge and interesting. Or maybe you simply want your site to not look like a SharePoint site. Regardless of the reason, you've decided that controlling the look and feel of your SharePoint site is important.

The goal of this book is to provide you with all the tools you need to brand your SharePoint sites. This chapter starts at a high level with overviews of concepts you need to understand before diving into branding. (The topics will become increasingly more granular as the book progresses.) Whether you are unaccustomed to design work or someone who does SharePoint design full-time, there is something in this book for you. By the time you have completed all the chapters, you should have a solid understanding of the tools you can use, as well as how best to use them, in your own branding endeavors.

As your starting point, this chapter will give you, at the highest level, an understanding of what branding is and why it is important. You will get an idea of exactly what branding means, at least in the world of SharePoint, and gain some exposure to several of the SharePoint components that you will need to be familiar with in order to accomplish your own branding goals. By the end of this chapter, you should be ready to get started on your first branding tasks.

DEFINITION OF BRANDING

In general, *branding* is the act of creating a specific image or identity that people recognize in relation to a company or product. For example, nearly everyone recognizes the iconic design of a can of Coca-Cola, which always uses the same logo, font, and red-and-white color scheme. You could probably look at the logos for businesses like Target, McDonalds, and FedEx and, without reading any words on or around the logo, immediately identify them. These companies have chosen a marketing identity that enables the public to quickly and easily recognize them. This is branding. When referring to websites, branding usually involves the colors, fonts, logos, and supporting graphics that make up the general look and feel of the site.

Branding for SharePoint sites is similar to branding for any other sites, except that branding for SharePoint includes the creation of master pages, page layouts, Cascading Style Sheets (CSS), Web Parts, and eXtensible Stylesheet Language Transformations (XSLT). In fact, everything a user sees on the screen contributes to the user experience, which helps to define the branding for a site. This could also include the correct use of corporate logos or other graphics, whether this means you are doing this because of strict corporate guidelines or merely because you don't want to look like every other SharePoint site. Regardless of your reason for wanting to affect the design of your site, you need to be familiar with the concepts of SharePoint branding.

To better understand branding, it might be easier if you can actually see it in practice. Figure 1-1 is a Team site in Windows SharePoint Services (WSS) 3.0, and Figure 1-2 shows the look and feel for the same site in SharePoint 2010. As you can see, Microsoft has used branding to distinguish between two major versions of its product. If you were to walk by two laptops, one with WSS loaded in the browser and the other with SharePoint 2010, it wouldn't be difficult to determine which site is which. The colors are different; the fonts are different; the graphics are different; even the basic layout of controls is different. The same content might be in both, but the presentation is unique to each site. This is a smart, and common, use of branding.

FIGURE 1-1

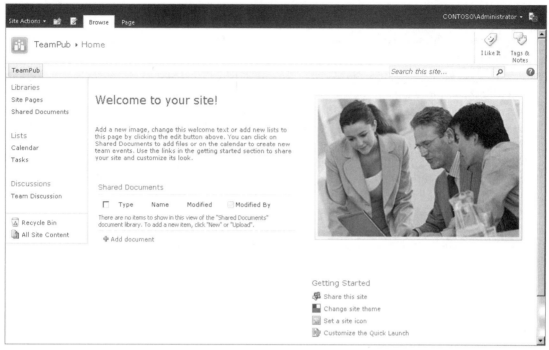

FIGURE 1-2

Some business texts describe branding as the "feeling" users get when they see something, such as a product or even a website. Normally these books are referring to external sites for commercial products, but the concept applies to internal sites, such as intranets, as well. In other words, branding is not merely cosmetic, because the key to any successful SharePoint implementation is whether users actually use the site — in other words, user adoption. How users feel about the site is an important factor in driving user adoption.

WHY BRAND SHAREPOINT?

To brand or not to brand, that is the question. For most organizations the answer is usually to brand. Probably most of you reading this have already made up your mind that you are going to brand your SharePoint site for one reason or another. But there are many different reasons companies choose to brand and some of them might be similar to your reasons, and some might be very different.

For most organizations, the most common reason to brand a SharePoint site is to make it unique. Out of the box, SharePoint 2010 is not visually compelling. In fact, its look and feel is intentionally bland, as it is assumed that most companies are going to customize it. Indeed, making it "not look like SharePoint" is a basic request. You likely want to brand SharePoint to make it consistent with the corporate image and marketing standards you have established for your organization.

The previous section mentioned that branding is often associated with how a user feels about a company or product. Obviously, companies want to evoke different feelings in different types of users. For example, a company might want to brand its intranet site to help convey to employees a sense of collaboration, teamwork, and even family. While that might sound a little touchy-feely or unrealistic, consider the alternative — a sterile, poorly branded intranet that doesn't reflect the company's image or purpose. Although a company with such a site may not cause its employees to walk out the door, a SharePoint intranet site that is effectively branded has a positive effect on employees, in much the same way that a nicely decorated room creates a welcoming, harmonious effect.

Conversely, if your company has a public-facing Internet site, you likely want to target a completely different audience. In most cases the goal for a public-facing Internet site is to communicate to this external audience information about your company, such as its services or products. In these cases, your online presence is a critical component of your corporate identity, and there's no way the out-of-the-box SharePoint branding is going to cut the mustard. The design options for public-facing SharePoint Internet sites are virtually unlimited. Examples include everything from local government sites, schools, and universities to small, family-run businesses, huge, global companies, nonprofit organizations, and many others (see Figures 1-3 and 1-4).

Although SharePoint is purchased for a variety of reasons, most companies are seeking the business benefits such as document management, process improvement, or enterprise search that it provides. The point here is that the people who are actually using SharePoint care very little about the underlying technology as long as it helps them get their job done. From a branding perspective, this points to another reason why companies brand: to improve usability. Improving usability could mean simply organizing the elements of the page in an efficient manner, or increasing the size of the fonts in the navigation, or something far more complex, such as customizing the ribbon interface.

The subject of branding covers a wide range of topics. Each SharePoint implementation has unique requirements and poses unique challenges when it comes to creating a user interface. Nonetheless, effective branding doesn't have to be overly complex. Regardless of your reasons for branding or your branding prowess, SharePoint provides a wealth of options.

FIGURE 1-3

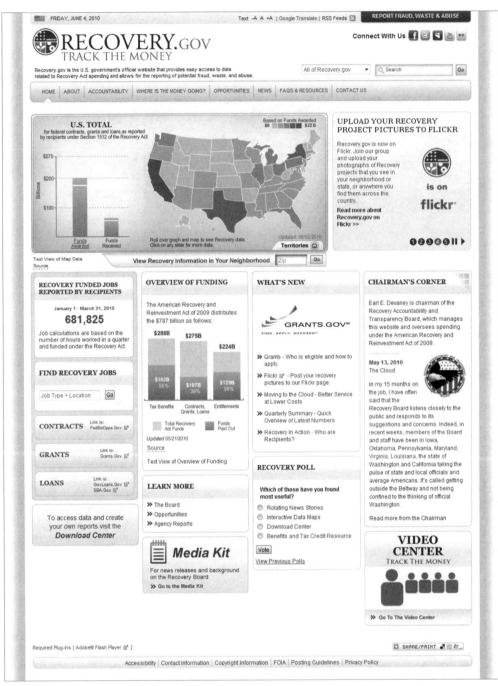

FIGURE 1-4

SHAREPOINT 2010 VERSIONS

Like its predecessor, SharePoint 2010 is available as two distinct products:

➤ **SharePoint Foundation 2010** — The new version of the free Windows SharePoint Services version 3 (WSS)

➤ **SharePoint Server 2010** — The new version of Microsoft Office SharePoint Server 2007 (MOSS)

Although SharePoint Server 2010 is more expensive than SharePoint Foundation 2010, it includes the Publishing Features, which has several useful additions for branding projects:

➤ The Web Content Management (WCM) functionality provides users with a robust publishing platform. This means that users can author pages with rich and structured content and publish the pages in a controlled way using out-of-the-box workflows.

➤ SharePoint Server contains more robust options for navigation. This gives users more control and provides greater flexibility than what is provided out-of-the-box by SharePoint Foundation.

➤ SharePoint Server also enables site administrators to easily change a master page for any site, and all of its subsites, from a SharePoint site's settings page.

➤ SharePoint Server enables more flexibility with themes, including the capability to change the colors and fonts in the SharePoint Web user interface, as well as the capability to apply a theme to all subsites at the same time.

For a more detailed comparison of the different versions of SharePoint 2010, see http://sharepoint .microsoft.com/en-us/buy/Pages/Editions-Comparison.aspx.

From a branding perspective, SharePoint Server 2010 provides many more options for creating highly styled sites than SharePoint Server 2010. Therefore, many of the examples throughout this book are geared towards sites with publishing enabled. However, in most cases the examples will still apply to a nonpublishing site with minimal changes to the steps. The only exception to this would be when the examples cover functionality that is available only with SharePoint Server 2010. Where possible throughout the book, we will try to highlight different approaches for achieving the same results in SharePoint Server and SharePoint Foundation.

TYPES OF SHAREPOINT WEBSITES

Although all SharePoint installations are unique, they all fall into one of three categories: intranet, Internet, or extranet. Each of these SharePoint sites has a different audience and, therefore, different design considerations as part of the planning phase.

The following sections discuss the typical considerations for each of the three environments. However, at a higher level, each environment is made up of many SharePoint sites and each of these sites is usually designed to primarily facilitate either *communication* or *collaboration*. It is certainly possible to do a little bit of both, but in terms of the core decisions being made about branding, most sites will favor one more than the other. For example, most of the sites on an organization's intranet would fall under the category of a collaboration site, as this is where most users store content and collaborate with others on their day-to-day tasks. However, the intranet home page for most companies is usually designed as a place to convey information to employees, such as the latest company news, announcements, or events. When users open their browser, they are taken to this home page where they are presented with all of this information, and from there they navigate to another area of the intranet to do work and collaborate.

Unfortunately, branding projects often overlook the importance of determining whether the intended purpose of a site is either collaboration or communication. To understand why it is so important, consider what you'd expect to find on the home page of your intranet site compared to what you'd expect to find on the main page for your department site. You would probably expect the intranet home page to be more highly styled, with a focus on communicating information. Conversely, you would expect the main page for your department to focus on the actual documents and content you work with on a daily basis. Obviously, your specific situation might be slightly different, but the point is clear: There's a distinct difference in the intended purpose of a site designed purely for communicating information in a one-way fashion verses a collaboration, which is designed for more of a two-way flow of information.

From a technical standpoint, sites designed primarily for communication or collaboration require different SharePoint templates, which require different approaches to branding. Templates are discussed later in this chapter, but consider that the approach for branding a SharePoint site based on the Publishing Portal template, which is designed for public-facing sites, is different from branding a Meeting Workspace template, which is designed purely for internal collaboration.

 Planning for branding is discussed in more detail in Chapter 3.

Intranet Sites

Intranet sites are typically available only to employees and partners who are connecting locally to the network or using a virtual private network (VPN). The focus of intranet sites is to facilitate information delivery and collaboration for specific sets of users. They often have many content authors, as well as many users who will be consuming content and collaborating on new content.

Unlike public Internet sites, the browsers and system capabilities of intranet sites are usually controlled by the IT department. This makes designing a SharePoint intranet easier because fewer variables need to be considered. For example, if your organization supports only one browser, you have to design and test with only that one browser.

As mentioned in the previous section, most intranets are designed to facilitate communication, but the vast majority of sites that are created are of the collaboration variety. Usually this means using the Team site template or some custom variation. This is especially true for SharePoint Server 2010 implementations. If you are using SharePoint Foundation 2010, your options are more limited than with SharePoint Server (because of the lack of publishing functionality) and you'll most likely use all Team site templates (refer to Figure 1-2). Often, it is important to add a certain amount of corporate branding even to intranet sites. Figure 1-5 shows an example of a custom-branded SharePoint intranet site. This site used a custom master page, CSS, and images to create a new look and feel.

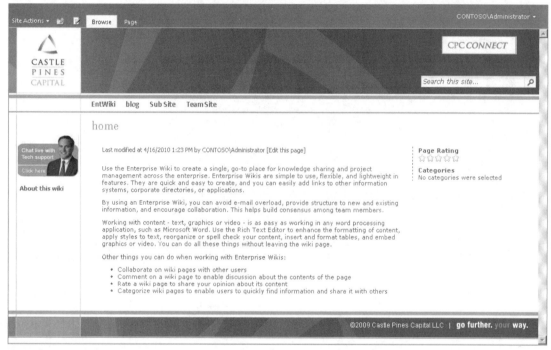

FIGURE 1-5

Internet Sites

Internet sites are public facing, and typically have anonymous users visiting them using a variety of Internet browsers. These sites are usually driven by marketing, with few content authors and tightly controlled content.

Typically, public-facing Internet sites offer the opportunity to create highly stylized designs. They pose a much greater design challenge than internal-facing sites because it is much more difficult to control the clients who access the site. In other words, additional effort has to be taken to ensure that the site is displayed properly across all types of browsers, and conforms to whatever compliance standards need to be met for the given site. Not only is the creative effort usually higher for an Internet site than for an intranet site, but the actual implementation effort is also usually higher because of the added complexity.

One example of corporate-branded Internet sites that were built with SharePoint is Chilis.com (see Figure 1-6). It has a highly customized user interface, so much so in fact that, without some poking around in the HTML source, it is hard to see any evidence that they are even using SharePoint.

FIGURE 1-6

Extranet Sites

Extranet sites combine the security and collaboration of an intranet site with the more heavily emphasized branding found in Internet sites. The goal for most extranet sites is to enable external partners to collaborate with an organization. This is usually accomplished by having a public-facing Internet site that users access initially. Once on the site, users enter a username and password in order to access a secure site, where they can collaborate with users from inside the company. For example, a manufacturing organization might have an extranet site to allow distributors to log in and place orders or to get other information to help them sell the organization's products.

The biggest challenge with extranets is usually security. Most organizations want external users to be able to log in to see what they need to see, but no more. Maintaining this balance of security can be tricky. From a branding perspective, it usually means that you must ensure that your branding is consistent across all areas of the site, especially those that business partners will be using.

HOW BRANDING WORKS IN SHAREPOINT

Before diving into the specifics of creating branding in SharePoint 2010, it's important to understand some of the key ways in which branding can be applied in SharePoint. The following sections examine these key concepts in detail.

Themes

Imagine that you want to make some changes to spruce up your home. Maybe your house has a dated feel to it, and you want to make some changes that can be done relatively quickly and easily. Your budget is limited, so you decide to paint the walls with a brighter and more appealing color. In SharePoint terms, this would be equivalent to applying a *theme*. Technically speaking, themes can be thought of as changes that are applied to the existing look and feel through the use of CSS. In SharePoint 2007, themes played a similar function, but behind the scenes, they worked completely differently than they do in SharePoint 2010.

In SharePoint 2007, themes were stored on the server in the `SharePoint 12` folder (the root folder for SharePoint), and consisted of XML, CSS, and images that were applied over the top of the default master page and CSS. (It was also possible to make some themes that would really be stretching the analogy of painting the walls of your house.) The downside with SharePoint 2007 themes is that they were fairly complicated, and often required someone to make changes to files on the server if you weren't able to find an out-of-the-box theme to suit your needs; and frankly, it wasn't very easy to find a theme that met your needs unless your company's colors included some pretty shocking colors like bright red or neon green. At the end of the day, even though themes were a more simplistic alternative to creating a custom master page, they still weren't something the average user wanted to implement.

In SharePoint 2010, themes are created with the Microsoft Office client software (2007 and above), using either Word or PowerPoint to create `.THMX` files that describe the 12 theme colors and two fonts available in the new SharePoint themes. Once created with Office, they can be loaded into SharePoint 2010 and applied to any site by site owners.

Along with the capability to create themes in the Office client, the Server version of SharePoint 2010 enables site owners to modify the themes — i.e., the colors and fonts — directly in the SharePoint Web user interface (see Figure 1-7), and the changes can be viewed immediately.

FIGURE 1-7

The new theming engine effectively eliminates the entry barrier to creating simple color and font changes in SharePoint. Now, anyone with rudimentary knowledge of how themes work in Office can create a SharePoint theme in minutes, instead of hours.

It is important to realize, though, that themes do not affect the layout of a page. In other words, regardless of which theme you select, the controls on your pages will always be laid out in the same basic area. If you want to change the layout of the page, then you need to use *master pages*.

 You can learn more about using themes in Chapter 5, "Simple Branding."

Master Pages

Let's revisit the analogy in the previous section of making some changes to your house. If applying a theme is comparable to painting the walls, then using master pages is comparable to altering the physical structure of the house. By changing the physical structure of your house, nearly anything is possible. Want to add a new room or knock down some walls? No problem. The sky is the limit as long as you have the right skills or can find a good general contractor to help you get the job done. The same is true with master pages in SharePoint.

Remember the good old days of classic web design, all the way back to the late 1990s and early 2000s, when web pages were created with the look and feel hard-coded in each and every page? Changing the footer, for example, typically required you to access every page in the site, repeating the same change on each one, and then uploading them back to the server. This very tedious manual process created many opportunities to introduce errors.

With the advent of ASP.NET 2.0, master pages were introduced to alleviate this problem. Just like in a typical ASP.NET website, master pages enable designers and developers to create a consistent look and feel for all the pages in a SharePoint website. Every page on a SharePoint site references a master page. When a page is loaded in a browser, SharePoint merges the master page with the page, and the resultant styled page is returned to the user. The result is that master pages enable organizations to create a consistent look and feel across all sites, which is a far better approach than was available in the past.

Figure 1-8 shows the relationship between master pages and page content.

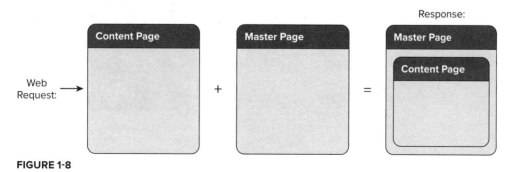

FIGURE 1-8

In the typical SharePoint site, master pages define the outer shell of the website. Sometimes called the *chrome*, this shell defines much of the overall look for every page loaded in the site. Master pages include HTML; SharePoint-specific controls (navigation, search, etc.); and *content placeholders*, containers used to load specific pieces of content from the referring content. A content placeholder is essentially a named container that is used to render various pieces of content. The most common example of this is `PlaceHolderMain`, which exists on every page layout. This is the content place-holder where field controls, Web Part zones, and anything else that is to be rendered in the central area of the page typically would exist.

SharePoint comes with a few out-of-the-box master pages that can be used for website branding right away. The following list describes some of the more important out-of-the-box master pages:

➤   `v4.master` — This is the default master page that is used for many of the site templates used by SharePoint 2010, and is the page shown earlier in Figure 1-2.

➤   `nightandday.master` — This master page is accessible only in a SharePoint Server 2010 site that has the Publishing Feature enabled. Unlike `v4.master` (which is geared toward intra-net sites), this master page is styled in a more simplistic way and is more appropriate for an Internet site. Because the underlying code for the master page is well organized, this can be a good place to look when you are first learning about master pages. Figure 1-9 shows the `nightandday` master page.

➤   `minimal.master` — This master page is used only on pages that have their own navigation or need extra space (such as dedicated application pages or the search center). Unlike the concept of minimal master pages in SharePoint 2007, this master page is not intended to be the starting point for branding, as it lacks several common SharePoint controls. Figure 1-10 shows the minimal master page.

FIGURE 1-9

FIGURE 1-10

Content Pages

As discussed in the previous section, master pages define the outer shell of a SharePoint page; but the body of the page itself is important too. Depending on the purpose of your site (collaboration vs. communication) and the site template you've chosen, you will have different types of content pages available to you. In fact, there are three main types of content pages in SharePoint Server 2010:

➤   Publishing pages (SharePoint Server 2010 only)

➤   Web Part pages

➤   Wiki pages

Each type of page has different options and a different intended use, so your functional requirements will dictate which page is right for each scenario.

Publishing Pages

Publishing pages are available only in SharePoint Server 2010 on sites where the Publishing Feature is enabled. The Publishing Feature enables authors to create pages that have an approval workflow so that content can be reviewed and approved before being published. For example, you might create a page announcing a new policy, but the new page would need to be approved by your manager before it could be viewed by others on the website.

Publishing pages are created by using page templates called *page layouts*. If master pages create the outer shell of a SharePoint page, then page layouts define the body of a page. They enable content authors to create pages that contain text, HTML, graphics, rich media, and more.

To continue with the house analogy we've used throughout the chapter, imagine a room with furniture in it — perhaps a couch and a few chairs and tables. The room would be similar in concept to a page in SharePoint; the pieces of furniture would be the various fields on the page. Applying a new page layout would be similar to rearranging the furniture in the room. The room is still the same and the pieces of furniture are still the same, but they are laid out differently and ultimately have a different look and feel.

Several out-of-the-box page layouts can be used right away in a SharePoint Server site, but also remember that designers and developers can always create their own custom page layouts. For example, when a user creates a new page in SharePoint Server, the same content can be arranged as a news article or as a welcome page, based on the page layout that is selected.

Figure 1-11 shows the relationship between master pages and page layouts.

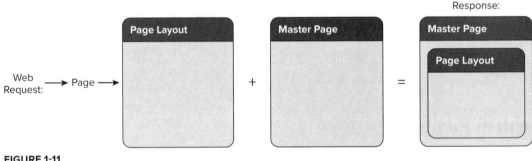

FIGURE 1-11

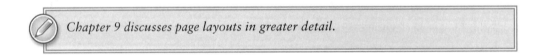

Chapter 9 discusses page layouts in greater detail.

Along with defining how content is arranged on a page, page layouts also define the location of editable fields and Web Parts. *Web Parts*, which can be thought of as self-contained widgets of functionality, can be arranged in pages through the use of *Web Part zones* that are defined in page layouts. Web Part zones enable content authors to add and arrange multiple Web Parts vertically or horizontally.

Publishing pages are the most highly structured of the SharePoint content pages. Not only do they provide a fairly strict template for creating content, but the approval workflow helps to prevent unwanted content from ever being seen. Because of the structure provided by publishing pages, they are best suited for sites where communication is the primary goal.

Web Part Pages

The function of Web Part pages is fairly obvious by their name. They are pages that contain Web Part zones, where Web Parts can be placed that display things like list data, images, rich media, or other functionality. Any user with the proper permissions, usually the site owner, can create and edit Web Part pages.

Web Part pages are most appropriate when you simply need a page to display some information via Web Parts. Because the goal of Web Parts is to deliver functionality to the page, often by displaying content from lists and libraries, in most cases the Web Part page itself wouldn't be the place where actual collaboration occurs. Additionally, it lacks the structure and formalized publishing process that you get with a publishing page. Both SharePoint Server 2010 and SharePoint Foundation 2010 support Web Part pages.

Wiki Pages

The word "wiki" is Hawaiian for quick. The goal of a wiki site is to enable users to quickly create content and collaborate with other users; thus, wikis tend to be informal and unstructured.

In SharePoint 2007, the most commonly created type of site across most implementations was the Team site, which was designed to be a place where teams could collaborate. In SharePoint 2010, the new Team site template now puts the wiki functionality front and center as a way to make it easier for teams to collaborate (see Figure 1-12). From a branding perspective this is an important new addition to SharePoint 2010 for the simple fact that Team sites will likely be the most common type of site that's created across your organization — assuming you are using SharePoint for your intranet.

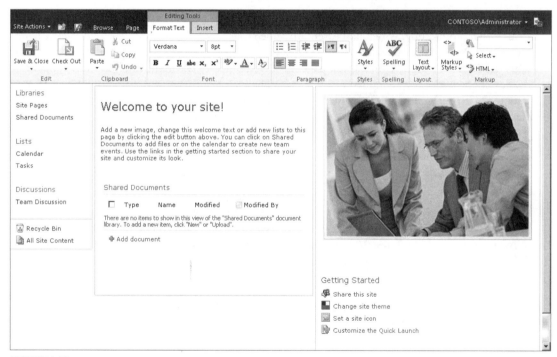

FIGURE 1-12

Wiki pages are available in SharePoint Foundation and SharePoint Server 2010. Specifically for SharePoint Server 2010, the Enterprise Wiki template supports the capability to create and use page layouts with wiki pages.

Wikis are a great way to collaborate with others on a project. They are also very useful for creating knowledge bases or other repositories for storing and sharing information.

Cascading Style Sheets

CSS is pervasive in SharePoint branding. Almost every aspect of SharePoint is styled by CSS. All the SharePoint controls that are loaded by a master page are styled by CSS, as well as many Web Parts — even SharePoint themes apply to specially commented CSS files in SharePoint 2010. Because of the importance of CSS in SharePoint, a sound understanding of it is crucial to becoming skilled at branding in SharePoint. If you aren't a CSS guru, that's okay. Parts I and II of this book discuss techniques for branding that don't require too much heavy lifting with CSS. Chapter 5, "Simple Branding," is specifically geared toward users who want to customize their SharePoint site but aren't fifth-degree CSS ninjas.

 For more information on learning CSS, check out Professional CSS: Cascading Style Sheets for Web Design, Second Edition, *by Christopher Schmidt.*

Unlike SharePoint 2007, which had essentially one large core CSS file that was loaded for each page, SharePoint 2010 splits its default CSS across several smaller CSS files that are loaded according to what controls are available on a given page; however, much of the main CSS for SharePoint still resides in one core CSS file named `corev4.css`. The intent of this new division of labor is to load only the CSS that's necessary to render a given page, whereas the old method simply loaded the entire massive CSS file every time, whether you needed it or not.

When creating a heavily branded SharePoint site, it is often critical to create custom CSS to style not only the page design, but also the out-of-the-box SharePoint controls. The primary means for loading custom CSS in SharePoint is by referencing it from a custom master page.

SharePoint Server provides a secondary means to load CSS on publishing sites, known as *alternate CSS*. Alternate CSS can be applied to any of the out-of-the-box master pages or any custom master page easily through the SharePoint Server Web user interface. This can be particularly useful for mimicking the old SharePoint 2007 themes concept by applying CSS and background images to the default `v4.master` page using Alternate CSS.

 Custom master pages are discussed in more detail in Chapter 8, "Master Pages." You can learn more about alternate CSS in Chapter 5, "Simple Branding."

APPROACHES TO BRANDING IN SHAREPOINT 2010

As you embark on your SharePoint branding project, keep in mind that the people involved likely have different skill levels and often different ideas about how intricate the design should be. The SharePoint branding role in an organization often falls to traditional web designers or a lucky member of the SharePoint team who gets to don the branding hat. The ultimate goal for branding SharePoint in an organization could be as simple as just putting the company logo at the top of each page, or it could be as complex as creating a high-volume, public-facing SharePoint site. Whatever the goal, the first step in any project is to understand the level of effort required to achieve it. Fortunately, there are several ways to approach branding in SharePoint 2010 — from those that are simple and quick to those involving highly skilled designers and generous deadlines.

Following are three different approaches for creating branding in SharePoint:

➤ **Low effort** — Typically, this approach includes all the branding tasks that an end user with limited training could perform. By utilizing the out-of-the-box branding, even someone with little knowledge of traditional website development and design can create a customized site. Using the out-of-the-box functionality, users can select master pages and themes or create their own custom themes. It is even possible to add a logo image to the top of every site by simply uploading an image and changing the reference in one of the menus.

➤ **Medium effort** — This approach is good for adding some level of unique branding to a site without spending the time and effort needed to create a custom master page. A medium level of effort would typically involve a power user and could be done using SharePoint Designer 2010. These users could make basic changes to the CSS or HTML of a site or even copy and modify the out-of-the-box master pages or other SharePoint pages to create custom branding for their site.

➤ **High effort** — If your design requirements cannot be met by any of the other approaches, then your only option is the high-effort approach. This involves creating custom master pages, custom CSS, and potentially some custom page layouts. This approach is good for people who are experienced with traditional website design and have some knowledge of SharePoint or ASP.NET master pages. It is also well suited for public Internet sites and highly styled internal employee portals.

Which option you choose is likely going to depend on the skillset of the resources doing the work and the budget for the project. Throughout this book we'll show different examples about what is possible for each of the approaches.

SUMMARY

This chapter provided a high-level look at SharePoint branding, including why it is important and what tools you need to be familiar with in order to brand your own sites. After seeing some examples of how others have applied SharePoint branding, it is hoped that you have gained a little inspiration from those sites. If you were unfamiliar with branding from previous versions, you now know that SharePoint branding is merely modifying some SharePoint assets, like master pages and themes, as well as some web standards, such as CSS and images, to make your site uniquely yours.

The information in this chapter is simply an introduction to branding. As you continue through the book, each chapter will take you a little further on the journey into SharePoint branding.

What's New in SharePoint 2010

WHAT'S IN THIS CHAPTER?

➤ New features in SharePoint 2010

➤ Changes to the branding story

➤ Migrating from SharePoint 2007 to SharePoint 2010

This chapter discusses the major changes to the branding story in SharePoint 2010 and provides an overview of SharePoint concepts. If you are new to SharePoint or SharePoint branding, this chapter should serve as a good first step in your learning process. If you've used SharePoint previously, you'll notice several changes to many pieces of functionality you may already be familiar with.

OVERVIEW OF NEW FEATURES IN SHAREPOINT 2010

When the earliest versions of SharePoint were released around 1999, the product was designed to be a web-based document management tool that would provide collaboration to users across an organization. As the product evolved, each version of SharePoint became easier to use to create a custom user interface (UI). However, for the most part, customization of the UI was tricky at best and often involved modifying system files and overriding a lot of CSS. The end result still could easily be identified as SharePoint, which limited its appeal as a platform for sites that required a customized UI.

The release of Microsoft Office SharePoint Server (MOSS) 2007 signaled a big change in the SharePoint branding story. Essentially, MOSS was the combination of SharePoint Portal Server 2003 and Microsoft Content Management Server (CMS) 2002. MOSS was built on top of ASP.NET 2.0 and enabled developers and designers to take advantage of all the great functionality available with that new framework, such as master pages. MOSS retained (and improved) the collaboration functionality of earlier versions but added web content management functionality. More specifically, creating custom UIs was now easier; the SharePoint UI could now be customized just like any other ASP.NET application. Templates were included with the product that were designed to be used with public-facing websites. Most important, because the product could be modified to "not look like SharePoint," it became much more viable for use with public-facing websites. The flexibility to use SharePoint as both an organization's internal site and its external site helps to fuel its popularity to this day. Figure 2-1 shows one of the more prominent examples of a heavily styled Internet SharePoint site.

FIGURE 2-1

The capability to customize the SharePoint UI has improved significantly over the life of the product, which has evolved from an internal document management tool with almost no flexibility to customize the UI to the robust platform that is SharePoint 2010 which offers nearly endless options to customize the UI. Collaboration is still SharePoint's main purpose, but significant additions and improvements have been made to the branding experience in SharePoint 2010.

Changes to the User Experience

If you are already familiar with SharePoint 2007, it won't take long for you to notice that significant changes have been made to the user experience (UX) in SharePoint 2010. For starters, several items that you have likely become accustomed to seeing in a given location are no longer where you expect them. For example, the Site Actions button, which has traditionally been in roughly the same location at the top-right corner of most SharePoint pages has been relocated to the left side of the page.

The most significant change to the UX may be the addition of the Fluent UI control platform, more commonly referred to as the *ribbon*. The ribbon, shown in Figure 2-2, was first introduced in Microsoft Office 2007 as a way to provide more efficient access to the most frequently used controls. Use of the ribbon is becoming pervasive across many Microsoft platforms. Even Microsoft Paint in Windows 7 boasts a ribbon interface. The goal of the ribbon in SharePoint was to make it easier to perform the most common tasks, which in many cases can be done with a single click. For example, when editing a page, users can click an icon at the top of a page to edit it, and then click once again to exit edit mode.

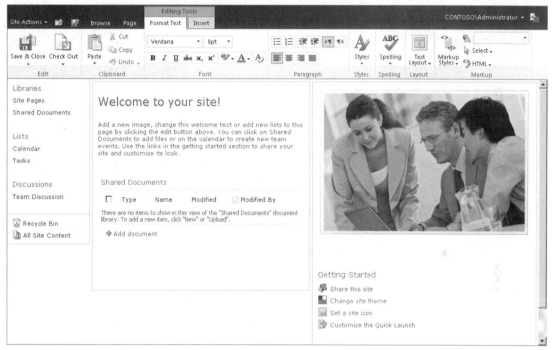

FIGURE 2-2

Much like the response most users had when they first saw the ribbon in Office 2007, it does take some getting used to. As a general rule, the most common tasks are easier with the ribbon, although some of the less common options might require a few more clicks to get to compared to SharePoint 2007.

The overall goal of the UX platform is to make it easy for users to complete most tasks without exiting the current context in which they are working. For example, in SharePoint 2007, when users tried to add an image to a page using a page layout, they would be directed to several different pages throughout the process and at the end wouldn't be returned to the page layout they were editing. They would have to manually browse back to the page and then finish editing it. The process was very confusing. In SharePoint 2010, when users want to perform the same task, a dialog box appears that allows them to complete the task without leaving the current page (see Figure 2-3). The ribbon is fully extensible and can be customized to add buttons and functions as needed. This topic is covered in detail in Chapter 12, "Page Editing and the Ribbon."

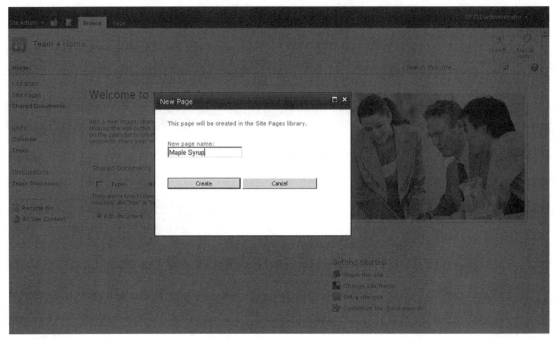

FIGURE 2-3

Because the UX has changed so significantly in SharePoint 2010, there certainly will be growing pains. In addition to all the new SharePoint 2010 functionality that users will need to learn, they'll also have to relearn how to do many of the common tasks they've become so familiar with in SharePoint 2007; but once they start using the new UX, they should come to appreciate SharePoint 2010's high level of usability.

Browsers and HTML Standards

In the past, SharePoint has always provided the best user experience to those using Internet Explorer. For organizations that needed to support multiple platforms, this caused issues with SharePoint because users who weren't using Internet Explorer to access SharePoint were at a disadvantage; they weren't able to use all the features of the product. SharePoint 2010 provides improved support for browsers other than Internet Explorer. In fact, since the earliest public previews of SharePoint 2010, Microsoft has provided many of their demos using Mozilla Firefox 3.5 (see Figure 2-4).

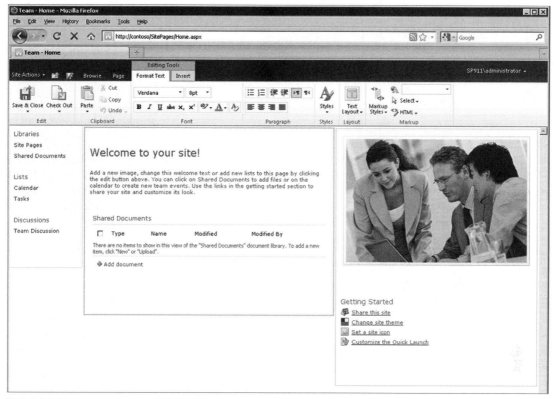

FIGURE 2-4

Browser support for SharePoint 2010 can be divided into three categories:

➤ **Supported** — A supported web browser is a web browser that is known to be fully tested with all features and functionality to work with SharePoint Server 2010. If you encounter any issues, support can help you to resolve these issues.

➤ **Supported with known limitations** — A supported web browser with known limitations works with most features and functionality; however, if there is a feature or functionality that does not work or is disabled by design, documentation on how to resolve these issues is readily available.

➤ **Not tested** — A web browser that is not tested means that its compatibility with SharePoint Server 2010 is untested, and there may be issues with using the particular web browser.

SharePoint Server 2010 works best with up-to-date, standards-based Web browsers. The following are supported browsers running on the Windows operating system:

➤ Internet Explorer 7 32-bit

➤ Internet Explorer 8 32-bit

The following are supported browser options with known limitations:

➤ Internet Explorer 7 64-bit

➤ Internet Explorer 8 64-bit

➤ Firefox 3.6 32-bit on Windows operating systems

➤ Firefox 3.6 on non-Windows operating systems

➤ Safari 4.04 on non-Windows operating systems

SharePoint 2010 does not support Internet Explorer 6 for publishing site scenarios (such as Internet-facing ".com" sites). The Web Content Management features built into SharePoint Server 2010 provide a deep level of control over the markup and styling of the reader experience. Page designers can use these features to help ensure that the pages they design are compatible with additional browsers, including Internet Explorer 6, for viewing content. However, it is the page designer's responsibility to create pages that are compatible with the browsers that they want to support.

For full browser support information visit `http://go.microsoft.com/fwlink/?LinkId=190341`.

Note that Internet Explorer 6.x is not among the list of browsers; it is not supported. IE 6 was originally released in the summer of 2001 and it fails to conform with many modern web standards. Dropping support for it was a necessary step in order for SharePoint 2010 to become more standards compliant. Although a few companies will be forced to upgrade from Internet Explorer 6, most readers of this book will probably be happy to learn they won't have to deal with it anymore.

The code generated by SharePoint 2007 often frustrated users. There were tables galore, which were deeply nested and difficult to style, and in general the HTML techniques that were used didn't conform to common standards. Additionally, there were large amounts of CSS, which made it complicated to make even simple changes. All these issues together made it very difficult for designers and developers to get up to speed with customizing the SharePoint UI. The good news for web designers and developers is that SharePoint 2010 now outputs cleaner HTML code to the browser and organizes the CSS and JavaScript better.

The following code snippets show the HTML outputs to the browser for the top navigation, also referred to as the *global navigation* in sites with the Publishing Feature activated. This is the navigation that runs horizontal at the top of all default SharePoint sites. The first sample is from SharePoint 2007, and the second sample is the eqivalent code from SharePoint 2010. You'll notice how much cleaner the code that is output by SharePoint 2010 is; specifically, the navigation is essentially an unordered list. The code in the first sample is filled with nested tables that are much more difficult to style.

SHAREPOINT 2007

```
<TD id="onetIdTopNavBarContainer" WIDTH="100%"
class="ms-bannerContainer">
  <table class="ms-bannerframe" border="0" cellspacing="0"
  cellpadding="0" width="100%">
    <tr>
      <td nowrap="nowrap" valign="middle"></td>
      <td class="ms-banner" width="99%" nowrap="nowrap"
      ID="HBN100">
        <table id="zz1_TopNavigationMenu"
```

```
        class="ms-topNavContainer zz1_TopNavigationMenu_5 zz1_
TopNavigationMenu_2"
      cellpadding="0" cellspacing="0" border="0">
        <tr>
          <td onmouseover="Menu_HoverRoot(this)"
          onmouseout="Menu_Unhover(this)"
          onkeyup="Menu_Key(this)" id="zz1_TopNavigationMenun0">
            <table class="ms-topnav zz1_TopNavigationMenu_4
ms-topnavselected zz1_TopNavigationMenu_10"
            cellpadding="0" cellspacing="0" border="0"
            width="100%">
              <tr>
                <td style="white-space:nowrap;">
                  <a class="zz1_TopNavigationMenu_1 ms-topnav zz1_
TopNavigationMenu_3 ms-topnavselected zz1_TopNavigationMenu_9"
                  href="/Pages/default.aspx" accesskey="1"
                  style="border-style:none;font-size:1em;">
                  Collab</a>
                </td>
              </tr>
            </table>
          </td>
          <td style="width:0px;"></td>
          <td>
            <table border="0" cellpadding="0" cellspacing="0"
            width="100%" class="zz1_TopNavigationMenu_5">
              <tr>
                <td style="width:0px;"></td>
                <td onmouseover="Menu_HoverStatic(this)"
                onmouseout="Menu_Unhover(this)"
                onkeyup="Menu_Key(this)"
                title="Document Center site"
                id="zz1_TopNavigationMenun1">
                  <table class="ms-topnav zz1_TopNavigationMenu_4"
                  cellpadding="0" cellspacing="0" border="0"
                  width="100%">
                    <tr>
                      <td style="white-space:nowrap;">
                        <a class="zz1_TopNavigationMenu_1 ms-topnav zz1_
TopNavigationMenu_3"
                        href="/Docs"
                        style="border-style:none;font-size:1em;">
                        Document Center</a>
                      </td>
                    </tr>
                  </table>
                </td>
```

SHAREPOINT 2010

```
    <div id="zz14_TopNavigationMenuV4" class="s4-tn">
      <div class="menu horizontal menu-horizontal">
        <ul class="root static">
          <li class="static selected">
            <a class="static selected menu-item" title="Home"
            href="/Pages/default.aspx" accesskey="1">
```

```
        <span class="additional-background">
          <span class="menu-item-text">Portal</span>
          <span class="ms-hidden">Currently selected</span>
        </span>
      </a>
      <ul class="static">
        <li class="static">
          <a class="static menu-item"
          href="/entwiki/Pages/Home.aspx">
            <span class="additional-background">
              <span class="menu-item-text">Ent Wiki</span>
            </span>
          </a>
        </li>
        <li class="static">
          <a class="static menu-item"
          href="/PressReleases/Pages/default.aspx">
            <span class="additional-background">
              <span class="menu-item-text">Press Releases</span>
            </span>
          </a>
        </li>
        <li class="static">
          <a class="static menu-item" href="/Pages/Article.aspx">
            <span class="additional-background">
              <span class="menu-item-text">Article</span>
            </span>
          </a>
        </li>
        <li class="static dynamic-children">
          <a class="static dynamic-children menu-item"
          href="/subsite/Pages/default.aspx">
            <span class="additional-background">
              <span class="menu-item-text">Subsite</span>
            </span>
          </a>
          <ul class="dynamic">
            <li class="dynamic">
              <a class="dynamic menu-item"
              href="/subsite/subsubsite/Pages/default.aspx">
                <span class="additional-background">
                  <span class="menu-item-text">Sub Subsite</span>
                </span>
              </a>
            </li>
          </ul>
        </li>
      </ul>
    </li>
  </ul>
</div>
</div>
```

The CSS files have also been reorganized by splitting them into multiple files so that the browser only downloads what is needed to render the page. If you look in `C:\Program Files\`

Common Files\Microsoft Shared\Web Server Extensions\14\TEMPLATE\LAYOUTS\1033\ STYLES, you will see all the various CSS files that are used to style the different parts of SharePoint. In SharePoint 2007 these styles were combined into a single large CSS file. The problem with this was that every time a SharePoint page was loaded, this entire CSS file would load, regardless of whether the different pieces were being used or not. From a performance perspective, this caused the size of SharePoint pages to be unnecessarily large. As a performance-tuning technique, many developers tried to prune the pieces they didn't need, which was effective but involved modifying system files, which is not supported by Microsoft.

Conversely, each control in SharePoint 2010 is responsible for requesting which CSS it needs to render properly; therefore, depending on which controls are on the page, you might see a different combination of CSS files being referenced. For example, if you were to view source on the HTML produced by a Team site, you'd see it references corev4.css, search.css, and wiki .css; but if you were to look at the source for the Publishing Portal, you'd also see controls .css and page-layouts-21.css in addition to the others.

How much of a savings does the new method provide over the old method? In most cases, if you were to compare the 2007 version of a site to its 2010 equivalent, there isn't much savings with respect to the page size or speed at which the page is rendered. However, separating the CSS out into different files prevents the 2010 version from being even larger.

 This topic of Cascading Style Sheets is covered in more detail in Chapter 7, "Cascading Style Sheets in SharePoint 2010."

New SharePoint Controls

To provide many of the rich new features for SharePoint 2010, a number of new controls have been added for use in master pages. The following table highlights most of the new controls:

CONTROL	DESCRIPTION
SharePoint:SPShortcutIcon	Sets the favicon in the top left of the browser URL bar
SharePoint:CssRegistration After="corev4.css"	Tells SharePoint what to load after Corev4.css
SharePoint:SPRibbon	Adds the Fluent UI (the ribbon) to the page
SharePoint:PopoutMenu	Adds the breadcrumb that, when clicked, shows the pop-out that displays your current location in the site in a hierarchical tree structure
SharePoint:SPRibbonPeripheralContent	Adds various items that are attached to the ribbon
SharePoint:PageStateActionButton	Loads the page edit and save icon button near the top left of the page

continues

(continued)

CONTROL	DESCRIPTION
SharePoint:LanguageSpecificContent	Displays content specific to the selected language
Sharepoint:DeveloperDashboardLauncher	Launches the developer dashboard (which is hidden by default but can be enabled with STSADM or PowerShell)
SharePoint:ClusteredDirectionalSeparatorArrow	Loads the arrow near the site icon after the page title
SharePoint:AspMenu UseSimpleRendering="true	Renders tableless navigation
SharePoint:VisualUpgradePreviewStatus	Displays the Visual Upgrade status in the status bar
SharePoint:VersionedPlaceHolder UIVersion="3"	Enables the capability to target page elements to v3 or v4 capabilities
SharePoint:ClusteredSPLinkButton	This is how SharePoint 2010 makes use of CSS sprites.
SharePoint:DeveloperDashboard	Loads the actual developer dashboard at the bottom of the master page. This is hidden until the launcher is clicked.
SharePoint:WarnOnUnsupportedBrowsers	Displays a warning to users who are trying to access the site with an unsupported browser (e.g., Internet Explorer 6)
wssuc:MUISelector	Sets the MUI language selected that shows up in the welcome menu if language packs are installed
SPSWC:MySiteCssRegistration	Allows the use of specific CSS.

 The topic of master pages and their controls is covered in more detail in Chapter 8.

Themes

In previous versions of Windows SharePoint Services (WSS) and SharePoint Server, themes were a common way to quickly change the look and feel of a site. A site owner had the capability to choose from one of the many out-of-the-box themes available. Although this was quick and easy, these out-of-the-box themes often didn't suit the organization's corporate brand. For these situations, the options were either to create a custom theme, which required development and could be challenging for those unfamiliar with the process, or to just live with the out-of-the-box options.

SharePoint 2010 introduces a new theming engine that makes it much easier for users to create a custom branded UI. The theming engine uses the .thmx Open XML file format, which is already used by Office programs like Word 2007 and PowerPoint 2007 to create themes. Users create a new theme by selecting 12 colors and two fonts (see Figure 2-5). SharePoint 2010 generates new CSS, which is applied to the site, replacing the existing colors and fonts with the ones selected in the new theme. The themes are saved to the theme gallery so that other users can reuse the custom themes that have been created. If you've already created a custom theme for PowerPoint presentations or Word documents, those same themes can also be imported into SharePoint 2010!

FIGURE 2-5

Rather than adding another CSS file on top of all the existing SharePoint CSS, as was the case in SharePoint 2007, the new themes replace CSS in the existing SharePoint CSS files on-the-fly. They are marked with variables and use a comment-based design that is more standards compliant and provides more flexibility. This is beneficial because the browser doesn't have to download the extra CSS file, which makes the page load faster. Because these comments are replaced on-the-fly, the new themes can be used not only to skin the master page, but also to change anything that takes advantage of the theme comments. The new theming engine will make it easier for information workers to create a custom branded SharePoint site consistent with your organization's standards, and more advanced users will be able to leverage the more powerful capabilities to extend the custom branding to the content.

 Themes are discussed in greater detail in Chapter 5, "Simple Branding."

Wiki Pages

Wikis were first available with SharePoint 2007 as a WSS site template. Companies used them to create dynamic knowledge bases and as a way to create constantly evolving content. In many organizations the wiki was a popular way for teams to collaborate.

One of the more significant changes to SharePoint 2010 is that the wiki functionality has been combined into the Team Sites template, enabling users to combine the best parts of both the wikis and team sites (Figure 2-6). Users will be able to begin editing content on a team site with a single click. The process for adding content to the wiki has been improved; users can simply add images, list views, or even Web Parts directly into the wiki without the need for a Web Part zone or specialized field control. As content is entered, users can see a live preview of the changes; and when complete, the changes can be saved again with a single click.

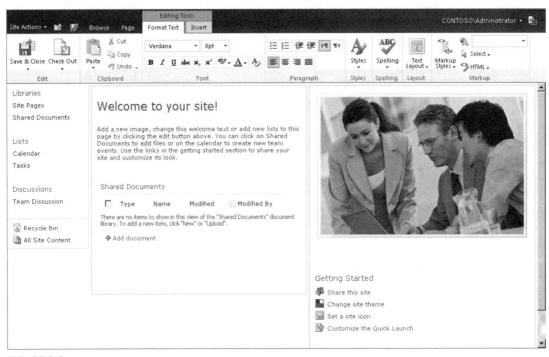

FIGURE 2-6

The new wiki functionality has also been merged with the Collaboration Portal from MOSS 2007. Many companies used the Collaboration Portal template with MOSS 2007 as the starting point for their corporate intranet. The Collaboration Portal has now been replaced by a new template called the Enterprise Wiki. This new template, like its predecessor, is available only with SharePoint Server and has publishing enabled.

The biggest difference between these templates is that the Enterprise Wiki uses page layouts for content, whereas the Team Site template uses text layouts. A text layout is basically just a wiki page, but unlike wiki pages in SharePoint 2007, they enable users to select from eight different options (see Figure 2-7), which provide much more flexibility than the previous version of SharePoint, where users couldn't change the page without resorting to custom methods. The biggest downside to text layouts is that it is not possible to create new text layouts. If you don't like the options that are available out-of-the-box, you are out of luck. If more flexibility is required than what the text layouts afford, the next best option is to enable the Publishing Features on the site, which provides the capability to use page layouts, which *can* be customized (see Figure 2-8).

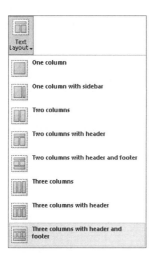

FIGURE 2-7

FIGURE 2-8

 Wiki pages are discussed in more detail in Chapter 5, "Simple Branding."

Client Object Model and Silverlight Web Parts

SharePoint 2007 really didn't offer an easy way to update information stored in SharePoint without using some type of compiled code, such as an event receiver or a workflow. This often required access to data via a web service or traversing through the SharePoint object model to finally arrive at the object to be changed. The process was complex for developers, and created plenty of opportunities to make mistakes along the way. In addition, the process frustrated administrators because even simple changes meant adding another DLL to the global assembly cache (GAC) on the server. Surely, there had to be an easier way. Technically, there were other ways to update content by using client-side techniques like jQuery or Silverlight, but developers still needed to jump through a number of hoops to get those techniques to work.

SharePoint 2010 has its own client object model that allows Silverlight or JavaScript to easily access SharePoint data. This new object model provides a simple API to add, retrieve, update, and manage data in SharePoint using code that does not require any compiled code. Web developers will be happy because the process to update data in SharePoint is now easier than ever before; and because all the updates take place on the client side, data can be updated instantly without the need for a page refresh, enabling the creation of more rich and dynamic applications. Administrators will be excited that their servers won't be cluttered with countless custom DLLs in the GAC.

SharePoint 2010 also takes advantage of Silverlight throughout the platform. You can see this most obviously in the Create Site dialog — notice the animation when you select a group of templates. The Create Site dialog is all made possible with Silverlight. If you don't have Silverlight on your client, the menus will still work but you'll miss out on the exhilarating experience of seeing your template icons sliding onto the screen.

The Silverlight experience isn't limited to just the menus. A Silverlight Web Part is included out-of-the-box, which makes integrating Silverlight applications easier than ever. Previously, integrating Silverlight applications took so many extra steps that developers were dissuaded from attempting to use it. Rich web-based applications aren't just reserved for fancy Internet sites; any organization can take advantage of dynamic dashboards and other ways to visualize data that will further drive return on investment (ROI) across the platform.

Working with the Client Object Model is discussed in more detail in Chapter 13, "The Client-Side Object Model and JQuery."

Digital Asset Management

Rich media is becoming more commonplace in all types of organizations, and that trend is expected to continue for the foreseeable future. This includes things like imagery or videos for marketing, or screencasts for training purposes. SharePoint 2010 provides a number of enhancements for storing, serving, and using rich media across an organization.

The asset library has been improved to allow for thumbnail-centric views, metadata extraction for images, and RSS/podcasting support. All of this has been added while retaining the traditional capabilities of a document library, such as the use of content types, workflows, and so on.

The SharePoint Media Player is built with Silverlight and allows videos to be played from SharePoint or other remote locations (Figure 2-9). The interface is customizable using Microsoft Expression Blend, and it can be extended via the new client-side object model. The Media Player can be used either as a Web Part or as a Publishing Field control.

Support for media has also been added to the Content Query Web Part (CQWP), which provides a way to dynamically serve up media based on the filter criteria set in the Web Part. The CQWP also supports the capability to stream content, as opposed to waiting for the entire content to download before it is displayed to users — a big change from how media was handled in SharePoint 2007.

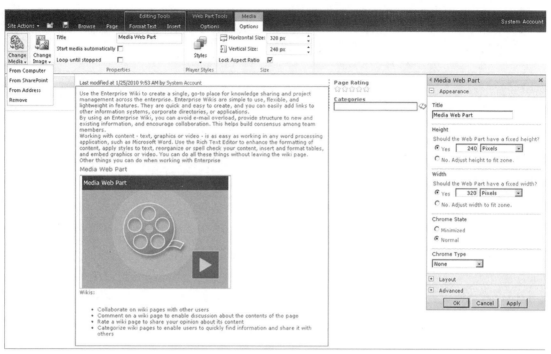

FIGURE 2-9

Usage Analytics

Although usage analytics is traditionally considered an administrative topic, in many cases it is the web designer or developer who has to field questions when they arise. These days, businesses expect to get Google Analytics-style usage reporting. SharePoint 2010 provides this sort of reporting out-of-the-box by logging usage and performance information into the SharePoint Logging Database. This logging is enabled by default and it is possible to read, query, and build reports directly from this usage database as needed. The types of events that are logged include page requests, feature use, search query usage, site inventory usage, timer jobs, and rating usage (see Figure 2-10).

Additional usage analytics are provided by the *developer dashboard*. This dashboard shows detailed information about each page load, enabling you to identify and troubleshoot performance issues. The dashboard is disabled by default but it can be enabled using STSADM or PowerShell.

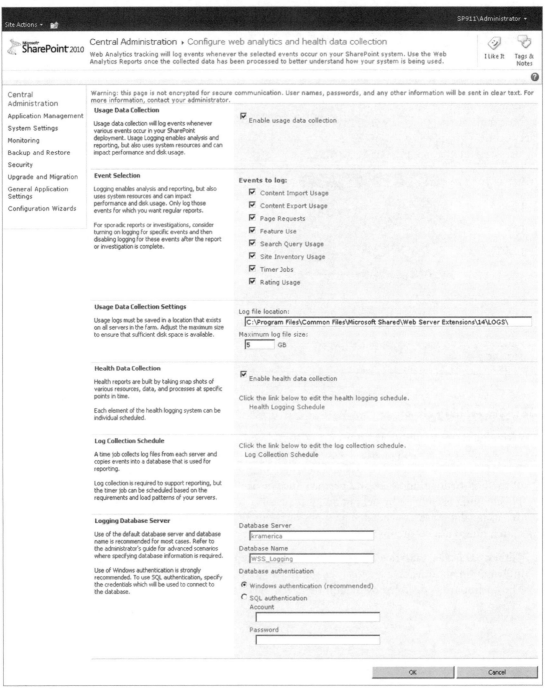

FIGURE 2-10

Multi-Lingual User Interface (MUI)

Many organizations have employees who speak different native languages, and another new feature of SharePoint 2010 is the Multi-Lingual User Interface (MUI), which dynamically changes elements of the user interface based on the language specified by the user. With MOSS 2007, multi-lingual capabilities were addressed with a feature called variations (still available in SharePoint 2010), which basically creates a separate site for each language. MUI is different in that it allows a single site to support multiple languages. When a user visits a site with MUI enabled, SharePoint automatically checks the language specified in the browser settings and different aspects of the site can be shown in the user's selected language. The following table highlights the various areas that are MUI enabled:

Application Content	Menus
	Controls
	Custom Actions
	Site (Title, Descriptions, Icon Description)
	Lists (Title, Description)
	Global navigation/Top Link bar (Links)
	Current Navigation/ Quick Launch (Links, Headings)
	Global Breadcrumb
	Local Breadcrumb
	Managed Metadata (Taxonomy)
	Site Content Types (Name, Description, Groups)
	List Content Types (Name, Description)
	Site Columns (Name, Description, Groups)
	List Columns (Name, Description)
Settings and Help	Settings Pages
	Help
	Images
Developer Content	Features
	Solutions

Obviously, MUI has an impact on the user interface; from a branding perspective, it enables dynamic modification of site elements according to the language specified. For example, you could change a logo at the top of the site to better support a different language. Any of the elements defined in the preceding table could tap into the MUI capabilities.

MUI is not meant to be used as a replacement for variations; rather, it is an enhancement to the multi-language capabilities of SharePoint. For many multi-language scenarios, variations and MUI will be used together to create the final solution.

Accessibility

Another area of significant improvement is SharePoint accessibility. The *Web Content Accessibility Guidelines (WCAG)*, published by the W3C's Web Accessibility Initiative, were created to make web content more accessible, mostly for disabled users but also for all types of user agents. In other words, the WCAG enables developers to create a site that can be accessed by a multitude of users — whether they are visually impaired or using a mobile phone or even a different browser. SharePoint 2010 has been designed to more closely follow industry web development standards (XHTML), which also enables delivering an interface that is WCAG 2.0 AA compliant. When the first details about SharePoint 2010 began to emerge, there was some confusion regarding exactly what was meant by saying that the new version would be "standards compliant." Although the HTML generated by SharePoint 2010 is significantly cleaner than previous versions, it is not XHTML compliant and will not pass any of the various compliance validators.

With SharePoint 2007, lack of better accessibility was a frequent complaint and often prevented many organizations from using the product because of strict guidelines they were required to adhere to. For example, a government agency might require that all their websites be WCAG-compliant. Some organizations even heavily modified SharePoint 2007 to ensure that the HTML code it was generating was compliant. This was an extremely time-consuming, and therefore expensive, undertaking, making it impractical for most organizations. The new accessibility features of SharePoint 2010 should not only increase its adoption in the marketplace, but also change the product's overall branding potential, as it is now easier for designers to create sites that function uniformly across more browsers.

HOW THE BRANDING STORY HAS CHANGED

The SharePoint branding story has improved significantly with every release. Although the jump in the improvements from SharePoint 2003 to 2007 probably represents an overall bigger change to the branding story itself, the changes in SharePoint 2010 are significant in other very important ways. With SharePoint 2007 the platform went through a massive change that allowed designers to create SharePoint sites that could be designed to look like any other .NET website. The options were nearly limitless. However, even though it was possible to create nearly any design in SharePoint, the techniques required to create the design were not ones that traditional web designers would find familiar. With SharePoint 2010, the platform itself and the techniques required to customize the UI will feel more familiar to designers who are trying to customize it for the first time. And designers who have experience working with the SharePoint UI will be excited about the cleaner HTML and better cross-browser support, which should reduce the amount of time spent tweaking designs to get them just right. SharePoint 2010 also now makes it possible for non-designers to more easily create custom branded sites with the use of the new theming engine and the new controls available for editing content. The branding story for SharePoint 2010 represents changes that should positively impact all users.

Changes to Master Pages

Like the previous version of the product, SharePoint 2010 still makes use of master pages. Additionally, it is still true that you cannot render a page in SharePoint without a master page.

However, several enhancements have been made with respect to how the master pages work in SharePoint.

One of the biggest changes is that now application pages use a dynamic master page defined on a per-site basis. Application pages are those whose URL contains the _layouts directory. A good example of an application page is the Site Settings page (`settings.aspx`). In SharePoint 2007, the only options for modifying the look and feel of application pages were to modify the `application .master` file on the SharePoint server, which was not a supported behavior by Microsoft, or to create a custom theme. When applied, custom themes did provide styling to the application pages, but creating custom themes that matched a custom master page was often tricky or required double the work. Not only does SharePoint 2010 add greater flexibility in terms of how branding is applied to these system pages, it also provides a fail-safe mechanism: If an error occurs in the master page used by application pages, SharePoint will automatically fall back to using the system's `v4.master` master page so that the pages can still be accessed.

Out-of-the-box, SharePoint 2010 ships with several master pages. The two most useful master pages are:

➤ `v4.master` — The `v4.master` master page should be considered the new equivalent of `default.master` from previous versions. It displays a traditional UI that is well suited to intranets, and it is available in both SharePoint Foundation and SharePoint Server 2010 (see Figure 2-11).

➤ `nightandday.master` — The `nightandday.master` master page is designed for use with Internet sites and large corporate intranet sites, and is available only in SharePoint Server when publishing is enabled (Figure 2-12).

FIGURE 2-11

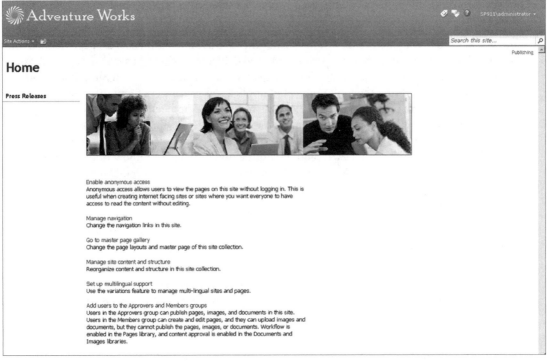

FIGURE 2-12

The HTML used in this master page is much cleaner than the out-of-the-box master pages from the previous version, which makes it a good example to learn from and extend for custom branding projects. The master page itself is very basic-looking, most likely because the SharePoint development team assumed that the vast majority of organizations will prefer to create a unique site, rather than use a boilerplate created for them.

Both of the new master pages in SharePoint 2010 work with the new themes, unlike SharePoint 2007, which required `default.master` in order for the themes to work properly.

 To learn about additional specific changes to master pages, see Chapter 8, "Master Pages."

Standards Compliance in SharePoint 2010

The improvements to accessibility in SharePoint 2010 were covered earlier in this chapter, but how do these changes impact the overall standards compliance story? The easiest way to understand the impact of standards is to consider how the branding process usually worked with SharePoint 2007. Designers often would create a mockup of the site, create the HTML, and then integrate the HTML into a

SharePoint master page and page layout. As a final step, they'd test the design in all of the organization's supported browsers — typically, both Internet Explorer and Mozilla Firefox. Then they would identify some subtle design elements that didn't match exactly, requiring a frustrating process of massaging the HTML and CSS to ensure that the design was rendered uniformly across different browsers.

Creating custom designs in SharePoint 2010 should be a simpler process for designers. Because the HTML is cleaner, it should be easier for designers to create the look and feel they want — without having to wrestle with the code as much as they did in the previous version. And once the design is implemented, it is more likely to look the same across multiple browsers.

Some designers might still be unhappy that despite all the improvements to SharePoint 2010, it still is not 100 percent XHTML-compliant. Although that's true, many improvements have been made, such as cleaner HTML rendered by most of the controls and fewer tables in the design. As a general rule, the new controls being written for SharePoint will produce XHTML-compliant code; it is the older controls that are generating noncompliant code. Over time, those will be replaced, but for now the changes to standards compliance in SharePoint 2010 are a big step in the right direction even if it won't pass an XHTML validator.

Themes Use the New Engine

The new theme engine in SharePoint 2010 is a huge change to the branding story for a number of reasons. The main reason is that it enables users to quickly create a site with branding that matches their organization's corporate branding by clicking a few buttons. In just a few minutes, even non-technical users can apply custom branding to all their SharePoint sites. This significantly lowers the entry barriers for SharePoint branding.

Because the new theming engine is dramatically different from the one used by previous versions of SharePoint, organizations with existing custom themes will not be able to carry them forward to SharePoint 2010. If this describes your scenario, you have two options for applying your branding to this version of the product: Create a custom master page or try to match your color scheme by creating a new v4 theme. Keep in mind that the older theme engine allowed much greater control over the UI, enabling the creation of themes that significantly changed the look and feel of the site. The SharePoint 2010 theme engine is easier to use, which will be good for most users, but other than changing a few colors and fonts, it provides less flexibility in terms of customization. The gap between what's possible with a custom theme and a custom master page is now much larger. In short, the price of easily creating themes is fewer options, and creating custom master pages is still an advanced topic.

MIGRATING FROM SHAREPOINT 2007 TO SHAREPOINT 2010

SharePoint 2007 has been reported to have more than 100 million users worldwide. Therefore, the odds are good that in addition to new users, many organizations will be upgrading to SharePoint 2010. Because this is a book about SharePoint branding and design, it is not possible to provide exhaustive detail about the upgrade process here; however, it is important to understand at a high level the steps involved and how the migration can impact branding.

Hardware and Software Requirements

Before discussing the upgrade process, it is important to take a look at the hardware and software requirements for SharePoint 2010:

	PRODUCTION	DEVELOPMENT
Operating System	Windows Server 2008 RTM or R2 (64-bit only)	Windows Server 2008 RTM or R2 (64-bit only)
Database Server Software	SQL Server 2005 SP2 or later (64-bit only)	SQL Server 2005 SP2 or later (64-bit only)
	SQL Server 2008 SP1 CU2 or later (64-bit only)	SQL Server 2008 SP1 CU2 or later (64-bit only)
CPU	2.5 GHz Quad Core	2.5 GHz Dual Core
RAM	8 GB	4 GB

Source: http://technet.microsoft.com/en-us/library/cc262485(office.14).aspx

Note that it is also possible to install SharePoint 2010 on Windows 7 64-bit for development purposes.

You might notice from the preceding table that SharePoint 2010 requires a 64-bit OS and the 64-bit version of SQL Server 2005 or 2008. This is going to be an important consideration for companies that want to upgrade from a 32-bit version of SharePoint. There's no getting around it: SharePoint 2010 is not compatible with a 32-bit environment. If this is the case for your organization, it is important to carefully plan your migration strategy to include new software — and maybe new hardware if your current environment doesn't meet the minimum requirements. If you are planning to run a development environment, the new requirements make it particularly tricky if you have a laptop because of the RAM requirements. If you are shopping for a new laptop, just be careful to look at the maximum amount of RAM the new laptop supports.

Overview of Migration Steps

The first step in any migration is to verify your configuration and start preparing for the actual migration. This begins with making sure that Service Pack 2 has been applied to SharePoint 2007. This adds a new STSADM command called the Pre-Upgrade Checker. This tool will provide valuable information about your SharePoint farm, including the following:

➤ All servers and the total amount of content

➤ Search configuration info

➤ Alternate access mappings

➤ All Features

➤ Site definitions

➤ Language packs

In addition, the Pre-Upgrade Checker will also identify other potential issues such as large lists and missing upgrade dependencies. The valuable information provided by this tool will enable administrators to determine which steps are required to complete the migration.

For more information about the Pre-Upgrade Checker, see `http://technet` `.microsoft.com/en-us/library/dd789638.aspx`.

After identifying any potential issues and addressing them, the next step is to determine which upgrade method would make the most sense for your environment. There are two primary methods for upgrading from SharePoint 2007 to SharePoint 2010:

> ➤ **In-place upgrade** — Use the in-place upgrade method if your goal is to upgrade your farm using the hardware on which it is currently installed.

> ➤ **Database attach upgrade** — The database attach method enables you to back up content databases from SharePoint 2007, move them to a new farm, and attach the database to SharePoint 2010. The database will be automatically upgraded when it is attached to the new farm.

Which method is right for your farm? The first consideration would be to look at your existing servers and compare it against the recommendations for SharePoint 2010. Many organizations will need to move to new operating systems or versions of SQL to support the new 64-bit requirements, or simply move to Windows Server 2008. If your current environment requires new hardware or software, the database attach method would be the best option. If your environment already meets the requirements for SharePoint 2010, the in-place method might be a good fit.

Overview of Visual Upgrade

Microsoft has added a new option during the migration process called the *Visual Upgrade.* Essentially, there are two pieces to the upgrade: the database component and the UI parts. Visual Upgrade makes it easier for users to upgrade from SharePoint 2007 by providing support for Office SharePoint Server 2007 master pages and CSS. This means that if you choose to use the Visual Upgrade feature, once you've upgraded your SharePoint implementation you will still be able to view your site using the Office SharePoint Server 2007 branding assets. The goal of the Visual Upgrade feature is to enable organizations to upgrade to SharePoint 2010 to take advantage of most of the new functionality while providing some time to get these branding assets updated. As mentioned throughout this chapter, a significant number of changes have been made to the UX that require new controls in the master pages in order to work. For example, if you were to use the Visual Upgrade feature, your site would look exactly like it did in SharePoint 2007 — you wouldn't have the ribbon but you would have all the new options available under the Site Settings menu.

An upgraded site can exist in one of three states: Office SharePoint Server 2007 (Visual Upgrade), SharePoint 2010 preview mode, and SharePoint 2010. The preview mode enables administrators to view the site in the SharePoint 2010 user interface before committing to it. This setting is specified in each individual website, providing granular control of the Visual Upgrade experience.

SUMMARY

A vast number of new features and enhancements specifically related to the user experience have been added to SharePoint 2010. The Fluent UI, or ribbon, is the most obvious change. Every user who interacts with SharePoint 2010 will encounter the ribbon as soon as they try to make any changes. Although this will likely cause some grumbling as users learn to use the new interface, it does reduce clicks and make it easier to perform many common tasks.

The addition of the new theming engine will make it possible for more users to create custom branded sites by choosing a few colors and fonts. This task was previously much more complicated, and creating a SharePoint site with colors that match your organization's branding standards is now easier than ever before.

Perhaps the most significant changes are those related to standards. SharePoint 2010 is now compliant with WCAG 2.0, which will make it easier for everyone to access content in SharePoint. The master pages are now XHTML-compliant, so most modern browsers will present SharePoint in the same way. The improvements to standards compliance means cleaner HTML, which in turn means better cross-browser support and an overall easier experience when creating custom UIs in SharePoint. This should also benefit designers and web developers who are new to the platform because the HTML they will be working with is similar to what they would traditionally expect with other platforms.

Users who will be upgrading from SharePoint 2007 can take advantage of the Visual Upgrade feature to help make the upgrade process less painful. Visual Upgrade separates the upgrade of the database from the upgrade of the UI elements, enabling users to take advantage of all the powerful new capabilities of SharePoint 2010 while their old UI is updated to the latest version.

PART II
Branding Basics

3

Planning for Branding

WHAT'S IN THIS CHAPTER?

➤ How planning now alleviates pain later

➤ How to gather requirements for a SharePoint project

➤ Considerations when estimating a SharePoint project

➤ Creating a wireframe in Visio

➤ An overview of how to create realistic design comps

➤ Considerations when converting a design comp into working HTML

This chapter discusses the process of properly planning for SharePoint branding. In many ways, this topic is similar to the planning that would go into any software project, but the steps involved are often unique for creative projects. Even if you are experienced with planning typical design projects, this chapter will provide information for properly planning for SharePoint branding projects.

WHY PLAN FOR BRANDING?

Having read through the first two chapters now, you are probably eager to jump right into SharePoint Designer and start creating master pages for SharePoint. While this is certainly a tempting proposition, in any project of reasonable size it would probably be a mistake. The process of actually creating a brand in a SharePoint site involves several steps, including creating master pages, page layouts, CSS, and more. By effectively planning your branding before starting it, you have proactively considered exactly what you want to create and how it will be produced. Any adjustments or changes that are discovered during the planning process can be realized with much less effort than having to deal with them inside of SharePoint.

For example, if the planning process is skipped and the client decides that they hate the shade of blue that they themselves had chosen (don't laugh, it's happened before), you could be stuck spending hours changing CSS and images, checking them into SharePoint, approving files, refreshing your browser, and then potentially repeating the process a few more times as the changes are refined. If instead you utilize a planning phase, the client should notice the "offensive" blue color after looking at a static mockup of the design, and it could be changed quickly in a graphic design program.

In many ways, change is the reason why planning for branding is necessary. Enterprise websites frequently change, and the sooner a change can be caught in the design process, the easier it will be to effect. Beyond this, by planning for branding, questions are asked and approvals are given, thus avoiding many issues that may have gone unnoticed until later in the project — when making changes is a much harder pill to swallow.

Given that upfront planning clearly makes a lot of sense for most SharePoint websites, how much planning is needed? Do you need to spend months and months of daylong meetings? Not necessarily. Depending on the size of the project, the intricacy of the SharePoint site, and the amount of people involved (often known as *stakeholders*), planning for branding could take months, just a few days, or even hours. The next few sections discuss some of the key steps you should take when planning for branding. Although it may seem like a lot, keep in mind that smaller projects can get away with doing only a portion of them. For example, if your branding project requires only small changes to the out-of-the-box user interface, there is probably no need to go through the full process of making design comps. In many ways, the decision for how much planning is needed for a project will be unique for every project. The key to this process is to carefully consider your branding *before* actually executing it in SharePoint.

REQUIREMENTS ANALYSIS

Whether your SharePoint branding project is a site for 10 users or 10,000 users, before the project can be considered complete, certain requirements will undoubtedly need to be met. This is why the first step of almost any project, whether it is a SharePoint branding project or not, should be some amount of requirements analysis. Requirements analysis involves gathering and understanding the specific needs of a project. Typically this process includes asking a lot of questions and breaking larger problems into more manageable pieces to gain a better understanding of them. Requirements should not be vague or lofty ideas; instead, they should be both measurable and actionable. To put it another way, for a requirement to be useful, you should be able to tell when it has been accomplished successfully. If the requirement has no success criteria, it should be broken down into smaller, more discrete requirements that do.

Consider the following two example requirements. The first is ambiguous and not very measurable which makes it very difficult to know when the task is accomplished; whereas the second certainly can be measured for successful completion:

➤ **Requirement #1** — The project must have special business-to-business functionality.

➤ **Requirement #2** — The project must allow partners to log in remotely and manage their product lines.

Throughout the requirements analysis process, some requirements may end up being less important than others, and eventually they may be dropped or moved to a later phase. The result of the requirements analysis process should be a list of needs that can be broken down into quantifiable tasks that measure the success of a project.

When gathering project requirements, it is important to involve all the project stakeholders. Stakeholders are people or groups that have a vested interest in the project's success. They may be affected by the project directly, such as an executive or manager, or indirectly, such as users who will depend on the final product. Figure 3-1 shows some of the potential stakeholders for a project.

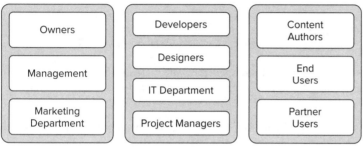

FIGURE 3-1

Keep in mind that adding stakeholders to the requirements gathering process can mean more time to complete the process and increased complexity. In fact, depending on the project, some stakeholders can actually be detrimental to successful requirements analysis. For example, the owner of a company may be too abstracted from day-to-day operations to give meaningful feedback, or certain employees, such as those recently hired, may not be able to offer a valuable opinion regarding the project. Determining the right stakeholders can be a difficult task, but at the end of the day, if someone has enough influence to change the project in later stages, it's a good idea to include that person early on. The reason is obvious: By involving the appropriate stakeholders early in the requirements analysis process, you can avoid making those dreaded, and costly, last-minute changes to a project to meet a critical need.

The following sections discuss the most important aspects of the requirements gathering that are necessary before starting any SharePoint branding project.

SharePoint Version

One of the first decisions to make is which version of SharePoint will be used for the project: SharePoint Server 2010 or SharePoint Foundation 2010 (or an older version like Microsoft Office SharePoint Server 2007 or Windows SharePoint Services 3.0)? Although SharePoint Server 2010 is more expensive than SharePoint Foundation 2010, it includes the Publishing Feature, which has several useful additions for branding projects:

➤ Navigation can be more easily controlled from the Web user interface and more options are available to the designer.

➤ Publishing sites enable you to change a master page by using the Web user interface. While you could use custom code to perform this task in SharePoint Foundation, it is not included out-of-the-box.

➤ Publishing sites enable more flexibility with themes, including the capability to apply the theme to all subsites at the same time.

➤ Publishing sites enable developers and designers to create page-level templates by using page layouts. Non-publishing sites utilize the wiki page concept of "text layout," which is similar to page layouts except that they are not configurable.

Type of SharePoint Website

Typically, SharePoint sites are set up as one of three types of website: public-facing Internet sites, internal-facing intranet sites, and extranets, which are have aspects of both. The users of each of these types of websites differ vastly. Here is a quick breakdown of some of the differences between them:

➤ **Internet sites** — These sites are usually marketing driven and typically have tightly controlled content with few content authors. They tend to be more stylistic than intranet sites, and are targeting a much wider spectrum of users. Because Internet sites are public facing, developers have no control over the type of browser or the screen resolution that will be used to visit the site.

➤ **Intranet sites** — These sites typically sit behind a corporate firewall and are specifically tailored to help internal users work in a more collaborative and efficient manner. Intranet sites usually have many content authors and numerous employees who are consuming documents and collaborating. Because these sites are internal facing, companies can control browser and screen-resolution requirements if desired.

➤ **Extranet sites** — These sites are a hybrid of the previous two. They are typically intranet sites that have a separate area for external users to authenticate into. From a branding perspective, the extranet area can be the similar to an Internet site or an intranet site, depending on the particular objective for the extranet. Sometimes an extranet can be collaborative and sometimes it can be simply information that is published to external users.

Targeted Browsers

Another important decision to make is which browsers and operating systems will be targeted by your branding. Although many people may say that a website should support all browsers equally, it is often impractical to test each and every browser for pixel-perfect display. This is why it's a good idea to decide early what browsers and operating systems will be supported by your SharePoint site. As mentioned earlier, this decision is typically much more important for public-facing Internet sites, for which you have no control over what browser users will be using to access the site. Conversely, corporations can dictate strict browser requirements for intranet sites; and prohibit unsupported browsers from accessing the system.

One typical way of choosing a level of supported browser is to consult industry websites that track this information across extremely large usage statistics. One such site is W3Counter.com; here are their published browser statistics as of May 2010 (`http://w3counter.com/globalstats.php`):

BROWSER VERSION	MARKET SHARE
Internet Explorer 8.0	25.35%
Firefox 3.6	20.67%
Internet Explorer 7.0	12.74%
Internet Explorer 6.0	7.64%
Firefox 3.5	6.81%
Chrome 4.0	6.49%
Safari 4.0	5.05%
Firefox 3.0	2.98%
Chrome 5.0	1.84%
Firefox 2.0	1.68%

As discussed in Chapter 2, SharePoint 2010 supports, with some minor limitations, most modern browsers. Other older or less popular browsers like IE6 are *not* supported by SharePoint 2010. This makes deciding not to support these browsers in your SharePoint site a lot easier because Microsoft doesn't support them either, but it might be helpful to provide a message to these users that it is time to upgrade their browser. This concept is discussed further in Chapter 8.

Screen Resolution

You also need to decide what screen resolution will be targeted for your SharePoint branding. Until a few years ago, computer monitors supported only a limited number of screen resolutions, mostly 800×600 or even 640×480. However, as LCD monitor prices have decreased significantly, it's not uncommon to see website visitors browsing at resolutions of 1920×1200 or higher. Currently, most web designers consider 1024×768 to be the most common screen resolution, followed closely by 1280×800.

As you create your branded SharePoint website, it is important to balance the desire to display large amounts of information with common user screen resolutions. This becomes even more important when you consider that users often install scrollbars and special toolbars that take up a portion of the screen real estate.

 Most of the examples in this book use a target browser size of 1024×768.

Information Architecture

Along with the physical appearance of a SharePoint site, another important aspect is the amount of information it will contain and how that information will be organized. *Information architecture* is the term used to describe a blueprint for outlining how information should be stored and organized.

This process is particularly important in content management systems like SharePoint, which often contain websites with hundreds or thousands of pages and documents. For the users approaching this mountain of information, the act of finding what they want can be similar to finding the proverbial needle in a haystack. Imagine going to your local grocery store for your favorite cereal and finding that the products were shelved randomly, in no logical fashion, just placed on the shelves in whatever order they arrived. It might take you an hour just to find your box of cereal. Luckily, grocery stores organize their products so that you can easily navigate them. Website information can be treated much the same way. If it is placed randomly, users will have a difficult time finding what they want. The key to designing a website that makes it easy for users to find the information they need is to create an effective taxonomy.

Taxonomy is the science of classifying and organizing things, and it is a core component of information architecture. In science it is often used to organize, or classify, plants and animals in a hierarchy based on their relationships. You may remember a famous taxonomy from science class: kingdom, phylum, class, order, family, genus, and species. This same method can be applied to a corporate SharePoint site, in this case organizing content by business units, functional role, or even an alphabetical directory.

When creating a taxonomy, it is important to think about the website's audience. How will they use the site? Are they familiar with your internal organizational structure or will they be expecting information to be organized differently? Different roles inside of an organization may use information differently. Executives may be looking for strategic information while workers on the floor may need specific information to do their job.

This structure will eventually manifest itself in the SharePoint site's navigation. Chapter 6 looks at SharePoint navigation in detail. Keep in mind that providing multiple forms of navigation could be beneficial. Some users may feel comfortable using the primary navigation, while others may prefer to search. Your site may even contain information that is so important it should "roll-up" to a top-level page from where the content is located. In these cases, a SharePoint Web Part would be perfect.

 You can learn more about Web Parts in Chapter 10, "Web Parts and XSLT."

Common SharePoint Branding Questions

The previous sections covered a few of the most important questions you need to answer in a SharePoint branding project requirements analysis process, but several others are helpful as well. Although each project is different, here is a list of some common questions:

➤ Is there an existing website or SharePoint site that the new SharePoint site will replace?

➤ Will master pages or SharePoint themes be used to create the branding? Will both be required?

➤ How will the pages of the site be created? Is there a person or team responsible for creating the content and entering data?

➤ Will this be a new design or will it be based on some existing branding?

➤ According to what criteria will the branding be judged a success? What goals does it need to address?

➤ Is there an existing corporate style guide that needs to be followed?

➤ Are there any existing branding or marketing materials that can or should be used, such as corporate logos?

➤ Are there any stylistic requirements, such as preferred or disliked colors, fonts, or imagery?

➤ Who will the audience be? What will they be looking for in the website? Are they corporate users? Are they teenagers? Would a cutting-edge, modern design speak to them or would a tried-and-true corporate layout be better?

➤ What sort of navigation is required? Horizontal navigation? Vertical navigation? Both? Are dynamic drop-downs or fly-outs desired for submenu items?

➤ Are custom page layouts required? Do they require custom content types?

➤ Are there any specific requirements for Web Parts to roll up content? Will they require custom development or just styling?

➤ Will any third-party Web Parts or controls be needed?

➤ Who will be approving the new branding?

➤ How will the branding be deployed to the production SharePoint server?

➤ What is the time frame to deliver the new branding?

Note that requirements analysis can be either a formal process, involving scheduled meetings and full documentation, or a brief process, involving very few key stakeholders and some quick decisions. Either way, the result should be a better understanding of what will actually be built — in this case, how SharePoint will look and behave.

PROJECT ESTIMATION

In many ways, project estimation for SharePoint is the same as any other IT project. Constraints such as due date, feature scope, and budget impact the estimation process greatly. These three common constraints are often interconnected; when one becomes more aggressive, it could affect the other two. Figure 3-2 shows the relationship between these three constraints.

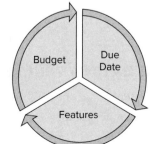

For instance, the budget could be too low to accommodate all the desired requirements. This would indicate that the scope needs to decrease. Alternatively, the timeline for delivery could be very aggressive, which could translate into more hours or workers being assigned to the project.

FIGURE 3-2

The topic of project estimation, in theory and in practice, could fill an entire book. A comprehensive discussion is therefore impossible within one chapter. In general, however, the process should involve the following steps:

1. Decide on a high-level project timeline. When will the project start and when do you estimate it will end?

2. Break down the requirements into specific tasks.

3. Estimate the amount of time each of those tasks will take.

4. Determine which resources will be working on each task. Will certain tasks require specialized skills? If so, be sure to account for the availability of someone with those skills.

5. To the extent possible, determine any roadblocks or risks you might face, and attempt to troubleshoot them proactively.

6. Allow enough time to include all phases of traditional development, including any necessary extra planning, building the branding and the SharePoint site, testing and review, making any necessary adjustments, and deploying the project to a production environment.

SharePoint projects have specific factors that could impact project estimation. The following is a list of some things that should be considered:

➤ Will the project involve creating custom master pages, or will it just use a SharePoint theme?

➤ What is the skill level of the designers and developers involved in the project? Do they have experience with SharePoint?

➤ How will the project be deployed to a production server? Will files just be customized with SharePoint Designer, or will a solution package be created?

➤ How complex is the design that is being attempted?

➤ How many different areas of SharePoint will be branded?

➤ How many Web Parts will need custom styling?

➤ How flexible is the due date and budget?

Even after thinking through all of this, estimates can still be wrong! SharePoint projects tend to have a lot of moving parts. Team members are often very dependent on each other's specific skill sets. Rarely in a SharePoint project will every task be accomplished by the same person; the server administrator who installs SharePoint will most likely not be the same person who designs the branding. Whether this is your first SharePoint project or your fiftieth, some amount of estimate padding is a good idea to account for any unseen problems.

CREATING WIREFRAMES

The previous sections have discussed many aspects of planning a branding project, but the next few sections will focus on the more creative aspects of planning. The creative planning process for larger websites often begins with the creation of several black-and-white wireframes. *Wireframes* are skeletal page designs; they capture the layout and flow of a website without focusing on colors and graphics.

At this point, you might be wondering why you should create a static, black-and-white wireframe when you plan to create a dynamic, full-color website. The major reason for creating wireframes before full-color comps is to ensure that all the stakeholders and decision makers focus on the layout and page flow, rather than get hung up on whether cornflower blue is better than robin's egg blue. This allows for quicker iteration between ideas because creating black-and-white wireframes is faster than creating full-color designs. In some cases, wireframes should be built for every page on a website, whereas in other cases you can get by with just making wireframes for the major sections of the site. The decision for whether wireframes should be made for every page will be different for every project, but it generally is based on how different all the pages will be and how granular you want to get with the planning process.

Before delving into the process of creating a wireframe, however, take a look at a sample wireframe for Randy's Waffles (the fictitious company that will be used in several examples throughout this book) created in Microsoft Visio. Figure 3-3 shows a sample website page wireframe.

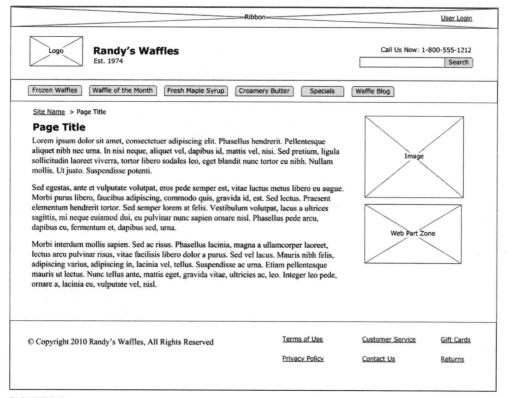

FIGURE 3-3

Notice that the focus of a wireframe is the placement of page content and functionality, not stylistic colors or fonts. By creating wireframes such as this, you enable the project's stakeholders to quickly visualize, and hopefully approve, the site's general layout. This gives designers a lot of latitude to create a branded SharePoint design using whatever styles they would like, because as long as it matches the approved wireframes, the design will meet the project's needs.

Wireframes can be created in a number of different ways, from simple pen and paper diagrams to dedicated software programs like Microsoft Visio or Adobe Illustrator. Visio is particularly well suited for this task because it includes prebuilt shapes or stencils that can be used to piece together typical Web user interfaces. Figure 3-4 shows the Visio Shapes Window with some common web shapes available for use.

 A particularly useful set of stencils is the GUUUI Web Prototyping Tool, found at www.guuui.com/issues/02_07.php. *It includes common browser and page shapes for websites.*

When creating a brand for SharePoint, a key consideration is what pieces of SharePoint functionality will be supported by the design. A typical SharePoint page is made up of several controls and other pieces of functionality. Some of these functional controls are required in order for SharePoint to be used, but others are purely optional, based on your own project requirements. This is particularly true for public-facing Internet sites; several pieces of SharePoint functionality are not appropriate to show to anonymous public website viewers. For instance, by default, the help button in the top-right corner of the typical SharePoint user interface contains help for SharePoint itself, not the website that users are currently viewing.

Figure 3-5 shows the default SharePoint user interface (based on v4.master), with each of the major areas of functionality labeled.

FIGURE 3-4   **FIGURE 3-5**

The following table describes each of these major functional areas:

1	The Ribbon	Also known as the Fluent User Interface, the ribbon is the contextual menu at the top of the SharePoint 2010 page that is used to interact with the current page or activity.
2	Site Actions	A drop-down menu, used primarily by authenticated users for managing many aspects of the SharePoint site.
3	Global Breadcrumbs Pop-out	This pop-out menu is the replacement for the global breadcrumbs in SharePoint 2007. It shows a hierarchical view of the current site with links to its parent sites.
4	Page State Action Button	A contextual shortcut button that often displays a quick link for editing and saving the page.
5	Ribbon Contextual Tabs	These tabs allow the user to switch between major sections of the ribbon. They are contextual based on the current activity on the page.
6	Welcome Menu	This control shows the current user name and has a drop-down for My Site, My Profile, My Settings, Sign in as Different User, and Sign Out. When users are not logged in, the control shows the Sign In link. If language packs are installed, this control also allows users to switch their language.
7	Developer Dashboard Launcher	This button is hidden by default and can be activated with STSADM or PowerShell. Clicking the button displays the developer dashboard, which is typically shown at the bottom of the page.
8	Title Logo	This is the main site icon that is shown by default in SharePoint. It can be changed by setting the Logo URL from Site Actions ➪ Site Settings ➪ Title, description, and icon.
9	Breadcrumb	Specific to the default v4 master page, this is a combination of the site title and the current page's title that is designed to look like a traditional breadcrumb.
10	Social Buttons	Social media buttons that are used to mark the page as liked or to add tags and notes.
11	Top Link Bar	Also known as the top navigation bar or global navigation, this is the primary horizontal navigation for the site.
12	Search Area	Comprised of a search box to enter search terms and a button to start the search. If SharePoint is configured to show search scopes, they will appear to the left of the search box.
13	Help Icon	The help icon links to the SharePoint 2010 product help documents. Often hidden for public-facing Internet sites.
14	Quick Launch	Also known as the left navigation or current navigation. It is typically used for secondary vertical navigation to show pages related to the current location.

continues

(continued)

15	Tree View	Displays a Windows Explorer–style tree view representation of the current site. Often hidden for public-facing Internet sites.
16	Recycle Bin	A link to a collection of items that were recently deleted from the site. Often hidden for public-facing Internet sites.
17	All Site Content	Known as the View All Site Content button in SharePoint 2007, this links to the All Site Content page of the SharePoint site. Often hidden for public-facing Internet sites.
18	Body Area	This is the main content placeholder. It is required for rendering the actual content of the current page.

When creating wireframes for your SharePoint site, consider that not all of this functionality needs to be supported in your SharePoint branding. Also, it is important to remember all the different types of content that are supported in SharePoint 2010. It is easy to forget that content authors could be creating wiki sites, blog sites, meeting workspaces, and many other types of content other than just the traditional content pages.

Looking at the wireframes for Randy's Waffles again, note that not every single piece of SharePoint 2010 functionality is going to be included on this site. Figures 3-6 and 3-7 show the home page wireframe and a subpage wireframe, respectively.

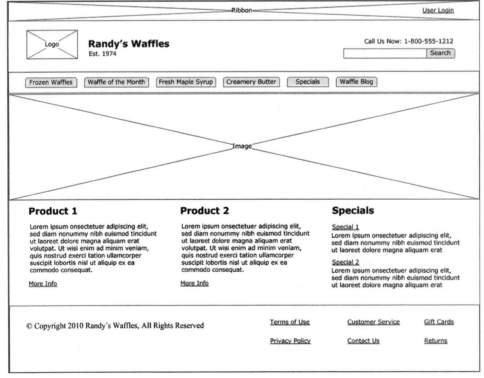

FIGURE 3-6

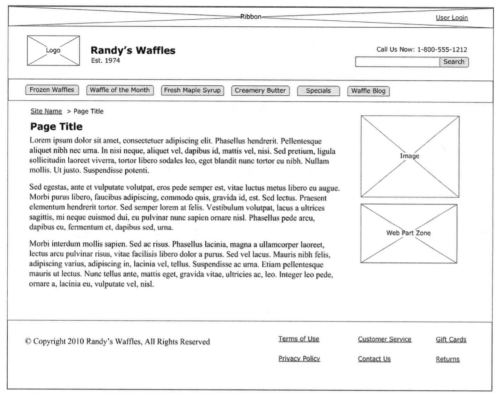

FIGURE 3-7

You can see that some of the functionality that won't be included in this design is the left navigation, the Tree View, the Recycle Bin, and the All Site Content link. Because this wireframe is diagramming the public Internet site for Randy's Waffles, this functionality would probably only confuse anonymous Internet visitors who are not familiar with SharePoint. Conversely, if you were to create wireframes for Randy's Waffles intranet pages, they would probably include most of these functional elements because intranet users may need them to collaborate more efficiently with each other.

Another thing to notice in these wireframes is that the body content areas are filled with fake text. This technique is known as *greeking* because it uses text in Greek or Latin (as shown in the figure) in a pseudo random pattern to fill in the blocks of text. Much like other aspects of the wireframes, the goal here is get decision makers to focus on the general layout, rather than the actual text in the document. Greeking works better than just filling in the text blocks with "Content goes here" because it more accurately mimics the size and spacing of actual body content. Rather than make up greeked text by hand, resources like Lorem2 (`http://lorem2.com`) provide stock greeked passages of varying size for anyone to copy and paste into their wireframes and design comps.

 The Visio wireframes for Randy's Waffles are available for download, with the rest of the examples in this book, at Wrox.com.

By creating wireframes early in a SharePoint branding project, decisions about what should be on the page and how it should be generally arranged on the screen can be discussed and agreed upon. When it's time to actually create the user interface, the designer will be able to focus purely on the creative aspects of the design rather than get mired in functional requirements.

CREATING REALISTIC DESIGN COMPS

Creating wireframes is certainly a valuable process for planning a new SharePoint website; however, for any serious branding effort, you will need to make decisions based on creative concepts such as colors, font, and images. Before actually creating a brand in SharePoint, much like with wireframes, it would be good to have a way of creating realistic mockups of what the final website will look like. This is where *design comps* (sometimes known as *prototypes*) come into play. Unlike wireframes, design comps are intended to mimic the final branding of the actual SharePoint site as closely as possible without actually creating any code. Design comps should include all of the things that make up a final design, such as colors, fonts, form elements, photos, and anything else that will appear on the final rendered website page.

Many programs are available to create realistic design comps. (You could even use a pencil and paper if you want a sense of nostalgia.) While you could use something like Microsoft Paint, which has been included with every copy of Windows since version 1.0, there are some compelling reasons to seek out a more advanced solution. Design programs such as Microsoft Expression Design 3.0 and Adobe Photoshop CS4 are shining examples of modern software that is geared toward creating design comps (among many other things). Both programs provide capabilities that aid in creating and maintaining reusable realistic design comps. Figure 3-8 shows the Randy's Waffles design comp in Photoshop CS4.

FIGURE 3-8

Features of Modern Design Programs

The following sections highlight some of the features that make using a modern design application ideal for creating design comps.

 The examples in this section use Photoshop CS4. Similar functions are available in Expression Design 3.0 for everything discussed here.

Layers and Layer Groups

Unlike Microsoft Paint, where all design elements share the same "flat" surface, modern design programs utilize layers to separate elements. Layers create the illusion that each successive group of elements is floating above the previous group. Each layer can be manipulated or even deleted completely independently of the other layers. This flexibility enables designs to evolve over time with changing business or organizational requirements, and layers can be hidden or changed to accommodate these changes without redoing the entire design. Layers also provide the capability to create realistic visual effects such as adding depth with drop shadows. Figure 3-9 shows the Layers menu in Photoshop CS4.

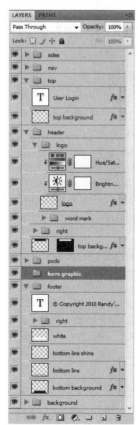

Editable Text

In a modern design tool like Expression Design or Photoshop CS4, text is not static. Not only can you control the font face, weight, size, color, and style, you can also change and rearrange the text at will without affecting the surrounding layout. Figure 3-10 shows text being edited in Photoshop CS4.

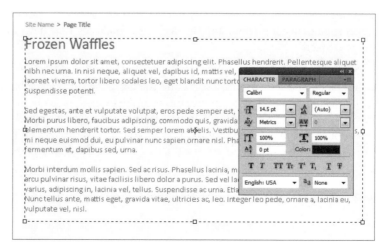

FIGURE 3-9   **FIGURE 3-10**

When working with text for design comps in Photoshop, a common "gotcha" is anti-aliasing. Anti-aliasing is a mechanism that reduces distortion of text and images at lower resolutions. While this is generally helpful for creating pleasing designs, it can create unrealistic expectations regarding how your final text will look in a browser. Because Internet Explorer doesn't anti-alias the same way as Photoshop, sometimes text in Photoshop will seem smoother than the same text in Internet Explorer. It's important to try a few different anti-aliasing settings in Photoshop and try to match how text normally looks in a browser. This usually means that very small text may need to have its anti-aliasing set to "None." Figure 3-11 shows the anti-aliasing menu for text in Photoshop CS4.

Making the Design Comp Realistic

With all the amazing things you can do in Expression Design and Photoshop, it's tempting to go crazy creating the world's most uniquely branded website. However, it's important to remember that the design comp is meant to imitate what can actually be created in a SharePoint 2010 website. Ultimately, learning whether something is easily creatable in SharePoint will take some time to get the hang of. One good method for learning this is to look at the functionality provided in the out-of-the-box master pages, both `v4.master` and `nightandday.master`. For example, if you are planning to use SharePoint's own top navigation functionality, it will be difficult to support very long navigation item titles. This is because the horizontal navigation rendering in SharePoint does not wrap multiple lines of text per item by default.

FIGURE 3-11

As you are creating your design comp, it's a good idea to consider how the various elements in your design will be created in SharePoint. Will the elements use out-of-the-box SharePoint functionality with some styles applied to them, or will they require some amount of custom code? If they can be accomplished with Web Parts, will they require custom XSLT for styling? All of the answers to these questions aren't needed immediately while creating the design comp, but the project's schedule and budget should be considered, and the design's complexity may need to be scaled back to accommodate these factors.

As the design comps are completed, key stakeholders may need to be engaged again to sign off on the final look and feel. Are the colors and the design in line with what they were hoping for? If not, it's not uncommon to have a few iterations of the design comps before they are fully agreed upon and finalized. While this can certainly be time-consuming, ultimately it's much better to work these issues out earlier in a design tool than try to adjust master pages and CSS later. Figures 3-12 and 3-13 show the final design comps for the Randy's Waffles home page and subpage, respectively.

FIGURE 3-12

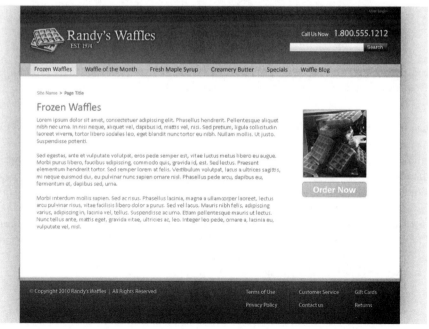

FIGURE 3-13

The layered Photoshop design comps for Randy's Waffles are available for download with the rest of the examples in this book at Wrox.com.

Note that this design comp is highly stylized relative to the out-of-the-box SharePoint branding. If your project needs to make only minor changes to the v4.master master page styling, you could create a design comp by starting with a screenshot of an existing SharePoint page. From there, you could use a design program to replace only the areas that are going to change. This technique could be used to quickly and easily create realistic design comps for the kind of simple branding that is discussed in Chapter 5.

CONVERTING DESIGN COMPS INTO WORKING HTML AND CSS

Now that the realistic design comps have been created and agreed upon, it's time to finally start writing code! However, as with the other concepts in this chapter, an ounce of pre-SharePoint work could save a pound of pain later. If your branding project is more than just simple adjustments to the out-of-the-box SharePoint branding, it's a good idea to create a functioning HTML version of the design comps. Also, because this will be a modern web design, you will need a healthy amount of CSS as well, to position and style your elements. The good news is that the HTML and CSS you create here can actually be used in your SharePoint branding as the basis for a custom master page and custom CSS. Chapter 8, "Master Pages," talks about this topic further.

 This section discusses some of the key concepts for creating a working HTML and CSS version of the design comp. Most of these concepts focus on considerations that need to be made specifically for a SharePoint project. It is assumed that you already have a good understanding of basic HTML and CSS concepts. If you need a refresher on these topics, check out Beginning Web Programming with HTML, XHTML, and CSS *(Wrox, 2008).*

Much like creating wireframes and design comps, there are several ways to create HTML and CSS. The most basic method is to use Notepad or another text editor that is already included on your computer for manually writing HTML and CSS. This works fine for small HTML projects, but for anything of significant complexity, a dedicated HTML editing program is extremely helpful. Again, Microsoft and Adobe have two of the most popular options for working with HTML: Microsoft Expression Web 3.0 and Adobe Dreamweaver CS4, both of which are more than capable of creating HTML and CSS for this project. The primary benefits of such software are that they provide code completion for HTML and CSS as well as a WYSIWYG (What You See Is What You Get) visual design view. While SharePoint Designer contains these features as well, the 2010 version is really not intended for working with HTML and CSS outside of a SharePoint server.

DOCTYPEs and SharePoint 2010

Before starting any HTML web page, you first must decide which DOCTYPE will be used. A *DOCTYPE* is a piece of code that is declared at the top of a document that instructs browsers or other software to use a specific language to interpret the rest of the included code. If you haven't heard of DOCTYPEs, you may be thinking that all browsers already understand HTML, so why the need to declare a DOCTYPE at the top? Although you can create HTML for SharePoint or anything else that has no DOCTYPE declared, this method could cause the browser to render the page in unexpected ways. In fact, without any other intervention, an HTML page without a DOCTYPE is rendered by Internet Explorer in what's known as *Quirks mode*. Quirks mode is similar to how IE 5.5 rendered pages, which can't be a good thing; it was released ten years ago after all!

Several DOCTYPEs are available that will render your code in predictable ways. The following is a list of the most popular DOCTYPES in use today:

➤ **HTML 4.01 Strict** — Allows all HTML elements but does not allow deprecated elements such as the <font> tag.

➤ **HTML 4.01 Transitional** — Allows all HTML elements including deprecated elements.

➤ **XHTML 1.0 Strict** — Similar to HTML 4.01 Strict, but all tags must be well-formed XML. Deprecated elements are allowed but must also be well-formed XML

➤ **XHTML 1.0 Transitional** — Similar to HTML 4.01 Transitional, but all tags must be well-formed XML. Deprecated elements are allowed but must also be well-formed XML

So, which DOCTYPE is right for creating HTML that is destined to be used in a SharePoint 2010 site? In SharePoint 2007, this topic was much more subjective, but in SharePoint 2010, Microsoft's own master pages all use the XHTML 1.0 Strict DOCTYPE. It stands to reason that Microsoft's latest controls are built to work best using this DOCTYPE, so it is recommended that you stick to it. All the examples in this book will use the XHTML 1.0 Strict DOCTYPE.

Before moving on to the next topic, it's worth saying a few words about W3C Compliance. Many web designers use various forms of W3C HTML validators to ensure that their HTML adheres correctly to their chosen DOCTYPE. (The W3C's own validator can be found at http://validator.w3.org.) The nice thing about validating your HTML in a validator is that, in theory, if your HTML is valid and your site has a valid DOCTYPE, then any browser that is coded to display valid HTML properly will render yours the same. The bad news is that when you actually create your branding in SharePoint 2010, the resulting page will not properly validate as XHTML 1.0 compliant. This is because several legacy ASP.NET controls used in SharePoint 2010 do not produce valid XHTML code. Does this mean that W3C compliance should be ignored in SharePoint branding projects? Not at all. Microsoft's goal is to ensure that any new control they create for SharePoint in the future will be XHTML compliant, and in theory software updates could get SharePoint to be fully compliant. Beyond that, by creating HTML and CSS that is XHTML compliant, you are, in effect, ensuring that everything you created should work the same in most modern browsers.

The sample HTML that is provided with this chapter for Randy's Waffles is fully XHTML 1.0 compliant. Figure 3-14 shows the result of the W3C validator for the HTML for Randy's Waffles.

FIGURE 3-14

Most web development programs make using a DOCTYPE as easy as simply choosing the DOCTYPE when you create a new HTML file. The DOCTYPE is placed on the first line of the HTML. A typical blank XHTML 1.0-compliant HTML file would look like this:

```
<!DOCTYPE html PUBLIC "-//W3C//DTD XHTML 1.0 Strict//EN"
    "http://www.w3.org/TR/xhtml1/DTD/xhtml1-strict.dtd">
<html xmlns="http://www.w3.org/1999/xhtml">
<head>
<meta http-equiv="Content-Type" content="text/html; charset=utf-8" />
<title>Untitled Document</title>
</head>

<body>
</body>
</html>
```

Compatibility Mode in Internet Explorer 8

Another topic related to DOCTYPEs is compatibility mode in Internet Explorer 8 (IE8). Microsoft introduced this feature to help with the display of web pages that were coded to older versions of Internet Explorer. Compatibility mode tells the browser how to interpret and render a website through the use of a `meta` tag named `"X-UA-Compatible"`, which is placed in the `<head>` section of a web page:

```
<meta http-equiv="X-UA-Compatible" content="IE=8" />
```

There are several supported compatibility modes for Internet Explorer 8:

COMPATIBILITY MODE	DESCRIPTION
IE=5	IE5.5/Quirks rendering mode
IE=7	IE7 Standards rendering mode
IE=EmulateIE7	IE7 Standards or Quirks rendering mode, depending on the DOCTYPE
IE=8	IE8 Standards rendering mode
IE=EmulateIE8	IE8 Standards or Quirks rendering mode, depending on the DOCTYPE
IE=edge	Uses the latest rendering mode, which is currently IE8 Standards Mode

An interesting aspect of compatibility mode is that Microsoft maintains a list of sites that are known to load poorly in IE8, and instead automatically loads them in the IE7 emulation mode. Also, by default, any site that is local to the browser's intranet zone is also loaded automatically in IE7 Emulation mode.

Because SharePoint 2010 was created with IE8 in mind, all of the out-of-the-box master pages that Microsoft provides with SharePoint 2010 have the compatibility mode set to IE=8, which locks IE8 and future versions of IE into rendering the page in IE8 Standards rendering mode regardless of which DOCTYPE is applied. Keep in mind that other browsers such as Mozilla's Firefox or Google's Chrome do not use this `meta` tag to determine a rendering mode, so a DOCTYPE still needs to be declared. To ensure compatibility with future versions of Internet Explorer, always set the compatibility mode `meta` tag when creating HTML for use in SharePoint.

Table-less Design

When it comes to modern website design, no other topic has generated as much debate as that of table-less design. Back in the early days of web development, when Internet Explorer was young and Netscape was still a contender, almost all website layouts leveraged tables to create a rich user interface. Over time, as browsers have evolved, so has their support for CSS-based page layout. Because HTML tables were originally intended for displaying truly tabular data, it can be argued that HTML tables that are used for page layout are inappropriate from a readability and semantic point of view. In recent years, web designers have begun to embrace CSS for any sort of decorative layout, using HTML tables only with actual grids of data.

With SharePoint 2010, Microsoft has also embraced this concept in its own HTML design. Unlike SharePoint 2007, where HTML tables were rampant throughout the code, SharePoint 2010 uses tables for layout only in legacy controls that were not rewritten for various reasons. When you are creating HTML for use in a SharePoint design, it is best practice to use as few HTML tables as possible to lay out the page elements. The example HTML for Randy's Waffles that is used in this chapter was created without the use of any HTML tables.

Slicing Images from the Design Comp

Web pages typically aren't just gigantic single images that load in the middle of the browser; instead, they consist of many smaller images and text. Now that you are creating the HTML and CSS, the design comp will come in handy for making all these individual images that will make up the web page. This process of saving smaller web formatting images is sometimes referred to as *creating slices*.

Most modern design programs, including Photoshop CS4 and Expression Design 3, support the capability to save images in all three major web formats: GIF, JPEG, and PNG. The following table describes the differences between these formats and which format is best for a specific image.

FORMAT	DESCRIPTION
GIF	Limited to 256 colors with transparency. Good for images that have a small amount of color, or images for which exact colors are critical. This format is also good for images that need transparency or animation. The primary way to reduce the file size of GIF is by reducing the number of colors it supports.
JPEG	Supports compression but does not support transparency. Because this format supports millions of colors, it is better for photos. Also, because compression can be adjusted, file sizes can be reduced while maintaining a relative amount of quality and color. Does not support animation.
PNG	Supports millions of colors and transparency. This format is the newest of the three and in some ways it was intended to replace GIFs (though without support for animation). Until recent browser versions, PNG was not fully supported in a reliable way. Because SharePoint 2010 does not support Internet Explorer 6 (one of the primary browsers that did not support PNGs fully), Microsoft has decided to use PNGs heavily in their designs.

In Photoshop CS4, the primary means for saving web-formatted images is to use the Save for Web & Devices menu (see Figure 3-15). Always choose the image type that balances quality with size to ensure that the result is both visually appealing and quickly downloadable.

When saving web slices, the following guidelines can help you achieve the best results:

➤ **Backgrounds** — When saving an image that will appear in the background of other elements, be sure to hide any elements from the design comp that are floating over the background before saving it. If a background has a repeating pattern, best practice is to save a small sliver of the graphic and use the `background-repeat` property of CSS for filling a larger area; this allows the file size to be smaller.

➤ **Text that can't be replicated easily on all computers** — Heavily stylized text or text that uses very specific fonts is sometimes best saved as an image. This image can be used loaded on the page instead of letting the browser try to render the text.

➤ **Photos, logos, and buttons** — These are typically independent design elements and should be saved separately from the rest of the design. Sometimes they will need to be saved with transparency so that they can float over backgrounds.

The Randy's Waffles example uses a total of 17 image slices, including backgrounds, text, photos, buttons, and logos.

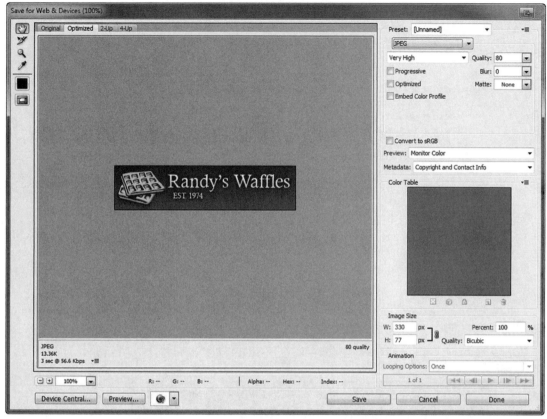

FIGURE 3-15

Creating the HTML and CSS

Putting everything you have learned in the previous sections together with existing knowledge of HTML and CSS techniques should enable you to create HTML versions of the design comps that mimic them closely. As stated before, the HTML and CSS that were used to create Randy's Waffles are available for download with the code examples from this chapter. The following code snippet shows a portion of the HTML for the home page:

```
...
<div class="customPageWidth">
 <div class="customTop customPagePadding">
  <a href="#" class="customLogin">User Login</a>
 </div>
 <div class="customHead customPagePadding">
  <a href="#" class="customLogo" title="Back to Home"></a>

  <div class="customHeaderRight">
   <div class="customPhone"></div>
   <div class="customClear"></div>

   <div class="customSearch">
```

```
       <div class="customSearchBox"><input type="text" value="" size="15" /></div>
       <div class="customSearchGo" title="Go"></div>
      </div>
      <div class="customClear"></div>
     </div>
    </div>
    <div class="customNav customPagePadding">
     <div class="customTopNavHolder">
      <div class="customTopNavItem"><a href="#">Frozen Waffles</a></div>
      <div class="customTopNavItem"><a href="#">Waffle of the Month</a></div>
      <div class="customTopNavItem"><a href="#">Fresh Maple Syrup</a></div>
      <div class="customTopNavItem"><a href="#">Creamery Butter</a></div>
 ...
```

code snippet Chapter 3/HTML Mockup/index.html

Notice that this HTML uses no tables for layout and instead makes frequent use of <div> tags and CSS to arrange the elements in an appealing manner. Also, all CSS class names are prefixed with the word "custom." This is helpful because you will be sharing CSS class names with Microsoft when using this code in SharePoint, and this way there is little chance for running into instances where class names conflict.

Figure 3-16 shows the HTML and CSS loaded in Firefox. Notice that it looks remarkably similar to the design comp created earlier, and that's the point.

FIGURE 3-16

Testing in Multiple Browsers

Chapters 8 and 9 discuss converting an HTML and CSS design into functioning SharePoint 2010 branding. Before that happens, however, it's a good idea to test your HTML in as many browsers as possible (or at least all the browsers that your organization plans to support). Again, this will save you the pain of testing and fixing things later in SharePoint. The easiest way to test your HTML in other browsers is to download and install each browser and compare how they render your design comp. The following is a list of most major browsers and the URL from which you can download them:

➤ **Internet Explorer 8** — www.microsoft.com/windows/internet-explorer/default.aspx

➤ **Firefox 3.5** — www.mozilla.com/en-US/firefox/

➤ **Safari 4** — www.apple.com/safari/

➤ **Chrome 3** — www.google.com/chrome

Another option for testing your HTML and CSS in various browsers is to use Microsoft's Expression Web SuperPreview. This program is available in two versions: a free version called Expression Web SuperPreview for Internet Explorer (http://expression.microsoft.com/en-us/dd565874.aspx), and a more advanced version that includes Expression Web 3 called Expression Web 3 SuperPreview (www.microsoft.com/expression/try-it/).

SuperPreview simplifies the process of testing and debugging by enabling you to view your web pages in multiple browsers simultaneously and even compare them to a design comp. The full version supports simultaneous display of the following browser renderings:

➤ Firefox 3.5.5

➤ Internet Explorer 6

➤ Internet Explorer 8 (IE7 compatibility mode)

➤ Internet Explorer 8

➤ A design comp

The free version works almost identically but shows only the Internet Explorer browsers. Figure 3-17 shows the Randy's Waffles web page loaded in both Firefox and Internet Explorer 8 at the same time using SuperPreview.

FIGURE 3-17

SUMMARY

Planning for any project is all about clarifying your goals and mitigating changes and problems early, before they become more difficult to deal with during implementation. The same is true for SharePoint branding projects. This chapter discussed several steps that you should take before actually creating your branding to plan for it more effectively.

By performing requirements gathering, creating wireframes, creating realistic design comps, and finally creating working HTML and CSS, your project will start off on the right foot. With the plan in place, you are ready to create branding for SharePoint. In the following chapters you will do exactly that, starting with more basic SharePoint branding and working toward fully branded SharePoint sites with custom master pages and page layouts. The next chapter introduces SharePoint Designer 2010, which makes all that possible.

SharePoint Designer 2010 Overview

WHAT'S IN THIS CHAPTER?

➤ The history of SharePoint Designer

➤ New changes in SharePoint Designer 2010

➤ An overview of the new user interface

➤ Branding with SharePoint Designer 2010

➤ Views and the XSLT List View Web Part

➤ Restricting access to SharePoint Designer 2010

SharePoint Designer (SPD) 2010, the latest version, includes many changes and improvements, and it remains an important tool for customizing the look and feel of SharePoint. This chapter takes you on a tour of the major changes to SPD 2010, focusing on its branding-related functionality.

HISTORY OF SHAREPOINT DESIGNER

Before the advent of SPD, there was a product called Microsoft FrontPage. For many web designers, the mere mention of FrontPage conjures up bad memories; and while it is true that the origins of SPD can be traced back to FrontPage, it has come a very long way. Although the product originally was an ugly duckling of sorts, it has evolved into a powerful tool — not only for branding, but also for managing your SharePoint sites and improving business processes in your organization.

FrontPage was designed to be a powerful tool that made creating websites easy; but with great power comes great responsibility. This mantra has been a recurrent theme of the product throughout its evolution. In the early days of FrontPage, its ease of use led to a large number of websites that all looked very similar. Most of us could easily identify a FrontPage website because of the overuse of its themes. In fact, FrontPage had such a bad reputation with some web designers that there have been stories of job applicants not being hired for simply listing proficiency with the product on a resume.

FrontPage was also the tool of choice for customizing sites in SharePoint 2003. At the time, branding wasn't a key focus for SharePoint, and FrontPage was really among the only options for most. Although FrontPage had its quirks, such as rewriting HTML, it seemed to do the job just fine. However, it wasn't until organizations started to upgrade to SharePoint 2007 that the full extent of FrontPage's deficiencies were realized. Entire migration efforts were made significantly more difficult because of how FrontPage customized sites.

Around the same time SharePoint 2007 was released, FrontPage was split into two products: Microsoft Office SharePoint Designer 2007 and Expression Web Designer. As you've probably noticed, the name FrontPage is missing from both product names. This was an intentional way of signifying a new beginning for the products. SPD 2007 was designed to be the primary development tool for users to customize the user interface of SharePoint, but also to build applications to improve business processes without having to write any code. SPD 2007 was created to give business users the ability to create functionality that previously required a developer.

Even with the name change, SPD 2007 wasn't able to shake all the negative perceptions. Although many users described SPD 2007 as a powerful product, they also tended to describe it as being quirky. Common complaints included instances where HTML was rewritten or functionality in the product seemed unreliable. For example, to export a file from SPD 2007, many users would go to the File menu and click Export. Unfortunately, this would often inject code into the file that would break it when it was imported into another system or editing tool such as Visual Studio. Instead, it was more reliable to use the Save As function, which achieved the desired result of getting the file out of SharePoint. These types of quirks existed throughout the product and often gave users the impression that this new product was just FrontPage with some added SharePoint functionality.

The other big issue with SPD 2007 was related to governance. Any user who had Site Owner access to a site could use SPD to modify the site. It wasn't uncommon for a user without proper training to open a site with SPD and accidentally cause issues. Administrators found it challenging to balance the need to give users access to their SharePoint sites while restricting the use of SPD. In many cases, organizations chose to avoid installing SPD on machines.

Fortunately, the issues that plagued the two previous versions have been resolved. SPD 2010 has been redesigned to specifically address the frustrations and complaints that users have had with previous versions, and the current product provides some welcome, fundamental changes.

WHAT'S NEW IN SHAREPOINT DESIGNER 2010

SPD 2010 has undergone significant changes. Users who open the product will note that SPD is now squarely focused on one thing: SharePoint. You'll notice that SharePoint information is front and center, whereas the previous version opened to a blank web page.

SPD 2010 is most definitely a tool for managing SharePoint. The product is now more of a management suite for SharePoint than its name might indicate. In fact, when most users hear the name

SharePoint Designer, they immediately associate the tool with a web editor for SharePoint. It is still a tool for customizing the look and feel of SharePoint, but SPD now enables users to manage almost all aspects of their sites quickly and easily. You can create sites and manage users, lists, and libraries without even leaving SPD. It is a powerful tool for branding, creating workflows, and connecting to external data sources, so if those were capabilities you were using previously, nearly everything has been improved across the board.

Another big change to SPD 2010 is how access to the product can be controlled. Although this isn't a specific change to the product, this enhanced level of control will enable organizations to deploy SPD to users confidently, knowing that they can govern more effectively how the product is used.

Overview of the New User Experience

When you open SPD 2010 for the first time, you'll immediately notice that the user interface has changed. At the top of the screen is the ribbon, which should be no surprise, but you'll also see that the entire user interface has been updated.

With SPD 2010, it is possible to make most settings changes to a SharePoint site directly from the tool itself. Previously, in SharePoint 2007, if you wanted to make a change to the settings of a list, you needed to open a web browser, go to the list settings page for the list, and then make the change. Most changes that were previously made through the web browser can now be centrally accessed and changed through SPD 2010. This is a big help if you are trying to make several changes to different aspects of your site. The new user interface not only makes it easy to make the changes, but also makes the process of making the changes far more efficient than in the past.

To open SPD 2010, click Start ➪ All Programs ➪ SharePoint, and then click Microsoft SharePoint Designer 2010.

The first screen that appears is the Sites page of the Microsoft Office Backstage view. As shown in Figure 4-1, the screen is divided into four self-explanatory areas: Open SharePoint Site, New SharePoint Site, Recent Sites, and Site Templates.

FIGURE 4-1

You must be connected to a site to use SPD 2010. Although it was possible to edit local copies of master pages or page layouts with SPD 2007, this is no longer possible. For example, you can't e-mail yourself a copy of a master page and edit it at home if you don't have access to a SharePoint server there. If you try to edit the file without first opening a site, you get the error shown in Figure 4-2.

If this is the first time you've opened SPD, no sites will be listed under the Recent Sites section. To open a site, click the Open Site button. When the Open Site dialog opens, enter the URL for a site and then click Open.

The site will open to what is referred to as the *site settings* page. This page displays information about your site, such as the title, description, and URL, as well as subsites and other details. This page is the central location from which all changes to your site will be made.

FIGURE 4-2

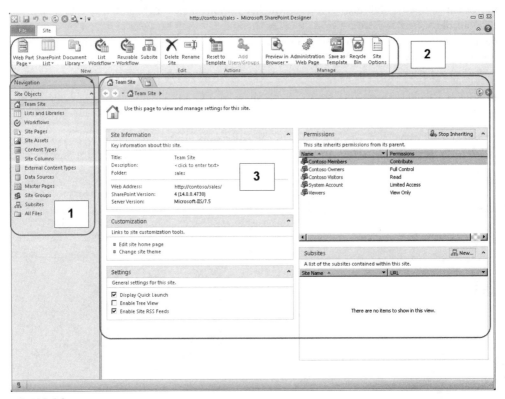

FIGURE 4-3

With the site open, you can see that the new user interface is divided into three sections, as shown in Figure 4-3:

➤ **The Navigation pane (1)** — This pane contains links to the elements that make up a site, including lists, libraries, master pages, page layouts, workflows, content types, and so on. Clicking a link takes you to a gallery page.

➤ **The ribbon (2)** — Selecting an object in SPD causes the ribbon to display menus and options for customizing that object. The ribbon is also used to create new objects.

➤ **The gallery and summary pages (3)** — This main area in the center of the screen displays the lists of each component type, along with summary information. A gallery page shows a list of all the items of a selected type. A summary page shows the attributes of a selected element.

The Navigation pane provides a convenient way to get to different areas of the site. No matter which gallery is selected, the Navigation pane is always visible. Users can quickly jump between the different areas of the site or click the first Site link (listed first in the Navigation area in Figure 4-3) to return to the site settings page for the site.

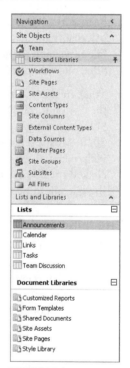

The gallery pages show a high-level view of each component of a certain type. For example, when you click Lists and Libraries in the Navigation pane, the gallery will display all the lists and libraries in a site. When an item in the gallery has been selected, the context of the ribbon will change to show buttons and functionality related to the selected gallery. For example, when you view the Lists and Libraries gallery, the ribbon displays buttons that enable you to create new lists and libraries; when you view the Master Page gallery, the context of the ribbon changes to display different operations related to master pages.

Another new feature that can be especially helpful for branding projects is the capability to *pin* a gallery, which will open a "mini-gallery" below the Navigation pane. To pin a gallery, hover your mouse over the link for it; you should see a pin icon, as shown in Figure 4-4. Simply click the pin icon to open the mini-gallery, which will continue to be displayed even if another gallery is selected. This makes it easy to access the items in a pinned gallery at any time.

FIGURE 4-4

Breadcrumbs, Tabs, and Navigation

Although the Navigation pane of SPD 2010 will probably be the most common way you get around your SharePoint site, there are other new ways to move around. As you browse through your SharePoint site, you'll find that the interface works similarly to how a browser works. For example, as you click around to different areas of the site, new tabs open so that you can maneuver between different files. When you are browsing on the Internet, each tab in your web browser maintains its own history; for example, you can click the back button on each tab to return to the last site you visited. Each tab in SPD 2010 works in exactly the same way; simply press the back button in the toolbar under each tab to return to the previous page. Additionally, if your mouse has forward and back buttons, you can use them to move between the page histories, as in Figure 4-5.

There's also a breadcrumb navigation that shows where you are within the site. For example, if you are looking at the Shared Documents, the breadcrumb has a link for each level in the hierarchy. In addition, the breadcrumbs themselves can be expanded. For example, from Shared Documents, you can click the drop-down for Lists and Libraries in the breadcrumb and go directly to the Announcements list as in Figure 4-6.

FIGURE 4-5

The File Tab

The File tab in the upper-left corner of SPD 2010, located at the top of the ribbon, has similar options to the File menu that has been in the left-most position in toolbars in Microsoft applications for many years. The File tab enables you to open new sites, close SPD, and add pages and items.

You can also use the File tab to change the option for SPD and the Help files for SPD, including the version number for SPD 2010. Most users typically look for the

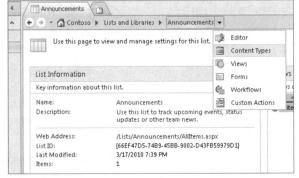

FIGURE 4-6

Help menu along the top toolbar, so the new location takes a little getting used to. Also, once you've clicked the File tab and want to return to your site, you can click the tab immediately to the right of the File tab to be returned to the page you were viewing before clicking the File tab.

Checking and Changing the Current User

When you open SPD, it usually logs you in to the sites you are trying to access with the same credentials used for the machine you are currently logged into. If you aren't automatically logged in, you'll need to enter the credentials you'd use to access SharePoint to open the site. In some cases, you might want to log in as a different user, perhaps to test user permissions or to test another user's access. Although checking the current user's account and switching to another user's account is very easy, it is not necessarily obvious.

With SPD open, note the small person icon in the lower-left corner, as shown in Figure 4-7. Hovering your mouse over this icon will display the name of the user currently logged in. Clicking the icon enables you to log in with a different account.

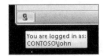

FIGURE 4-7

BRANDING WITH SHAREPOINT DESIGNER 2010

When most people see the name "SharePoint Designer," they probably assume the product has something to do with designing websites. This is probably a fair assumption, since we are talking about a product that has its roots in FrontPage, a tool for designing websites. As further evidence, when you first opened SPD 2007, you were presented with a blank HTML page, as opposed to something specific to SharePoint. Although the overall focus has shifted away from being just a page editor for SharePoint, make no mistake: SPD 2010 is still the primary tool for customizing the SharePoint user interface.

How does SPD 2010 fit into the branding process? It is often the first (and many times only) tool used to create a custom branded SharePoint site. As you read this book you will most certainly see examples that don't include SPD, but for many projects they will start with this tool.

You are likely already at least somewhat familiar with the basic building blocks for branding in SharePoint: master pages, page layouts, and CSS. (Each topic is discussed in more detail later in the book.) The following describes SPD's role with respect to these aspects of the branding process:

➤ **Master pages** — For many simple projects, SPD can be used to copy one of the existing OOTB master pages, which can then be further customized. More advanced projects might use SPD to start a new master page from scratch. Although it is possible to use other tools such as Visual Studio, with SPD you can view any changes immediately as you refine your designs.

➤ **CSS** — Similar to master pages, for more simple projects it is often easier to modify CSS directly from SPD so that changes can be more easily viewed. For more complex projects, the CSS might initially be created outside of the tool, and then brought in later in the process to be finalized when changes can be more easily made.

➤ **Page layouts** — SPD is the easiest tool for creating page layouts. It provides a wizard for creating the page layout, associating it with a content type. Once the page layout has been created, you can use SPD to drag field controls onto it, and then style the controls using custom HTML or CSS.

Although SPD often is the starting point for SharePoint branding, in many cases it makes sense to export your files to a non-SharePoint application. In previous versions, this was fairly straightforward, but it is less obvious with SPD 2010. The easiest way to export files from the Master Page Gallery (usually master pages or page layouts) is to go to the gallery by using the web browser itself from site settings and manually download each file. Another option is to copy the code and create a new file. It should also be noted that if you click on the master page link in the Navigation pane, there will be a button in the ribbon at the right called Export File. It is strongly recommended that this option be avoided because it causes additional code to be injected into the file to be exported, which can break the master page.

For downloading other files the process is simpler: If you browse to the document library in a web browser, click the Library tab in the ribbon, and then click the Open in Windows Explorer button from the Connect & Export section. This will open a File Explorer window that will allow you to drag the files to a new location on your machine. You can use this process to quickly upload files to SharePoint; just make sure that you check in and publish files if content approval is enabled for the library.

Modifying CSS

The SharePoint user interface uses CSS heavily to create the look and feel. Have you ever viewed a SharePoint site with no CSS? It doesn't look like much at all. It's just a pile of text on a white background, lacking any "look and feel." Making changes to the look and feel of a SharePoint site usually requires modifying some CSS, as nearly everything you see in a SharePoint site has CSS applied to it. For example, imagine that you want to make a minor change like hiding the All Site Content link in the left navigation. This requires modifying some CSS. To do so, you basically have two options: edit the out-of-the-box CSS provided by SharePoint or create your own custom CSS. As a general rule, you should never modify system files, and changes you make should be by creating your own custom CSS.

CSS is covered in much greater detail later in this book, but at this point you should understand that each object in SharePoint uses one or more CSS styles. For the preceding example of the All Site Content link, because of the cascading nature of CSS, whichever style is applied to the object last is the one that is applied. (There are definitely some exceptions to this, but for simplicity that is good enough for now.) In order to apply your own styling to an object, you merely have to ensure that your custom CSS is applied after the system CSS. SPD 2010 makes it easy to apply your custom CSS in two ways:

➤ **Apply the styles inline** — You can add your CSS directly to the master page. The term *inline* is used because the CSS is actually referenced inline within the HTML tag on the master page. Using this means that any updates to the CSS require modifying the master page.

➤ **Create a custom CSS file** — You can also place styles in a separate CSS file and reference it in the master page. As long as the CSS is called after the out-of-the-box CSS applied by SharePoint, the custom styles will be safely applied. You can modify the CSS by changing the CSS file, which makes it easier to make changes. Additionally, the CSS can be referenced by other master pages, enabling style reuse. This is the preferred approach for creating custom CSS.

Added to SPD 2010 are some features that make it easier to work with CSS. For example, Skewer Click enables you to determine which style is being applied to a given element. When you click the Skewer Click button in the ribbon, you can select an element on the page to display the specific CSS style being used to style that element. Once the style has been identified, you can apply your own style to the element. SPD 2010 simplifies the process of creating your own custom CSS. The following example will walk you through the process of using the Skewer Click functionality.

Working with Master Pages and CSS

Master pages are covered in much more detail in Chapter 8, but the following example will walk you through the process of making some common changes with SPD 2010. The example demonstrates how to add a footer to a custom master page, as well as how to hide the All Site Content and Recycle Bin links from the left navigation using custom CSS.

Before beginning this example, make sure you are logged in as a user who has permission to edit master pages. Also, this example makes changes to a site using the Team Site template. If your site uses a different template the steps might differ slightly.

1. Open your site in SPD and click the Master Pages link in the Navigation pane.

2. Right-click v4.master and select Copy. Then right-click and paste another copy of the file into the Master Page Gallery.

It is recommended that you always make copies of any out-of-the-box files before making changes to them.

3. From the Master Page Gallery, click next to the filename for the master page that was just created. From the ribbon, click the Rename button in the edit section of the toolbar, and then rename the file **CustomFooter.master**.

4. From the ribbon, click the Edit File button.

5. Ensure that either the Split view or Code view is showing. Near line 624, after `<SharePoint:DeveloperDashboard runat="server"/>`, add the following code snippet, as shown in Figure 4-8:

```
<div class="s4-notdlg" style="clear: both; background-color:
        #FEAD30; padding: 10px;">
    &copy; Copyright 2010 Contoso Manufacturing
</div>
```

 For demonstration purposes, this example applies the CSS inline. It is generally preferable to add custom CSS by referencing a specific CSS class that can be used throughout the page or from other pages.

FIGURE 4-8

6. After you've made the change, save the file by clicking the Save icon in the upper-left corner of the screen. You will get a dialog that warns you that you are about to customize the file from the site definition. Click Yes to continue.

7. Click the Master Page link again from the Navigation pane on the left to return to the Master Page Gallery.

8. To apply the changes to the site, select CustomFooter.master. Then, from the ribbon, click the Set as Default button.

If you open your site in the web browser, you'll see that a footer has been applied to your site, as shown in Figure 4-9. If your browser is already open to the site, you might need to press F5 to refresh your browser.

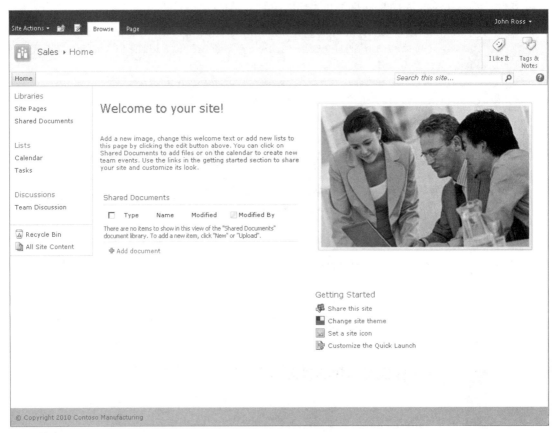

FIGURE 4-9

Now that the footer has been added, let's hide the Recycle Bin and All Site Content links from the Navigation pane. Many organizations make this change because they think the links in the Navigation pane are confusing or add too much clutter.

1. Click Master Pages from the navigation panel at the left. Edit the `CustomFooter.master` file again from SPD in the master page gallery.

2. Select CustomFooter.master and click the Edit File button from the ribbon.

3. Ensure that either the Split view or Code view is showing. Near line 624, after `<SharePoint:DeveloperDashboard runat="server"/>`, add the following code snippet (refer to Figure 4-8):

```
<div class="s4-notdlg" style="clear: both; background-color:
        #FEAD30; padding: 10px;">
    &copy; Copyright 2010 Contoso Manufacturing
</div>
```

4. From the ribbon, click the Skewer Click button, as shown in Figure 4-10. This enables you to see the CSS that is currently applied to a specific object. Note that Skewer Click can be used only when you are in design or split view for a page.

5. Before you can edit the CSS, you must first add a new panel to SPD. From the ribbon, click the Style tab and select the CSS Properties button, as shown in Figure 4-11.

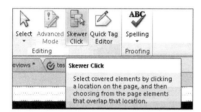

FIGURE 4-10

FIGURE 4-11

6. Hover your mouse near the locations for the Recycle Bin and All Site Content links. You should see the name `PlaceHolderQuickLaunchBottom` appear faintly. Select it and another window will open and display a list of styles. Click the style called `ul.s4-specialNav...`, as shown in Figure 4-12.

7. When the new panel opens, you'll see that the top section is called Applied Rules, as shown in Figure 4-13. The style you want to modify (`.s4-specialNavLinkList`) should already be selected. It may be difficult to read the entire name of the style, but you can make the right panel a little wider. Right-click the style and select New Style Copy.

8. At the top of the New Style dialog, shown in Figure 4-14, set the new style to be defined in the current page, check the box to "Apply new style to document selection," select Layout under category, set the visibility to hidden, and then click OK.

FIGURE 4-12

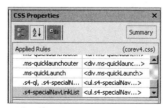

FIGURE 4-13

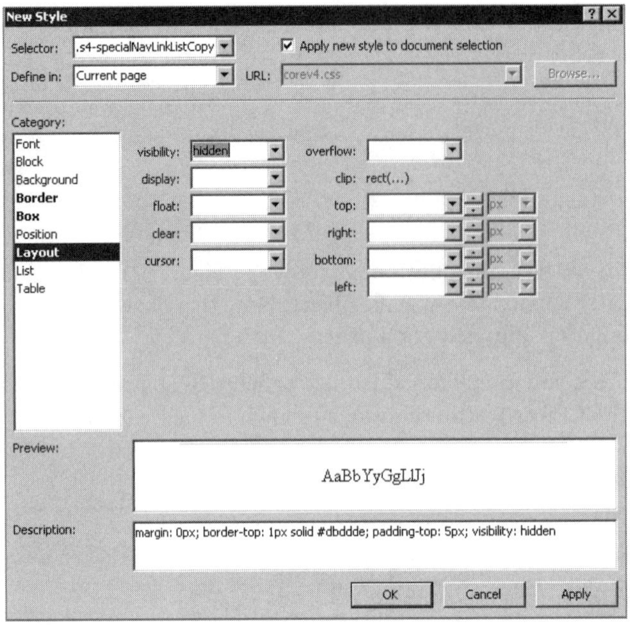

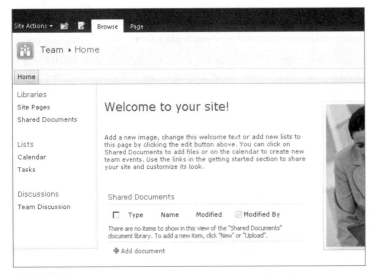

FIGURE 4-14

9. Save the changes made to the master page by clicking the Save button in the upper-right corner.

When you view the site now, the links for All Site Content and Recycle Bin will be hidden, as shown in Figure 4-15. You might get a warning after you save the file that says, "Saving your changes will customize this page so that it is no longer based on the site definition." Click Yes to continue.

FIGURE 4-15

This example used the Skewer Click functionality to identify the CSS currently applied to an object and then used the New Style Copy feature to safely override the SharePoint CSS to hide the All Site Content and Recycle Bin links. The new features of SPD 2010 make it easy to safely make changes to the CSS in your SharePoint site.

When you used the New Style Copy functionality, SPD made a copy of the style you wanted to edit. Then the reference to the CSS file on the object was automatically updated to point to the styles you were adding inline at the top of the master page. If you were to look back at your master page, you would see that SPD made a copy of `.s4-specialNavLinkList` and added it near the top of the page. If you look at the Code view of the master page, you'll see that the following code has been added near the top:

```
    <style type="text/css">
.s4-specialNavLinkListCopy
{
    margin: 0px;
/* [ReplaceColor(themeColor:"Light2-Lightest")] */        border-top: 1px solid #dbddde;
    padding-top: 5px;
    visibility: hidden;
}
</style>
```

The style was appended with the word `Copy`. This is done automatically when you use the New Style Copy function. However, it is necessary to check the "Apply new style to document selection" option to change the reference to point to your new style. If you don't check the box, you would need to update the references manually to point to your new styles. For this example, not checking the box would add your code to the top of the master page, but the Recycle Bin and All Site Content links won't be hidden until the reference to `.s4-specialNavLinkList` is changed to `.s4-specialNavLinkListCopy`.

USING VIEWS AND THE XSLT LIST VIEW WEB PART

List views and data views are some of the ways that content from lists and libraries is displayed to users. Essentially, these views provide a look at the content in a list or library. A SharePoint Designer view is similar to a filter in Excel. For example, suppose that you have a library containing 100 documents from different departments across the organization. You could create a view that shows only the documents from HR, which might be 20 documents. However, each view can be filtered in different ways to show the content in a different way.

In SharePoint 2007, views were created primarily in the web browser, but now you can create them directly from SPD 2010. From the Navigation pane, select any of the items from the Lists and Libraries gallery and you'll see the list of views on the settings page. To create a new view, click the New button in the top-right of the Views section and enter a name for the view. Once the new view has been created, it will be added to your list of views.

All views in SharePoint 2010 are based on XSLT and can be customized from SPD. This is a big change from the views in SharePoint 2007, which based them on CAML (Collaborative Application Markup Language), making them difficult to customize. All views now use the XSLT List View Web Part, which means that in addition to adding filter criteria to the data, it is also possible to apply custom grouping, sorting, as well as conditional formatting. Users who are familiar with the Data View Web Part (DVWP) will find the functionality very similar. All this can be done without having to write any code, but if you happen to be an XSLT ninja, you could create and apply more advanced customizations to views.

Those of you familiar with the DVWP in SharePoint 2007 know that although you could do a lot with it, once it was deployed it wasn't easy to update without going back to SPD 2007 to make the changes. The new XSLT List View Web Part provides much the same capability to customize functionality as the DVWP, but it also enables you to edit and modify the Web Part through the SharePoint user interface. In fact, if you have some basic views mixed in with custom views with conditional formatting, you can easily switch between them without issue.

Editing Views with SharePoint Designer 2010

This example walks you through the various options available in SPD 2010 for creating and editing views and forms. You will create a list, add a few fields, edit the view to add conditional filtering, and then create a custom view. Although views can still be created through the user interface, as they were in SPD 2007, SPD 2010 provides more power and flexibility through the use of the new XSLT List View Web Part. This example shows off these new capabilities and demonstrates some concepts that can be reused and expanded in your organization.

As with previous examples in this chapter, the following example assumes that you are using a site based on the Team site template. The steps required when using a different template might vary.

1. Open SPD 2010 and connect to a site.

2. From the Navigation pane, click Lists and Libraries to open the gallery.

3. To create a new list, click the Custom List button on the ribbon.

4. Name the list **Waffle Sales**, and then click OK. The new list should be added to the gallery.

5. Click the name of the list to open its summary page.

6. From the summary page's Customization section located in the middle of the center panel, click the "Edit list columns" link. This opens the editor for this list. There should already be a column on the list called `Title`.

7. Single-click the name of the column and change it to **City**.

8. For the next column, click the Add New Column button on the ribbon and select to add a Choice column. The Column Editor dialog shown in Figure 4-16 opens, in which you can customize the options for the drop-down. For the options, enter the months of the year on separate lines.

9. While still in the Column Editor, delete the value from the "Default value" field, leaving the field empty, and then click OK. You'll be returned to the screen showing the columns on the list. Be sure to name the new column **Month**.

10. Add one more column. For this column, set the column type to Number. Call it **Units Sold**.

FIGURE 4-16

11. After the list is created and the fields are updated you need to save the list in order for the changes to be applied. Click the Save icon in the upper-left corner of the browser, or press Ctrl+S.

12. Click Lists and Libraries from the navigation panel at the left and then click the name of the `Waffle Sales` list to get to the list settings page. Click the All Items view to edit it, as shown in Figure 4-17. In a production environment, however, the best practice would be to create a new view, rather than modify this one.

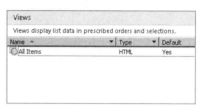

FIGURE 4-17

13. The XSLT List View Web Part will open. For this example, we'll be customizing the view, and it can be easier to make these changes if the view has some data in it, so you can add your own values. To have SPD 2010 add some test data, click the Design tab in the ribbon and put a check in the box to show Sample Data.

The first step will be to remove the attachments column on the left. It is possible to delete the elements themselves, but it is a little easier to simply remove the column. From the ribbon, press the Add/Remove Columns button. This will open the Displayed fields dialog. Select Attachments from under displayed fields and then press the Remove button. Once complete, press the OK button.

Once the column has been removed, you are going to make an empty new column on the left. Click with your mouse somewhere in the City column, and then right-click and select Insert ➪ Column to the left.

14. Select the left cell on the first row with data below the headings. It is important to select the whole cell. (Note that if the whole cell is selected, it will be gray. Otherwise, only the border will show, but the center will be white.) If the cell isn't selected, click the small "td" tab above the cell, as shown in Figure 4-18. To add conditional formatting to this cell, click the Conditional Formatting button in the Options tab of the List View Tool that is highlighted in the ribbon. Then choose Format Column.

FIGURE 4-18

15. In the Condition Criteria window, shown in Figure 4-19, use the following criteria for the condition:

➤ **Field Name** — Units Sold

➤ **Comparison** — Less Than

➤ **Value** — 100

When you are done, click the Set Style button.

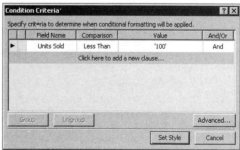

FIGURE 4-19

16. In the Modify Style window, as shown in Figure 4-20, choose the Background category. Change the background color to #FF0000 (red), and then click OK. You'll be returned to the view.

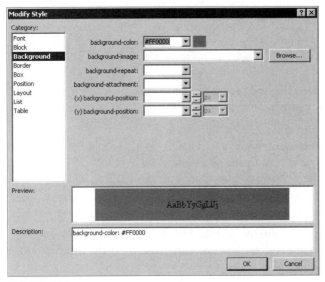

FIGURE 4-20

17. Save the changes to the view by clicking the Save button in the upper-left corner.

18. If you browse to the list now you'll notice that any items for which the Units Sold are less than 100 are highlighted (red), as shown in Figure 4-21. (This is similar to how you could create a simple KPI for any list or library, no matter which version of SharePoint you used.) If your list doesn't have data, now would be a good time to add some new items to the list and test out the new view.

FIGURE 4-21

The final step is to create a custom view that shows only the values of the employees who have given themselves a low rating. To do this, follow these steps:

1. Click Lists and Libraries and open the settings page for the `Waffle Sales` list. In the Views section, click the New button to create a new view. The Create New List View dialog will open. Name the view **Low Sales** and click OK.

2. The new view will be created and appear in the list of views. Click the new name of the new view to edit it.

3. Click the Filter button on the ribbon, as shown in Figure 4-22. If you don't immediately see it, select the Options tab under List View Tools. If you don't have data in the list, refer to step 13 in the previous example to add sample data.

FIGURE 4-22

4. For the Filter Criteria, set the values to the following criteria:

➤ **Field Name** — Units Sold

➤ **Comparison** — Less Than

➤ **Value** — 100

5. Click OK. Before viewing the changes, click the Save button in the upper-left corner.

The new view has been created. To test it, open the site in the web browser again and navigate to the list. When the list opens, it will show the All Items view by default. To switch to the new view, hover your mouse over the All Items link in the breadcrumb (see Figure 4-23). You'll be able to switch to the Low Sales view, which will now display only the entries with sales less than 100.

FIGURE 4-23

This example walked through some common ways to edit and customize views. However, we only scratched the surface of what is possible. Once you've created your custom view, you can simply drop it onto any page in your site, just as you've always done with any view you've created, and the custom formatting that you defined will be displayed.

WORKFLOWS

After branding, creating custom workflows might be the second most commonly used capability of SPD. SharePoint provides several out-of-the-box workflows that can be configured through the web interface, but their flexibility is relatively limited. Organizations use SPD to create custom no-code workflows that provide more flexibility to automate business processes.

Significant improvements have been made to workflows in SharePoint Designer 2010; the following sections provide a brief overview.

New Types of Workflows

One of the biggest limitations of workflows in SPD 2007 was that they were directly tied to lists or libraries, which made them very difficult to reuse. SPD 2010 enables you to add new types of workflows that address these limitations. The following types of workflows are supported by SPD 2010:

➤ **List workflows** — These are workflows that are directly associated with a list. This was the only type of workflow supported by SPD 2007.

➤ **Reusable workflows** — These are workflows that can be associated with many lists, or libraries. Reusable workflows are based on a specific content type and can be reused throughout your SharePoint sites as needed.

➤ **Site workflows** — These workflows are not associated with a specific list or content type.

➤ **Globally reusable workflows** — When you look in the Workflow gallery in SPD, you'll notice that the out-of-the-box workflows (Approval, Collect Feedback, and Collect Signatures) are listed as Globally Reusable Workflows. These workflows can be edited with SPD or used as the basis to create new workflows. When working with these workflows, it is best to create a copy of the workflow and make any modifications to the new copy.

For business users and nondevelopers, these new workflow capabilities provide more powerful options to automate business processes without writing custom code.

Workflow Designer

The Workflow Designer, the interface used to create workflows, has been completely changed for SPD 2010. The Workflow Designer enables you to visualize an entire workflow on a single screen, which makes it easier to create the workflow and ensure that all the necessary conditions and actions are included.

SPD 2010 uses rule-based declarative workflows. This means that when a workflow is being run on an item, for each step in the process each condition is evaluated one at a time.

To view the Workflow Designer, click the Workflows link in the Navigation pane to open the Workflow gallery, and then click one of the workflow buttons in the New section of the ribbon. With the Workflow Designer open, you can add conditions and actions to your workflow steps:

➤ **Conditions** are the rules or criteria that are applied to the workflow. When the workflow is started, the conditions are compared against the item being processed by the workflow. If the condition is found to be true, then whatever is contained within the condition is processed. Conditions are compared in order, starting with the first condition, then the second, and so forth. To see a complete list of conditions, click the Condition button on the ribbon.

➤ **Actions** determine what activities are performed by the workflow. Common examples include sending an e-mail or setting a value in a field. Actions can be applied without the use of conditions. To see a complete list of the actions available for workflows, click the Actions button on the ribbon.

When a condition or action is added to your workflow, it includes a link that when clicked enables you to define what is happening. The whole process is very similar to what happens when you create a rule in Microsoft Outlook. If you were to create a workflow that required sending an e-mail, then after adding the send an e-mail action you'd click the link, which opens a dialog to define the recipient, subject, and body of the message.

For companies that purchase SharePoint, improving business processes through workflows often represents a significant source of ROI (return on investment), which is one of the most important things that the stakeholders who are supporting SharePoint are looking for. Many organizations use workflows to automate processes that previously were paper based or otherwise required manual effort to keep track of. Some common examples of workflows that could be automated would be a process to track an employee onboarding, expense reports, or many common HR type processes. You could probably quickly think of one or more processes that you are currently tracking using e-mail or a basic spreadsheet that's stored on someone's machine.

SPD 2010 workflows enable you to track and provide a history for a process. In addition, a workflow enables you to design a process so that other users can manage it passively. That is, the process can proceed even if you aren't around, which provides greater efficiency.

Workflows in SharePoint 2010 can now be designed in Microsoft Visio 2010 and then imported into SharePoint Designer 2010, where they can be further defined and customized. It is even possible to import workflows from SPD into Microsoft Visual Studio 2010, where a developer can make additional changes. Combining SharePoint's powerful workflows with SPD 2010 opens a new world of possibilities for what can be done without writing any code — and even if you are a developer it is the ideal starting point for your custom workflow.

 For more information on creating workflows in Visio, see
`http://blogs.msdn.com/b/visio/archive/2009/11/23/`
`sharepoint-workflow-authoring-in-visio-premium-2010-part-1.aspx.`

CONNECTING TO DATA SOURCES

Another area of improvement with SharePoint Designer 2010 is around connecting to data sources. "Data source" is a generic term in SPD 2010 that refers to any content, whether it resides in SharePoint or another system. External systems could include SQL Server, a web service, an RSS feed, or many other LOB applications. The following sections discuss the different types of data source connections as well as using SPD 2010 to connect to external data sources.

Data Source Connections

If you click the Data Sources link in the Navigation pane (on the left in SharePoint Designer), you'll see the gallery of various data sources. By default, only lists and libraries are displayed, but several other data sources are supported depending on the buttons in the ribbon. The following are examples of supported data source connections:

➤ External database

➤ SOAP web service

➤ REST web service or RSS feed

➤ XML file connection

Clicking any of the buttons in the ribbon opens a wizard that walks you through the process of connecting to each of the various data sources. Once the connection to the data source has been made, you can use SPD to combine the data from multiple sources into a single application. This is sometimes referred to as a *mashup* or *composite application*. An example of this would be if you combined customer address information from a SQL Server table with Bing maps to create a visual representation of where your clients were located.

External Data Integration

The Business Connectivity Service (BCS) is a new feature in SharePoint 2010 that enables SharePoint to connect with line of business (LOB) applications such as SQL Server, PeopleSoft, Oracle, and others. SharePoint Server 2007 included functionality referred to as the Business Data Catalog (BDC), which was very similar, although it presented several challenges that made it difficult for many organizations to implement.

The BDC required an XML file called an *application definition*, which helped to define the connection between SharePoint and the LOB system. The problem was that the application definition was very complex to create. It was possible to create it manually but not very practical, and usually required the assistance of a third-party tool. The other big issue with the BDC is that once you were able to connect to the LOB, system data was pushed in only one direction to SharePoint. This enabled SharePoint to search data coming from these systems, but you weren't able to edit the data in SharePoint and write it back to the LOB system without custom development.

The BCS in SharePoint 2010 addresses both of these issues. The process for connecting to LOB systems has been greatly simplified and can easily be done directly from SharePoint Designer 2010. Once the connection has been created, the data can be surfaced in an external list, allowing users to interact with the external data in the same way they could if they were editing a SharePoint list. In fact, users can even make changes to the external list and the changes will be written back to the LOB system.

 For more information on the BCS, see `http://msdn.microsoft.com/en-us/magazine/ee819133.aspx`.

RESTRICTING ACCESS TO SHAREPOINT DESIGNER

As mentioned previously, effectively governing the use of SPD 2007 was difficult for organizations, making them wary of allowing its widespread use. When Microsoft began to allow free downloading of SPD in April of 2008, the negative feelings and concerns among IT professionals were only increased.

Users with appropriate access permissions could do whatever they liked with SharePoint Designer 2007. There was no real granular control. A user with SPD installed and site owner permissions had virtually unlimited control of a site. Organizations were forced to either block the use of SPD by preventing it from being installed (which wasn't always possible), to prevent any user other than someone in IT from having full control of a site, or to define the acceptable usage of SPD within a governance document. To be fair, there were other ways to prevent site access with SPD, but these required changes typically made by developers and therefore were beyond the capabilities of most server administrators. In short, although it was possible to govern the use of SPD 2007, it was more effort than most companies were willing to expend.

One of the most significant improvements to SPD 2010 is that you can easily control its use. Administrators can now control not only who uses SPD 2010, but also how it is used. This increased granular control enables, for example, the use of SPD but not the customization of files. Greater control doesn't mean that all the risks associated with using SPD are eliminated; it simply means it is now much easier to control the risks.

SPD 2007 offered the Contributor Settings feature, which wasn't heavily used and, since the settings were fairly complex and didn't integrate with permissions, it was possible to bypass them and still make changes. Another important aspect to the way that SPD access is controlled with SharePoint 2010 is that these settings integrate directly with the SharePoint permissions model. Therefore, they effectively prevent unwanted changes to sites and cannot be bypassed.

SharePoint 2010 allows access to SPD 2010 to be controlled at two different levels:

➤ **Central Administration** — Accessed from the General Application Settings menu, this enables farm administrators to control SPD at the web application level. Disabling the options here prevents site collection administrators from enabling the functionality from within a site collection. Site collection administrators cannot make edits with SPD either.

➤ **Site Collection** — Accessed from the Site Collection Administration section in Site Settings, this enables site collection administrators to control SPD access for designers and site owners. When disabled, only site collection administrators can make customizations.

SharePoint 2010 has the following settings in both Central Administration and at the site collection level to control how SPD can be used:

➤ **Enable SharePoint Designer** — Determines whether SPD can be used at all.

➤ **Enable Detaching Pages from the Site Definition** — Allows edited pages to be customized, which detaches them from the site definition.

➤ **Enable Customizing Master Pages and Layout Pages** — Enables the Master Page link from the Navigation pane; when disabled, it prevents users from updating master pages and layout pages.

➤ **Enable Managing of the Web Site URL Structure** — Enables the All Files link on the Navigation pane, which allows users to manage all the folders and files for a given site. This is useful for advanced configuration and modification of a site and should be reserved for experienced users to prevent someone from accidentally modifying or deleting system files.

The following example walks through the process of updating the SPD settings from Central Administration:

1. Open Central Administration from your SharePoint server by clicking Start ⇨ All Programs ⇨ Microsoft SharePoint 2010 Products ⇨ Microsoft SharePoint 2010 Central Administration.

2. Click General Application Settings in the Navigation pane.

3. From the SharePoint Designer section, click Configure SharePoint Designer Settings, as shown in Figure 4-24.

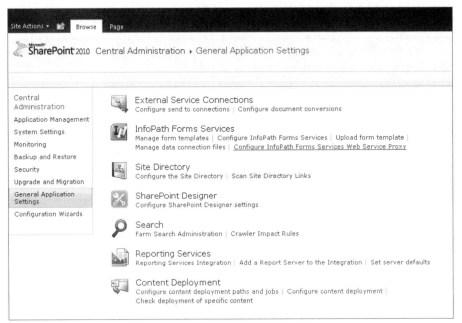

FIGURE 4-24

4. From the Settings page, select the appropriate web application from the drop-down at the top right. By default, all the options should be selected. Leave the first box checked, which enables the use of SPD, but remove the checks from the other boxes, as shown in Figure 4-25. Click OK.

5. To test the changes, navigate to the URL of the site collection in your web browser to be used for testing, and log in as a site collection administrator. For this example, use `http://contoso`.

   For this example to work, the ID used must be a site collection administrator. If you were to test with an account that has more permissions (such as a farm administrator account), you might not notice any changes. Because farm administrator accounts have more rights to the site collection, these changes won't impact the capability of those administrators to use SPD.

6. From the Site Actions button, choose Edit in SharePoint Designer, as shown in Figure 4-26.

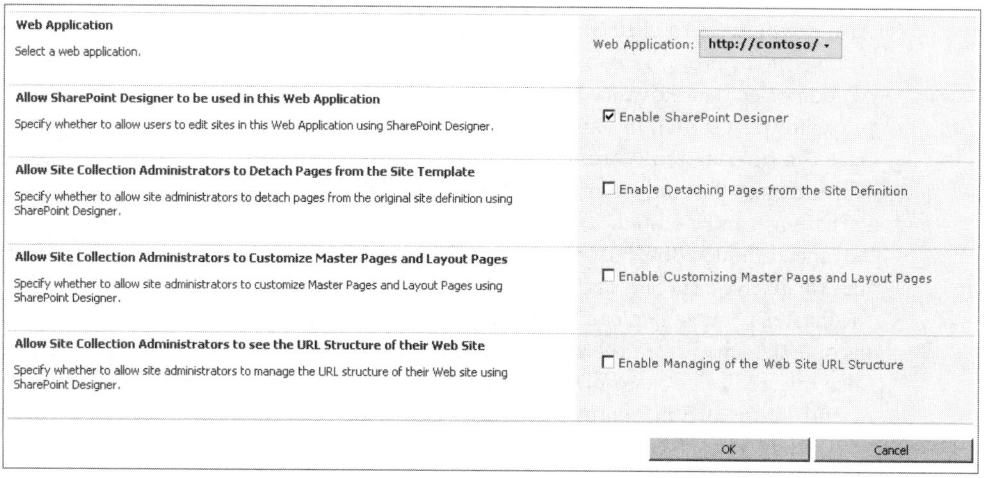

Web Application

Select a web application.

Web Application: **http://contoso/** ▾

Allow SharePoint Designer to be used in this Web Application

Specify whether to allow users to edit sites in this Web Application using SharePoint Designer.

☑ Enable SharePoint Designer

Allow Site Collection Administrators to Detach Pages from the Site Template

Specify whether to allow site administrators to detach pages from the original site definition using SharePoint Designer.

☐ Enable Detaching Pages from the Site Definition

Allow Site Collection Administrators to Customize Master Pages and Layout Pages

Specify whether to allow site administrators to customize Master Pages and Layout Pages using SharePoint Designer.

☐ Enable Customizing Master Pages and Layout Pages

Allow Site Collection Administrators to see the URL Structure of their Web Site

Specify whether to allow site administrators to manage the URL structure of their Web site using SharePoint Designer.

☐ Enable Managing of the Web Site URL Structure

[OK]   [Cancel]

FIGURE 4-25

SPD should open. Note that the Master Page, Page Layouts (only displayed in sites with Publishing enabled), and All Sites links should be missing from the Navigation pane, as shown in Figure 4-27. If the links are still there, verify that you are logged in as a site collection administrator, not a farm administrator. You can check by clicking the icon in the lower-left corner of the SPD window, which displays the name of the logged-in user (as explained in the earlier section "Checking and Changing the Current User").

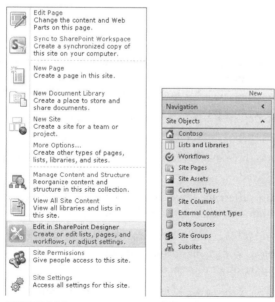

FIGURE 4-26   **FIGURE 4-27**

Also, if you were to click Site Pages and try to edit the `home.aspx` page, you would notice that Advanced mode is grayed out, as shown in Figure 4-28. The page can be edited in Normal mode only, which means that only content in Web Part zones can be edited. Conversely, Advanced mode allows users to edit the files themselves, such as the page itself or the master page, which causes the files to become detached from the site definition

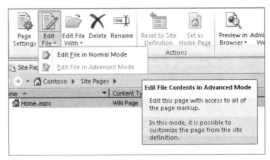

FIGURE 4-28

(also referred to as customizing the page). If this setting is enabled, it is important to sufficiently train all SharePoint Designer users to use the tool responsibly, in accordance with your organization's governance policies.

7.   To test what happens when you completely disable SPD access, close the instance of SPD that you were using for the previous example. It's okay to leave your web browser open.

8.   Repeat steps 1–3 and remove the check from the Enable SharePoint Designer box. Click OK.

9.   Repeat step 5. Now when you try to open SPD, you should see the prompt that Web Site Editing Is Disabled, as shown in Figure 4-29.

FIGURE 4-29

SUMMARY

This chapter focused on the new capabilities of SPD 2010, with a specific emphasis on the topics most closely tied to branding. Although the name of the product has "design" in the title, it is no longer a tool just for customizing the user interface for SharePoint. Users who are familiar with the previous version of the product will notice that SPD 2010 includes several improvements:

➤   The user interface for SharePoint Designer 2010 has been redesigned to focus on the various SharePoint objects, rather than serve as a page editor.

➤   The user interface is separated into three main areas: the Navigation pane, the ribbon, and the galley/summary pages.

➤   SPD is an invaluable tool for many different tasks across the organization for all users, including information workers, administrators, and developers.

➤   SPD can be used as the starting point for creating your custom SharePoint branding elements regardless of the size of your project. For smaller projects it might be the only tool you use, whereas larger projects might require other tools at some point.

➤   SPD is especially effective when you want to apply branding changes to your site and immediately see those changes.

➤ You can create and customize XSLT list views through SPD. The views enable you to add grouping, sorting, filtering, conditional formatting, and other customizations.

➤ Declarative workflows created with SPD enable you to create no-code solutions in order to streamline business processes.

➤ Connections to data sources can be made right from SPD, including LOB systems such as external databases, REST web services, SOAP web services, and XML files.

➤ Access to SPD can be controlled by farm administrators from Central Administration, or by site collection administrators from the Site Settings page.

To prevent users from getting into trouble, you can restrict SPD by customizing specific pages, or more broadly by removing the permission to use SPD altogether.

5

Simple Branding

WHAT'S IN THIS CHAPTER?

➤ Using the ribbon to create and edit web page content

➤ Using SharePoint 2010 themes to apply colors and fonts to a SharePoint site

➤ Using Cascading Style Sheets with SharePoint 2010

➤ Creating a simple master page with minor changes to the default look and feel

A primary focus of this book is to help users of all levels of experience learn to make changes to their SharePoint user interface. This chapter is designed to provide an introduction to creating SharePoint branding — without getting bogged down in learning all the nuts and bolts. Whether you are new to SharePoint or a site owner who just needs to make your site look more like your existing corporate look and feel with colors and minor branding, this chapter is a great place to start.

As discussed in Chapter 1, there are three approaches to branding in SharePoint 2010. See Figure 5-1 for a reminder.

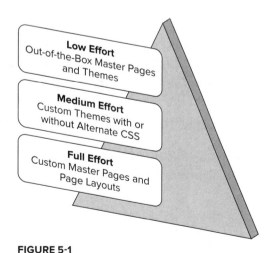

FIGURE 5-1

This chapter focuses on the upper portion of the triangle — the low and medium effort approaches to branding — diving only briefly into the full effort approach. The next section will begin this discussion by looking at the simplest form of branding — editing page content.

EDITING PAGES

Probably the easiest way to add some style to SharePoint is to just jump in and start editing pages using SharePoint's Web user interface. With SharePoint 2007, the page-editing experience was vastly different among the different editions of SharePoint. For Windows SharePoint Services 3.0 (WSS 3.0), much of SharePoint's focus was on document collaboration, and included only simple web page editing capabilities. SharePoint Server 2007 publishing sites had a nicer page-editing experience, but this difference often led to confusion, as one SharePoint website could have some publishing sites and some non-publishing sites. Alternatively, pages throughout SharePoint 2010 share an enhanced editing experience that allows for the rapid creation of web page content, which is similar to working with Microsoft Word 2007 or 2010. Also, by default, pages in SharePoint 2010, including Foundation and team sites, are actually wiki pages, which means they include basic wiki technology to allow rapid page linking (discussed later in the chapter). When SharePoint Server is used to create publishing pages, the page editing experience includes some extra functionality regarding publishing and approval workflows, as well as the concept of page layouts, which represent an enhanced type of page template.

 Page layouts are discussed in much more detail in Chapter 9.

The next section discusses using the SharePoint ribbon to edit page content in SharePoint 2010. The options displayed in the ribbon vary according to which version of SharePoint you are running, as well as your permissions for a particular site collection. For this chapter, a site collection administrator account was used when viewing the ribbon. If your user has limited permissions, your options may be different from those described in this chapter.

Another factor that changes the options on the ribbon is whether a SharePoint site is a publishing site or not. To see the publishing options in the ribbon, you need to have SharePoint Server 2010 and a site that has the Publishing Feature enabled. There are two ways to create a publishing site in SharePoint Server 2010:

➤ From Central Administration, you can create a new site collection based on either the Enterprise Wiki or Publishing Portal site templates. These two site templates have publishing enabled by default.

➤ If you have an existing non-publishing site collection, you can activate two features to enable publishing. From Site Settings ➪ Site collection features, activate the SharePoint Server Publishing Infrastructure Feature, and from Site Settings ➪ Manage site features, activate the SharePoint Server Publishing Feature.

Whenever the ribbon is configured differently between SharePoint editions or between publishing and non-publishing sites, the differences are called out in the next section.

Understanding the Page-Editing Experience

The page-editing experience in SharePoint 2010 is controlled primarily by the ribbon. Because the ribbon is contextual, you won't actually see page-editing options until a page is in edit mode. There are three main ways to put a page into edit mode in SharePoint 2010:

➤ Click Site Actions ⇨ Edit Page (see Figure 5-2).

➤ Click the edit icon (the small paper and pencil at the top, next to the Browse tab), as shown in Figure 5-3.

➤ Click the Page tab at the top of the ribbon, and then click Edit (see Figure 5-4).

FIGURE 5-2

FIGURE 5-3

FIGURE 5-4

With the page in edit mode, SharePoint places the cursor at top of the first editable area on the page, and the ribbon is opened with the Format Text tab selected (see Figure 5-5).

FIGURE 5-5

You can immediately begin typing in the editable area; page editing in SharePoint is very similar to editing a document in Microsoft Word. Note that if you click outside of an editable area, the ribbon will revert back to the Browse tab, effectively hiding the ribbon. The next few sections discuss the various tabs that are available when editing page content, focusing specifically on options that are relevant to branding.

The Format Text Tab

Figure 5-6 shows a typical Format Text tab.

FIGURE 5-6

This tab contains many of the basic options for editing content on the page, including the following groups:

Edit

The Edit group includes options to save the page, stop editing, and check in/check out. Checking out a page locks it for editing so that no one else can edit it until it is checked back in. Note that when edited, publishing pages automatically start in the checked out state.

Clipboard

The Clipboard group enables you to paste in content from other websites or documents (either by trying to retain the formatting or just pasting in plain text), and to copy information to the clipboard for pasting inside of the page or somewhere else. This group also contains the undo and redo options for quickly cycling through the history of changes in the content area. The paste option is particularly useful for bringing in existing content; SharePoint will attempt to retain the existing formatting, including references to images if they are web-based.

Font

The Font group is very similar to what you will find in the latest Microsoft Word releases. This group enables you to change how the text looks; here are some of the options:

➤ **Font face** — You can enter any font name, select from theme fonts, or select from several standard fonts. Note that whether a font will be displayed properly is ultimately determined by the user's operating system.

➤ **Font size** — You can enter any size with a valid CSS unit of measure or you can select from several standard point sizes.

➤ **Bold, italics, underline, strikethrough, subscript, superscript** — Applies the specific style to the selected text.

➤ **Highlight color** — Enables you to apply a highlight color from standard colors, theme colors, or enter any color via its hex value.

➤ **Font color** — Enables you to apply a font color from standard colors or theme colors, or to enter any color via its hex value.

➤ **Clear formatting** — Clears all formatting and returns the selected text to the default format.

Paragraph

The Paragraph group is also very similar to Microsoft Word; it enables you to change the way text content is arranged on the page. Here are some of the options in the Paragraph group:

➤ **Bullets** — Create bulleted lists.

➤ **Numbering** — Create numbered lists.

➤ **Outdent/indent** — Increase or decrease the indent level of the paragraph.

➤ **Bi-directional text layout** — Switch the paragraph between left-to-right display and right-to-left display. This feature is primarily used for sites that are intended for specific foreign languages that read right-to-left.

➤ **Paragraph alignment** — Set the paragraph alignment to Left, Center, Right, or Justify.

Styles

The Styles group enables you to format text content with various prebuilt visual styles. Chapter 12 discusses how custom styles can be added to this list for all content authors to use. This is a great way to enforce consistency across page content.

Spelling

As you might have guessed, the Spelling tab enables you to spell-check your page content against several installed languages. SharePoint will scan the page content and underline errors with a red dotted line. Clicking on the red dotted line enables you to select from a list of possible corrections.

You can hide the red dotted lines by clicking Spelling ⇨ Remove Spelling. Spell-checking is available only for SharePoint Server publishing sites.

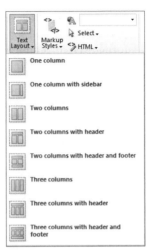

Text Layout

Text Layout includes several preconfigured content layouts that can easily be switched from the ribbon. Figure 5-7 shows the Text Layout options. Text Layout is available only in non-publishing sites; publishing sites have their own type of layout known as Page Layouts, which are available on the Page tab. The text layout functionality is useful because authors can see their content easily in several configurations without the need for creating custom page layouts.

Markup

The Markup group has several useful features for creating page-level branding:

FIGURE 5-7

➤ **Markup Styles** — Enables you to format text content with various prebuilt visual styles, much like the Styles button, except it surrounds the selected content with specific HTML tags as well as styles. Chapter 12 discusses how custom markup styles can be added to this list for all content authors to use. Like styles, markup styles are a great way to enforce consistency across page content.

➤ **Languages** — This option adds a Lang attribute to the HTML of the selected text, which can be used by browsers and search engines to handle the text differently based on a language code.

➤ **Select** — Select can be used to move the selection from the current item to its HTML parent elements. This can be helpful for applying formatting or styles to more than just the current selection.

➤ **HTML** — HTML has two options. First, you can select the Edit HTML Source option, which is great for those who have a good understanding of HTML coding and want to create or copy and paste very specific HTML layouts. The second option is Convert to XHTML, which can be used with Edit HTML Source to ensure that the entered HTML is fully XHTML compliant. Convert to XHTML will remove any elements that are not compliant with XHTML standards.

The Insert Tab

Figure 5-8 shows a typical Insert tab.

FIGURE 5-8

The Insert tab is used to add various elements to the page content. Elements you can add include the following:

➤ **Table** — Enables you to add HTML tables of various sizes to the page

➤ **Picture** — Enables you to add an image to the page. It can be uploaded from the client computer, linked from a web URL, or selected from SharePoint directly (available only for SharePoint Server publishing sites). Unlike previous versions of SharePoint, images can be uploaded and added to the page in one action.

➤ **Video and Audio** — Available only for SharePoint Server publishing sites, this option adds a Media Web Part to the page, enabling you to provide video and audio on your SharePoint site.

➤ **Link** — Enables you to add a link to the page either by specifying a URL or by directly selecting something on the SharePoint server (available only for SharePoint Server publishing sites).

➤ **Uploaded File** — Uploads a file to SharePoint and adds a link to the file on the page.

➤ **Reusable Content** — Available only for SharePoint Server publishing sites, enables a specific list named Reusable Content to be used to inject snippets of HTML or content on the page. You can add HTML content to the Reusable Content list from Site Actions ➪ View All Site Content ➪ Reusable Content.

➤ **Web Parts** — Enables you to add Web Parts to the page. Unlike in previous versions of SharePoint, Web Parts do not need to be placed in Web Part zones in SharePoint 2010. Web Parts are a type of self-contained widget that provide extra functionality to the page. To learn more about how Web Parts can be used for branding, see Chapter 10.

➤ **Existing List** — Inserts an existing SharePoint list onto the page.

➤ **New List** — Creates a new list and inserts it on the page.

When selected on the page, all these elements (except Reusable Content) add a special Tools tab to the top of the ribbon with specific options for adjusting that particular item. Figure 5-9 shows the Table Tools tab.

FIGURE 5-9

The Page Tab

Figure 5-10 shows a typical Page tab.

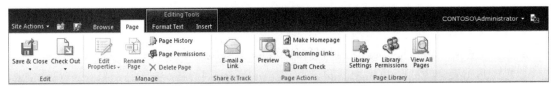

FIGURE 5-10

The Page tab is used to view and edit various properties of the page and the library that it lives in. The tab begins with the same Edit Group that is in the Format Text tab, which includes options for saving the page, stop editing, and check in/check out. The Page tab also has the following features:

➤ **Edit Properties** — Only available for SharePoint Server publishing sites, this enables you to view or edit the underlying page metadata properties, including the content type on which the publishing page is based.

➤ **Rename Page** — Available on all sites except publishing sites. This only allows you to rename the page. Note that you cannot rename the home page.

➤ **Page History** — Shows the history of what has been changed on the page.

➤ **Page Permissions** — Loads the permissions settings for the page.

➤ **Delete Page** — Enables you to delete the page after confirming the "Are you sure?" message.

➤ **E-mail a Link** — Opens a new e-mail with a link to the page included automatically in the body.

➤ **Alert Me** — Only available for sites with publishing enabled, this allows you to set up e-mail alerts for the page or to manage all your existing alerts. Alerts can e-mail you immediately, daily, or weekly based on changes made to the page.

➤ **Preview** — Only available for sites with publishing enabled, this presents a preview of the current version of the page, as viewers will see it, in a new window.

➤ **Page Layout** — Only available for sites with publishing enabled. Page layouts provide a type of page-level templating that allows content authors to create pages with specific layouts that can be controlled by developers or designers. Chapter 9 discusses in detail how to create and use page layouts.

➤ **Make Homepage** — Replaces the site's home page with the current page. This changes the page that is displayed when you browse directly to the top of the current site.

➤ **Incoming Links** — Provides a list of all pages that link to the current page.

➤ **Draft Check** — Only available for sites with publishing enabled, this runs a process that detects and highlights, with a red, dotted border, unpublished content on the current page. The highlight remains visible until the unpublished content is published or the Draft Check button is deselected from the ribbon.

➤ **Library Settings** — Opens the library settings for the current page.

➤ **Library Permissions** — Opens the library permissions for the current page.

➤ **View All Pages** — Opens a view of all pages in the current library.

The Publish Tab

Figure 5-11 shows the Publish tab for a SharePoint Server publishing page.

FIGURE 5-11

Only available for sites with publishing enabled, the Publish tab enables you to publish the page, submit it for approval, and even unpublish the page. For publishing sites, pages must be published before site visitors can see your changes. If the approval workflow is turned on for the Pages library, the published page must also be approved before site visitors can see the changes.

The Browse Tab

Figure 5-12 shows the Browse tab.

FIGURE 5-12

The browse tab hides the ribbon and shows the typical browsing experience. To get the ribbon back, click one of the other tabs again.

As you can see, the ribbon provides a lot of functionality for editing pages in SharePoint 2010. In the next section you will see an example of putting all this to use to create engaging page content.

Creating Branded Page Content with the Ribbon

In this example you will use the ribbon to create page content that is styled to match with the SharePoint site. Because SharePoint content is often copied and pasted from other sources, part of the example uses content provided in a pre-created Microsoft Word document that is available with the downloads for this chapter. The example should be created from a team site in either SharePoint Foundation or SharePoint Server. If you have a publishing site, you should start by creating a subsite based on the Team Site template; otherwise, the Text Layout steps will not be the same. To get an idea of what the example will look like, see Figure 5-13.

Here are the steps for recreating this page in your SharePoint site:

1. Click Site Actions ⇨ New Page. This causes the New Page dialog box to appear over the page. In this dialog box, for New page name, enter **About Us**, and then click Create.

2. When the page opens, note that the cursor is automatically placed in the main body field. The ribbon is set to the Format Text tab (see Figure 5-14).

3. Open Microsoft Word 2007 or later, and then open `About Randys Waffles.docx` from the chapter downloads (see Figure 5-15).

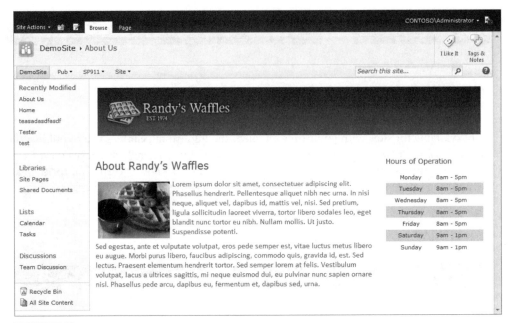

FIGURE 5-13

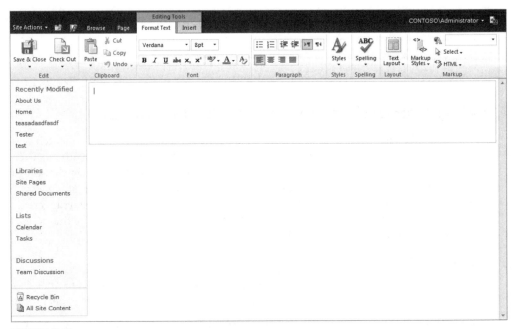

FIGURE 5-14

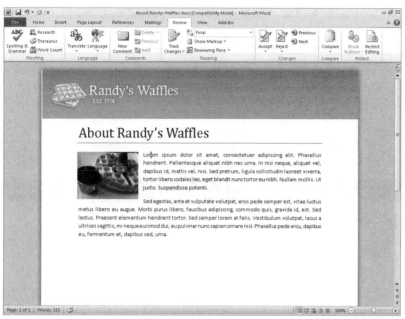

FIGURE 5-15

4. Select all the title and body content and copy and paste it into the new About Us page in SharePoint 2010.

As shown in Figure 5-16, some of the formatting is retained from Word, but the images aren't added and the styles don't really match well with the SharePoint site. If a broken image is added to the page, just select it and click Delete. Let's see if we can improve the look and feel using the SharePoint page-editing features.

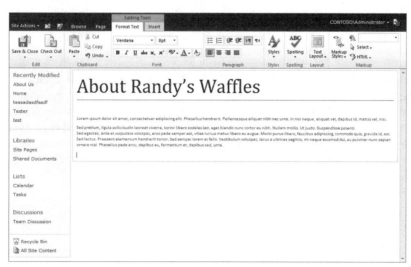

FIGURE 5-16

5. Select the title "About Randy's Waffles." From the ribbon, click Markup Styles ⇨ Colored Heading 1. This will apply a built-in HTML markup and style to create a unified look. If you prefer, you can add your own markup styles, which are discussed in Chapter 12.

6. To make the body font more readable, select everything but the title; and then, from the ribbon, click Markup Styles ⇨ Paragraph and then click the Font Size drop-down and select 12pt. You may also need to clean up the spacing between the paragraphs by adding or removing breaks with Delete and Enter.

The page is starting to look better (see Figure 5-17), but let's add some images to give it a bit more visual interest. The images are available with the downloads for this chapter.

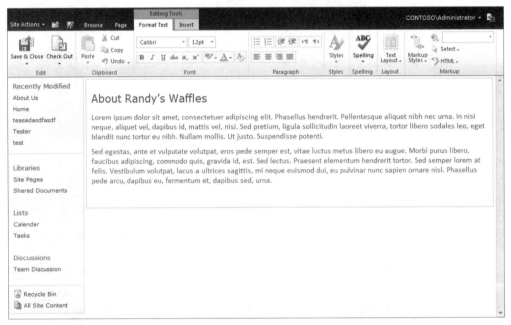

FIGURE 5-17

7. Place the cursor in front of the title on the page. Then, from the ribbon, click Insert ⇨ Picture ⇨ From Computer. Click the Browse button and select `PageBanner.png` and leave the rest of the settings the same, and click OK. On the next menu you can choose to rename the image, but for this example you can leave it the same and click Save. Notice that SharePoint 2010 uploads the image and places it in the page content near where the cursor was placed (see Figure 5-18).

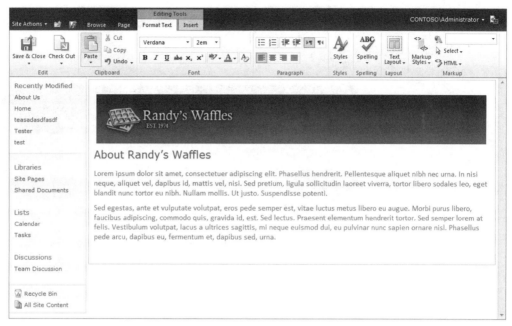

FIGURE 5-18

8. To add the waffle image to the body area, click to the left of the first character in the first paragraph of text, and from the ribbon click Insert ⇨ Picture ⇨ From Computer. Click the Browse button and select WafflePhoto.png and leave the rest of the settings the same, and click OK. On the next menu click Save.

9. This photo is too large and needs to be resized. From the Design tab on the ribbon, change the Horizontal Size to 150px and press Enter. Because the size ratio is locked, the width and height change accordingly.

10. Click on the waffle image in SharePoint and from the ribbon click Position ⇨ Left. This places the image to the left of the text. A small gap is introduced before the first paragraph begins; you can click to the left of the first character and press Backspace twice to get rid of it.

11. If you want to save your progress so far, from the ribbon click Save & Close ⇨ Save & Keep Editing.

Everything is looking good now (see Figure 5-19), but what if you want to add the hours of operation to the page? You could just place it after everything else on the page, but a better solution would be to utilize Text Layout to change the page to a two-column layout and add the hours to the right-hand column.

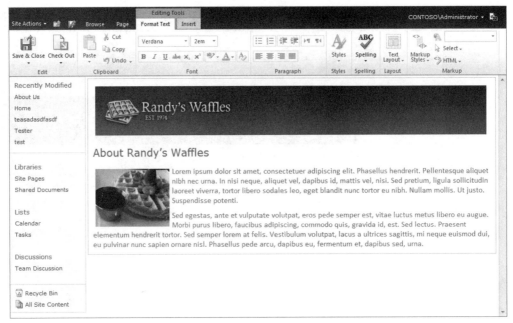

FIGURE 5-19

12. From the ribbon, click Text Layout ⇨ Two columns with header. Figure 5-20 shows the new layout in action; the right column is not very easy to see but it is there.

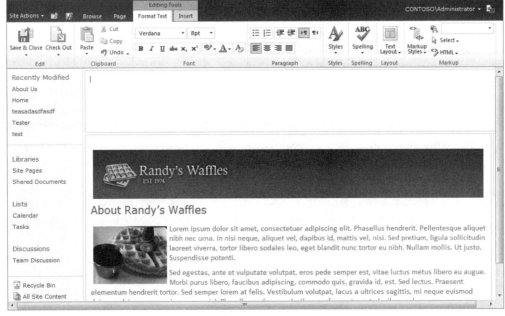

FIGURE 5-20

13. Because this layout has a specific area for a header, click on the banner image and drag it to the header area. Firefox users will need to cut and paste the banner image instead of dragging it. Remove any extra space that remains at the top of the left-hand area by pressing Backspace. Figure 5-21 shows what the page looks like now.

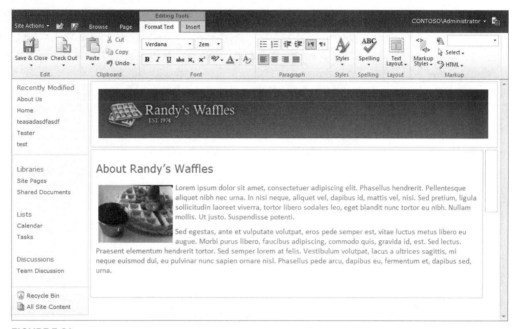

FIGURE 5-21

14. To add some heading text and a table for the hours of operation, click the right-hand area and type **Hours of Operation**; then select the text, and from the ribbon click Markup Styles ⇨ Colored Heading 2.

15. Press Enter after the Hours of Operation text. Then, from the ribbon, click Insert ⇨ Table and select Insert a 2 × 7 Table. Figure 5-22 shows the ribbon selection.

16. Before entering data, from the ribbon click Table Tools ⇨ Design and uncheck Header Row and Footer Row. This will ensure that all the rows have the same styling.

17. Enter the days of the week in the left column (Monday, Tuesday, etc.), and the opening and closing times in the right column (e.g., 8am–5pm). Figure 5-23 shows an example.

18. To apply some styling to the table, from the ribbon click Table Tools ⇨ Layout. For the table width, type **200 px** and press Enter. This will set the width so that it doesn't fill all the available space. Next, from the ribbon, click Table Tools ⇨ Design ⇨ Styles and select Table Style 2 - Light Banded.

19. That's it for the About Us page. From the ribbon, click Save & Close or click the smaller Save & Close button next to the Browse tab at the top of the ribbon. Figure 5-24 shows the final page design.

FIGURE 5-22

FIGURE 5-23

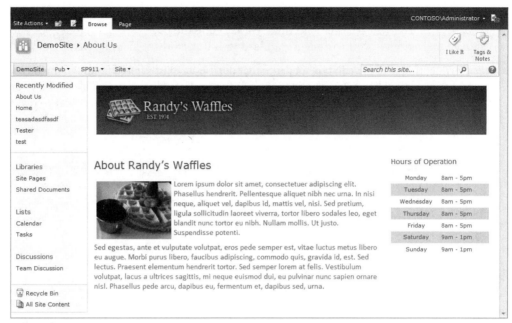

FIGURE 5-24

Creating Wiki Links

While you can certainly do a lot of things with page content in SharePoint 2010 using the ribbon, the introduction of wiki pages throughout SharePoint 2010 provides one more feature that hasn't been discussed yet. Wiki pages enable you to use *wiki links*. Wiki links provide a standard way to quickly mark links on pages using a syntax that is shared among many wiki software products.

To create a wiki link in SharePoint 2010, simply begin editing any wiki page, and in an editable text area type two left brackets ([[). Once the brackets are typed, SharePoint loads a list of available items for linking; you can click through the various levels and eventually select something to link (see Figure 5-25).

FIGURE 5-25

Once something is selected, just press Enter and SharePoint will finish the link with two right brackets (]]). You will see this wiki link syntax while the page is in edit mode, but when the page is saved and browsed you will see a standard web link to the item you selected.

It's worth noting that you can type in pages that don't even exist yet and SharePoint will save the link and display a dotted line below the link text. When this dotted line item is clicked, SharePoint will create the new page and the link will continue to function properly. This is a great way to make links to items that you know will need to be created in the future when content becomes available.

 If for some reason you need to type two brackets in page content but you are not trying to create a wiki link, you can escape them by typing a backslash before the two brackets. For example, \[[will display just [[when the page is saved and browsed.

SHAREPOINT 2010 THEMES

As mentioned in Chapter 1, when talking about SharePoint branding, a house analogy often is used. Master pages can be thought of as the blueprints, whereas SharePoint themes can be thought of as simply painting the walls. From a technical standpoint, SharePoint themes are simple color and font changes that can be applied to a SharePoint site via Cascading Style Sheets (CSS). Themes are not a new concept for SharePoint, but they have changed significantly in SharePoint 2010.

SharePoint 2007 themes were often considered difficult to build because they involved editing files in the SharePoint root (the 12 folder), including configuration files, XML, CSS, and images. When themes were applied in SharePoint 2007, the theme's CSS was applied after the out-of-the-box SharePoint CSS, thus overriding it. This was effective but ultimately resulted in a lot of extra data being sent to end users when a page first loaded, often 1000s of lines of extra CSS.

Alternatively, SharePoint 2010 themes are created using the Microsoft Office client software or the SharePoint Server 2010 web interface. The 2007 and later versions of Microsoft Word, Excel, and PowerPoint can create themes using twelve colors and two fonts that can be saved as .THMX files. SharePoint 2010 allows site collection owners and designers to load these .THMX files and use them as themes that can be applied throughout SharePoint. Unlike in SharePoint 2007, the new themes do not apply CSS after the core CSS; instead, SharePoint actually looks for a special type of CSS comment and injects the new colors and fonts into a line below the comment in the core CSS so that only one file has to be loaded by the web browser. You will learn more about theme comments later in this chapter.

 If you are familiar with how themes worked in SharePoint 2007, you may be surprised to see that custom background images are not included in the SharePoint 2010 themes. One way to remedy this is to utilize custom background images with custom CSS, possibly applied with SharePoint Server publishing's Alternate CSS feature. Although there are no custom images in SharePoint 2010 themes, an interesting feature does enable you to tint existing custom images with theme colors. Both of these concepts are discussed later in the chapter.

When following along with the theme demos in this chapter, note that SharePoint Foundation 2010 does not support showing themes for anonymous users. However, themes will work fine for anonymous users in SharePoint Server 2010.

Applying Themes

To get started working with themes in SharePoint, you don't have to concern yourself with creating custom themes right away. Twenty pre-built themes are available out-of-the-box in SharePoint 2010. The following example shows how to apply one of these 20 themes to SharePoint:

1. Click Site Actions ➪ Site Settings, and under Look and Feel, click Site Theme.

2. Notice that 20 out-of-the-box themes are available. Click through them and on the left you can see a preview of the colors and fonts that will be used on the site (see Figure 5-26). You can apply the selected theme to the site immediately by clicking the Apply button.

FIGURE 5-26

With the theme applied, you should notice that many of the colors have changed throughout the SharePoint site. To return to the default theme, simply return to the Site Theme settings page and select Default (no theme), and then click Apply.

Note that SharePoint Server includes more options on the Site Theme settings page than SharePoint Foundation, including the capability to change the theme color and fonts from the Web user interface as well as a theme preview. If the SharePoint Server site has the Publishing Feature activated, you can also apply the theme to all sub-sites below the current site.

Creating Custom Themes with the Office Client

The next step in working with themes in SharePoint 2010 is to create your own theme using the Microsoft Office client. Here are the steps for creating a Microsoft Office theme for use in SharePoint 2010 using PowerPoint 2010. (These steps are very similar when working with Word, PowerPoint, or Excel 2007 and higher.)

1. Open PowerPoint (2010) and either create a new PowerPoint file or use an existing PowerPoint presentation.

2. On the ribbon, switch to the Design tab and click Colors, and then select Create New Theme Colors (see Figure 5-27).

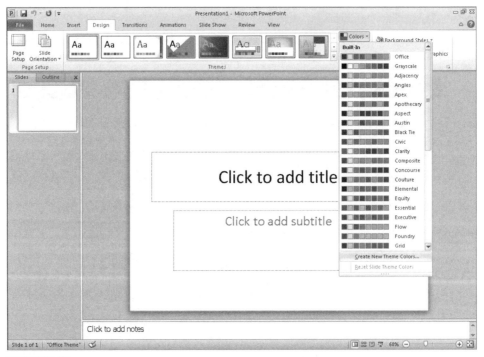

FIGURE 5-27

Notice that there are two dark and two light Text/Background colors, six Accent colors, and two Hyperlink colors. One thing to consider here is that the Accent 1 through 6 colors correspond well to the bullet indention levels in PowerPoint, but they are more subjective in SharePoint. Some experimentation is typically needed before getting the right combination. One good strategy is to pick colors that are similar or complementary. Figure 5-28 shows the menu for creating new theme colors. (This figure loses some impact in a black-and-white screenshot.)

3. After choosing your theme colors, click Save.

4. Back on the ribbon, click Fonts ➪ Create New Theme Fonts (see Figure 5-29).

Notice that there are options to set both the Heading and Body font and that the selections include many of the fonts installed on the client computer. Because these fonts will be used in SharePoint and loaded from an Internet browser, it is best practice to pick fonts that are common across multiple operating systems (such as Verdana, Arial, and Times). Figure 5-30 shows the Create New Theme Fonts dialog.

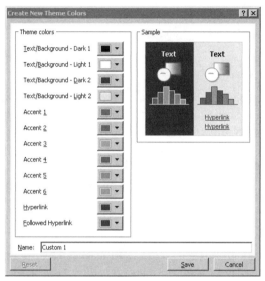

FIGURE 5-28

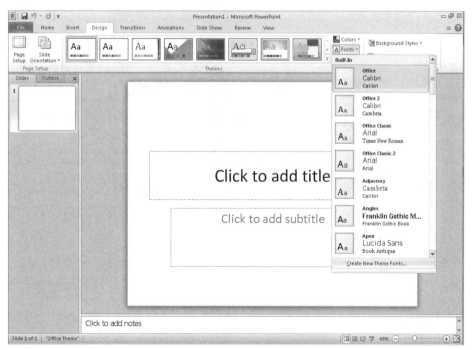

FIGURE 5-29

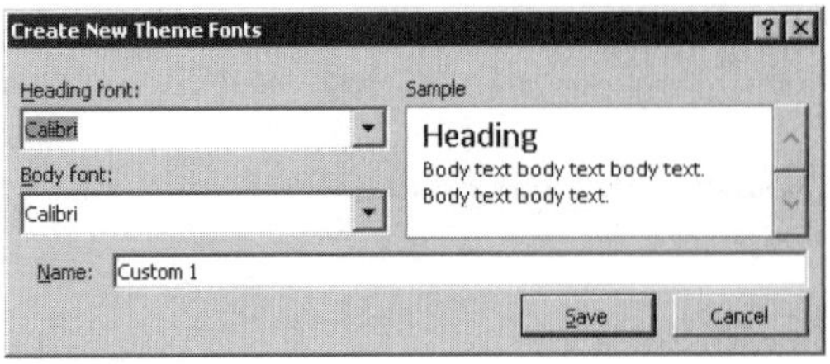

FIGURE 5-30

5. After selecting the two fonts, click Save.

6. Up until now, your selections were being saved in the local PowerPoint file. To export the theme for use in SharePoint, click the small "more" button (the downward-pointing arrow) on the right side of the Themes section of the Design tab in the ribbon (see Figure 5-31).

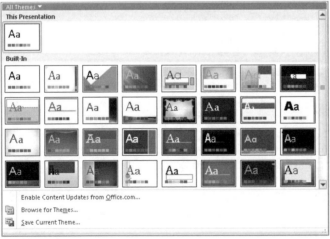

FIGURE 5-31

7. At the bottom of the All Themes dialog, shown in Figure 5-32, click Save Current Theme, select a location, name it **demo.thmx**, and click Save. This saves the .THMX file so that it can be used in SharePoint.

FIGURE 5-32

8. Open a SharePoint 2010 site in a browser, log in, and click Site Actions ➪ Site Settings ➪ Galleries ➪ Themes. This will load the document library view of the available themes.

9. To add the new theme, from the ribbon select Documents ➪ Upload Document (see Figure 5-33).

FIGURE 5-33

10. From the Upload Document dialog, click Browse, find the saved `demo.thmx` file, and click Open. Then click OK in the Upload Document dialog.

11. When the save dialog opens, you can change the filename here or just save the selection by clicking Save. Now the new theme is ready to be selected for use in SharePoint.

12. To select the theme, click Site Actions ➪ Site Settings ➪ Look and Feel ➪ Site Theme.

13. From the Select a Theme section of the Site Theme page, select your new theme, "Demo," from the list. If you have SharePoint Server, you can preview the theme by clicking Preview. You don't have to preview it, though; you can just apply it to the site immediately by clicking the Apply button.

Because this book is in black and white, a screenshot would look exactly the same as a non-themed SharePoint site; you'll have to try it yourself to really see the results.

 The out-of-the-box SharePoint v4.master *look and feel does not actually use any fonts that are applied from a custom theme. Although this certainly reduces the usefulness of themes with the default look and feel, theme fonts work with* nightandday.master, *and, as you will see later in the chapter, you can use themes with your own custom CSS. In these cases, you can use the two theme fonts, if you like.*

Modifying Themes in SharePoint Server

SharePoint Server 2010 has unique functionality that allows you to adjust the theme color and fonts directly in the Web user interface. SharePoint Foundation users are limited to editing SharePoint themes using the Office client software.

To change the theme attributes in SharePoint Server 2010, simply click Site Actions ➪ Site Settings ➪ Look and Feel ➪ Site Theme. From there, the Customize Theme section will display all of the same options that are available from the Office client software. Figure 5-34 shows the Customize Theme options.

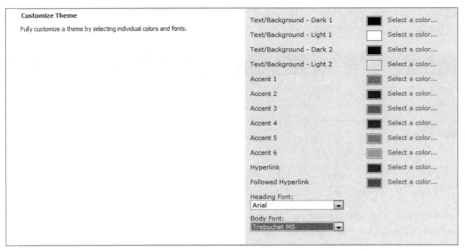

FIGURE 5-34

The color picker is a very useful addition to this dialog. You don't have to rely on previous knowledge of how colors are defined in web pages. To open the color picker, click Select a color from the Site Theme page. Figure 5-35 shows the color picker in the Colors dialog box.

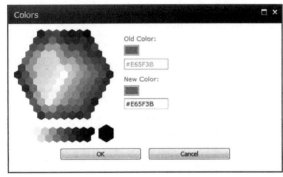

FIGURE 5-35

Along with the twelve colors, the two font options can be changed as well. Note that all the fonts installed on the server are available for selection. Of course, you should be careful not to pick a font that is completely inappropriate for viewing content on the Web, like Wingdings. (See the earlier note for information on where the theme fonts will show in SharePoint.)

As mentioned earlier, if you have a publishing site in SharePoint Server you can apply the theme to the current site and reset all of the subsites below it to the same theme. There was no equivalent option in SharePoint 2007 themes, and it can be quite useful for projects with many subsites. After all of the changes are made, clicking Apply will refresh the site with your new color and font selections.

The next few sections discuss topics that are a little more advanced, including CSS and master pages. Along with these more advanced topics, you will learn more about how themes are applied in SharePoint 2010, as well as how to use the theme colors in your own custom CSS. This chapter serves only as an introduction to the topics of CSS and master pages, however. For more information on CSS, see Chapter 7; for more information on master pages, see Chapter 8.

OVERRIDING CSS

Throughout SharePoint, CSS is probably the most prevalent method of applying branding. Thus, when creating a heavily branded SharePoint site, you will often need to apply your own custom CSS. Chapter 7 discusses CSS in more depth, but for the purposes of this chapter, just know that CSS utilizes sets of style rules that are applied to HTML to change the page rendering. Because CSS cascades by nature, if more than one CSS rule matches the same element and all other aspects are the same, the rule that is defined last will be the rule that applies to the element.

There are a few ways to apply custom CSS in SharePoint. One common mistake is to just log in to the server and find and edit the core SharePoint CSS file (`corev4.css`) in the SharePoint root. This should be avoided because it is problematic in terms of supportability. If Microsoft releases an update for SharePoint (which is inevitable), the `corev4.css` file in the SharePoint root is likely to be overwritten. Also, changes to this file will apply branding to all web applications on the farm, which is probably not the desired behavior.

Instead of editing the core CSS file, you should be overriding the default SharePoint styles. This entails creating your custom CSS using the same CSS selectors provided out-of-the-box in SharePoint and then ensuring that your CSS is loaded after the core CSS. SharePoint 2010 provides two primary means for overriding SharePoint's CSS with your own:

➤ **Alternate CSS** — This method enables you to easily apply custom CSS to a particular site and all subsites below it. However, without writing custom code, alternate CSS is available only from the SharePoint Web user interface in a SharePoint Server publishing site. If you have SharePoint Server, alternate CSS is an easy way to ensure that custom CSS is loaded last.

➤ **CSS applied via custom master page** — Through the use of a custom master page and the `CssRegistration` tag, you can ensure that custom CSS is always loaded after the SharePoint core CSS. This method is particularly well suited to creating custom branding because often a custom master page is specifically tied to one or more custom CSS files. By applying the CSS with `CssRegistration`, the two will always be applied together.

Alternate CSS is discussed in greater detail later in this chapter, and applying CSS with custom master pages is discussed in Chapter 8.

Tools for Working with CSS

Understanding how CSS is used in the default SharePoint look and feel can be challenging for both beginners and experienced SharePoint branders. This is because the typical SharePoint 2010 page has more than 5,000 lines of CSS code applied to it at any one time. Luckily, the following tools can help you analyze a SharePoint site and identify the CSS classes so that you can override them:

➤ **Internet Explorer 8 Developer Tools** — Formerly a separate download for IE7 called IE Developer Toolkit, this is now included with every copy of Internet Explorer 8 (IE8). You can activate it by clicking Tools ➪ Developer Tools.

➤ **Firebug for Firefox** — This is a third-party add-on for Firefox that can be downloaded from www.getfirebug.com.

One very useful feature of both tools is the capability to point to an area of the rendered page inside the browser and see a breakdown of what CSS is being applied to that area and how CSS rules are being overridden. Firebug is particularly powerful because it enables you to actually temporarily manipulate the CSS and see the results in real time in your browser. Because of differences between the way that different browsers render pages, both tools are often required to truly understand all of the styles that are being applied to a SharePoint site. Once the styles are identified, you can move them into a custom CSS file and apply them to SharePoint to make the overrides permanent.

> *The previous chapter showed how you can use SharePoint Designer 2010's Skewer Click feature, another great option for working with CSS in SharePoint 2010.*

CSS Tools Example

In the next section you will be working with alternate CSS to override the default SharePoint 2010 header look and feel. How can you best determine what CSS needs to be overridden to make that change? The IE Developer Tools and Firebug can both help; here is an example of using both to identify the proper CSS:

IE Developer Tools

1. Open Internet Explorer 8 and browse to your SharePoint site.

2. Click Tools ➪ Developer Tools and use the Select Element by Click feature, which is the little arrow on the left. Blue rectangles will appear around areas of the design as you move your mouse around.

3. Try to highlight the entire header portion of the page (the area vertically between Site Actions and the top navigation). One easy way to select the entire header is to move the mouse to the left of the SharePoint site icon.

4. After clicking on the area, you can see (on the right side of the Developer Tools window) that the CSS class .s4-title is applying a background image (see Figure 5-36). This is the class that you would want to override with your own CSS to override the existing header styles.

FIGURE 5-36

Firebug for Firefox

1. Ensure that Firebug has been installed in Firefox.

2. Open Firefox and browse to your SharePoint site.

3. Click Tools ➪ Firebug ➪ Open Firebug and click Inspect from the left-hand menu in the Firebug panel. Blue rectangles will appear around areas of the design as you move your mouse around.

4. Try to highlight the entire header portion of the page again. Like the previous example, one easy way to select the entire header is to move the mouse to the left of the SharePoint site icon.

5. When you have clicked on the area, you can see on the right side of the Firebug panel that, like the previous example, the CSS class .s4-title is applying a background image (see Figure 5-37).

Firebug also enables you to manipulate the CSS values and see the results right away. To try this out, make sure .s4-title is still selected, and on the right-hand panel click 64px, next to min-height. You can press the up and down arrows to see the changes in real time in the browser. You can also type values with a form of IntelliSense as well. Any changes made here are only temporary; they will disappear when the browser is refreshed. You can, however, select classes in the right-hand panel and copy and paste them into your own custom CSS once they look correct in the browser.

FIGURE 5-37

Applying Alternate CSS

Alternate CSS is a feature of SharePoint Server publishing sites that enables you to apply custom CSS to a site using the SharePoint Web user interface. Alternate CSS is a great way to add background images and other minor stylistic changes to SharePoint that can't be done with just a theme. Also, because the new theming engine in SharePoint 2010 enables you to use comments to change colors on-the-fly, alternate CSS provides an easy way to leverage that feature. You will learn more about applying theme comments in the next section.

 SharePoint Foundation 2010 does not have a menu in the Web user interface for switching to alternate CSS.

The following example describes how to utilize the Web user interface in a SharePoint Server publishing site to apply a custom header background graphic using alternate CSS. You will need to have a SharePoint Server site with publishing enabled for this example. If you have SharePoint Foundation, you can still do something similar but you need to apply the custom CSS from a custom master page.

The files for the examples in this chapter are available for download with the rest of the examples in this book at Wrox.com.

1. Create a file named **Alternate.css** on your desktop.

2. Add some CSS to set the background color and a background image:

```
.s4-title {
        background:#ff9b21 url(Header.png) repeat-y scroll 0 0;
}
```

3. Save the CSS file.

4. For the example, you need a header background image that is fairly wide to stretch the length of the browser window. Download "Header.png" from the files for this chapter.

Figure 5-38 shows the header image. (Because the book is black and white, the figure doesn't really do it justice.)

FIGURE 5-38

5. To upload the files to a folder in the site collections Style Library, first browse to your SharePoint Server site and click Site Actions ➪ View All Site Content.

6. From Document Libraries, click Style Library.

7. From the ribbon, click New Folder, name it **Themable**, and click Save. Then click on the new Themable folder.

The Themable folder is used in this example so that theme comments can be applied in the following example. If you have no intention of using theme comments, you can just skip this step, but it will change the alternate CSS URL that should be used in step 12.

8. From the ribbon, click New Folder, name it **Demo**, and click Save, Then click the new Demo folder.

9. From the ribbon, click Upload Document and upload both `Alternate.css` and `Header.png`.

10. After the files are uploaded, you need to ensure that they are published. To do this, click next to each of the filenames in SharePoint; then, on the ribbon, click Publish. When the dialog appears, click OK.

11. To apply the alternate CSS to SharePoint, click Site Actions ➪ Site Settings, and under Look and Feel click Master page.

12. For the alternate CSS URL, click Browse, select `/Style Library/Themable/Demo/Alternate.css`, and then click OK.

13. Click OK to apply the alternate CSS.

As shown in Figure 5-39, the header background image should be changed to the custom image. Again, the black-and-white figure doesn't capture the full impact of the change. To really see the change, you will need to try the example yourself.

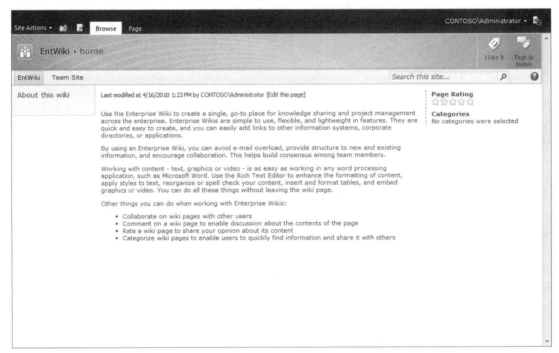

FIGURE 5-39

There is a problem in the current implementation of how background images are applied when the Themable directory is used. You will learn more about theme comments in an upcoming section, but it's important to note that for the previous example, you need to make sure that no theme is applied to the site. If a theme is applied to a site that uses the preceding alternate CSS in the Themable directory, the custom background header graphic will not show. This problem has to do with how SharePoint looks for theme comments in a themable folder. Since the previous example doesn't have any theme comments, SharePoint gets confused and has problems showing the image. Hopefully, this problem will be resolved in one of the future updates to SharePoint 2010. Alternatively, if you want to use themes with custom CSS that has no theme comment, you can just place the CSS outside of the Themable folder in the Style Library.

In an upcoming example, you will add theme comments to the preceding example. With the theme comments added, themes can then be safely applied to the site, and the background image will show properly.

Replacing the Site Icon with a Custom Logo

Another simple change you can make to your SharePoint branding is to replace the site icon with a custom logo. This is easy enough to do in SharePoint Foundation or Server; the following steps describe how to change the site icon to the Logo.png image from the chapter downloads:

1. Make sure you have downloaded Logo.png from the chapter files.

2. Browse to your SharePoint Server site and click Site Actions ➪ View All Site Content.

3. From Document Libraries, click Style Library ➪ Themable ➪ Demo.

4. From the ribbon, click Upload Document and upload Logo.png.

5. To ensure that the uploaded logo is published, click next to the filename in SharePoint; then, on the ribbon, click Publish. When the dialog appears, click OK.

6. Click Site Actions ➪ Site Settings, and under Look and Feel click Title, description, and icon.

7. For Logo URL and Description, enter **Style Library/Themable/Demo/Logo.png** and click OK.

Figure 5-40 shows the new site logo. In the next section, you will see how you can add theme comments to the custom CSS to allow the header image to be recolored by a SharePoint 2010 theme.

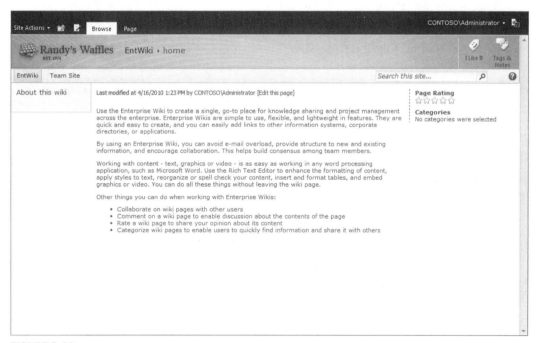

FIGURE 5-40

Understanding Theme Comments

As stated earlier, when a theme is applied to a SharePoint 2010 site, SharePoint looks for specific CSS markup comments in the out-of-the-box SharePoint CSS as well as for custom CSS and replaces colors and fonts in the line directly below each of the comments. Here is list of the tokens that SharePoint will look for:

➤ **ReplaceFont** — Replaces fonts with one of the two font options.

➤ **ReplaceColor** — Replaces colors such as backgrounds and fonts with one of the twelve color options.

➤ **RecolorImage** — Recolors images using one of three methods: Tint, Blend, or Fill.

Each of these theme comment tokens has specific parameters that are acceptable; the following sections discuss the options for each.

ReplaceFont

The two available fonts are referred to by the following names:

➤ **MajorFont** — Corresponds to the Heading font.

➤ **MinorFont** — Corresponds to the Body font.

Here is an example of how the comments would look in CSS:

```
/* [ReplaceFont(themeFont: "MajorFont")] */
font-family: verdana;

/* [ReplaceFont(themeFont: "MinorFont")] */
font-family: arial;
```

When SharePoint encounters the first comment, it replaces Verdana with whatever is set as the Heading font and replaces Arial with whatever is set as the Body font.

ReplaceColor

The twelve available colors are referred to by the following names:

➤ Dark1, Dark2

➤ Light1, Light2

➤ Accent1, Accent2, Accent3, Accent4, Accent5, Accent6

➤ Hyperlink, FollowedHyperlink

As shown in Figure 5-41, each of these colors has five shade values that can be applied:

➤ Lightest

➤ Lighter

➤ Medium

➤ Darker

➤ Darkest

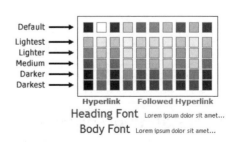

FIGURE 5-41

You can select these options on the theme settings page by choosing Site Actions ⇨ Site Settings ⇨ Site Theme.

Clearly, you can create a wide variety of colors with themes. The following are all valid color syntax:

```
/* [ReplaceColor(themeColor:"Accent1")] */
color: #ABABAB;

/* [ReplaceColor(themeColor:"Dark1")] */
color: red;

/* [ReplaceColor(themeColor:"Hyperlink")] */
color: white;

/* [ReplaceColor(themeColor:"Accent6-Lightest")] */
color: black;

/* [ReplaceColor(themeColor:"Accent6-Darker")] */
color: black;
```

Also, interestingly enough, you can achieve even more color variations by utilizing `themeShade` and `themeTint` to darken and lighten colors, respectively. These two properties accept values between 0.0 (maximum change) and 1.0 (no change). The following are two examples of using this method to achieve specific theme colors:

```
/* [ReplaceColor(themeColor:"Accent1",themeShade:"0.8")] */
color: red;

/* [ReplaceColor(themeColor:"Accent1",themeTint:"0.35")] */
color: red;
```

The first comment darkens Accent1 a little, while the second comment lightens Accent1 a lot. This setting can be confusing because the values are not applied directly as decimal percentages; instead, they are applied exponentially. You can think of `themeTint` and `themeShade` as values representing the amount of luminosity applied to the color, with larger numbers leading to more of the original color remaining after the change. The previous method of stating Lighter, Lightest, and so on is shorthand for specific `themeShade` and `themeTint` values.

As noted earlier, the concepts of Accent1–6 correspond nicely to PowerPoint and Word bullet indentions, but they aren't necessarily an obvious mapping to SharePoint. In some cases a color's usage in the default SharePoint CSS may make sense, and in others it may seem arbitrary. For example, one common pattern in the out-of-the-box SharePoint branding uses Dark1 and Dark2 for text colors, while Light1 and Light2 are often used for background colors. When applying colors to SharePoint with themes, you will likely need a fair amount of trial and error before achieving the perfect color scheme.

RecolorImage

`RecolorImage` uses the same color options available for `ReplaceColor`, except they can be used to affect images in three specific ways:

➤ **Tinting** — Applies the theme color to the image by shifting its colors to the selected color. The details of the image remain but its colors will be comprised entirely of shades of the selected color.

➤ **Blending** — Applies the theme color to the image by mixing its original colors with the selected color. The details of the image remain, as well as some aspects of its original coloring. Results can be interesting when using blending; you may need to experiment to get a nice result.

➤ **Filling** — Applies the theme color entirely for the height and width of the image. Filling results in a rectangle that is 100% comprised of the exact selected color.

Here are some examples of the `RecolorImage` syntax:

```
/* [RecolorImage(themeColor:"Accent1",method:"Tinting ")] */
background-image:url("banner1.png");

/* [RecolorImage(themeColor:"Accent1",method:"Blending ")] */
background-image:url("banner2.png");

/* [RecolorImage(themeColor:"Accent1",method:"Filling ")] */
background-image:url("banner3.png");
```

Lastly, you can use `RecolorImage` with `includeRectangle` to recolor only a specific rectangular portion of a background image. This could be useful in cases where one part of a banner needs to change color but the rest should remain the same. Here is an example of `includeRectangle`:

```
/* [RecolorImage(themeColor:"Accent1",method:"Tinting",includeRectangle:
   {x:0,y:0,width:100,height:50})] */
```

In the preceding example, the tinting will occur only in a rectangle that starts at the top-left corner of the image (determined by the *x* and *y* coordinate) and extends 100 pixels wide and 50 pixels high.

Themable Locations

Themes will apply these color changes to your own custom CSS if you use the aforementioned comments, but the CSS must be located in a "themable" location. The following locations and any subfolders beneath them are valid themable locations:

In the SharePoint root folder:

➤ `14\TEMPLATE\LAYOUTS\1033\STYLES\Themable`

At the top level of a site collection:

➤ `/Style Library/Themable/`

➤ `/Style Library/~language/Themable/`

Note that the `/Style Library/~language/Themable/` directory is created automatically on SharePoint Server. Also, ~language is a language code; for United States English, this would equate to `/Style Library/en-us/Themable`

`Style Library/~en-us/Themable` is not created by default on SharePoint Foundation, and `Style Library/Themable` is not created by default for either Foundation or Server. The good news is that you can create a folder named **Themable** at the root of the Style Library, and SharePoint will know to make it available for theme comments.

Using Theme Comments in Custom CSS

Because the CSS in the previous alternate CSS example was placed in a themable directory in the Style Library, you can apply SharePoint 2010 theme colors simply by adding some CSS comments. The following example takes the alternate CSS from the previous example and adds one theme comment that will tint the header background image:

1. On your desktop, open the `Alternate.css` file that you used previously.

2. Modify the code to have a `RecolorImage` comment that will tint the `Header.png` image the color of Accent 6:

```
.s4-title {
        /* [RecolorImage(themeColor:"Accent6", method:"Tinting")] */
        background:#ff9b21 url(Header.png) repeat-y scroll 0 0;
}
```

3. Save the CSS file.

4. Browse to your SharePoint Server site and click Site Actions ➪ View All Site Content.

5. From Document Libraries, click Style Library ➪ Themable ➪ Demo.

6. From the ribbon, click Upload Document and upload the new version of `Alternate.css`. Ensure that "Add as a new version to existing files" is checked and click OK.

7. To ensure that the file is published after it is uploaded, click next to the filename in SharePoint; then, on the ribbon, click Publish. When the dialog appears, click OK. Notice that the header doesn't look any different; it won't until you apply a theme.

8. Click Site Actions ➪ Site Settings, and under Look and Feel click Site theme.

9. Select the Cay theme (note that it sets a green color for Accent 6), and click Apply.

When the theme is applied, SharePoint encounters the comment in your custom CSS and knows to make a new version of the header image tinted in the color of Accent 6. (Unfortunately, a black-and-white screenshot won't enable you to see the color change, but if you follow the steps in your SharePoint Server site you can see that the header has changed color.) You can use this same method to try some of the other theme comments that were described earlier in the chapter.

CREATING SIMPLE CUSTOM MASTER PAGES

The topic of master pages can certainly be complex (which is why all of Chapter 8 is dedicated to them). Despite their complexity, however, you can modify the out-of-the-box master pages without diving too deeply into fully studying them. The `v4.master` and `nightandday.master` out-of-the-box master pages can be good starting points for custom branding, as long as you only need to make minor changes. Be aware, though that the out-of-the-box master pages basically have zero comments and their formatting is very specific to their particular look and feel. Chapter 8 discusses other options that are more appropriate for creating highly branded master pages. That said, if you only need to make minor changes, or add/remove something, you should be fine starting with an out-of-the-box master page.

The following example uses SharePoint Designer 2010 to create a new master page using `v4.master` as a starting point to create a centered, fixed-width layout. This type of design is popular for public-facing sites that use a more structured look and feel. Although this example uses a SharePoint Server 2010 publishing site, if you have SharePoint Foundation 2010 you can still accomplish the same branding (although some of the steps may be different).

1. Open SharePoint Designer 2010 and load the SharePoint Server 2010 publishing site.

2. From the Site Objects menu on the left, click Master Pages (see Figure 5-42).

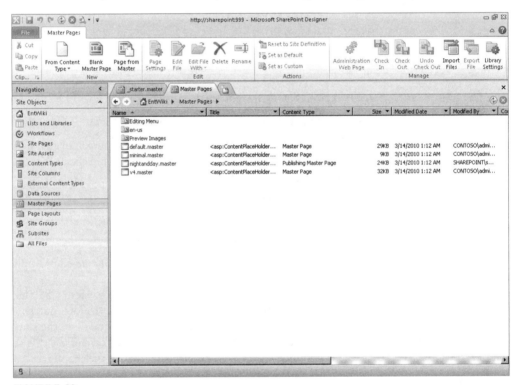

FIGURE 5-42

3. From the list of master pages, click next to `v4.master`. Then, from the ribbon, click Copy and then Paste. This will create a duplicate of `v4.master` named `v4_copy(1).master`.

4. Click Rename from the ribbon and then rename `v4_copy(1).master` to `v4_centered .master`.

5. Click `v4_centered.master` and the click Edit File from the ribbon. When a prompt asks if you want to check it out, click Yes.

6. Change the background color to maroon. Near line 36, add `style="background-color: maroon;"` to the `<body>` tag, as shown here:

```
<body scroll="no" onload="if (typeof(_spBodyOnLoadWrapper) != 'undefined')
    _spBodyOnLoadWrapper();" class="v4master" style="background-color:
maroon;">
```

7. Add a surrounding `<div>` tag that centers the inner page and makes the background white. Near line 37, add the following bold line between the `<form>` tag and the `<asp:ScriptManager>` tag:

```
<form runat="server" onsubmit="if (typeof(_spFormOnSubmitWrapper) != 'undefined')
    {return _spFormOnSubmitWrapper();} else {return true;}">

<div style="width: 960px; margin: auto; background-color:white;">

<asp:ScriptManager id="ScriptManager" runat="server" EnablePageMethods="false"
    EnablePartialRendering="true" EnableScriptGlobalization="false"
    EnableScriptLocalization="true" />
```

8. Close out the previous `<div>` by adding a `</div>` near line 626, after the `<SharePoint:DeveloperDashboard>` tag:

```
<SharePoint:DeveloperDashboard runat="server"/>
</div>
```

9. Add a class called `s4-nosetwidth` to the main page `<div>`. This is required to make a SharePoint 2010 master page that has a fixed width. Otherwise, SharePoint will take over and inject a variable width to the page. Near line 293, change `<div ID="s4-workspace">` to `<div ID="s4-workspace" class="s4-nosetwidth">`:

```
<div ID="s4-workspace" class="s4-nosetwidth">
```

10. Save the master page by pressing Ctrl+S. If you are warned that the page will no longer be based on a site definition, simply click Yes to continue.

11. Right-click `v4_centered.master` in SharePoint Designer and select Check In. Then select Publish a major version. SharePoint will warn that "This document requires content approval. Do you want to view or modify its approval status?" Click Yes, and a browser window will open to the Approval status page.

12. Click the arrow that appears to the right of `v4_centered` and select Approve/Reject (see Figure 5-43). From the next screen, click Approved and then OK. This will allow other users to see the changes.

13. Now you need to apply the custom master page to your SharePoint site. Click Site Actions ⇨ Site Settings. Under Look and Feel, click Master page.

14. Select `v4_centered.master` for both the Site Master Page and System Master Page. Ensure that the alternate CSS URL is set to "Use Microsoft SharePoint Foundation default styles" (see Figure 5-44). Finally, click OK.

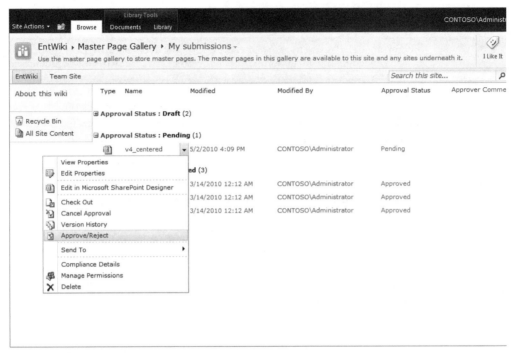

FIGURE 5-43

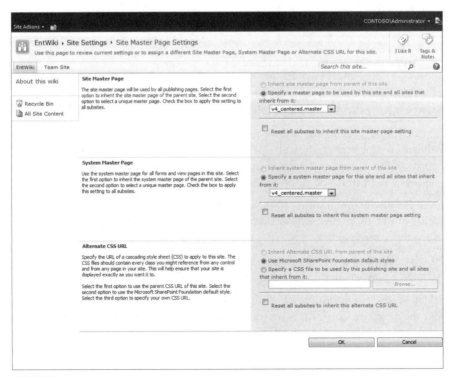

FIGURE 5-44

This will apply the new master page throughout the site, even to the Site Settings pages. Figure 5-45 shows the new fixed-width master page. The screen width in the screenshot is low; you can just barely see that the main page width is smaller than the full screen width. The dark areas on the sides of the screenshot are the background, while the large white area in the middle is the actual page width. If you were to view this example on a higher resolution monitor, the middle section would stay the same width, whereas the dark sides would expand to fill the whole screen.

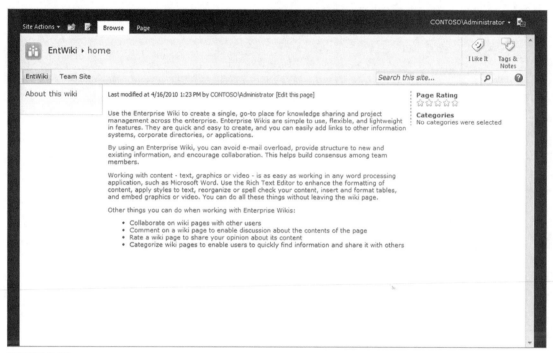

FIGURE 5-45

SUMMARY

SharePoint 2010 branding doesn't have to be complex. There are many ways to apply colors, fonts, and stylistic formatting that don't require a deep understanding of the inner working of master pages. This chapter discussed some of the easier approaches to SharePoint 2010 branding, including page customization, themes, alternate CSS, and even how to make minor changes to existing master pages. You can use these techniques either together or separately to create SharePoint branding in a short amount of time — and in some cases, even if you have little knowledge of traditional web development.

Future chapters will dive deeper in to some of these topics. For example, Chapter 7 will help you understand how CSS works in SharePoint 2010, and Chapter 8 looks at master pages in much more detail. What you've learned in this chapter should pique your interest enough to forge on and learn about how more involved custom branding is created for SharePoint 2010.

Working with Navigation

WHAT'S IN THIS CHAPTER?

➤ General navigation considerations and planning

➤ SharePoint-specific navigation issues

➤ Navigation controls in SharePoint 2010

➤ Creating custom navigation controls

When planning for branding, many people think of the graphics and colors that make a site look nice, or maybe they think of the layout schema — where to place design elements, whether the layout should be fixed width or fluid, and how to address browser inconsistencies. What is often overlooked is navigation. However, it is only logical that you would brand your navigation along with the rest of your site, as it represents a critical aspect of the entire design.

Clearly, applying design elements to your navigation controls requires some consideration. If you do not take into account the design and functionality of your navigation, your navigation controls may not resemble the rest of the site you have so meticulously planned.

But that is only part of navigation design. With any branding project, SharePoint or otherwise, the *usability* of the site is critical. Can visitors find the information they seek, make a purchase, or simply use the site easily and effectively? A good designer will consider the flow of information and the ease of use for the visitor when planning the design of any website or application.

As you go through this chapter, you will get an overall understanding of what you should think about when planning navigation in your SharePoint site, what controls are available to you to help with your navigation plan, and how to handle navigation issues that are not covered by the default navigation controls in SharePoint 2010.

PLANNING SITE NAVIGATION

When you are planning a SharePoint site, careful thought needs to be given to how users will experience it and how they will find the information that is important to them. In Chapter 3 you learned about information architecture and taxonomy, two topics that can be thought of as the early stages of planning a navigation structure. Designing an information architecture will help you determine what the hierarchy of your SharePoint environment will look like. The goal with a SharePoint information architecture is to ensure that your content is well organized, has enough room for all the various types of content in your organization initially, and will provide room for long-term growth as the amount of content increases over time. Information architecture is designed with two primary functions in mind:

➤ **Findability** — Users must be able to find the content they are looking for; they should be able to navigate the structure in a logical manner.

➤ **Usability** — Once the content is found, it should be retrievable in a useful format.

By planning for navigation ahead of time you avoid potential problems down the road for your SharePoint site, particularly the following:

➤ **Duplication of content** — This makes it difficult for users to determine which version of content is correct and current.

➤ **Poorly designed navigation** — This makes it difficult for users to find important sites and information.

Much like a traditional construction project, the goal here is to build your SharePoint site once and let it grow naturally over time. By effectively planning your navigation before implementing it, you are helping to ensure the process is as smooth as possible.

When designing your information architecture, you should take several things into consideration, including the following:

➤ Existing sites and their content

➤ User requirements

➤ Business requirements

➤ Security requirements

Existing Sites and Their Content

If you have an existing site with relevant content, this is a great place to start when planning your site's new information architecture. In fact, after analyzing the content and current navigation, your existing site may provide a reasonable structure for your information architecture with little to no change. However, make sure you do analyze it to ensure that it is set up in a way that makes sense and that it will continue to work with the new site. Examining log files can help you get a sense of what is being accessed the most frequently and the least, which can help you plan how navigation should be organized moving forward. If changes need to be made, this is the time to make them.

But this is just the starting point. Remember that your new site will likely host new information that isn't already a part of your existing site. Try to take into account the plausible and likely additions to the content of your site at this stage and make sure the information architecture you create is robust enough to handle these content changes over time. While this may prove hard to predict, thinking about existing content and what may become future content is a great place to get started on creating your eventual information architecture.

User Requirements

Navigation is the cornerstone of any good information architecture. The consumers of your site will use whatever information architecture you put in place to find the information they need (or that you want to disseminate). If you fail to meet their needs, the information architecture cannot be a success.

So what kind of hierarchy do users want to see in the site navigation? Does it make sense to create sites for each business unit in the company (e.g., Human Resources, Payroll, IT, etc.)? Or would it make sense to have sites broken out by employee types (e.g., Employees, Supervisors, Executives, etc.)? For public-facing sites it may make sense to organize the sites by product lines or even just sites for related pages.

The easiest way to determine this is to ask the users who will be interacting with your site. If possible, try to get answers to the following questions:

➤ What information do you need to complete your normal daily tasks?

➤ Is the current application missing anything?

➤ Do you prefer to browse to or search for the information you need?

Getting feedback to questions such as these can identify any problems that users are experiencing with the current information architecture, enabling you to fix them proactively.

Business Requirements

A critical step in planning your information architecture is to determine what, if any, business requirements are in place that may dictate how the navigation works on your site. You will need to find out from the decision makers how the information should flow throughout the site and who should get to see it.

Specifically, you need to find out the following:

➤ What information will be presented to the users of the site?

➤ What information is most important?

➤ How should information be compartmentalized?

➤ Will information be shared across business units, isolated within each unit, or a combination of both?

Once you have the answers to these questions, you will have a good idea of what management expects in terms of site navigation. Combined with the user requirements and any existing architecture, you have a pretty good foundation for the new information architecture of your site.

Security Requirements

Securing content is a critical piece of any web application. Security might dictate that content be divided into manageable groups that can be accessed only by certain groups. This could help determine which nodes are created in the site hierarchy of your information architecture. For example, it might make sense to have an Executive site that contains dashboard and other planning data used by the executive team of the corporation that would be available only to members of a particular security group. In this scenario, maintaining the security of this information only requires maintaining this one security group, rather than maintaining the security of individual pieces of information.

UNDERSTANDING SHAREPOINT 2010 NAVIGATION

By default, SharePoint 2010 implements a dynamic navigation system that automatically changes what is shown as sites and pages are created in a site collection. This can be a very useful feature because content authors are typically not thinking about navigation as they are creating sites and pages. Sometimes, however, you may wish to control the arrangement of navigation manually, and you will learn more about that process later in the chapter.

Navigation links in SharePoint 2010 are also security sensitive. If a user doesn't have the appropriate permissions to view a particular site or page, the navigation link will be unavailable for that user. This feature, known as *security trimming,* is useful because without it the user sees an error if they browse to those pages (either through navigation or manually). By automatically security-trimming links, users are spared the indignity of being denied access to items they cannot visit!

SharePoint 2010 also includes an option for turning off security trimming for a site collection. This allows users to select navigation links for pages that will display "Error: Access Denied." From the error message, users can e-mail an administrator to request access to the page. To find the option for turning off security trimming, click Site Actions ⇨ Site collection navigation, and then uncheck the option for Enable security trimming, and click OK. Note that turning off security trimming may affect other aspects of SharePoint beyond just the main navigation, so be sure to thoroughly test your site after selecting this option.

For the following example, use either a SharePoint Foundation or SharePoint Server team site:

1. Click Site Actions ⇨ New Site.
2. From the Create dialog box, select Team Site. For the Title enter **Nav Test** and for the URL name enter **NavTest**.
3. Click Create.
4. Navigate back to the parent site.

Notice that the top navigation has gained a link for the new site, Nav Test (see Figure 6-1).

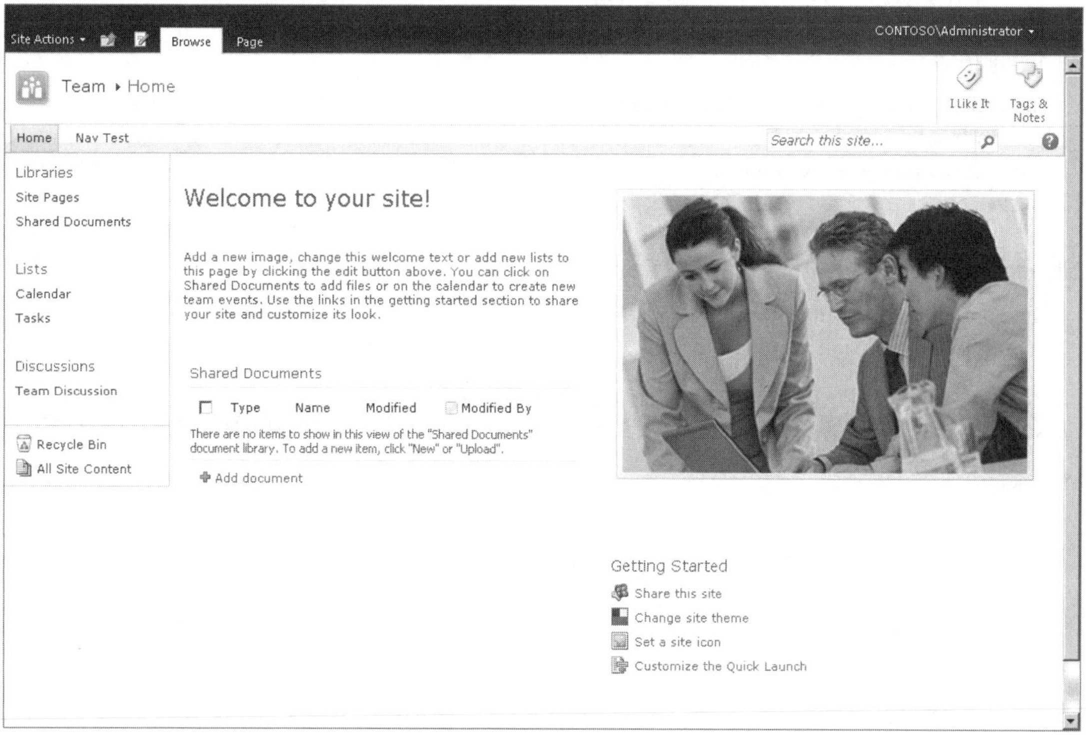

FIGURE 6-1

By default, both SharePoint Foundation and SharePoint Server will show new sites in the top navigation. SharePoint Server publishing sites will also show new pages in the top navigation, but you need to change the default settings as described in the next section.

> *SharePoint separates content by site collections; this separation also applies to navigation. This means that by default SharePoint shows navigation for only the current site collection. Later in the chapter you will learn more about advanced ways of handing cross-site-collection navigation.*

Managing Navigation with the SharePoint Web Interface

The two different versions of SharePoint 2010 give designers different navigation controls. SharePoint Foundation provides relatively simple control over navigation, whereas SharePoint Server publishing sites provide a more robust collection of settings that enable you to control the navigation more granularly. This difference even extends to the menu items available for navigation in the Site Settings.

Another major difference between SharePoint Foundation and SharePoint Server navigation is that the top navigation in a SharePoint Foundation site is limited to showing only one level of navigation by default. As you will see later, SharePoint Server provides drop-downs for more levels in the top navigation.

Whether you are using SharePoint Foundation or SharePoint Server, the capability to manage navigation from the web interface is a valuable feature when building a usable navigation structure. The following sections describe how you interact with both SharePoint Foundation and SharePoint Server publishing navigation from the web interface.

SharePoint Foundation Navigation

The Navigation Settings for SharePoint Foundation 2010 are divided into two links in the Site Settings menu under the Look and Feel heading: the Quick launch and the Top link bar (see Figure 6-2).

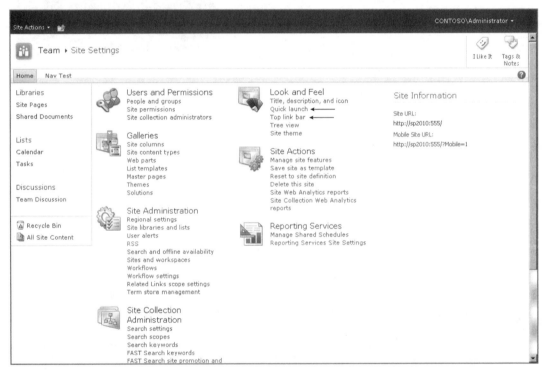

FIGURE 6-2

The top link bar provides menu navigation at the top of the page, usually for links that are just below the current location; the Quick Launch links, typically located on the left side of the page, usually contain links to important content. The following two sections describe the two navigation menus available from the Site Settings menu in SharePoint Foundation 2010.

Top Link Bar

When you first load the top link bar settings page, it displays all the existing top navigation items, which typically includes all the sites that have been created so far (see Figure 6-3). From here you can add new navigation links or change the order of the items.

FIGURE 6-3

In SharePoint Foundation, adding a new navigation link is fairly bare bones; you can enter a URL and a description. The URL can be to any website or to an existing page in SharePoint, but you need to know the URL, as there is no browse feature like there is in SharePoint Server publishing navigation. This simply adds a link to the list of navigation items.

You can also edit the existing links by clicking the little page and pencil icon to the left of the item. If the item was created automatically from a site, you can only change the description or delete the link. If the item was manually created from New Navigation Link, then you can also change the web URL or the description (see Figure 6-4).

Lastly, you can change the order of the items by clicking Change Order from the main top link bar page. This brings up a list of all the links; use the Link Order drop-downs on the left to indicate the desired order (see Figure 6-5). Click OK to see the results.

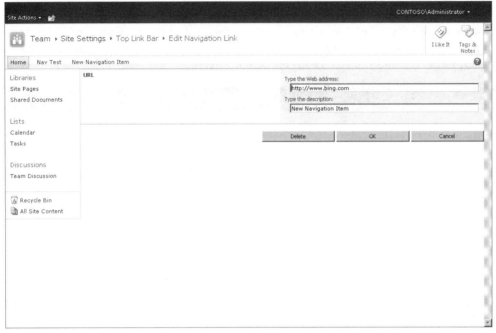

FIGURE 6-4

FIGURE 6-5

Quick Launch

The Quick Launch settings page is very similar to the top link bar settings page except you can also create headings from the New Heading button. This is available because SharePoint Foundation shows two levels of navigation in the Quick Launch menu, unlike the top link bar which shows only one level of navigation. Navigation links can be arranged under the headings, which creates the two levels of navigation. The addition of headings means that the New Navigation Link and Change Order buttons both gain options for ensuring that the items are arranged under the heading of your choice.

By adding headings and navigation links, the Quick Launch menu can be built to suit your site's navigation needs. The following example shows how to create a heading and navigation item for the Quick Launch:

1. If you haven't already, click Site Actions ➪ Site Settings, and under Look and Feel click Quick Launch.

2. Click New Heading.

3. For each heading you need to enter a Web address URL; you cannot leave it empty. If you don't want the heading to go anywhere in particular, just enter "/", which is a link back to the root of the site. If you do want the heading link to go somewhere, enter a valid URL like `http://www.microsoft.com` here.

4. Enter a description. This is the actual text that will appear for the link, so choose something descriptive. In this case just enter "Demo Heading" because this is a test item.

5. Click OK.

6. Click New Navigation Item.

7. For the Web address, because we are creating an actual navigation link, we need to enter a real URL. This can either be a link to an external website or a page in the existing site. For this example, type **http://www.bing.com**.

8. Enter a description, which will be the text that is displayed for the link. Enter **Bing**.

9. Select a Heading for the new link. In this case select the newly created Demo Heading.

As you create these items, you can see them appear in the Quick Launch menu. Figure 6-6 shows the new heading and link in the Quick Launch on the left side of the page.

To reorder the new heading and link to put them at the top of the Quick Launch, follow these steps:

1. From the Quick Launch settings page, click Change Order.

2. You will see a list of the Quick Launch items, with numbers in drop-downs next to them. Demo Heading and Bing should be at the end of the list. Click the drop-down to the left of Demo Heading and change it to 1. This will dynamically reorder the other items (see Figure 6-7).

3. Click OK to save the changes.

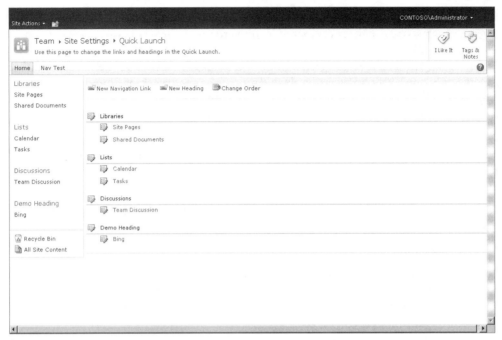

FIGURE 6-6

FIGURE 6-7

SharePoint Server Publishing Navigation

SharePoint Server has more robust navigation settings available to publishing sites. To follow along with this section you will need a SharePoint Server publishing site. You can learn more about creating a SharePoint Server publishing site from the beginning of Chapter 5.

The first difference, compared to SharePoint Foundation navigation, is that instead of two different menu items under Site Settings, SharePoint Server publishing sites have just one option titled Navigation. This one settings page has options for both the *global navigation* and the *current navigation*. These typically correspond to the top and left navigation, respectively, but they can be rearranged from a custom master page. Also, by default SharePoint Server sites can show multiple levels of dynamic top and left navigation. These are displayed as either drop-downs for the top navigation or fly-outs for the left navigation. When subsites are created they are automatically displayed as dynamic navigation items for the top navigation.

 One common question that comes up with SharePoint Server publishing sites is whether you can manually create multiple levels of dynamic navigation items from the Navigation Settings page. This menu only allows you to manually create one level of heading that has one level of links below it. This means that you can create only one level of dynamic drop-downs or fly-outs manually. If you want more levels of dynamic navigation, you must create the subsites and sub-subsites that correspond to the navigation you want to show.

The following sections describe the options on the Navigation Settings page for a SharePoint Server publishing site. Figures 6-8 through 6-15 use an Enterprise Wiki site template.

Global Navigation

Figure 6-8 shows the Global Navigation section of the Navigation Settings page.

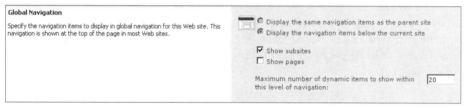

FIGURE 6-8

These settings typically affect the top navigation. You can set the navigation to display the same items as the parent site (if you are looking at the top-level site this option is grayed out). By default, only subsites are displayed on the top navigation. You can change this to show pages as well by clicking the checkbox next to Show pages. Lastly, this section enables you to set the maximum number of dynamic items that can be displayed within the level of navigation. This option can be useful to limit the number of drop-downs that would be necessary for sites that have numerous subsites and pages.

Current Navigation

Figure 6-9 shows the Current Navigation section of the Navigation Settings page.

Current Navigation

Specify the navigation items to display in current navigation for this Web site. This navigation is shown on the side of the page in most Web sites.

- ○ Display the same navigation items as the parent site
- ○ Display the current site, the navigation items below the current site, and the current site's siblings
- ● Display only the navigation items below the current site

- ☐ Show subsites
- ☐ Show pages

Maximum number of dynamic items to show within this level of navigation: 20

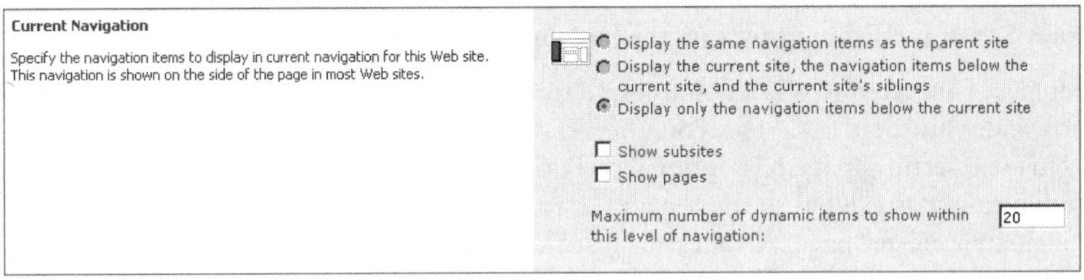

FIGURE 6-9

These settings are typically displayed in the left side navigation, the area known as the Quick Launch in Foundation sites. It contains similar settings to the Global Navigation settings just described, with the addition of options to either show the navigation for the current site, the items below it, and its siblings, or simply display all the navigation items below the current site.

Sorting

Figure 6-10 shows the Sorting and Automatic Sorting sections of the Navigation Settings page.

Sorting

Specify how subsites, pages, headings and navigation links should be sorted when displayed in navigation.

- ● Sort automatically
- ○ Sort manually
  - ☐ Sort pages automatically

Automatic Sorting

Automatically sort the navigation items by title, creation date, or publication date.

Sort by:

Title

- ● in ascending order (A,B,C or 1,2,3)
- ○ in descending order (C,B,A or 3,2,1)

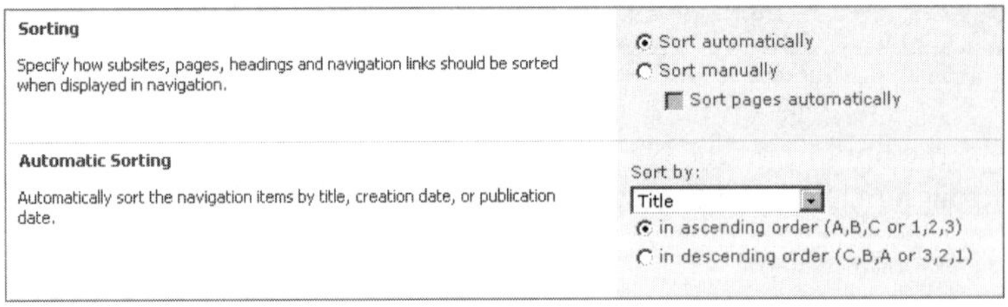

FIGURE 6-10

Sorting can be set to either automatic or manual. When set to automatic, additional options appear for sorting the items by either Title, Created Date, or Last Modified Date, as well as sorting in ascending or descending order. If pages are set to show in the previous sections, there is also an option to sort the pages automatically.

Navigation Editing and Sorting

Figure 6-11 shows the Navigation Editing and Sorting section of the Navigation Settings page.

This section is most similar to the basic options that are available for SharePoint Foundation navigation settings. In this section, you can add headings and links, delete items that were added manually, edit items that were edited manually, hide items that were created automatically (pages and sites), and move items up and down in the order. Unlike the SharePoint Foundation navigation settings, when sites and pages are created in SharePoint Server publishing, they can be set up to show automatically in the SharePoint navigation. Although you can hide these automatically created navigation items, you cannot completely delete them from the list of navigation items because the pages and sites that they represent would still exist. Hiding some of the sites or pages can be useful when too many items are displayed in the navigation.

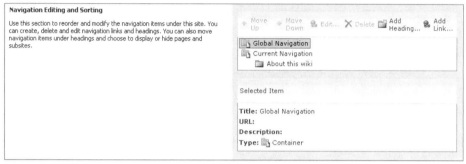

FIGURE 6-11

Because this menu represents both the top and left navigation, you will see areas of the menu that correspond to both of them — Global Navigation and Current Navigation, respectively. You need to make sure you have the current one selected when adding headings and items manually.

The following example shows how to add headings and links to the global navigation at the top of a SharePoint Server publishing site:

1. If you are not already on the Navigation Settings page, click Site Actions ➪ Site Settings; and under Look and Feel, select Navigation.

2. From the Navigation Editing and Sorting section, select Global Navigation.

3. Click the Add Heading... button.

This will allow you to enter the following settings (see Figure 6-12 for an example):

➤ **Title** — The text that shows for the heading.

➤ **URL** — Unlike SharePoint Foundation, you can leave this blank if you don't want a link. Also, SharePoint Server publishing allows you to click the Browse button to find pages that exist within your current site, which is a really useful feature.

➤ **Open link in new window** — A check box indicating whether the link will open in a new window (if there is a link).

➤ **Description** — This will show as the Title for the navigation item in the HTML source of the page. This text is displayed when the user hovers the mouse over the item.

➤ **Audience** — By assigning an audience to a heading or item, you are effectively hiding it from everyone except users who are members of the selected audience group.

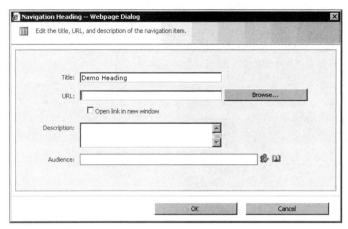

FIGURE 6-12

4. For the Title enter **Demo Heading,** and leave the URL blank to make a Heading that has no link. You can leave everything else empty and click OK. This adds the Demo Heading under Global Navigation and selects it.

5. Click the Add Link… button.

6. This menu item looks similar to the heading menu. For Title, enter **Demo Link,** and then for the URL click the Browse button and select one of the items in the Pages section of your site. This will enter a full URL for the item. You can remove the `http://SERVERNAME` portion of the link to make it relative to the server root.

7. Leave the rest of the settings blank and click OK. This creates the new Link under the Demo Heading (see Figure 6-13).

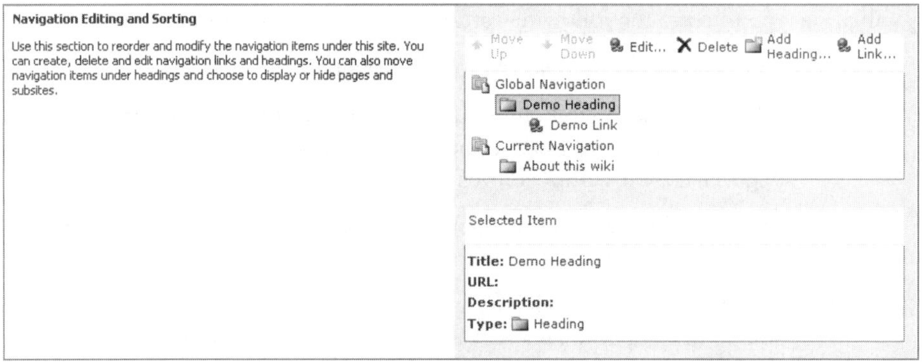

FIGURE 6-13

You could click the Move Up or Move Down buttons to move the link or heading up or down in the list (assuming you have more than one item). You can also click the Edit button to change the items, or you can click the Delete button to remove them. When you click OK at the bottom of the Navigation menu, the changes are made to the SharePoint global navigation. Figure 6-14 shows the updated navigation at the top of the page. Notice that the link shows up as a drop-down under the heading.

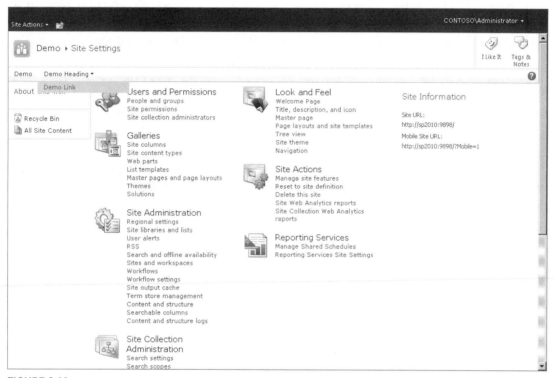

FIGURE 6-14

You will learn more about how this behavior is controlled by code in the master page later in this chapter.

Show and Hide Ribbon

Figure 6-15 shows the Show and Hide Ribbon section of the Navigation Settings page.

Show and Hide Ribbon	Make "Show Ribbon" and "Hide Ribbon" commands available
Specify whether the user has access to the "Show Ribbon" and "Hide Ribbon" commands on the Site Actions menu.	○ Yes ● No

FIGURE 6-15

Use this section to indicate whether content authors have access to buttons for hiding and showing the ribbon from the Site Actions menu. This can be useful for users who are new to the ribbon. Generally speaking, though, even with this option set to No, users will still be able to access the ribbon whenever they need to interact with it.

Showing and Hiding the Tree View and Quick Launch

Both SharePoint Foundation and SharePoint Server have an item in the Site Actions menu called Tree view. However, this item controls the hiding and showing of both the tree view navigation and the Quick Launch or current navigation. Figure 6-16 shows the Tree view menu.

By default, this menu is set to show the Quick Launch and hide the tree view. You can change these settings by toggling the check boxes and clicking OK. The tree view is similar to what the tree view looked like in SharePoint 2007, and is best suited for intranet scenarios because it is more like an Windows Explorer view of the site than anything a typical public-facing Internet user would expect to see. Figure 6-17 shows a typical SharePoint Foundation site with the tree view enabled.

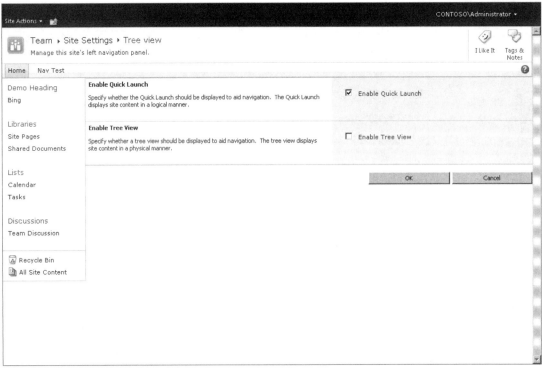

FIGURE 6-16

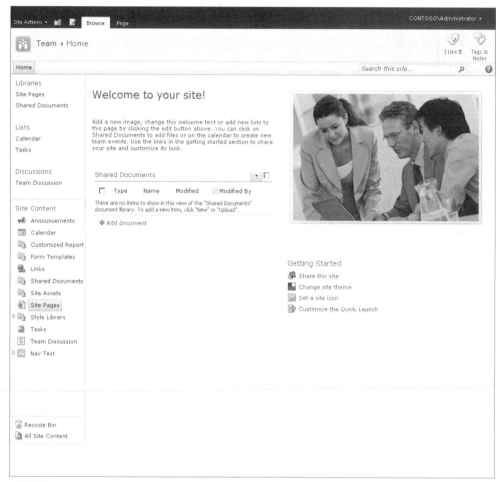

FIGURE 6-17

TYPES OF SHAREPOINT NAVIGATION

To fully understand how navigation works in SharePoint 2010, it's important to understand the various types of navigation that can be found on a SharePoint page. You already learned about the two most famous types of navigation, global and current navigation. The following sections briefly describe each of the other available navigation elements in SharePoint 2010.

Breadcrumb Navigation

Breadcrumb navigation displays a dynamically generated set of links that show users their current position in the site hierarchy. A hierarchically oriented breadcrumb in a pop-out menu is available in the out-of-the-box SharePoint 2010 user interface at the top left of the ribbon on most pages. This breadcrumb navigation is created from the `ListSiteMapPath` control.

Navigation Web Parts

SharePoint 2010 has introduced several new Navigation Web Parts that page administrators can add to pages to provide a richer navigation experience to users. Some of these new Web Parts, such as the Table of Contents Web Part, generate a dynamic list of links based on the site hierarchy. Others, like the Summary Links Web Part, rely on manual entry of navigation links. These Web Parts can be placed directly on specific pages to add additional navigation options to users.

Metadata Navigation

A new feature of SharePoint 2010 is *metadata navigation*, which enables administrators to set up metadata columns in libraries and lists that can be used as filtering options for those objects in the viewer — for example, your site might have a custom list called Contacts that is used to store basic contact information for various groups of people. In this list, you could set up a field for Contact Type, which might include values like Employee, Contractor, Vendor, and so on. When set up properly, the navigation hierarchy would display in the Quick Launch toolbar. This means that while you would still see the link for Contacts that would take you directly to the list viewer for the Contacts list, the link would also expand to show each of the metadata fields. This means that a user could expand the metadata fields for the Contacts list, see a category called Employee, and click it to go directly to a filtered listing of the Contacts list with only those entries tagged as Employee in the Contact Type field. This can greatly improve the navigation experience for many users.

SHAREPOINT NAVIGATION CONTROLS

The various types of SharePoint navigation discussed in the preceding section are represented behind the scenes in SharePoint by various *controls*. The following sections describe these controls.

AspMenu

The `AspMenu` navigation control is not new; if you have worked with navigation in previous versions of SharePoint, you are probably comfortable with this control. In fact, if you have done any kind of navigation controls in any ASP.NET application, you are probably at least familiar with `AspMenu`. This server control provides a menu that can be aligned either horizontally or vertically on the page. When bound to a site map provider, the control will display the navigation nodes in a menu that can be displayed statically or with client-side fly-out and drop-down menus. You will learn more about how this control is used in master pages later in the chapter.

SPTreeView

Like the `AspMenu` control, the `SPTreeView` control for SharePoint 2010 is not new; you have likely seen it before in previous versions of SharePoint. This control is often used as a substitute for the more common SharePoint Quick Launch navigation when the site owner would rather have collapsible nodes rather than just summary links for the site-specific navigation. The tree view can be enabled by clicking the link of the same name under the Look and Feel section on the Site Settings page.

ListSiteMapPath

The `ListSiteMapPath` navigation control is a new SharePoint 2010 server control. This control inherits from the SiteMapPath control used for breadcrumbs in SharePoint 2007 and provides a pop-up, hierarchical view of where the current page is located in the site collection. Like the SiteMapPath, you can click on any displayed link to navigate to a different page or site.

Navigation Web Parts

There are several Web Parts that provide additional navigation features for sites with publishing enabled. These new Web Parts can be added directly to a page just like any other Web Part (you can read more about adding Web Parts to a page in Chapter 10). You can find these new Web Parts in the Navigation category of Web Parts when you are in page edit mode.

Included in these new Navigation Web Parts are the following:

➤ **Table of Contents** — Creates a list of links that can span across your entire site collection and can be configured to show links up to three levels deep. This Web Part can display both dynamic links (based on the navigation hierarchy of your site) and static links that you add manually. However, security trimming is applied only to dynamically created links.

➤ **Summary Links** — This Web Parts provides an easy way to manually add a list of links to any page. These links can be managed and grouped as needed. However, because these links are added manually, no security trimming is applied.

SITE MAP PROVIDERS

SharePoint uses the site map provider to pull data from the content database and represent it as a hierarchical listing of nodes with the type `SiteMapNode`. The SharePoint 2010 master pages discussed in this book have navigation controls that use five different standard site map providers:

➤ `SPSiteMapProvider`

➤ `SPContentMapProvider`

➤ `SPNavigationProvider`

➤ `CurrentNavigation`

➤ `GlobalNavigation`

For most scenarios, these five options will be sufficient for use as the back end for your navigation controls. However, in some cases, you may need to go beyond the default providers. The next section discusses one such example and the solution.

SharePoint Navigation and Multiple Site Collections

SharePoint navigation, by default, is primarily focused on navigation within a site collection. However, it is not uncommon to have an information architecture that requires navigation across multiple site collections. To handle this requirement, you could manually create the navigation across all site collections so that all site collections have identical navigation. While this would work, there are at least two problems with this approach. First, with manual entries for your navigation, you no longer have any security trimming support, which means whatever you add to your navigation is available to anyone who uses it. Second, and maybe more important, this scenario would be a nightmare to maintain. If you make even one change in your navigation, you have to update your navigation links in every site collection, not an ideal situation.

Fortunately, SharePoint enables you to create consistent navigation across site collections by using the XML site map provider. The XML site map provider builds the hierarchical navigation links based on an XML file, which can be centrally located via a web service and shared among site collections. This makes maintenance easier because you can modify one file in one location and apply it across all site collections. However, this solution does not help the security trimming issue, as you cannot security trim this type of site map provider. Therefore, if you need to implement security trimming across your site collections, this still may not be the ideal situation.

There is at least one other solution, though: the custom sitemap provider. This is more work but, done correctly, you can use a custom back end (e.g., Microsoft SQL Server) to maintain all of your navigation links *and* you can keep your security trimmings in place. This solution involves writing custom code and is the most laborious to set up initially, but the payoff can be worth it if the other sitemap providers do not meet your needs.

Regardless of your navigation needs, several options are available in SharePoint 2010 to make your requirements a reality. In many cases the default sitemap provider will meet your needs; but when it doesn't, alternatives are available to create the navigation you need.

An example of creating a custom XML site map provider is beyond the scope of this book. For a tutorial on how to create one, see Sahil Malik's blog post: `http://blah.winsmarts.com/2010-5-Security_Trimmed_Cross_Site_Collection_Navigation.aspx`. *While the post is focused on SharePoint 2007, the steps for SharePoint 2010 would be similar.*

WORKING WITH NAVIGATION IN MASTER PAGES

You will learn more about working with the code of master pages in Chapter 8, but for now it's important to understand how the navigation is created. SharePoint master pages utilize the `AspMenu` control to render top and left navigation for SharePoint sites. When creating a fully branded SharePoint site, it may be necessary to adjust the settings in this control to change how the navigation is displayed to users. The default top navigation control in the v4 master page looks like this:

```
<SharePoint:AspMenu
    ID="TopNavigationMenuV4"
    Runat="server"
    EnableViewState="false"
    DataSourceID="topSiteMap"
    AccessKey="<%$Resources:wss,navigation_accesskey%>"
```

```
UseSimpleRendering="true"
UseSeparateCss="false"
Orientation="Horizontal"
StaticDisplayLevels="2"
MaximumDynamicDisplayLevels="1"
SkipLinkText=""
CssClass="s4-tn"/>
```

The following list describes some of the more important properties for the AspMenu control:

➤ DataSourceID — Sets the ID of the data source that the navigation will use. This date source is defined somewhere in the master page as either an <asp:SiteMapDataSource> or a <PublishingNavigation:PortalSiteMapDataSource>. This data source in turn will reference a site map provider as described earlier in the chapter.

➤ UseSimpleRendering — Controls whether the navigation will use simple rendering or not. When set to True, the navigation will use an HTML unordered list and CSS hover states for a more modern rendering. When set to False, the navigation will use the old SharePoint 2007 rendering method of nested tables with JavaScript. You will learn more about this property momentarily.

➤ Orientation — Controls whether the navigation will be rendered horizontally or vertically

➤ StaticDisplayLevels — Controls how many levels of navigation are shown by default. For example, setting this to 2 would cause SharePoint to show navigation items for the current site and the subsites directly underneath it.

➤ MaximumDynamicDisplayLevels — Unlike StaticDisplayLevels, this controls how many levels of navigation will show as drop-downs or fly-outs when the user's mouse hovers over navigation that has items below it. If StaticDisplayLevels is set to 2 and MaximumDynamicDisplayLevels is set also set to 2, SharePoint will show the first two levels of items by default and then show drop-downs or fly-outs for the next two levels. In this example, anything below the fourth level will not be shown.

➤ CssClass — Sets the CSS class that will surround the entire navigation menu.

Simple Rendering

The UseSimpleRendering property was added to the AspMenu control for SharePoint 2010. When set to True, the SharePoint navigation will render the menu with simple modern HTML code, leveraging unordered lists instead of nesting a ton of tables. This has the benefit of reducing the page weight, and makes styling with CSS much easier than in previous versions. The following is an example of some of the output when UseSimpleRendering is on:

```
<li class="static dynamic-children">
 <a class="static dynamic-children menu-item" href="http://www.bing.com">
  <span class="additional-background">
   <span class="menu-item-text">Heading</span>
  </span>
 </a>
 <ul class="dynamic">
  <li class="dynamic">
```

```
    <a class="dynamic menu-item" href="/page.aspx">
     <span class="additional-background">
         <span class="menu-item-text">Item</span>
         </span>
    </a>
   </li>
  </ul>
 </li>
```

This can be compared to a similar example of the navigation source with simple rendering turned off, like SharePoint 2007 would have rendered it:

```
<table>
 <tr>
  <td onmouseover="Menu_HoverStatic(this)" onmouseout="Menu_Unhover(this)"
onkeyup="Menu_Key(this)" id="zz1_GlobalNavn3">
    <table class="customTopNavItem zz1_GlobalNav_4" cellpadding="0" cellspacing="0"
border="0" width="100%">
     <tr>
      <td style="white-space:nowrap;">
       <a class="zz1_GlobalNav_1 customTopNavItem zz1_GlobalNav_3" href="http://www.bing.
com" style="border-style:none;font-size:1em;">Heading</a>
      </td>
     </tr>
    </table>
   </td>
  </tr>
  <tr onmouseover="Menu_HoverDynamic(this)" onmouseout="Menu_Unhover(this)"
onkeyup="Menu_Key(this)" id="zz1_GlobalNavn27">
   <td>
    <table class="customTopNavFlyOutItem zz1_GlobalNav_6" cellpadding="0" cellspacing="0"
border="0" width="100%">
     <tr>
      <td style="white-space:nowrap;width:100%;">
       <a class="zz1_GlobalNav_1 customTopNavFlyOutItem zz1_GlobalNav_5"
href="/page.aspx" style="border-style:none;font-size:1em;">Item</a>
      </td>
     </tr>
    </table>
   </td>
  </tr>
</table>
```

As you can see, the simple rendering is much cleaner than the table structures that were used in SharePoint 2007. If you are used to how SharePoint 2007 navigation was styled, there are some changes to the new simple rendering style. You will learn more about CSS in the next chapter, and Chapter 8 includes examples of how to style the new simple rendered navigation, but for now here is a portion of the CSS code that would style the main top navigation items:

```
.s4-tn li.static > .menu-item {
 color:red;
}
.s4-tn li.static > .selected {
 color:lime;
}
```

In the preceding snippet, CSS child selectors (the greater than symbol ">") are being used to target specific sub-elements to differentiate between standard navigation items and the selected items. In the example, the standard links would be colored red; the selected ones would be colored lime. This is a departure from the way SharePoint 2007 navigation was styled, both because it contained many nested tables and because it adhered to an older CSS coding standard. For more information on how styles worked in SharePoint 2007, see Heather Solomon's blog post "CSS Reference Chart for SharePoint 2007" at `http://www.heathersolomon.com/content/sp07cssreference.htm`.

If this new, cleaner HTML scares you or you don't want to spend time converting your old CSS to work with the new simple rendering, you can always turn it off by setting `UseSimpleRendering` to `False`. This will cause `AspMenu` to render navigation exactly like it did in SharePoint 2007, removing the need to update any complex CSS previously created.

USING NON-SHAREPOINT NAVIGATION

Sometimes when working with a heavily branded site, particularly public-facing Internet sites, you want to create a unique navigation experience that is different from the out-of-the-box SharePoint navigation. Maybe you want to show images for navigation, or maybe you want to leverage a rich Internet technology like Microsoft Silverlight, Adobe Flash, or even some fancy jQuery.

This can be a very appealing way to create navigation because it means you can brand it completely and uniquely any way you want without worrying about how SharePoint does things. You can simply add whatever static HTML and code that is needed to create the navigation directly to a custom master page and apply it to your site. One excellent example of this technique is the Ferrari.com site shown in Figure 6-18. This site uses Flash for a lot of the visuals on the page, as well as jQuery-style navigation, which provides extra details for the selected menu item, including photos and multiple columns of links.

However, consider the major downside to this technique. If you don't use some kind of custom code to wire this custom navigation up to the out-of-the-box SharePoint navigation providers, you will lose many of the features discussed in this chapter. No longer will SharePoint add items automatically when sites and pages are created; security trimming will not be utilized; and you will lose the capability to manage the navigation sorting from a nice SharePoint menu.

Also, if your site uses a Silverlight or Flash menu, what happens if visitors do not have the player installed? Or they have a legacy player installed instead of the one required as part of your deployment? Can they still get to the site content? Can they view the navigation for the site? SharePoint 2010 has certain pages that leverage Silverlight to make it a responsive and rich application. However, Microsoft was careful to provide standard HTML and JavaScript versions of the same content that are displayed only when Silverlight isn't installed. If your site requires Silverlight, Flash, or jQuery for its navigation but a visitor does not have the appropriate browser settings in place to use those technologies, the result is a frustrated visitor. We all know what frustrated visitors do because we've all been there: They leave!

This isn't to say that you shouldn't use these rich and full-featured technologies. The point is that if you use a technology like Flash or Silverlight, make sure you have a method in place to gracefully handle visitors who cannot use the site navigation the way the design was intended. Test your site extensively to ensure that users can easily access its content.

FIGURE 6-18

SUMMARY

Navigation should never be an overlooked piece of the branding puzzle. Although factors such as colors, fonts, and positioning of the navigation controls are an important part of branding, they are just the beginning. The underlying architecture of the hierarchal data, as well as how the rendered HTML will be presented by the browser, are equally important aspects of any navigation branding effort, and can seriously impact the look and feel of a site. Done correctly, the result will be a useful, easily navigated site to which users will want to return.

Having finished this chapter, you should have a better understanding of the importance of navigation planning when branding your sites, as well as the robust tools available in SharePoint 2010 to help you successfully achieve that. This chapter also stressed the importance of CSS in regard to branding, in general, and navigation, in particular. The next chapter dives a lot deeper into CSS.

PART III
Advanced Branding

7

Cascading Style Sheets in SharePoint

WHAT'S IN THIS CHAPTER?

➤ A CSS primer

➤ How CSS is used in SharePoint 2010

➤ Using third-party tools to maintain CSS code in SharePoint 2010

Cascading Style Sheets, known simply as CSS, is considered a fundamental part of any web development. Depending on the web page creator's preferences, CSS may be used heavily or sparingly, but most web pages use it in some capacity. Historically, SharePoint has used it fairly heavily; and in SharePoint 2010, it has become more prevalent. Fortunately, some cool new tools have been added to make it even easier to manage.

This chapter provides an overview of what exactly CSS is, how it is used in SharePoint, and how you can manipulate its rules to brand your own SharePoint 2010 projects.

CSS PRIMER

CSS is probably at least somewhat familiar to you if you have ever created a web page. If you are a designer, you are likely intimately familiar with CSS. However, if you are among the developers trying to do SharePoint design, which is typically the group assigned to brand a SharePoint site, a deep understanding of CSS may not be in your toolbox. This section explains the general basics of CSS — that is, not necessarily SharePoint-specific. When you have finished reading this section, you will be better equipped to understand how SharePoint uses CSS, as well as how you can use CSS to brand your own sites.

If you are already comfortable with CSS, you can skip this section and move directly to the section "CSS in SharePoint" later in this chapter. Conversely, if concepts such as child selectors, adjacent sibling selectors, and pseudo classes are not familiar to you, this section explains these items, which are used fairly extensively in SharePoint 2010 and which are critical for any kind of branding you might do in that environment.

What Is CSS?

Simply put, CSS is a set of design rules for your web page. These rules can be classified into two main types:

➤ **Cosmetic** — These rules affect the appearance of the page, and include items such as color and font-size.

➤ **Structural** — These rules affect how your web application is organized, such as the positioning of elements and the basic layout of your page.

Most people who are familiar with CSS have probably at least used cosmetic CSS rules in their design. For example, the following would be a way to apply CSS cosmetic rules to an HTML element of your page:

```
<p style="color: Red;">Hello, World</p>
```

This example would create the phrase "Hello, World" written in red on your HTML page. While this is admittedly a pretty simplistic example, it illustrates how CSS is essentially used: to modify HTML markup and affect the elements of the page in some way.

Inline Style Sheets

In the previous example, the paragraph (<p>) HTML element has its markup modified to apply a CSS cosmetic rule color: Red by including the rule in the style property of the element.

This doesn't mean that you always apply CSS rules by setting them in the style property of every element you want to modify. This is *one* way to do it, but not the only way. In fact, it is probably the worst way to do it for at least a couple of reasons:

➤ **Bloat** — If you wanted to apply 10 rules to a paragraph, just imagine how long that style property would be; and if you wanted to apply those same rules to every paragraph on your page, that adds a lot of characters to your HTML rendering. As a result, the total load time is increased because you have added so much redundant code to your HTML markup. In fact, 10 rules isn't that much. When you consider that you might want to set the font, its size, its weight, its color, the alignment of the paragraph, and so forth, 10 rules add up pretty quickly. This can create very ugly code that will be a nightmare to maintain (and these are just six rules applied for each paragraph):

```
<p style="color: Red; font-family: arial; font-size: 14pt; font-weight: bold;
font-variant: small-caps; text-align: justify;">Hello, World</p>

<p style="color: Red; font-family: arial; font-size: 14pt; font-weight: bold;
font-variant: small-caps; text-align: justify;">Hello, World</p>
```

➤ **Lack of reusability** — As mentioned in the previous point, if you wanted to apply the rules for one paragraph to every paragraph on the page, you would have to include the style rules in each <p> tag, which would just bloat your page. Even worse, suppose you wanted to apply your style rules to every paragraph on every page in your site. That would mean creating those same rules in every <p> tag on every page you create now or in the future. Now imagine that management wants to change the font color from red to magenta. You now have to go through every page on your site and look for every <p> tag and then update the style rule. This is the stuff that breeds insanity in otherwise sane people.

Fortunately, you have two other ways to apply style rules: by using *internal style sheets* and *external style sheets*.

Internal Style Sheets

The term "internal style sheets" is a bit of a misnomer. It seems to imply that a separate file (or sheet) contains your rules. That isn't exactly what is going on; rather, it is a way of creating a set of rules in your HTML document that apply to all pertinent elements. To continue the example of the <p> tag from the previous section, you could create an internal style sheet to apply your rules and dramatically increase the readability of your HTML (and its maintainability):

```
<style>
p{
    color: Red;
    font-family: arial;
    font-size: 14pt;
    font-weight: bold;
    font-variant: small-caps;
    text-align: justify;
}
</style>

<p>Hello, World</p>

<p>Hello, World</p>
```

Here, you can see the internal style sheet encapsulated by the <style></style> tags. This example specifies that for this particular HTML document, every time the browser sees a <p> tag in the markup, it should apply these six rules. You can see that both paragraphs under that don't actually modify their markup to apply the rules. They are <p> elements, so they have the <p> element rules applied to them. It's that simple.

Best practice dictates that internal style sheets are placed inside of the <head> element on the page. This is the only valid way to include an internal style sheet for XHTML Strict DOCTYPEs. That being said, there are times when including an internal style sheet outside of the <head> is very helpful in SharePoint. You will see this technique used in Chapter 8.

Although internal style sheets can help solve the bloat problem, they don't address the issue of reusability. That's because if you wanted to apply these same six rules to the paragraph elements of all your pages, you would have to copy the internal style sheet to all your pages. Nonetheless, it is better than just hardcoding the rules inline (inside of your HTML tags). And, honestly, if you consider that you would have to put the same sets of rules in the internal style sheets of every page on your site, you aren't eliminating bloat. Sure, it is more streamlined than putting the rules in every element on every page, but it is still putting a lot of redundant code on every page.

External Style Sheets

External style sheets are pretty much what their name implies: a detached document containing a set of rules that you can reference from any web page in order to apply the rules to the elements of that page. To continue the example from the previous section, you could create a style sheet called `styles.css` that looked like the following:

```
p{
    color: Red;
    font-family: arial;
    font-size: 14pt;
    font-weight: bold;
    font-variant: small-caps;
    text-align: justify;
}
```

Notice the lack of `<style>` tags encapsulating the rules. When you use an external document, the tags are not necessary. In your HTML document, you simply add a reference to your external style sheet with code similar to the following:

```
<link rel="stylesheet" type="text/css" href="styles.css"/>
```

Like the internal style sheets, the best practice is to include this reference in the `<head>` section of your page. Note that this is the only valid way to add external style sheets in an XHTML Strict page. Also, like internal style sheets, an external style sheet added outside of the `<head>` section will display in most modern browsers.

CSS Conflicts

At this point, you may be wondering what happens if you have conflicting rules. For example, what if there are rules applied inline on the HTML element, a different set of rules applied through an internal style sheet, and still another set of rules applied by an external style sheet? Which rules prevail?

Well, like the answer to many good questions, unfortunately, it depends. A general rule of precedence is as follows:

➤ Apply external style sheet rules first.

➤ Apply internal style sheet rules next.

➤ Apply inline style rules last.

However, this order isn't etched in stone. In fact, only the last rule of precedence is important: Apply inline styles last. This means that if you have set up your rules in internal/external style documents, you can override them with your inline styles. Of course, the key word here is "can." Note I did not say "should." As discussed later in the "Best Practices for CSS" section, you *shouldn't* put style rules inline, but you *can.*

To understand the relationships between these rules, you need to understand the concept of order of precedence in CSS. Essentially, *order of precedence* defines which styles are applied when there is a conflict — hence the "cascading" part of Cascading Style Sheets.

Consider the earlier example, which uses an external style sheet (`styles.css`) with the following content:

```
p{
    color: Red;
    font-family: arial;
    font-size: 14pt;
    font-weight: bold;
    font-variant: small-caps;
    text-align: justify;
}
```

At this point, you probably have an HTML document with the following content:

```
<link rel="stylesheet" type="text/css" href="styles.css"/>

<p>Hello, World</p>
```

This, as you remember, creates the phrase "Hello, World" in red text in your browser.

Now modify your HTML document to have the following content:

```
<style>
p{
    color: green;
}
</style>

<link rel="stylesheet" type="text/css" href="styles.css"/>


<p>Hello, World</p>
```

If you followed this example exactly, when you load the page in your browser the text should still be red. However, now change the content of your HTML page to the following and see what happens:

```
<link rel="stylesheet" type="text/css" href="styles.css"/>

<style>
p{
    color: green;
}
</style>

<p>Hello, World</p>
```

The only thing that changes is the order of the CSS declarations in your HTML document. In the first example, your internal style sheet was created first and then you next referenced the external style sheet. In that example, the external style sheet rules prevailed. However, in this example, you put the internal style sheet rules after the reference to the external style sheet reference, and the internal style sheet rules prevailed.

It is critical that you understand this order of precedence as you work with branding. This example illustrated how you can override external style rules for a particular page if necessary. In practice, you should do this very sparingly, but it does give you an extra layer of control over your style rules.

It is also important to understand that this isn't just an internal vs. external style sheet conflict. What do you think would happen in the following example?

```
<link rel="stylesheet" type="text/css" href="styles01.css"/>
<link rel="stylesheet" type="text/css" href="styles02.css"/>
<link rel="stylesheet" type="text/css" href="styles03.css"/>

<p>Hello, World</p>
```

If each of the preceding three referenced external style sheets had a differing rule for the font color of your <p> element, which one would win? If you look at the order in which they are referenced, you will know the order in which they are applied to your page. In this example:

➤   `styles01.css` is applied first.

➤   `styles02.css` is applied next.

➤   `styles03.css` is applied last.

In other words, because `styles03.css` is applied last, it prevails. It doesn't matter what you set the font color to in `styles01.css` and `styles02.css`; if you set the font color to red in `styles03.css`, the font will be red (assuming you don't override these rules with inline CSS).

While it is important to understand conflict resolution, it is equally important to understand two other related concepts: aggregation and inheritance.

Aggregation

Aggregation simply means that in the absence of any conflict, all rules applied to an element from any source will be applied to that element. For example, in `styles.css`, modify your code to have only the following two rules:

```
p{
    color: Red;
    font-family: arial;
}
```

Now, in your HTML document, include the following content:

```
<link rel="stylesheet" type="text/css" href="styles.css"/>

<style>
p{
    font-size: 14pt;
    font-weight: bold;
}
</style>

<p style="font-variant: small-caps; text-align: justify;">Hello, World</p>
```

This example merely divides your rules. You now have two rules (`color` and `font-family`) set in the external style sheet, two rules (`font-size` and `font-weight`) set in the internal style sheet, and two rules (`font-variant` and `text-align`) set in inline styles. However, when you load your HTML document, all six rules are applied, or aggregated.

When you are creating new HTML documents, you need to be very conscious of what rules are being referenced to your document. Just because you have set up some custom styles for your page, it doesn't mean those are the only styles that will be applied. If you have an external style sheet reference that includes additional rules for your element, those will be applied as well. In that case, you have to ask, "Is this OK?" If not, you need to override the other rules through order of precedence, which resolves these types of conflicts.

Inheritance

Inheritance is similar to aggregation but not exactly the same thing. Inheritance means that an element can inherit CSS rules from another element just because it is encapsulated in that element. To see how this happens, modify your `styles.css` file to include the following content:

```
body{
    font-family: arial;
    font-size: 14pt;
}
p{

    color: Red;
    font-weight: bold;
    font-variant: small-caps;
    text-align: justify;
}
```

Now, in your HTML document, change your content to the following:

```
<link rel="stylesheet" type="text/css" href="styles.css"/>

Here is some non-paragraph text.

<p>Hello, World</p>
```

If you load the page in your browser, you will see that the first line ("Here is some non-paragraph text.") has the rules applied to it from the body rules (`font-family` and `font-size`) but has none of the rules applied to it from the `<p>` element rules because it is not a `<p>` element.

However, the `<p>` element includes all these rules, including the ones set for the body element. This is because the rules for the body are applied to all elements on the page. When the paragraph is rendered, it inherits those rules before applying its own style rules.

This does not mean that the parent element wins. In fact, if there is a conflicting rule, the child wins. In other words, the inherited value applies only when no conflicting rule is specified for an element.

To see how this works, if you set your `styles.css` to include the following rules, it would still render the font for the `<p>` element red even though a conflicting rule in the parent element has a higher order or precedence (because it is declared later in the document):

```
p{color: red;}
body{color: green;}
```

Again, this typically isn't a big concern in web application development. If a style rule matters, you set it specifically; therefore, inheritance won't be a factor. However, it's good to know that you don't have to set the `font-family` rule to Arial (for example) on every style rule. You can just set the `font-family` rule in the `body` rules and it will be applied to all HTML elements. Conversely, if you don't want a certain element to have the Arial font applied, you can override it with the rules for that element. This lets you set a style that can be reused throughout the site, which is obviously good for branding.

Elements, Classes, and IDs

Until this point, the discussion has focused on HTML elements. Elements are simply the available tag types you can provide in your HTML rendering. The following table describes a few of the more common elements:

ELEMENT	DESCRIPTION
a	Anchor (e.g., hyperlinks)
body	Body of an HTML document
div	Block generic container
h1	Heading
img	Embedded image
p	Paragraph
span	Inline generic container

You can find a full listing of all HTML elements at the World Wide Web Consortium (W3C) website: `www.w3.org/TR/REC-html40/index/elements.html`.

Of course, if the only way to apply CSS were directly to these elements, you would have some issues in your design. For example, most designs implement several different styles for the page hyperlinks. For the content of the page, they are styled one way; for navigation links in the header, they are often styled differently; and perhaps still another style is used for hyperlinks contained in the footer of the page. If you could apply styles only to an element — in this case, the anchor (a) element, which is used for links — how would you apply styles for each of the three scenarios just described? Sure, you could apply different style rules for each hyperlink using inline styles, but there's a much better way: using classes.

Classes in CSS enable you to specify that various elements should use certain styles that are different from the style rules applied to all similar elements. To see how this works, create an HTML document with the following content:

```
<style>
p{
    font-family: arial;
    font-size: 14pt;
    color: black;
}
.big{
    font-size: 30pt;
}
```

```
.red{
    color: red;
}
</style>

<p>This is my first paragraph</p>

<p class="big">This is my second paragraph</p>

<p class="red">This is my third paragraph</p>
```

This example has created rules that apply to all `<p>` elements (`font-family`, `font-size`, and `color`). However, it also created two classes: `big` and `red`. Classes, as shown in bold in the preceding code, are designated by a period and then the class name. Therefore, the class `big` is defined in CSS by using `.big`. The `<p>` element can then reference the class to modify its rendering.

In this example, the first paragraph just uses the default styling for the `<p>` element. The second paragraph, however, implements the `big` class by adding the `class` property to the opening tag and pointing it to the `big` class. This makes its text render in a 30pt font. The last paragraph implements the `red` class, which renders the font in red.

Unless otherwise specified, classes can be used for any element. For example, modify the preceding example to the following:

```
<style>
p{
    font-family: arial;
    font-size: 14pt;
    color: black;
}
.big{
    font-size: 30pt;
}
.red{
    color: red;
}
</style>

<p>This is a hyperlink: <a class="red" href="http://www.bing.com">bing</a></p>

<p class="red big">This is some big red text</p>
```

This example shows an anchor tag as well as a `<p>` tag implementing the `red` class. It also shows the second `<p>` element referencing both the `red` and `big` classes simply by including both class references in the `class` property of the `<p>` element's opening tag. This means that the second paragraph will be rendered with a very large, very red, font.

Note that you can create your class definition to apply only to a certain element. In the preceding example, the `red` rule set applied to both a `<p>` element and an anchor element. You can designate that a class apply only to a particular element in the CSS definition by appending the element type to the front of the class. For example, to have the red class apply only to <p> elements, simply change the preceding example to the following:

```
<style>
p{
    font-family: arial;
    font-size: 14pt;
    color: black;
}
.big{
    font-size: 30pt;
}
p.red{
    color: red;
}
</style>

<p>This is a hyperlink: <a class="red" href="http://www.bing.com">bing</a></p>

<p class="red big">This is some big red text</p>
```

Notice the part in bold. This example changed the CSS designation from .red to p.red. If you were to save this example and load it in your browser, you would see that the hyperlink is no longer red, even though the large text in the second paragraph still has the red styling. This example demonstrates how granular you can apply your CSS rules if necessary.

IDs are similar to classes in that they style an element differently from other similar elements on the page. However, the main distinction is that IDs are meant to style a single element on a page, whereas classes can be used multiple times on a page. In other words, the ID CSS reference is meant to match up with the ID for a single element on a page.

To see how this works, create an HTML document with the following code:

```
<style>
p{
    font-family: arial;
    font-size: 14pt;
    color: black;
}
#header
{
    font-size: 30pt;
    font-weight: bold;
    font-variant: small-caps;
}
</style>

<p id="header">This is the header</p>

<p>This is just a paragraph.</p>
```

Here, there are two paragraphs in the HTML markup. The first paragraph has an ID of header, while the second paragraph doesn't have an ID at all. In the CSS rules, you will see a reference to #header. This is how you designate an ID rule set. It means that when the browser runs across the header ID on a page, apply the rules in the #header rule set.

If you actually performed this example, you would see that the first paragraph is large and uses small-caps, while the second paragraph would have basically the same look and feel as the other examples in this chapter.

 In order for an HTML page to be 100% valid, IDs are not supposed to be reused throughout a document. Although you could actually reuse the same ID more than once and most browsers would display both just fine without error, you should avoid this practice. There is no guarantee that later versions of browsers wouldn't ignore a reused ID because it is not acceptable according to the W3C.

Selectors

If you have been following the chapter until this point, you have already been exposed to selectors; you just didn't know it. In CSS, a *selector* merely identifies to what the style rules should be applied. For example, consider the previous code example:

```
p{
    font-family: arial;
    font-size: 14pt;
    color: black;
}
```

In this example, the selector is the <p> element; thus, the style rules enclosed in the brackets apply to all <p> elements in the HTML document that uses this style sheet. This type of indicator is called a *type selector* because you are selecting a particular type of HTML element. You have also seen how to handle class selectors (e.g., .big) and ID selectors (e.g., #header) in the previous section.

However, this just scratches the surface of how you can select content for applying CSS rules. Within CSS 2.1 (the current version), you can do things like select only hyperlinks contained inside of a paragraph (so that you can style them differently from those not encapsulated by <p> tags). You can apply special formatting to areas based on the language preference (e.g., English, French, etc.) of the client browser accessing the page. You can even apply formatting to elements based on their included attributes (e.g., only select form elements with a type set to checkbox). CSS enables a high degree of granularity when deciding which styles to apply to your HTML content. The following sections will help you understand some of the common selectors used in current web designs.

Universal Selector

This selector, as the name suggests, is a wildcard character (*) that enables you to select everything. Often times, it is implied in other selectors. For example, in previous examples in this chapter you saw class selectors denoted as .big. You could extend this to actually include the universal selector, which would be *.big. This just means that the big class applies to all elements that reference it in their class attribute. Recall from the previous examples that it is OK to fine-tune your class selector to apply only to, say, <p> elements by including it in the selector (e.g., p.red). However, the absence of this qualification of the class implies that the universal selector is present.

In the real world, the only time you will typically see the universal selector is at the top of a CSS style sheet — often used similarly to the following:

```
*{ padding: 0px; margin: 0px;}
```

This line of code will strip out all margins and padding from all elements in your HTML document. This is often done to handle some of the nuances of browsers, which pad content by different amounts depending on the browser. In other words, if you load the page in Firefox, there will be a certain amount of padding around the edges of your content (and the header will not be adjacent to the top of the browser window). If you load the page in IE, it will have a different padding and, as such, will look slightly different. Load the page in still another browser, say Google Chrome or Safari, and it will look different still. This is because there are no widely accepted standards regarding how much padding is added to elements by default when an amount isn't specified in an HTML document's style rules. Therefore, designers remove all padding and margins as the first style rule and then add it back for each element as dictated by the design.

Grouping Selector

A grouping selector is a simple yet powerful selector available to developers implementing CSS 2.1 in their design. As the name implies, you can group like rules for different elements into one rule set. To illustrate this, look at the following code:

```
p{
    font-family: arial;
    font-size: 14pt;
    font-color: steelblue;
}
a{
    font-family: arial;
    font-size: 14pt;
    font-variant: small-caps;
    text-decoration: underline;
    font-color: darkgray;
}
```

In the preceding example, several style rules are redundant. For example, both rule sets are defining the font-family as Arial and the font-size as 14pt. While the other rules for each element are unique, it seems superfluous to repeatedly apply the same rules to different elements. Imagine if the design requirements change to specify a font-family of Tahoma. You would have to find all the places where the font-family was defined and update them.

As an alternative, you could use a group selector to group together like rules into one rule set. The preceding example could be simplified to something like this:

```
p,a{
    font-family: arial;
    font-size: 14pt;
}
p{
    font-color: steelblue;
}
```

```
a{
    font-variant: small-caps;
    text-decoration: underline;
    font-color: darkgray;
}
```

This code creates a new section for the grouping of p and a elements, and puts all the shared rules in that group. You set up the group by providing a comma-delimited list of all elements to which the grouping applies. Note that this example groups only the p and a elements, but you can group as many elements as you like.

The obvious advantage to grouping is that you define like rules only once. If the preceding design changes to require the Tahoma font, you simply have to change the p, a group and the update automatically filters down to both the p and a elements.

In terms of lines of code, this grouping example did not result in a difference (you took out two lines of code for each of two elements and created a new group with four lines of code); in larger projects, however, you will likely see a reduction in lines of code, which is always good (fewer lines of code equates to faster load times). For example, suppose that you were able to strip out these same two lines of code from 100 different rule sets. That would remove 200 lines of code and add back only four for the group, resulting in 196 fewer lines of code overall. Furthermore, when you change the group, you are able to update 100 rule sets. Clearly, the larger the project, the greater the advantage.

Child Selector

A child selector applies style rules to a selector (element, class, or ID) that is a direct child of another selector. For example, consider the following hierarchy of elements that might exist on a sample page:

```
<div id="P1">
    <span id="P1C1">
        <span id="P1C1C1"/>
        <span id="P1C1C2"/>
    </span>
    <span id="P1C2">
        <span id="P1C2C1"/>
        <span id="P1C2C2"/>
    </span>
    <span id="P1C3">
        <span id="P1C3C1"/>
        <span id="P1C3C2"/>
    </span>
</div>
<div id="P2">
    <span id="P2C1"/>
    <span id="P2C2"/>
</div>
```

You could, in your style sheet, set up a child relationship to select all span elements that are children of the div element with an ID of P1 by using code similar to the following:

```
#P1 > SPAN{color: red;}
```

Notice the greater than (>) symbol between #P1 and span. This is how you designate a child selector in CSS 2.1.

Therefore, using this example, the following span elements would be changed to red:

➤   #P1C1

➤   #P1C2

➤   #P1C3

However, the span elements that were children of these span elements (e.g., #P1C1C1) would not have the color red applied because they are not direct children of the #div1 element.

For more of a real-world example, enter the following code into an HTML document and load it in your browser:

```
<style>
    *{color: black;}
    #myTable > span{color: red;}
</style>

<div id="myTable">
<span id="span1">
    here is my first level
    <span id="span2">and here is my second level </span>
</span>
<span id="span3">and, finally, here is my third level</span>
</div>
```

Here, the first CSS rule using the universal selector changes the default color for all page elements to black. The second rule uses the child selector to change all child span elements for the #myTable ID to red. If you load this in your browser, you should see that #span1 and #span3 are red because they are direct children of #myTable, whereas #span2 is black because it is not a child of #myTable (it is a child of #span1).

Descendant Selector

Descendant selectors are similar to child selectors except that they do not require the sub-element to be a direct child of the parent element. A way to think about the difference between child selectors and descendant selectors is to consider what these terms mean in genealogy:

➤   My son is my descendant and my child.

➤   My grandson is my descendant but not my child.

To see how this works, modify the child selector example from the preceding section to resemble the following code:

```
<style>
    *{color: black;}
    #myTable span{color: blue;}
    #myTable > span{color: red;}
```

```
</style>

<div id="myTable">
<span id="span1">
    here is my first level
    <span id="span2">and here is my second level </span>
</span>
<span id="span3">and, finally, here is my third level</span>
</div>
```

Notice the new code (indicated by the bold text). This demonstrates how you create a descendant selector: List two elements together with a space between them. In this example, the style rules for this descendant selector rule set will apply to all span elements that are encapsulated by the #myTable element, regardless of whether they are direct children of the #myTable element.

If you load this example in your browser, you will see that nothing has changed for #span1 or #span3, but #span2 is now blue.

Note, however, the order in which the rules are defined in this example. If you included the descendant selector after the child selector, all the text would be blue. That's because first the document would apply the child selector rules and change #span1 and #span3 to red, then it would apply the descendant selector rules and change #span1, #span2, and #span3 to blue. Therefore, when you combine child and descendant selectors in your own projects, be sure to consider the order in which rules will be applied. Remember: A child is always a descendant, but a descendant is not always a child. If you fail to take this into consideration in your own projects, you will likely see some unexpected results.

Adjacent Sibling Selector

Adjacent sibling selectors are used to style an element that is directly subsequent to another element (both under the same parent element). Therefore, if you wanted to do something like change the h2 element that immediately follows the h1 element on your page to be in italics, you could specify this relationship in your style sheet using the following syntax:

```
h1 + h2 {font-style: italic;}
```

Notice the plus (+) symbol between h1 and h2; this indicates an adjacent child selector.

To continue the descendant child selector example, modify your HTML document to include the following code:

```
<style>
    *{color: black;}
    span + span{color: red;}
</style>

<div id="myTable">
<span id="span1">
    here is my first level
    <span id="span2">and here is my second level </span>
</span>
```

```
<span id="span3">and, finally, here is my third level</span>
</div>
```

In this example, the bold text demonstrates how to set up an adjacent sibling selector relationship for situations when one span element follows another span element in the same parent container. If you were to load this example in your browser, you would see that only #span3 includes the red color font because it is the only span element that follows another span element in the same parent container (#span1 follows a div and #span2 does not have the same parent as the other span elements — it is a child of #span1).

Attribute Selector

Attribute selectors are interesting in that they enable you to select elements based on what a particular attribute of that element is set to. For example, if you want to select all elements on a page that have their lang attribute set to "en-us", you could do that by using an attribute selector. These can be matched in four different ways:

SYNTAX	DESCRIPTION
[att]	Matches any element with this particular attribute (att) being set. For example, *[id] would select any element on the page that had the ID attribute set to something.
[att=val]	Matches any element that has its attribute (att) set exactly to the value (val) provided. For example, if you wanted to identify any elements with an ID of header, you could set up your selector as *[id="header"].
[att~=val]	Matches when an attribute (att) is set to a value that contains a series of words separated by white space and one of the words exactly matches the value (val). For example, if you wanted to find all elements that have the word header in the ID, you could set up your selector as *[id~="header "]. Using this example, you would match with id="header", id="header div", or id="header div element". You would not, however, match id="headers" because "header" and "headers" are not an exact match.
[att|=val]	Matches when the attribute (att) of an element begins with the value (val) provided and is immediately followed by the - character. This is used primarily to identify language properties for elements. For example, if you wanted to identify all elements with some form of English set for the lang attribute (e.g., en, en-US, en-cockney), you would set up your selector as *[lang|="en "].

This list illustrates that there are several ways to find what you want to style. For example, consider the following line of HTML code:

```
<div id="header" lang="en-US">Hello World</div>
```

If you want to style the preceding div, all the following selectors would affect it:

➤   *

➤   div

- ➤ `*#header`

- ➤ `#header`

- ➤ `body div`

- ➤ `body #header`

- ➤ `*[id="header"]`

- ➤ `*[id~="header"]`

- ➤ `div[id="header"]`

- ➤ `div[id~="header"]`

- ➤ `*[lang|="en"]`

- ➤ `div[lang|="en"]`

This isn't a completely exhaustive list, but you get the idea. This list also demonstrates why CSS can sometimes frustrate developers. Just because you create the `div` with an id of `header` and set up the `#header` selector doesn't mean that those rules will be the only ones applied. In fact, some other rules from other selectors will almost certainly affect your `div`. This can be a bit of a headache when you have stated that the color should be red but it is showing up purple because you have set the color to purple with another selector.

To see how this might work in a real scenario, put the following code into your own HTML document:

```
<style>
    div[lang|="en"]{color: red;}
</style>

<div id="header" lang="en-US">Hello World</div>
```

This should set the "Hello World" text to red because the selector matches the `lang` attribute, which is set to `"en-US"`.

Pseudo Classes

Pseudo classes are a way of going beyond the element's position in the document tree. For example, all the selectors described until this point identify an element according to where it resides in the document tree. This might mean that it applies to all like elements, or only to an element that follows a particular element, or only to an element that is a sub-element of some parent element. Regardless of how you have identified the element up to this point, it has followed a hierarchal ordering of the elements in an HTML document.

Pseudo classes enable you to go outside of this hierarchal ordering to grab an element based on other criteria.

The following table describes the pseudo classes available in CSS 2.1:

PSEUDO CLASS	DESCRIPTION
:first-child	Matches the first child element of a parent container and ignores all other instances of the element in that parent container. This is used in conjunction with the child selector; for example, to identify the first span element in a div container, you would set up your selector to remember the following: `DIV > SPAN:first-child`
:link	Matches a hyperlink (typically an anchor tag) that has not been visited previously, differentiated from hyperlinks that have been visited.
:visited	Matches a hyperlink that has been visited previously, differentiated from a hyperlink that has never been visited.
:hover	Identifies the client action of hovering the mouse over an element. Typically, this is used to identify when a client moves the mouse over a hyperlink on the page, but it can be used for any HTML element.
:active	Identifies when an element becomes activated by the user. This is typically used for the time between when a client clicks on a hyperlink and when it is released.
:focus	Identifies when an element has the focus, which includes keyboard events and other forms of text input (not just clicking the element with the mouse).
:lang	Matches the human language of the HTML document, if determined. Differs from the attribute selector of [lang=val] because the attribute selector looks only at the lang attribute of a particular element. While the :lang pseudo class also looks at this attribute, it also looks at things like the meta element of the HTML document, HTTP headers, and even XML:lang properties, if appropriate and available.

A typical example of using pseudo classes in your style sheet would be styling your hyperlink controls to appear differently based on when the hyperlink is static, when a user hovers over the hyperlink, and when the user actually clicks the hyperlink. To set this up, you might use code similar to the following:

```
<style>
    a:link, a:visited{color: darkgray;}
    a:hover{color: steelblue;}
    a:active{color: orange;}
</style>

<a href="http://www.bing.com">Bing</a>
```

In this example, you are grouping the :link and :visited pseudo classes for the anchor (a) tag to create one look for a resting hyperlink, regardless of whether the user has accessed the page or not. You are then changing the color of the hyperlink when the user hovers over it. Finally, you are providing still a different color when the user actually clicks the link (color that will be visible only until the user releases the button).

"!important" Is Very Important

You may have seen the term !important used in CSS, but what exactly is it and what does it do? !important was created to allow both users (through the use of a user style sheet) and designers to declare certain CSS rules as more important than all others. When a CSS rule is declared as !important, the usual cascade rules do not apply and the !important rule takes precedence. The following example shows how !important is used:

```
<style type="text/css">
        div {
                color: blue !important;
        }
        div {
                color: red;
        }
</style>

<div>
        This text should be red, but is actually blue.
</div>
```

The <div> tag text in this example should be red because the second CSS rule should override the first one; however, the !important rule takes precedence and makes the text blue instead.

Understanding the Cascade

Earlier in this chapter you learned about how CSS handles conflicts, but a deeper understanding of how CSS cascades can be helpful. This is particularly true for SharePoint due to the complex nature of the CSS that it loads. The cascade refers to the ability of CSS to allow some styles (typically those lower in the cascade) to take precedence over others. CSS uses the following set of rules to determine what CSS wins this battle for dominance:

1. Find all style declarations that are applied to the particular element.

2. Sort by origin and importance. When it comes to origin, the browser's default style sheet is least important, then the user's style sheet, and, finally, the style sheet that you as the page designer create is the most important. The other factor that applies at this step is the !important tag. As discussed earlier, properties marked as !important will take priority over other styles.

3. If the rule in question has the same origin and importance, use specificity to determine what wins the cascade. *Specificity* is a calculation that refers to how specific the selector in question is. Specificity is determined via the following equation:

(The number of ID selectors) x 100

+

(The number of Class selectors) x 10

+

(The number of HTML selectors) x 1

This gives you the specificity of a given selector. If two selectors are otherwise equivalent, the selector with the highest specificity will have its style applied to the element. For example, given the following:

```
.myClass div {
        color: blue
}

div {
        color: red
}
```

The first style will take precedence because it has a specificity of 11, whereas the second has a specificity of 1.

4. Finally, if all other steps are equivalent, the rule that is declared last is the winner.

You can use these steps to your advantage to ensure your own styles win the cascade and override out-of-the-box SharePoint styles.

Browser Wars

You may recall from the beginning of this chapter that CSS rules are divided into two main categories: cosmetic and structural. Cosmetic style rules affect things such as color, font size, and font decorations. It can include things like setting background colors and borders, as well as special font styling (small caps, italics, bold, etc.). For the most part, if you set up these rules, they will apply to all major browsers today.

Unfortunately, however, when you start getting into structural rules this isn't always the case. Structural rules are more useful for providing the layout of your HTML document. Things like element positioning and how elements interact with each other (e.g., whether they can be contained on the same line or subsequent elements are pushed to the next line) can be tricky, especially if you are targeting older browsers. In particular, Internet Explorer 6 or earlier makes most designers shudder. IE7 and later have made great strides in terms of compatibility with other CSS-friendly browsers (such as Firefox, Safari, and Opera); however, if you are using a version of IE older than IE7, you will have a lot of trouble making everything look the same if you are using only CSS.

If you have read Chapter 3, then you are already aware of the various browsers available and their relative popularity, and have taken that into consideration as you begin planning the branding project for your SharePoint 2010 site. It is critically important that you test your branded site extensively with as many browsers as possible, especially when you start adjusting structural CSS rules.

Please refer to Chapter 3 if you need more information about browsers and other considerations when planning your project.

CSS Developer Tools

As mentioned in Chapter 5, several CSS developer tools are available to help you in your branding projects. CSS can be frustrating and overwhelming at times, especially when you have many lines of code to maintain, and various inheritance and aggregation rules apply to elements that have not had any style applied to them individually. Furthermore, the long list of browsers (and all their versions) still active on the Web can make maintaining this code difficult. This is when CSS developer tools can be useful.

One of the most widely used tools for CSS troubleshooting is Firefox's Firebug (`https://addons .mozilla.org/en-US/firefox/addon/1843`). This tool was already introduced in Chapter 5, but you can see it in use later in this chapter as well.

Best Practices for CSS

This chapter has mentioned some CSS best practices along the way, but it might be a good idea to review the main suggestions in one place. With that in mind, here are some of the major things to remember:

➤ **Re-use code** — If you can group elements, share style sheets, and so on, your pages will load faster and maintenance will be easier.

➤ **Use shortcuts** — Similar to the preceding point, don't write unnecessary code. For example, instead style rules such as

```
padding-right: 5px; padding -left: 5px; padding -top: 5px; padding -bottom: 5px;
```

you could simply write the following for the exact same effect:

```
padding: 5px;
```

➤ **Use CSS for your structural layout** — This will create pages that load faster, are easier to maintain, and are more accessible to your users.

➤ **Never use inline styles** — Inline styles override everything, which completely negates any attempt at global branding. It also presents a maintenance issue because updating your site will potentially require touching a lot of pages (if not all of them). Don't do it.

➤ **Use external style sheets** — Keep design and content separate. Use one file or a few files to keep all your rules so that maintenance is easier. This will also result in better performance in terms of loading time.

➤ **Organize your CSS rules wisely** — This might mean splitting your rules into several CSS files. For example, you might have all structural/positioning rules in one style sheet, and all the cosmetic rules in another. That way, when you need to change the font from red to blue, you go directly to the cosmetic file. To increase the size of the header, you go directly to the structural file. This also helps to organize the rules within each file. Try to keep elements that go together grouped together in the file. For example, all the CSS rules that apply to the header region of the page should be near each other so you can find them easily when updating.

➤ **Comment your code** — This is important for all code, and CSS is no different. Although it is not shown in this chapter, you can add comments by introducing them with /* and ending them with */. For example, this would be a commented line of code in your CSS file:

```
/* this is my comment */
```

➤ **Remove all margins and padding and then add them back** — The first rule in your style sheet should be something like the following:

```
*{padding: 0px; margin: 0px;}
```

This will strip out all the default padding and margins added by different browsers. Because different browsers have different defaults, this enables you to essentially level the playing field between browsers. You can add back what you need for each element as you need it. Failure to strip padding and margins will result in your site appearing non-uniformly across the different browsers in which it is viewed.

➤ **Test, test, test** — Make sure you test with as many browsers as possible; and test often.

➤ **Use Firebug or IE Developer Tools** — Both are free, easy to use, and you can avoid a lot of headaches trying to get your styles right.

This isn't an exhaustive list of best practices but it is a good start. As you continue to learn CSS, you will almost certainly add your own best practices to this list.

Additional Resources for CSS

This chapter provides a crash course in some of the basics of CSS, but one chapter cannot do justice to all that there is to know about it. (CSS is truly a huge challenge, but it is also very rewarding once you start making progress.) It stands to reason that you will want to find out more about CSS after reading this section.

The first place to look is where the standards for CSS come from: the World Wide Web Consortium (W3C), at www.w3.org. Here you will find an abundance of articles and guidelines to help you understand the CSS standards; many of the caveats of CSS; and how it can be used in real-world applications. Some of the highlights include the following:

➤ **Accessibility** — www.w3.org/WAI/

➤ **CSS** — www.w3.org/Style/CSS/

➤ **CSS selectors** — www.w3.org/TR/CSS2/selector.html

➤ **A CSS validation application** — http://jigsaw.w3.org/css-validator/

Another great way to get free information about CSS is from the CSS Tutorials at W3Schools.com (http://w3schools.com/css/). The tutorials on this site are well organized and range from basic CSS demonstrations to more advanced topics. The site even includes quizzes and references — not only for CSS rules, but also for things like web-safe fonts and even color values (e.g., #FFFFFF = White). You will likely begin with the tutorials, but you will come back for the references. This is truly valuable (and free) information.

Finally, there are no better printed CSS publications than the books by Richard York:

➤ *Beginning CSS: Cascading Style Sheets for Web Design* (Wrox, 2007)

➤ *CSS Instant Results* (Wrox, 2006)

CSS IN SHAREPOINT

So, how important is CSS in SharePoint? There seems to be a misconception among many developers that CSS is for designers and that enterprise portals just don't need it, but at least with SharePoint sites, that just isn't the case.

Consider, for example, SharePoint 2007. If you did any branding in that version, you are probably familiar with core.css and its nearly 5,000 lines of CSS rules. That file alone proved to be very daunting to many developers, but it also indicated that CSS is just as important to enterprise portal solutions as it is for the artistic web designer. In fact, it could be argued that it is even more important when you consider that a portal may contain literally thousands of sites, and therefore an exponentially greater number of pages. For example, if you want the body font to be the same from page to page, it's much more efficient to wrap it in some shared CSS rules than to hard-code the font properties on each page.

With that in mind, you can probably anticipate the role played by CSS in SharePoint 2010. The default corev4.css file (the new core.css) weighs in with just under 8,000 lines of code, almost doubling core.css from SharePoint 2007.

In addition to the heavier corev4.css file, if you look at the rendered page in a default installation of SharePoint 2010, you are likely to see something resembling the following near the top of your page:

```
<link rel="stylesheet" type="text/css"
    href="/_layouts/1033/styles/Themable/search.css?rev=DEoJG7NxjizWXwVceBbl%2Fg%3D%3D"/>
<link rel="stylesheet" type="text/css"
    href="/_layouts/1033/styles/Themable/wiki.css?rev=1JBDhRqaR21D5CLFiCimoA%3D%3D"/>
<link rel="stylesheet" type="text/css"
    href="/_layouts/1033/styles/Themable/corev4.css?
    rev=N2DtekLllkxi1g1b%2B7kf%2FQ%3D%3D"/>
```

While the last link probably won't surprise you, the first two links might. References to search.css (weighing in at just under 3,000 lines of code) and wiki.css (barely 50 lines of code) are pulled in dynamically, depending on what is being presented on the page. For example, if search were not enabled, search.css would not be referenced. However, with these two additional CSS references, the number of lines of CSS code added to this page now is well over 10,000. That is a lot of CSS!

And that's just the beginning. When you start delving into these files, you will understand why the primer in this chapter is so vital for branding. The CSS rules have matured significantly since SharePoint 2007, including fairly complicated selectors such as the following:

```
*:first-child + html[dir="rtl"]
```

In SharePoint 2007, you never saw things like adjacent child selectors or the first-child pseudo class. In fact, for the most part, in SharePoint 2007, you didn't really need to understand much more than element, class, and ID selectors to understand `core.css`. In SharePoint 2010, however, to truly be proficient at updating the look and feel of the SharePoint 2010 portal, you need a deeper foundation in CSS. (If you skipped the primer for CSS at the beginning of this chapter, you might consider at least perusing it.)

Another tangible example of CSS's importance can be found by comparing the layout architecture of the SharePoint 2007 master page and the new SharePoint 2010 master page. In SharePoint 2007, the master page created the structure of the page (positioning) through the use of tables. In SharePoint 2010, however, this is no longer the case. Instead, in the new master page (`v4.master`), positioning is determined through a series of `div` and `span` elements encapsulating large portions of the page content. While some tables are still used here and there for positioning, the use of tables for structure is significantly reduced.

Unfortunately, Microsoft still uses inline styles in the new master page (`v4.master`). In some instances, it probably doesn't matter much. For example, the following line of code ensures that the accessibility option is hidden from browsers using CSS:

```
<div id="TurnOnAccessibility" style="display:none" class="s4-notdlg noindex">
```

Although it does seem odd that the `div` is employing a class, and a reference could be added to some sort of class that sets the display property to `none`, in the grand scheme of things it probably doesn't really impact anything.

However, in some instances, this use of inline styles is a little more alarming. Consider this example:

```
<span style="top:12px;display:inline-block;position:relative;">
```

This line is hard-coded in the `v4.master` and results in some fairly heavy positioning. It may not seem like a big deal, but as soon as you start playing around with element positioning inside of your browser, it becomes a big deal. Moreover, because it is hard-coded in your master page, it isn't easily overridden with your internal or external style sheets, so this is something to be cautious about.

Despite this one drawback, there are a lot of remarkable things going on with regard to CSS and SharePoint. If you don't know CSS really well but plan to do SharePoint branding, it's time to hone your skills.

Working with corev4.css

As mentioned previously, the CSS file included by default with your SharePoint 2010 installation is `corev4.css`, which consists of almost 8,000 lines of code. While this can be daunting, you should familiarize yourself with this file if you plan to brand your own sites. While it is not feasible to explain all 8,000 lines of code in one section (or even one chapter or, probably, even one book), this section will help you get familiar enough with the file that you can make changes for your own projects.

If you wanted to find `corev4.css` on the actual SharePoint web server, you need to look in the following location:

```
<<Program Files>>\Common Files\Microsoft Shared\Web ServerExtensions\14\TEMPLATE\
LAYOUTS\1033\STYLES\Themable\corev4.css
```

While you could modify this file directly on the server, this is not considered best practice. Any modifications that you make will affect all web applications on this server. A better way to work with CSS in SharePoint is to override it from SharePoint Designer 2010 (SPD).

 The following example uses a SharePoint 2010 Team site to explain how the corev4 CSS works in as simple a setting as possible. If you use a publishing site to follow along with the example, the options may be different.

To modify `corev4.css` in SPD, open your site and then open one of its pages for editing (e.g., the site's home page). You can do this from the Home tab by clicking the "Edit site home page" link under Customization (see Figure 7-1).

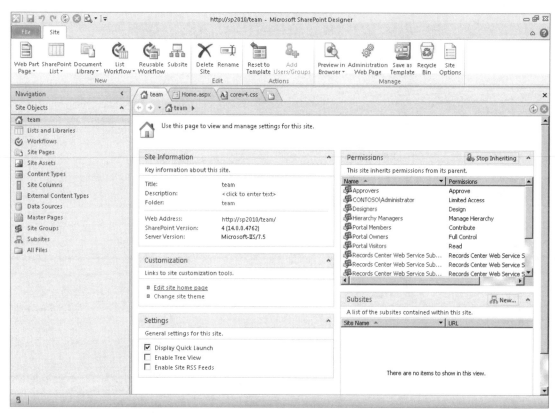

FIGURE 7-1

Once the page is opened for editing, make sure the Code view is visible (either through the Code view or Split view). If the Code view is not visible (meaning you can't see any HTML code in any pane open to you), click the Code button at the bottom of the designer pane to bring up the Code view. As you scroll through the code, you should see several CSS class references. For example, at approximately line 48, you will see a line of code starting with the following:

```
<div class="ms-webpartpagedescription">
```

The class name, `ms-webpartpagedescription`, is a hyperlink. Hold down the Ctrl button and click the hyperlink to open a copy of `corev4.css` in SPD that you can edit, as shown in Figure 7-2. You will see the rules defined for this class starting near line 638.

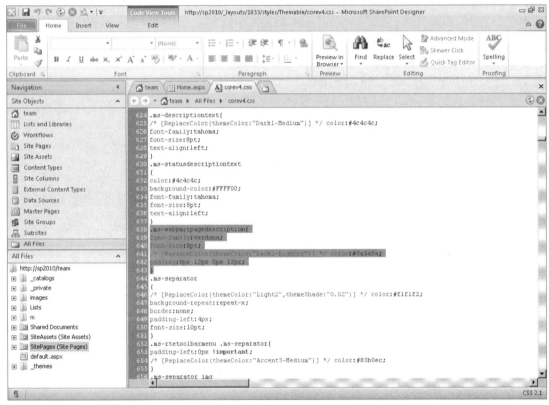

FIGURE 7-2

 Note that that there are references to other CSS files in the file you have open in SharePoint Designer. Therefore, when the CSS file loads, make sure it is `corev4.css`. Other CSS class hyperlinks could take you to files such as `wiki.css`. Just make sure you are in the right file before proceeding. If you wind up at another CSS file, simply close it and try another class reference.

At this point, without any modifications this set of rules provides most of the look and feel for your site collection, which (for frame of reference) should look like Figure 7-3.

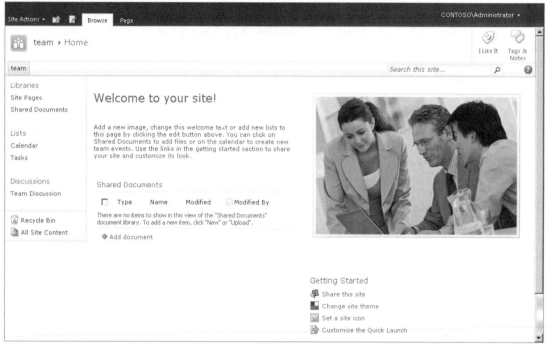

FIGURE 7-3

While in SPD, from this one file you can make edits to your site's appearance and layout that will affect everything in the site collection. As an example, navigate to the top of the file where the first rule creates a style reset for the site collection (strips out all margins from all elements):

```
body,form{
margin:0;
}
```

Change the `margin` to something that will be noticeable, such as `100px`. This will give every element a margin of 100px unless later overridden by another rule. When you go to save the file, the prompt shown in Figure 7-4 will remind you that you are customizing a SharePoint style sheet. Press Yes to continue. Once you have done so, refresh your site collection in your browser; it will now resemble Figure 7-5.

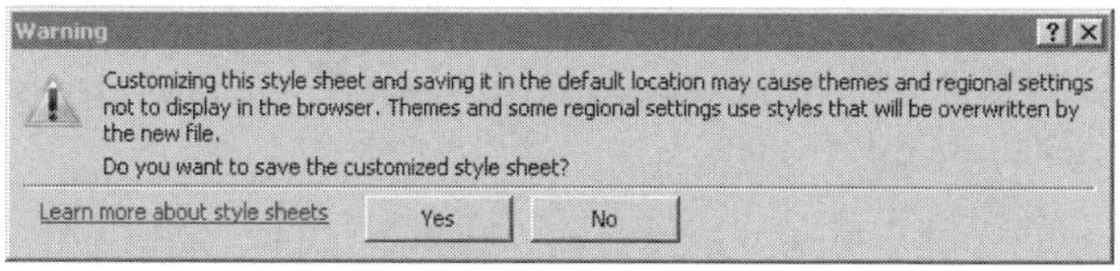

FIGURE 7-4

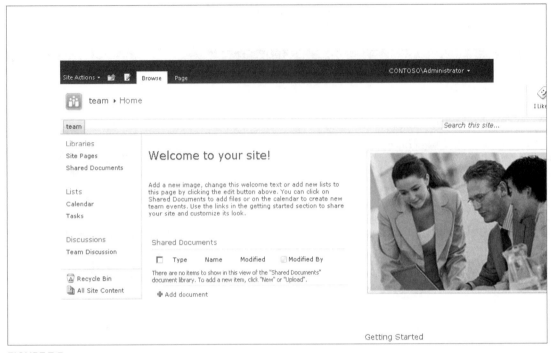

FIGURE 7-5

You may be wondering what exactly happened here when corev4.css *was saved. Did SharePoint Designer just change a file on the actual SharePoint server in the 14 folder? Not actually. If you were watching the top of SharePoint Designer, the filename and path are displayed. When the CSS file was first opened, the path was showing as something similar to* http://YOURSITE/ _layouts/1033/styles/Themable/corev4.css, *but when you made a change, SharePoint Designer actually made a copy of the* corev4.css *file and added it to a special folder named* _styles *inside the site collection. This can be confusing, but SharePoint Designer is doing this to protect you from accidently changing the CSS for all web applications on the server. SharePoint knows to apply this copied CSS file from the* _styles *directory for just this one particular site.*

You can see from this example the effect that setting the default margin for the site to 100px has. If you navigate through your site at this point, all the pages will have this obnoxious 100px margin enforced around the content of your page. This demonstrates how easy it is to change your default styling, and how big of an impact one small change can have.

Obviously, this is probably not a change you would want to keep, so feel free to change this line back to its initial value of 0, and resave your changes.

What changes *should* you make? Obviously, that depends on your own project and personal preferences. The bigger question is, how do you make changes to an element of your page when you don't know what styles are affecting the element? Consider, for example, the default home page from Figure 7-3. Maybe you would like to change the headers in the Quick Launch menu to have an italics style applied to them. How do you easily determine which styles are being applied to those headers so that you can make the necessary changes in `corev4.css`?

The easiest way is by using one of the CSS developer tools, such as the IE Developers Tools or Firebug for Firefox. You have already learned about both of these tools in Chapter 5, but the following example revisits Firebug to help explain how CSS is used in SharePoint 2010.

After installing Firebug, in the Firefox browser, click the small "bug" icon in the lower-right corner of the browser window to launch Firebug, which should make your browser window resemble Figure 7-6.

FIGURE 7-6

Once Firebug has launched, you can easily find out which styles are being applied to a particular element. Simply click the icon that looks like an arrow hovering over a box next to the Firebug logo at the top-left corner of the Firebug utility. This enables you to select any element in the browser window. Hover over the element you want to select (in this case, any of the headers in the Quick Launch menu), and then click that element. If you have done this correctly, Firebug should be updated to look more like Figure 7-7.

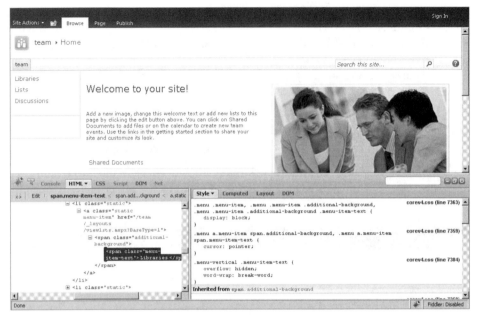

FIGURE 7-7

The right-hand pane of Firebug lists every rule from every source that is currently affecting the element — whether that's multiple external style sheets, internal style sheets, or inline code. Whatever CSS rules apply to this element will appear in this pane. In addition, and perhaps equally as useful, it will show the order in which these rules are applied, as well as which rules are not being applied because they are being overwritten by other rules.

If you scroll through the pane, you will come across the lines that are setting the cosmetic rules of the element, such as its `color` and `font-size` properties, as shown in Figure 7-8.

One of the really nice things about Firebug is that in addition to showing you all the rules being applied to an element, it also indicates exactly where that rule resides. For example, looking at Figure 7-8, you can see that this rule is being applied on line 2968 of `corev4.css`. With that information, you can return to SPD and navigate to around line 2900 of `corev4.css` to find the actual rule, which looks more like this:

```
.s4-ql ul.root > li > .menu-item,.s4-qlheader,.s4-qlheader:visited{
font-size:1.2em;
/* [ReplaceColor(themeColor:"Dark2")] */ color:#0072bc;
margin:0px;
padding:3px 4px 3px 10px;
border-width:1px 0px;
border-style:solid;
border-color:transparent;
word-wrap:break-word;
overflow-x:hidden;
}
```

Within this rule block, add the following new rule:

```
font-style: italic;
```

Now go back to your browser and refresh your page. It should look like Figure 7-9.

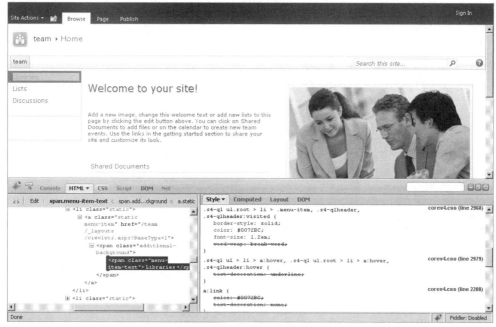

FIGURE 7-8

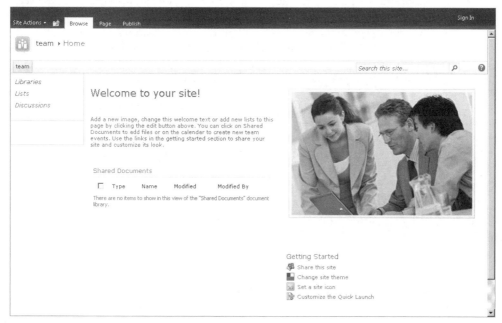

FIGURE 7-9

As you can see, the headers for the Quick Launch area are all now italicized.

You might have noticed when you looked at the actual CSS code in `corev4.css` that the `color` rule is a bit weird. Typically, the CSS rule for setting the color of an element resembles the following:

```
color: #0072bc;
```

This would set the foreground color for your element to #0072bc (a sort of steel-blue color); and if you referred back to Firebug (see Figure 7-8), that is how the rule appears. However, the actual code in `corev4.css` looks like the following:

```
/* [ReplaceColor(themeColor:"Dark2")] */ color:#0072bc;
```

This means that this color is a themed color that is initially set to color #0072bc. If you don't remember what this means, it is explained in more detail in Chapter 5. Just understand that the defined color can also be overridden by the colors defined in whichever theme is currently applied to the site.

Using this same approach, you can easily locate and modify any of the rules being applied to your site collection elements using Firebug and SPD. This makes managing an 8000-line code file (plus whatever other CSS external style sheets may be brought in) much more achievable. After all, if you can determine exactly which rules are being applied and exactly where you can find them, you can easily override them in a custom style sheet.

Custom Style Sheets

As mentioned at the end of the last section, you can create your own style sheets that override styles in `corev4.css` or any of the other standard SharePoint CSS files. You can also use a custom style sheet to provide additional style rules that are not currently included with the standard style sheets. For example, if you are creating custom Web Parts and need to have custom styles available to the rendered code from those Web Parts, a custom style sheet is probably a better solution than adding to one of the included SharePoint 2010 style sheets, if for no other reason than it is easier to maintain your custom style rules when they are in their own document.

As with any other external style sheet, you must ensure that you create your custom style sheet in a location that is available to web browsers. While you could reference a CSS file from several locations, probably the best place to store a custom CSS file is in the Style Library of your site collection. If you did this, you could reference your style sheet from within your master page with the following relative URL:

```
/Style Library/customstyle.css
```

Once you have created your custom style sheet, you can reference it in your master page with the following line of code:

```
<SharePoint:CssRegistration name="/Style Library/customstyle.css" runat="server"/>
```

One of the nicer enhancements to SharePoint 2010 is the capability to specify that your custom style sheet should be applied after another CSS file is applied. For example, if you want to ensure that your custom style sheet is applied after `corev4.css`, you can add the `After` attribute to the `CSSRegistration` tag and set its value to `"corev4.css"`:

```
<SharePoint:CssRegistration name="/Style Library/customstyle.css" After="corev4.css"
runat="server"/>
```

This ensures that your custom styles will be applied last, which, for the most part, means your styles will be applied even if they conflict with rules in other style sheets. If you have done any branding in previous versions of SharePoint, you will likely be ecstatic about this enhancement. You learn more about utilizing the `CssRegistration` tag in Chapter 8.

SUMMARY

CSS is used across all web development platforms to help create the look and feel of the pages displayed to the client. This can mean something as simple as formatting the font used on the page to something as complex as creating the exact positioning of content on the page using positional element rules. CSS isn't new and it isn't new to SharePoint, but it has come a long way since the original bits were offered almost 10 years ago.

If you have followed branding in SharePoint over the years, you will be either pleased or upset to see how much bigger a role CSS now plays in the branding of SharePoint sites. While previous versions used it fairly heavily, SharePoint 2010 takes it to an entirely new level. The selectors are much more complicated and the sheer number of lines of code has grown tremendously. However, with this added complexity there are some things that have gotten a lot better, such as SharePoint using fewer tables and less inline CSS. Also, because the underlying HTML is cleaner, the SharePoint CSS can take advantage of modern standard techniques for styling.

While knowing CSS is not something new to web developers, the level of proficiency required for SharePoint 2010 branding is increasing. This chapter showed you many of the selectors you will need to understand. It also showed you some of the ways SharePoint uses CSS in its deployments to stylize its appearance.

Although not knowing CSS will not prevent you from being a strong SharePoint developer, it will likely prevent you from being a strong SharePoint brander. Therefore, if you aspire to make your SharePoint 2010 sites look like they aren't SharePoint sites, you do need to understand CSS; and after reading this chapter, you should be well on your way.

Master Pages

WHAT'S IN THIS CHAPTER?

➤ An overview of how master pages work in ASP.NET

➤ How master pages use content placeholders and controls

➤ How master pages work differently in SharePoint 2010

➤ How master pages and page layouts work together

➤ How to create both simple and complex custom master pages

➤ How to solve common challenges that occur when creating custom master pages

In the previous chapter, you learned about how Cascading Style Sheets (CSS) work in SharePoint 2010. Even though CSS is an important concept in styling SharePoint sites, it can affect the overall look of a site only so much; CSS can only affect hiding and showing areas of a design, as well as changing colors and images. To truly make wide-sweeping changes to the user interface of a SharePoint site, master pages are the only way to go. Master pages are responsible for laying out the various pieces of functionality that are shown when SharePoint pages are browsed.

In this chapter, you will learn how master pages work in traditional ASP.NET applications and, more important, how they work in SharePoint 2010. You will also learn how master pages and page layouts differ, as well as how the various parts of master pages are handled in a SharePoint site. The chapter concludes with a tutorial on converting a standard HTML and CSS design into a corresponding master page and CSS.

UNDERSTANDING MASTER PAGES

If you remember the good old days of classic web design, web pages used to be created with the look and feel hard-coded in each and every page. This meant that when changes inevitably were needed, every single page on a website had to be changed accordingly. This was a tedious, error-prone process, which could even result in pages not looking the same.

To solve this problem, master pages were introduced with the 2.0 release of ASP.NET. Master pages are used to create a template that controls many aspects of the overall layout of many pages in an ASP.NET website. They are typically used as a shell to hold all the common HTML content, such as the DOCTYPE, meta information, CSS, navigation, footers, and the general layout of the major areas of the site. One website may have one master page that controls all the pages, or you can have several master pages that apply different layouts to different areas of your website. In addition to enabling easier website maintenance, master pages are especially helpful for creating a consistent look for large websites with many content authors of varying skill levels.

It's important to understand how master pages work before working with them in SharePoint. The next few sections discuss traditional ASP.NET master pages before diving into how master pages work in SharePoint.

Master Page Structure

From a coding perspective, a master page is a type of ASP.NET page that is written in either Visual Basic (VB) or C# and has a file extension of `.master`. Although you can use either language to create traditional ASP.NET applications, for SharePoint, Microsoft has chosen to stick to C#. All of the out-of-the-box SharePoint code uses C# and pretty much every example you see for custom SharePoint applications will be in C# as well. To get a better idea of what a master page looks like in traditional ASP.NET, the following illustrates a very simple master page:

```
<%@ Master Language="C#" %>
<!DOCTYPE html PUBLIC "-//W3C//DTD XHTML 1.0 Strict//EN"
"http://www.w3.org/TR/xhtml1/DTD/xhtml1-strict.dtd">
<html xmlns="http://www.w3.org/1999/xhtml">
<head>
 <meta http-equiv="Content-Type" content="text/html; charset=utf-8" />
    <title>Demo Title</title>
</head>

<body>
<form runat="server">
 <div>
  <asp:ContentPlaceHolder ID="MainBody" runat="server"/>
 </div>
 <div>
  <asp:ContentPlaceHolder id="Footer" runat="server">
   Copyright 2010 - Randy Drisgill
  </asp:ContentPlaceHolder>
 </div>
</form>
</body>
</html>
```

From this example, you can see that master pages begin with the @ `Master` directive that declares the language in which the master page will be written. In this case the master page is written in C#. There are two content placeholders in the body of the master page: One has no content and is closed immediately but the other has some default footer content. Otherwise, the rest of the master page code is comprised of standard HTML that is used to lay out the page.

Content Placeholders

Content placeholders define areas of a master page that can be replaced by information located on a content page. The master page's content placeholders receive their content from content controls that are placed on content pages. The content pages can override content in as many or as few of the master page's content placeholders as desired; this means that not every content placeholder in a master page needs to be overridden by content pages. Because of this, content placeholders can define some default content to show whenever a content page has no corresponding content. In the previous example master page, the Footer content placeholder provided the default content `Copyright 2010 - Randy Drisgill`.

Content Pages

On their own, master pages don't actually produce anything useful; in fact, browsing to a master page URL directly will cause the web server — in this case IIS (Internet Information Services) — to display an error. In traditional ASP.NET websites, content pages (files with an `.ASPX` extension) can refer to master pages for their layout. Users browse these pages, the page content is merged with the master page on-the-fly, and the resulting web page is displayed to the user. Figure 8-1 shows the relationship between content pages and master pages.

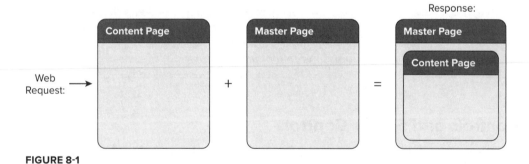

FIGURE 8-1

Content pages can declare a master page via an `@ Page` directive at the top of their code. Following is a simple content page:

```
<%@ Page Language="C#" MasterPageFile="demo.master" %>

<asp:Content ContentPlaceHolderID="MainBody" Runat="Server" >
 Hello World
</asp:content>

<asp:Content ContentPlaceHolderID="Footer" Runat="Server" >
 Copyright 2010 - Randy's Waffles
</asp:content>
```

Notice that the `@ Page` directive `MasterPageFile` property defines this page's master page as `demo.master`. Assuming the master page shown earlier was named `demo.master`, this content page would load that master page and use it to lay out its content.

Content pages that use master pages, like the one above, require that all content after the @ Page directive be located inside of <asp:Content> content controls. If anything is placed outside a content control, an error will occur. The content controls are tied to specific content placeholders with matching ContentPlaceHolderIDs. In this example, the content page would add the text "Hello World" where the MainBody content placeholder is located on the master page, and it would override the default content in the Footer content placeholder with "Copyright 2010 - Randy's Waffles." When loaded in the browser, the resulting page would have the following HTML in the main body:

```
<div>
 Hello World
</div>
<div>
 Copyright 2010 - Randy's Waffles
</div>
```

Although not every master page content placeholder needs to have a corresponding content control applied in a content page, the opposite is not true. Every content control defined in the content page must have a matching content placeholder in the applied master page; otherwise, an error will occur. In traditional ASP.NET applications, this can be easy to manage because you are in complete control over how master pages and content pages are set up. Because SharePoint is a dynamic environment, where content authors can change pages, page layouts, and master pages on-the-fly, this can be more challenging. You will learn more about this topic later in the chapter.

User Controls and Server Controls

Another important concept related to master pages is how controls are used to abstract complex code functionality. Before the creation of ASP.NET 2.0, developers who wanted to reuse code and HTML throughout a website would use a technique such as a classic ASP server-side include directive. These were often written in code with a statement like the following:

```
<!--#include file="inc_footer.aspx"-->
```

Later, this practice was largely replaced with the concepts of user controls and server controls. Developers use these controls to bundle HTML, existing ASP.NET server controls, and custom functionality into reusable components that can be added to master pages and content pages. User controls, which have a file extension of .ascx, are typically simpler than server controls. Server controls are coded and compiled into DLLs to be loaded on the web server. These controls enable master pages to provide large amounts of custom functionality while containing a relatively small amount of code for maintainability.

To use a control, you must first register it at the top of a content page or master page. This assigns a TagPrefix and a TagName, both of which are used to refer to the control in the page, as well as a src that points to the .ASCX control on the web server, or both a Namespace and an Assembly to point to a compiled DLL. Imagine that you had some prebuilt search functionality that was built as a custom user control named `searchbox.ascx`. To include this functionality on a master page or content page, you would first register the control near the top of the page, below the language declaration, as shown here:

```
<%@ Register TagPrefix="Custom" TagName="Search" src="searchbox.ascx" %>
```

To actually use the registered control, you use a combination of the `TagPrefix` and the `TagName`. The following example shows the control added to the page inside of a `<div>` tag:

```
<div id="header">
 <Custom:Search ID="mySearchControl" runat="server" />
</div>
```

When the page is loaded in a browser, whatever content the control is programmed to display will be added to the page inside of the `<div>` tags. Also, if the control were set up to receive custom properties, they could be applied when the control is added to the page. For example, if the search control has a property named `ButtonImage` to set the search button image, it could be added like this:

```
<Custom:Search ID="mySearchControl" ButtonImage="go.png" runat="server" />
```

SharePoint leverages this concept heavily to encapsulate much of the functionality in a SharePoint site. In the next section, which covers SharePoint master pages, you will notice that many controls are used.

MASTER PAGES IN SHAREPOINT

Because SharePoint was created with ASP.NET, master pages in SharePoint work much the same way that they do in traditional ASP.NET applications. Every page that is browsed in a SharePoint site uses a master page to lay out its content. One striking difference with master pages in SharePoint is that they are referenced by pages using one of four *tokens*, two of which are dynamic and two of which are static. These tokens are used in the `MasterPageFile` property of the @ `Page` directive at the top of SharePoint pages, rather than making a static reference to a specific master page on the file system.

The following *dynamic tokens* are available for SharePoint master pages:

> ➤ `~masterurl/default.master` — This dynamic token references whatever master page has been set as the System Master Page. This is the master page that is used for all pages in nonpublishing sites and in all forms, views, and settings pages in publishing sites. By default, it is set to `v4.master`.

> ➤ `~masterurl/custom.master` — This dynamic token references whichever master page has been set as the Site Master Page. This is the master page that is used by publishing pages. Typically, this is set to `v4.master`, but the Publishing Portal site template sets it to `nightandday.master` by default.

A SharePoint @ `Page` directive using one of these dynamic tokens would look like this:

```
<%@ Page MasterPageFile="~masterurl/default.master"%>
```

This would point to the master page that is set as the System Master Page. You will learn more about changing the Site and System Master Pages later in the chapter.

The following *static tokens* are available for SharePoint master pages:

➤ `~site` and `~sitecollection` — These two static tokens may be manually applied to pages to point to specific master pages using a relative reference to either the site or site collection root. Without using one of these static tokens, pages in SharePoint would be tied to their original location, and moving them would cause the master page to stop working. For example, if you used the following reference, your page would look for `Waffles.master` at the root of the site collection no matter where the page was located in the site hierarchy:

```
<%@ Page MasterPageFile="~ sitecollection/Waffles.master"%>
```

SharePoint Master Page Structure

Earlier you saw a sample ASP.NET master page, so now you can compare it with a sample SharePoint master page. Microsoft created a very simple SharePoint 2010 master page that can be found at `http://code.msdn.microsoft.com/odcSP14StarterMaster`. It contains too many lines of code to list here, but if you download it you can review it alongside the following discussion of its structure.

The first thing you may notice looking at the SharePoint master page is that it is generally much larger than the simple ASP.NET master page listed earlier. Like ASP.NET, it begins with an `@ Page` directive that declares the language as C#, and then several controls and assemblies are registered or imported. These controls and assemblies are what make SharePoint work, and they are sprinkled throughout the master page and arranged with HTML and ASP.NET to create all the SharePoint functionality that appears on the page.

One prevalent control is registered as `SharePoint`, and you will see tags listed as `<SharePoint:XYZ>`, where `XYZ` describes the control's functionality. Along with all this, JavaScript and CSS are declared, as well as standard HTML elements like all the meta tags at the top. Most of the content placeholders that are included in this master page are required by SharePoint.

Required Placeholders

SharePoint requires the inclusion of several content placeholders on a master page in order for it to function properly. If they are omitted, SharePoint will display a cryptic error message like the one shown in Figure 8-2.

Later in the chapter you will learn how to access the full error message so that you can actually identify which placeholder is missing. These placeholders are required because they are used on standard pages located throughout SharePoint. The following table lists the required content placeholders for SharePoint 2010, as described in the MSDN article "Upgrading an

FIGURE 8-2

Existing Master Page to the SharePoint Foundation Master Page" (`http://msdn.microsoft.com/en-us/library/ee539981.aspx`). Note that the first two are new content placeholders that did not exist in SharePoint 2007:

CONTENT PLACEHOLDER	DESCRIPTION
PlaceHolderQuickLaunchTop	The top of the Quick Launch menu
PlaceHolderQuickLaunchBottom	The bottom of the Quick Launch menu
PlaceHolderPageTitle	The title of the site
PlaceHolderAdditionalPageHead	A placeholder in the head section of the page used to add extra components such as ECMAScript (JavaScript, JScript) and Cascading Style Sheets (CSS)
PlaceHolderBodyAreaClass	The class of the body area
PlaceHolderSiteName	Name of the site where the current page resides
PlaceHolderPageTitleInTitleArea	Title of the page, which appears in the title area on the page
PlaceHolderPageDescription	Description of the current page
PlaceHolderSearchArea	Section of the page for the search controls
PlaceHolderGlobalNavigation	Breadcrumb control on the page
PlaceHolderTitleBreadcrumb	Breadcrumb text for the breadcrumb control
PlaceHolderGlobalNavigationSiteMap	List of subsites and sibling sites in the global navigation on the page
PlaceHolderTopNavBar	Container used to hold the top navigation bar
PlaceHolderHorizontalNav	Navigation menu that is inside the top navigation bar
PlaceHolderLeftNavBarDataSource	Placement of the data source used to populate the left navigation bar
PlaceHolderCalendarNavigator	Date picker used when a calendar is visible on the page
PlaceHolderLeftNavBarTop	The top section of the left navigation bar
PlaceHolderLeftNavBar	The Quick Launch bar
PlaceHolderLeftActions	Additional objects above the Quick Launch bar
PlaceHolderMain	The main content of the page
PlaceHolderFormDigest	The container where the page's Form Digest control is stored

continues

(continued)

CONTENT PLACEHOLDER	DESCRIPTION
PlaceHolderUtilityContent	Additional content at the bottom of the page. This is outside of the `form` tag.
PlaceHolderTitleAreaClass	The class for the title area. This is now in the `head` tag. Any customizations that add a Web Part zone in a content tag to this placeholder will cause an error on the page.

The following list also comes from the same MSDN article. This list shows content placeholders that are unused in SharePoint 2010, but are required for backwards compatibility when Visual Upgrade is used to show SharePoint 2007 visuals:

➤ PlaceHolderPageImage

➤ PlaceHolderTitleLeftBorder

➤ PlaceHolderMiniConsole

➤ PlaceHolderTitleRightMargin

➤ PlaceHolderTitleAreaSeparator

➤ PlaceHolderNavSpacer

➤ PlaceHolderLeftNavBarBorder

➤ PlaceHolderBodyLeftBorder

➤ PlaceHolderBodyRightMargin

With all these required content placeholders, you are likely wondering how you remove areas of functionality that aren't required for a specific branding project. Rather than delete required placeholders, you can hide them on the master page. The Starter master page from Microsoft utilizes CSS to hide the content placeholders, but a much better option is to put them in an `<asp:Panel>` whose visibility is set to `false`. The difference here is a subtle one; both methods hide the placeholders from users who are browsing the SharePoint site, but the latter method actually removes all the HTML that would be generated so that the page loads quicker in the user's browser. Anything placed in a nonvisible panel will be omitted from the HTML source of the SharePoint site.

The following code shows an example of a nonvisible panel hiding content placeholders:

```
<asp:Panel visible="false" runat="server">
 <asp:ContentPlaceHolder ID="PlaceHolderNavSpacer" runat="server"/>
 <asp:ContentPlaceHolder id="PlaceHolderLeftNavBarBorder" runat="server"/>
</asp:Panel>
```

In this example, the `PlaceHolderNavSpacer` and `PlaceHolderLeftNavBarBorder` will be omitted from the HTML and thus hidden from all users browsing pages that use this master page.

Master Pages and Application Pages

A major limitation to custom master pages in SharePoint 2007 has been rectified in SharePoint 2010. In SharePoint 2007, master pages did not apply any formatting or styling to application pages, which included the Site Settings, system pages, and several other key locations, all of which can be identified with /_layouts in the URL. These pages did not receive the custom master page because they were hard-wired to always use something known as application.master, which was shared across all sites on the farm. As a result, heavily branded sites often had a few rogue pages that stuck out like sore thumbs by showing the default yellow and blue look and feel.

In SharePoint 2010, custom master pages can apply to almost all pages on a SharePoint site, including the application pages. Note that in some cases a custom master page doesn't apply by default — for example, the error pages use a specific simple master page to ensure that you can always read the error page even if there is a major problem with your custom master page. You will learn more about applying master pages throughout a SharePoint site later in this chapter.

Page Layouts and SharePoint Master Pages

The introduction of page layouts to SharePoint Server publishing sites also affects SharePoint master pages. Page layouts can be thought of as templates for creating specially formatted content pages. You will learn a lot more about page layouts in the next chapter, but for now it's important to understand that you can use page layouts to create multiple types of pages, from article pages to welcome (home) pages. Page layouts control the inner layout of a page in SharePoint, whereas master pages control the outer layout. Figure 8-3 shows the relationship between a master page and a page layout when rendered in SharePoint.

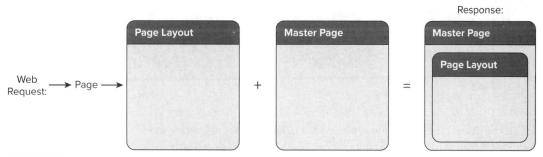

FIGURE 8-3

When creating custom master pages, you need to decide where your master page design ends and your pages or page layouts begin. The headers, navigation, and footers usually reside in the master page, but you are free to alter this arrangement if your design warrants it. Whether you use the master page or the page layout typically hinges on whether the page content will always be arranged in a uniform way. If so, the layout might be better suited for the master page. Conversely, if the arrangement of content is not the same on every page, the page layout may be more appropriate; otherwise, you will have to create more than one master page.

Figure 8-4 illustrates which areas of a custom branded SharePoint page are typically defined by the master page versus the page layout. Keep in mind that this figure is a simplified view; because content placeholders can be overridden throughout the master page, more areas of the layout can actually be controlled by the page layout. You can see that the master page reflects the outer shell of a design, which typically represents global elements for the entire site or site collection, whereas the page layout reflects how the inner content of a design is displayed, which typically represents dynamic, or changing, page content.

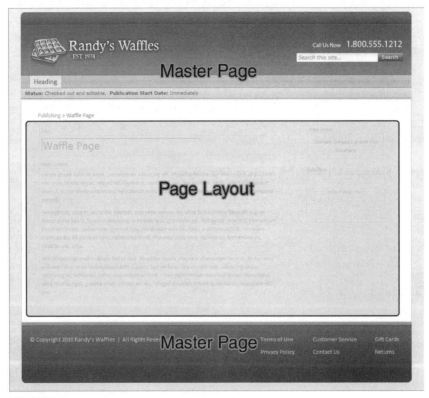

FIGURE 8-4

The choice between using a master page or a page layout often comes into play with public-facing Internet sites. Often, the home page for these sites looks drastically different from the subpages. How do you handle a situation like this, where the branding is so different in two areas of the same website? Sometimes the first solution that comes to mind is to just create a separate master page for both layouts. In practice, though, the best solution is to leverage page layouts whenever possible to create a different look and feel for the home page while still keeping the master page unified across all pages. This reduces the amount of maintenance that is needed because page layouts typically contain *much* less code than master pages.

The Master Page Gallery

While master pages in ASP.NET can be located anywhere within the website folder, both master pages and page layouts in SharePoint live inside of the Master Page Gallery. This is where you can find the out-of-the-box master pages, and where you should add any custom master pages that you want to apply to your SharePoint site. You can view the Master Page Gallery from either the SharePoint web interface or from SharePoint Designer. From the web interface, click Site Actions ➪ Site Settings, and under Galleries click Master pages and page layouts. Generally speaking, anything listed here with an extension of .master is a master page.

There are two ways to access the Master Page Gallery from SharePoint Designer 2010. One way is to follow these steps:

1. Open SharePoint Designer 2010 and load a SharePoint 2010 site.

2. From the Site Objects menu on the left, click Master Pages.

    This displays a filtered view of the Master Page Gallery that shows only valid SharePoint 2010 master pages.

Alternatively, you can access the Master Page Gallery from SharePoint Designer 2010 as follows:

1. Open SharePoint Designer 2010 and load a SharePoint 2010 site.

2. From the Site Objects menu on the left, click the small pushpin icon to the right of All Files. This shows a more advanced view of the SharePoint site collection.

3. From here, expand _catalogs ➪ masterpage (Master Page Gallery).

    Using this method provides a more realistic view of the Master Page Gallery, one that includes all the master pages as well as any page layouts.

Out-of-the-Box Master Pages

Chapter 1 provided a brief overview of some of the more important master pages that are available out-of-the-box in SharePoint 2010, but it's worth reintroducing them here. Note that SharePoint includes more master pages than those described here, but the others are specialized master pages that cannot be selected and applied to SharePoint by default. The first two master pages below are the most commonly used; the second two are used more for special circumstances, as described:

➤   v4.master — This is the default master page that is used for much of SharePoint 2010.

➤   nightandday.master — This master page is available only in SharePoint Server 2010 publishing sites. Much like the Blueband master page in SharePoint 2007, this master page is more appropriate for public-facing Internet sites.

➤   default.master — This master page is used only when a SharePoint 2007 site is being upgraded to 2010. It looks virtually identical to the default master page in SharePoint 2007. Note that this master page can be used only when SharePoint 2010 is in SharePoint 2007 mode via Visual Upgrade.

➤   minimal.master — This master page is used by SharePoint for sites that have their own navigation or that need extra space (such as dedicated application pages or the Search Center). Unlike the concept of minimal master pages in SharePoint 2007, this master page is *not* intended to be the starting point for general branding, as it is missing several common SharePoint controls. You would want to start from this master page only if you needed to apply custom branding to SharePoint sites that are already using the minimal.master, like the Search Center.

Applying Master Pages in SharePoint

Besides using custom code, there are two primary ways to apply master pages in SharePoint 2010: using the web interface in SharePoint Server publishing sites and using SharePoint Designer 2010.

Using SharePoint Server Publishing to Apply Master Pages

If you have a SharePoint Server publishing site, the web interface provides a very easy method for applying master pages. Note that with publishing enabled on the root site collection, the menus will be available for applying master pages throughout the site collection, including subsites that do not have publishing enabled. To change the master pages from the web interface, click Site Actions ➪ Site Settings, and then under Look and Feel, click Master page. Figure 8-5 shows the Site Master Page Settings page.

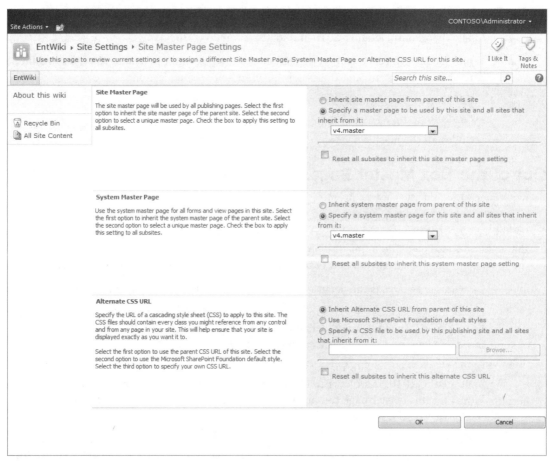

FIGURE 8-5

From this page you can change both the Site and System Master Pages, and you can also apply these selections to any subsites below the current site. Remember that from an underlying code perspective, the Site Master Page is ~masterurl/custom.master and the System Master Page is ~masterurl/default.master. In addition, as discussed earlier in the chapter, remember that the Site Master Page is used primarily by publishing pages, whereas the System Master Page is used throughout SharePoint, including non-publishing pages and the application pages, such as Site Settings.

Using SharePoint Designer 2010 to Apply Master Pages

If you don't have SharePoint Server or don't have publishing enabled, the next easiest option for applying master pages is to use SharePoint Designer 2010. To apply master pages from SharePoint Designer 2010, follow these steps:

1. Open SharePoint Designer 2010 and load a SharePoint 2010 site.

2. From the Site Objects menu on the left, click Master Pages.

3. In the main area of SharePoint Designer, click next to the name of a master page.

4. From the ribbon, in the Actions group you can click either Set as Default or Set as Custom. These options correspond to the System and Site Master Pages, respectively. If the master page is currently set as either of these options, the corresponding icon will be grayed out in the ribbon.

After setting the master page as either Default or Custom, you can browse back to your SharePoint site and see that the master page has changed. Note that in SharePoint Designer, you can also right-click the master page name and select either Set as Default Master Page or Set as Custom Master Page.

CREATING CUSTOM MASTER PAGES

When creating your own custom master pages, one of the biggest decisions you need to make is what SharePoint functionality you will include in your master page and how you will arrange it on the page. In Chapter 3, you learned how to plan for this functionality by reviewing the descriptions of the major functional areas in SharePoint 2010. Figure 8-6 highlights this functionality. (Refer to Chapter 3 for a refresher on each of these areas in SharePoint.)

In some cases this functionality is represented with content placeholders, and in other cases the functionality is included in a control. To learn more about how controls are used in master pages, you can explore the Starter master page discussed in the next section.

Because all this functionality is provided out-of-the-box, it's often impractical to start a new SharePoint master page from scratch. In reality, most custom SharePoint master pages are based on either one of the out-of-the-box master pages (as described in Chapter 5, "Simple Branding") or one of the Starter master pages that are made available to the SharePoint community. Typically, you would want to start with one of the out-of-the box master pages only if your desired design was similar to the existing out-of-the-box look and feel.

FIGURE 8-6

Using a Starter Master Page

As discussed earlier, in SharePoint 2007 Starter master pages were referred to as minimal master pages. The SharePoint community has adopted the new name of Starter master page because in SharePoint 2010 Microsoft already includes a master page named `minimal.master` that is intended for use sites like the Search Center.

Starter master pages are typically better commented than the out-of-the-box master pages, and have minimal styling and layout. However, they contain all the required content placeholders and have some of the functional SharePoint controls already loaded for easy use.

As of this writing, the following are two popular choices for **Starter** master pages in SharePoint 2010. You will recognize the first page from the "SharePoint Master Page Structure" section earlier in this chapter.

➤ **Microsoft's Starter master page** (`http://code.msdn.microsoft.com/odcSP14StarterMaster`) — This Starter master page was built for SharePoint Foundation 2010 but it will also work in SharePoint Server 2010. It is extremely minimal, with most of the elements hidden, and virtually no page formatting. For example, by default this master page does not even display the Site Actions button. Microsoft's Starter master page is a good beginning point for learning about SharePoint 2010 master pages.

➤ **My own Starter master pages** (http://startermasterpages.codeplex.com) — I have created a few Starter master pages: one for SharePoint Foundation 2010, one for SharePoint Server 2010 publishing sites, and some other minor iterations for specific cases. They are not as Spartan as Microsoft's Starter master page, and most of the common SharePoint functional controls are displayed.

A version of my Starter master page is included with the downloads for this chapter and is used for the rest of this chapter's examples. The following steps detail how to create a new custom master page based on a Starter master page in a SharePoint Server 2010 publishing site. This custom master page will be used for an example later in the chapter.

1. Open SharePoint Designer 2010 and load a SharePoint Server 2010 site.

2. From the Site Objects menu on the left, click Master Pages.

3. Click Blank Master Page from the ribbon and name it Waffles.master.

4. Click Waffles.master and then click Edit File from the ribbon. A prompt will ask if you want to check it out. Click Yes.

5. Download the Starter master page from the chapter downloads to your local computer and open the file in the text editor of your choice.

6. Copy the contents of StarterPublishing.master to the clipboard and switch to SharePoint Designer 2010. Then paste over the contents of Waffles.master, replacing the basic master page content that was included in Waffles.master.

7. Save the master page by pressing Ctrl+S.

8. Right-click Waffles.master in SharePoint Designer and select Check In. Then select Publish a Major Version. SharePoint will warn that "This document requires content approval. Do you want to view or modify its approval status?" Click Yes, and a browser window is opened to the My submissions page. From here, the files are grouped by their Approval Status.

9. Expand the Approval Status: Pending group and click the arrow that appears next to Waffles and select Approve/Reject. From the next screen, click Approved and OK. This will enable other users to see the changes.

10. From the browser, click Site Actions ➪ Site Settings. Under the Look and Feel section, click Master page.

11. Select Waffles.master for both the Site Master Page and System Master Page. Ensure that Alternate CSS URL is set to "Use Microsoft SharePoint Foundation default styles," and then click OK.

This will apply the new master page throughout the site, even to the Site Settings pages. Figure 8-7 shows the SharePoint site with the Starter master page applied. Notice that it contains very little styling or formatting.

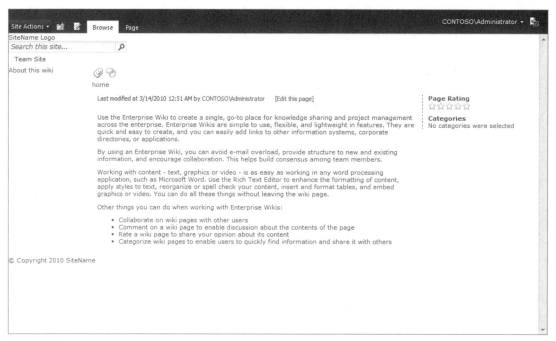

FIGURE 8-7

Next Steps

The Starter master page is like a blank canvas. By adding HTML for layout and CSS for styling, you can create almost any look. You can paste HTML into the Starter master page surrounding the various pieces of SharePoint functionality to arrange them as desired; and you can utilize the tools you learned about in Chapters 5 and 7 to work with the vast amounts of CSS used in SharePoint.

One common method for creating complex SharePoint branding is to first create the design using just HTML and CSS, and test it to ensure that everything looks right. By testing a design in HTML before applying it in SharePoint, you can quickly make a lot of design decisions without being slowed down by SharePoint check-ins and check-outs. From there, the HTML and CSS can be moved directly into the master page to apply layout and styling. After all the HTML and CSS is added, finishing the design is just a matter of tweaking the CSS to ensure that all the SharePoint-specific styling matches the rest of the design.

Later in the chapter you will use this process to make use of the HTML and CSS branding that was created in Chapter 3, "Planning for Branding," by implementing it in SharePoint using a Starter master page.

Upgrading SharePoint 2007 Master Pages

So far, you have learned about creating a new SharePoint 2010 master page; but what if you already have an existing branded SharePoint 2007 master page? Can you use these files with SharePoint 2010?

The answer is certainly yes, but you have a couple of options when using a SharePoint 2007 master page with SharePoint 2010. SharePoint 2007 master pages can be used immediately as-is if a SharePoint 2010 site is using Visual Upgrade to stay in SharePoint 2007 mode. However, because Visual Upgrade is meant to only be a temporary solution, SharePoint 2007 master pages should eventually be upgraded to work directly with the SharePoint 2010 visuals.

 For more information on the upgrading process, check out the MSDN article "Upgrading an Existing Master Page to the SharePoint Foundation Master Page," at `http://msdn.microsoft.com/en-us/library/ee539981.aspx.`

COMMON CHALLENGES FOR CUSTOM MASTER PAGES

When creating your own master pages for use in SharePoint 2010, some common obstacles often present themselves. The following sections describe some of these challenges and how you can work with them in SharePoint.

Turning on Full Error Messages

One of the first things you will realize when working on your custom master page is that when you make a mistake, SharePoint's default error messages are rather unhelpful. As mentioned earlier, if you omit one of the required content placeholders and browse a site that uses your master page, SharePoint will reply with simply "An unexpected error has occurred." The first time this happens, it's hard not to respond with some choice curse words and give up completely on SharePoint, but don't throw in the towel yet. SharePoint can actually return descriptive error messages, but they are turned off by default for security reasons. If you are working in a development environment, though, it's imperative to enable these full error messages.

Here are the steps for turning on the full error messages:

1. Log in to the physical SharePoint Server machine and navigate to the directory that holds your SharePoint website. It will most likely be located at `C:\inetpub\wwwroot\wss\VirtualDirectories\` and will be in a subdirectory with the port number of your SharePoint site. If you have trouble finding it, you can open IIS7 and in the Sites folder, right-click your SharePoint site, and then select Explore. This will take you directly to the directory that holds your SharePoint website.

2. Locate the file named `web.config` and open it for editing in Notepad.

3. Press Ctrl+F and find the line of code that contains the word "callstack." You will find a line that looks like this:

```
<SafeMode MaxControls="200" CallStack="false" DirectFileDependencies="10"
    TotalFileDependencies="50" AllowPageLevelTrace="false">
```

Change both the `CallStack` and `AllowPageLevelTrace` attributes from `false` to `true`.

4. Press Ctrl+F again and this time search for the word "errors." You will find a line that looks like this:

```
<customErrors mode="On" />
```

Change the mode from `On` to `Off`. This tells IIS not to show its customary basic error messages and to instead display the raw detailed error messages.

5. Save and close `web.config`. Note that this change will cause IIS to restart the web application in which your SharePoint site resides. Be careful when making edits to this file in production or shared development environments.

With these changes in place, browsing a page with an error will now reveal the complete error message.

Applying Custom CSS

As mentioned in Chapter 7, overriding the out-of-the-box SharePoint CSS is key to branding SharePoint sites. In previous versions of SharePoint, ensuring that your custom CSS was applied last (thus ensuring that it would override the out-of-the-box CSS) was a difficult process. In SharePoint 2010 Microsoft has added the `After` property to `<SharePoint:CssRegistration>` to force custom CSS to always load after a specific CSS file, such as the out-of-the-box `corev4.css`. Here is an example of how to apply custom CSS in a SharePoint 2010 master page:

```
<SharePoint:CssRegistration name="/Style Library/customstyle.css"
    After="corev4.css" runat="server"/>
```

The `After` property requires a more complete path to load CSS after files that are not the out-of-the-box CSS. The following code shows how to ensure that one custom CSS file is applied after another. Notice that the second one uses a more complete path for the `After` property because it is loading after a custom CSS file:

```
<SharePoint:CssRegistration name="/Style Library/customstyle.css"
    After="corev4.css" runat="server"/>

<SharePoint:CssRegistration name="/Style Library/secondfile.css"
    After="/Style Library/customstyle.css" runat="server"/>
```

SharePoint provides a token for making relative URL references for files such as CSS, known as `$SPUrl`*. You can use the token to create a reference to the root of either a site or a site collection by using either* `$SPUrl:~site` *or* `$SPUrl:~sitecollection`*, respectively. The following snippet shows* `$SPUrl` *being used in a* `CssRegistration`*:*

```
<SharePoint:CssRegistration name="<% $SPUrl:~sitecollection/
Style Library/
customstyle.css %>" After="corev4.css" runat="server"/>
```

Although this can be useful when deploying branding to a site collection that is not at the web application root, it does have a downside — namely, SharePoint Designer's Design view has trouble displaying some assets that are loaded via this method. Therefore, this chapter avoids using `$SPUrl` *in the examples.*

Working with the Ribbon

In SharePoint 2010 the ribbon is a prominent feature that takes up a large portion of the overall layout. While this may be intimidating from a code perspective, it's actually fairly easy to add the ribbon to a custom master page. The Starter master page includes a ribbon, but if you want to add the ribbon to your own master page, simply copy and paste the ribbon code from the default `v4.master`. The ribbon code is about 300 lines and begins with `<div id="s4-ribbonrow">` and ends with the two closing `</div>` tags that appear right before `<div id="s4-workspace">`. Typically, the default ribbon code should be a good starting point for most branding projects.

By default, the out-of-the-box master pages utilize the ribbon positioning system to cause the ribbon to "stick" to the top of the page no matter how much content has been scrolled. This feature actually involves turning off all the normal automatic browser scrolling functionality and then using JavaScript to analyze the current page size and location to reapply a custom scrolling method to the browser. This is why the out-of-the-box SharePoint user interface has a scroll bar located on the right just under the ribbon.

While this feature is very useful, it can often complicate the branding process for SharePoint 2010. The following sections discuss how to handle these complications.

Handling Fixed-Width Designs

One particularly surprising aspect of the ribbon positioning system is that it sets the height and width of the scrollable area automatically based on the height and width of the browser window. The out-of-the-box master pages all utilize 100% of the browser width for the design of the page. If you are building custom branding that is going to have a fixed-width design, like the currently popular 960-pixel-width grid design (`http://960.gs`), you will need to add a special CSS class to the workspace element of the master page. The workspace element is typically `<div ID="s4-workspace">` by default in SharePoint 2010. For a fixed-width design, you need to ensure that the element is changed to `<div ID="s4-workspace" class="s4-nosetwidth">`.

Handling the Ribbon for Anonymous Users

A common request with public-facing SharePoint 2010 designs is hiding the ribbon so that it takes up no space and is completely hidden to anonymous users. The SharePoint community has pioneered several methods for hiding the ribbon for anonymous users. One method involves using `<Sharepoint:SPSecurityTrimmedControl>` to trim the ribbon to show only for certain security roles. This method has the upside of completely removing the ribbon code from the HTML of the page; the downside is that you have to decide which security role should be required to see the ribbon. This can be tricky because the ribbon is needed in different scenarios that involve many different roles.

An easier method for hiding the ribbon is to use `<asp:LoginView>` to hide the ribbon with CSS for anonymous users. Hiding the ribbon has one "gotcha" in that it also causes the Sign In link to be hidden. Therefore, you need to add an HTML link to `/_layouts/authenticate.aspx`, which is the default page that allows anonymous users to log in. The following code snippet shows a sample `<asp:LoginView>` for hiding the ribbon:

```
<asp:LoginView id="LoginView" runat="server">
 <AnonymousTemplate>
```

```
<a href="/_layouts/authenticate.aspx">User Login</a>

<style type="text/css">
 body #s4-ribbonrow {
   display: none;
 }
</style>
</AnonymousTemplate>
</asp:LoginView>
```

Note that you can also add a `<LoggedInTemplate>` to introduce any specific code that should run only for users who are authenticated.

 If your SharePoint site is not currently set up to allow anonymous users, you can configure it to allow them by following the instructions in this blog post:

> http://blog.drisgill.com/2009/11/sp2010-branding-tip-9-turn-on-anonymous.html.

Turning Off the Ribbon Positioning System

Because of the way the ribbon positioning system uses JavaScript to control scrolling, sometimes a very complex CSS design can cause problems with the system. A common example is some of the methods that are used to "stick" a footer to the bottom of page content with just CSS. Sometimes these methods cause SharePoint to calculate the page height incorrectly. In these instances, you have two options: either change your CSS code or turn off the ribbon positioning system. By turning off the ribbon positioning system, you are telling SharePoint to let the ribbon scroll off the page when long pages are scrolled. Instead of having SharePoint manage scrolling, you let the browser do its standard scrolling behavior.

To make this change in a typical SharePoint 2010 master page like `v4.master`, follow these steps:

1. Remove or override the CSS that hides the out-of-the-box `body` overflow:

```
body { overflow:hidden; }
```

You can override this with the following:

```
body.v4master { overflow:auto; }
```

2. Remove `scroll="no"` from the `<body>` tag.

3. Remove `ID="s4-workspace"` from the `<div>` tag that surrounds the page content (located directly below the ribbon code in the master page). Alternatively, you can remove the entire `<div>` tag and its corresponding `</div>` if you prefer.

4. Save and Check-In and Approve the master page, and you will have a page that scrolls normally.

Working with Application Pages

Earlier you learned about how master pages apply to most pages in SharePoint 2010, including the application pages like Site Settings. One common "gotcha" with this behavior is that these pages have an extra level of error handling applied to them. Many simple errors, such as those that occur when you omit a required content placeholder, are not displayed; instead, SharePoint actually reverts to displaying the default v4.master page. This can be frustrating when you are creating your own custom master page because without any type of message, it's difficult to determine the source of a problem. If you run into this, your best bet is to make minor changes to your master page until it starts applying to these pages again. Often the problem lies with missing content placeholders, so that should be the first thing to check. Another common solution is to compare your custom master page with one that is known to work, like v4.master or a Starter master page.

Hiding Left Navigation

Another issue that arises when custom master pages are applied to the application pages can be seen when you want to hide all left navigation from your custom branding. The issue here is that many of the application pages, such as the People and Groups Site Settings page, require the Quick Launch bar for critical menu items. Therefore, how can you hide the left navigation in one part of the site and show it another using the exact same master page? One solution is to use content placeholders to your advantage. Because the left navigation lives inside a content placeholder that is overridden by the content pages that require special menus, you can remove the default menu controls that are typically applied. In addition, because the left and main areas of the page are controlled by CSS, some embedded CSS needs to be changed for these default styles.

The following example shows how you can hide the left navigation in either the default v4.master page or the Starter master page from this chapter:

1. Remove all the existing content and controls that are located inside of the PlaceHolderLeftNavBar content placeholder in the master page.

2. Add the following highlighted embedded CSS:

```
<asp:ContentPlaceHolder id="PlaceHolderLeftNavBar" runat="server">
 <style type="text/css">
  #s4-leftpanel {
   display: none;
  }
  .s4-ca {
   margin-left:0px;
  }
 </style>
</asp:ContentPlaceHolder>
```

Once this change is in place and the master page is saved and published, the default behavior of the PlaceHolderLeftNavBar content placeholder will be to hide the left navigation on any page that doesn't specifically override it. The reason this works is because the s4-leftpanel <div> that holds the left navigation is hidden, and the s4-ca <div> that holds the main page content has its margin changed to not add space for the left navigation anymore.

Turning Off Master Pages Applying to Application Pages

There may be times when you just don't want your custom branding to apply to the application pages — for example, if you have an extremely unique look and feel for your home page. You have two options for handling this situation. One, you can always not apply your custom master page to SharePoint as the System Master Page. This prevents the application pages from showing the custom branding, but it also prevents the branding from showing on any nonpublishing page too. The other way to stop master pages from applying to application pages is to just turn off the feature completely from Central Administration, as follows:

1. Open Central Administration on the SharePoint server.

2. Under Application Management, click Manage web applications.

3. Select the desired web application from the list, and then from the ribbon, click General Settings (see Figure 8-8).

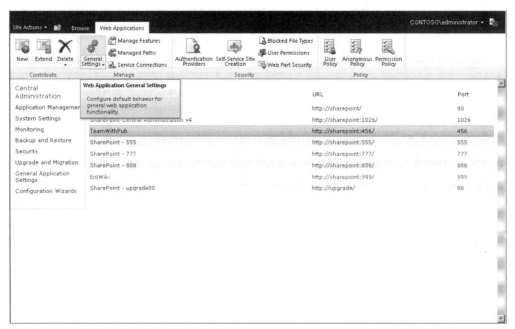

FIGURE 8-8

4. In the dialog that appears, scroll down to Master Page Setting for Application _Layouts Pages and select No (see Figure 8-9).

5. Scroll to the bottom of the dialog and click OK.

Now custom master pages for this entire web application will not apply to the application pages. This is the same way master pages behaved in SharePoint 2007.

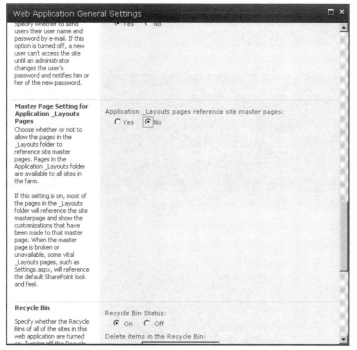

FIGURE 8-9

Handling Dialogs and Custom Branding

You may have noticed while working with SharePoint 2010 that many page activities don't actually open a new page but rather load in dialogs. These allow related menus and content to be loaded into a floating frame, which is essentially a modal window. Modal windows are secondary windows that gain focus over the main window; they must be interacted with or canceled before continuing. Dialog boxes in SharePoint 2010 can be dragged around within the browser window and even maximized to the full browser window size.

Although dialogs are certainly helpful, they present a unique challenge in the context of SharePoint branding because when a custom master page is applied as the System Master Page, by default, dialogs in SharePoint 2010 display all the master page branding, including logos, footers, and navigation. Figure 8-10 shows a dialog that is loading all the branding from a custom System Master Page.

Notice that the dialog doesn't look very good with all this branding inside of it. One option for handling this would be to not apply your custom master page as the System Master Page. But what can you do if you want your master page to show everywhere by setting it as the System Master Page but you don't want the branding to show in dialogs? Fortunately, Microsoft has provided a simple way to hide branding from dialogs. Anything that shouldn't show in a dialog can have a specific CSS class, s4-notdlg, added to its HTML element, and SharePoint will simply ignore that element only when showing dialogs. For example, if you want to hide a footer <div> from dialogs, you would add the special CSS class as follows:

```
<div class="customFooter s4-notdlg">Copyright 2010 Randy's Waffles</div>
```

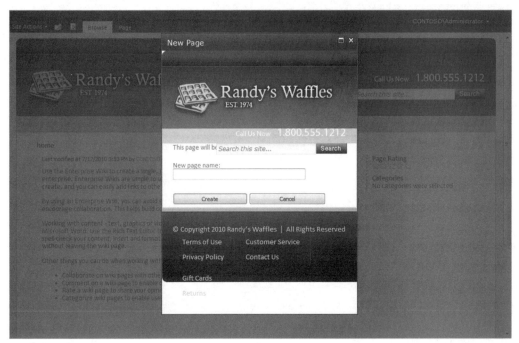

FIGURE 8-10

Because SharePoint dialogs will skip anything with the class of s4-notdlg, this <div> will not show in dialogs. Another important thing to consider when working with dialogs is that they may also be affected by styling applied to elements that you don't want to hide. This frequently happens when you apply padding, margins, or background colors to the main content <div>. To fix this, you may need to add some custom CSS that overrides this behavior only inside of the dialogs. In the following example, the left margin of the customBody <div> is being expanded to 120 pixels:

```
.customBody {
margin-left: 120px;
}
```

You wouldn't want this margin to apply to the dialogs as well. To override this, you would need to add CSS to override the customBody <div> only when it is inside of the ms-dialog element. The !important declaration is helpful for ensuring that the dialog specific CSS always takes precedent over anything else. The following code shows the dialog-specific CSS:

```
.ms-dialog .customBody {
margin-left:0 !important;
}
```

Handling Legacy Browsers

If you recall from Chapter 2, browser support in SharePoint 2010 has been greatly improved over SharePoint 2007; but for better or for worse, IE6 is not supported from a content-authoring perspective. While you could create a specific master page that would work for anonymous IE6 users, you would need a completely different master page for content authors. Therefore, it's generally not practical to create SharePoint 2010 master pages that support IE6. The good news is that Microsoft has provided a way to provide a simple message to users with legacy unsupported browsers like IE6:

```
<SharePoint:WarnOnUnsupportedBrowsers runat="server"/>
```

You can find the preceding line at the bottom of the out-of-the-box master pages as well as the Starter master page used in this book. Figure 8-11 shows the message as it appears in IE6.

If you want to turn off the message for all users, you can simply find the control at the very bottom of the master page and remove it.

FIGURE 8-11

Hiding the Name.dll ActiveX Control

If you are working on a public-facing Internet site, you should be aware that SharePoint may show a particularly annoying message at the top of Internet Explorer when users don't have the SharePoint Server added to their trusted sites list. The message asks the user to run the Name ActiveX Control add-on (see Figure 8-12).

> This website wants to run the following add-on: 'Name ActiveX Control' from 'Microsoft Corporation'. If you trust the website and the add-on and want to allow it to run, click here... ✕

FIGURE 8-12

This control enables presence information to be displayed for authenticated users in SharePoint, and typically shows their availability in external Instant Messaging programs from inside SharePoint. Because anonymous users will not be using this control, it's generally bad form to show this message to them. It's especially bad because the name of the ActiveX control and the message displayed might not be understandable to users who aren't familiar with SharePoint.

In SharePoint 2010 the message can be turned off from Central Administration ⇨ Manage Web Applications ⇨ General Settings. Simply set Enable the Person Names Smart Tag and Online Status for Members to No. This will turn off the presence information and remove the ActiveX message for the entire web application.

If you want to be 100% certain that the message doesn't show in a production environment and you are at the mercy of server administrators who may or may not deactivate the feature, you can still disable the message and functionality from a custom master page. Simply add the following code to your master page:

```
<script type="text/javascript">
 function ProcessImn(){}
 function ProcessImnMarkers(){}
</script>
```

This JavaScript code overrides the functions in SharePoint that cause this ActiveX message. The Starter master page included with this chapter already has this code applied to it. If your SharePoint project requires the presence information, you should remove these lines from your custom master page.

Showing a Favicon

Favicons are the little shortcut icons that appear in most modern browsers next to bookmarks, as well as in the address bar next to the site's URL and on browser tabs. SharePoint 2010 makes it very easy to add a favicon to custom master pages using the following code:

```
<SharePoint:SPShortcutIcon runat="server" IconUrl="/Style Library/Waffles/favicon.ico"/>
```

Using this line, the `IconUrl` should point to a valid favicon file located on the SharePoint site. If you need help creating a favicon, a free Photoshop plug-in is available from Telegraphics (`www.telegraphics.com.au/sw/`), and many websites enable you to generate favicons, without cost, directly from a web browser.

 When testing favicons, particularly with Internet Explorer, a lot of caching can get in the way of seeing actual results. If you are having trouble seeing a new favicon and you are certain that the code and the image are set up correctly, it may help to clear your browser cache, make a new bookmark, or even close and reopen the browser.

Working with Web Parts

Web Parts certainly provide a lot of flexibility for building a SharePoint site, but sometimes you want to display certain Web Parts across all site pages. SharePoint does not allow you to enter Web Part zones on master pages, and Web Parts that are outside of Web Part zones will not be editable by content authors when they put the page in edit mode. In order to enable content authors to con-figure or edit Web Parts, you must place them in Web Part zones on content pages or page layouts.

Although there is no way to get around this problem, there is one trick that can make Web Part zones appear to be located outside of the main content placeholder in the master page. As you learned earlier, content placeholders in master pages can be overridden by content on content pages and page layouts. For example, if you needed a Web Part zone to be located in the header portion of all pages, you could either create a new content placeholder or use an existing one, and move it to the header portion of the master page. Then, any content page or page layout could place a Web Part zone into the corresponding content control, thus effectively making the Web Parts in the zone appear to be located in the header part of the master page.

Working with Navigation

SharePoint navigation is covered in detail in Chapter 6, but recall that a few common navigation behaviors are controlled from the master page. Specifically, the `AspMenu` tag controls important features, such as which data source is used, whether the control uses simple rendering, whether the navigation is horizontal or vertical, and the number of levels of static and dynamic navigation that will show. Chapter 6 also covers the difference between simple rendered navigation and the old way that navigation was rendered in SharePoint 2007. Be sure to review Chapter 6 before implementing custom branded navigation in SharePoint 2010.

Adding a Custom Logo

You have a few options for adding a custom logo to a SharePoint master page. The two most obvious options are to set one with either an HTML `image` tag or a CSS background. Another very useful way of setting a custom logo for SharePoint is to use the `<SharePoint:SiteLogoImage>` control. This control enables you to set a default image for the master page that can be overridden by the SharePoint web interface from the Title, description, and icon Site Settings page. The following code sets the default logo image to `/Style Library/sitename/logo.png` and sets the link URL to the top level of the site collection:

```
<SharePoint:SPLinkButton runat="server" NavigateUrl="~sitecollection/">
 <SharePoint:SiteLogoImage  LogoImageUrl="/Style Library/sitename/logo.png"
runat="server"/>
</SharePoint:SPLinkButton>
```

This logo can then be overridden by clicking Site Actions ➪ Site Settings ➪ Title, description, and icon, and then adding a URL logo, which could be an image in the Style Library or anywhere else, and clicking OK. This method enables site owners to apply their own logo if they want, which could be a good thing or a bad thing depending on how tightly you want to control the way your corporate logo is shown throughout the site.

Adding Traditional Breadcrumbs

SharePoint 2010 includes a new style of breadcrumb navigation in the default user interface. In addition to the pop-out hierarchical global navigation at the top of the ribbon (see Figure 8-13), the header also provides a location indicator, which is a combination of the site title and the current page's title (see Figure 8-14).

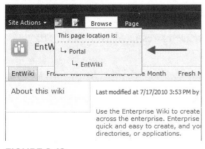

FIGURE 8-13

FIGURE 8-14

Although these are very useful, sometimes on public-facing Internet sites you may want to use a more traditional type of breadcrumb. Fortunately, you can use the old breadcrumb control from

SharePoint 2007. This can be added to either a custom master page or a custom page layout, depending on where you want the breadcrumb to show on the page:

```
<asp:SiteMapPath runat="server"/>
```

Figure 8-15 shows the more traditional breadcrumb being used on a SharePoint site.

FIGURE 8-15

Search Centers and Minimal.Master

There are three site templates to choose from when creating search sites in SharePoint 2010:

➤ Enterprise Search Center

➤ Basic Search Center

➤ FAST Search Center

Unlike most other sites in SharePoint 2010, these sites do not have `v4.master` or even `nightandday` `.master` applied to them; instead, they have `minimal.master` applied to them. If you have a custom master page that is based on `v4.master`, `nightandday.master`, or even one of the typical starter master pages and apply it to one of these search centers sites, you notice that the search center doesn't work properly. This is because the page layouts and pages that are created by default for these search center sites are hard coded specifically to work best with the way `minimal.master` is coded. SharePoint Server publishing sites are even more problematic because master pages can be applied to a parent site and then applied to all subsites below it, thus changing the search center from the default `minimal.master` to one that doesn't work. Sometimes when this happens, the problem can go unnoticed by the person who applied the master page. If it happens on your site, there's no need to panic because you can just reset the Site Master Page to `minimal.master`, using either the Master page Site Settings page or by right clicking `minimal.master` in SharePoint Designer and setting it as the Default Master Page.

If the search center sites are set up to work only with `minimal.master`, how can you make sure your custom branding is applied to them? Unfortunately, the answer is that you need to create a specific version of your custom branded master page that is based on the out-of-the-box `minimal.master`. The biggest difference between the typical SharePoint 2010 master pages and `minimal.master` is related to how the `PlaceHolderTitleBreadcrumb` content placeholder is used. In a typical SharePoint 2010 master page, the `PlaceHolderTitleBreadcrumb` is used to hold the pop-out breadcrumb menu at the top of the page. Alternatively, `minimal.master` uses `PlaceHolderTitleBreadcrumb` to hold parts of the main body content, including the search box that allows users to enter search terms. If you create a special master page for just the search center sites and base it on `minimal.master`, you can apply it to just search center sites while keeping your normal custom master page applied everywhere else.

Working with Mobile Devices

SharePoint has a special view that it can display for mobile devices. The mobile view has very minimal formatting and is focused on delivering information to small screen devices. In SharePoint 2007, you activated the mobile view for a site by navigating to the main URL and appending `/m` to the end. SharePoint 2010 handles this a little differently. First, the URL for the mobile view has changed; instead of adding `/m`, you have to add `?Mobile=1`. If you forget it, you can find this mobile view URL for any site by clicking Site Actions ➪ Site Settings. On the right side of the page, Site Information shows both the standard site URL and the mobile site URL. Figure 8-16 shows a typical mobile view of a SharePoint 2010 site.

In SharePoint 2010, when a SharePoint site is browsed, SharePoint identifies the browser's User Agent to determine whether it is a mobile device. If SharePoint 2010 can determine that a mobile device is in use, it will automatically display the mobile view of the site at all times. This can be very useful in an intranet setting, but for public-facing Internet sites, it's often desirable to show the standard view of the site, especially if a lot of custom branding has been applied. Unfortunately, if you want to turn off this default mobile view, there is no setting in Central Administration or in the site collection itself; instead, you must edit a file named `compat.browse`, which is located on the physical SharePoint server. Here are the steps for turning off the mobile view:

1. Log in to the physical SharePoint server and navigate to the directory that holds your SharePoint IIS website.

2. From this folder, navigate to the `App_Browsers` folder and locate the file named `compat.browse`.

3. Because you will be editing the file, it's probably a good idea to make a backup and store it somewhere, in case you want to go back to the original state.

4. Open `compat.browse` for editing in a text editor such as Notepad. This file has settings for many popular browsers, including most mobile browsers.

5. Find the section for the particular mobile browser for which you want to use the normal view and look for the following line:

```
<capability name="isMobileDevice" value="true" />
```

6. Change this setting to `false`, save the file, and then browse back to your SharePoint site from your mobile device to see the fully branded view of the SharePoint site.

While it may seem counterintuitive to say that the browser is *not* a mobile device, this is what is required to turn off the automatic mobile view in SharePoint. Figure 8-17 shows a branded SharePoint site loaded from a smart phone with the mobile view disabled.

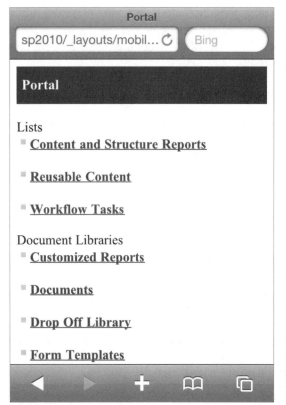

FIGURE 8-16

FIGURE 8-17

CREATING A FULLY BRANDED MASTER PAGE

The rest of this chapter focuses on creating a branded SharePoint publishing site based on the Randy's Waffles design that was created in Chapter 3. You will begin with the Starter master page and then add the HTML, CSS, and images that were created in Chapter 3. Finally, some adjustments will be made to the master page and CSS to create a master page that looks as similar as possible to the original HTML mockup. In the next chapter, you will complete the Randy's Waffles example by creating page layouts that will be used by the page-level branding.

To begin the example, you need to have a SharePoint Server publishing site with the Starter master page from this book applied. You can do this by following along with the earlier example in the section "Using a Starter Master Page."

Adding HTML Branding Assets

Because the Starter master page is the blank canvas with which you begin your branding, the first step is to add the branding assets (the CSS and images) that were already created for Randy's Waffles. These files are available with the downloads for Chapter 3. SharePoint Designer 2010 will be used to create a folder under the Style Library and add the files.

1. Open the publishing site that contains `Waffles.master` in SharePoint Designer 2010.

2. From the Site Objects menu, click the little pushpin icon for All Files, and from the All Files list in the main window, click Style Library.

3. Create a new folder by clicking Folder from the ribbon, and name the new folder **Waffles**.

4. Make sure you have copied the branding assets from the Randy's Waffles site that were created in Chapter 3 to your desktop or another convenient location. Click the new `Waffles` folder in SharePoint Designer and drag in all the images, `favicon.ico`, and `style.css` from your local copy of Randy's Waffles branding assets.

5. Select all the files that were added to the Style Library, and right-click and select Check In. From the Check In menu, select Publish a major version, and then click OK. Because the Style Library does not have an approval workflow applied to it, approving the files will not be necessary.

Building the Master Page

With the branding assets added to the Style Library, the next step is to open the Starter master page and start adding code from the HTML mockup. With the HTML added, you can begin to move pieces of the Starter master page around in the layout and make other changes as necessary to make the design functional in SharePoint. If you have trouble following along with these steps, the final versions of the files are available with the downloads for this chapter.

1. Make sure that `Waffles.master` is open in SharePoint Designer 2010, and then check out the file for editing by right-clicking on it and selecting Check Out. This will add a green check mark next to it, indicating that the file is checked out.

    The Starter master page contains several instances of the word "sitename" that should be replaced with the actual name of the project or folder that was created in the Style Library. The next step is to make those replacements.

2. Press Ctrl+F to find each of these instances. Here are the lines that will be updated, with the changes in bold:

```
<title runat="server"><asp:ContentPlaceHolder id="PlaceHolderPageTitle"
 runat="server">Randy's Waffles</asp:ContentPlaceHolder></title>

<SharePoint:SPShortcutIcon runat="server"
 IconUrl="/Style Library/Waffles/favicon.ico"/>

<SharePoint:CssRegistration name="/Style Library/Waffles/style.css"
 After="corev4.css" runat="server"/>

<SharePoint:SPLinkButton runat="server" NavigateUrl="~sitecollection/">
 <SharePoint:SiteLogoImage LogoImageUrl="/Style Library/Waffles/logo.png"
  runat="server"/>
</SharePoint:SPLinkButton>
```

By making these changes, the HTML page title, favicon, custom CSS style sheet, and site logo will all be configured. Because the corresponding files were already added to the Style Library, they will begin working once the changes are saved.

3. Now you should remove all the embedded CSS that is included in the <head> section of the Starter master page. Because you will have a dedicated custom style sheet for this master page, this embedded CSS can be moved there so that the CSS can be managed all in one place. Simply remove all the code from <style type="text/css"> to </style> in the <head> section of the Starter master page. You will add this CSS to the style sheet in step 8.

4. Copy and paste the entire body of the original HTML document (everything after the <form action="#"> tag and before the closing </form> tag) into the Starter master page underneath the <div id="MSO_ContentDiv" runat="server"> tag, located about halfway down the page.

This existing content will be used as a shell to hold various pieces of the Starter master page. In the next few steps, areas of SharePoint functionality will be moved from the lower parts of the master page into the pasted HTML code, and new functionality will be added as needed. The changed parts of the code are highlighted in the code snippets.

5. This process begins with the User Login button; it is one of the more complex steps because you will be adding an <asp:LoginView>, as described previously in the "Handling the Ribbon for Anonymous Users" section. Replace the simple HTML link with the <asp:LoginView>, as follows:

```
<div class="customTop customPagePadding">
 <asp:LoginView id="LoginView" runat="server">
  <AnonymousTemplate>
   <a href="/_layouts/authenticate.aspx" class="customLogin"
     title="User Login">User Login</a>

   <style type="text/css">
    body #s4-ribbonrow {
     display: none;
    }
   </style>
```

```
    </AnonymousTemplate>
   </asp:LoginView>
  </div>
```

This code will hide the ribbon for anonymous users and instead show them a simple user login link.

6. Because the `customTop` `<div>` should not show in the dialogs in SharePoint 2010, add the `s4-notdlg` CSS class:

```
<div class="customTop customPagePadding s4-notdlg">
```

7. Replace the static link and image HTML

```
<a href="#" class="customLogo"><img src="logo.png"
  alt="Back to Home" title="Back to Home" /></a>
```

with a `<div class="customLogo">`, and cut and paste the `<SharePoint:SPLinkButton>` and the `<SharePoint:SiteLogoImage>` from the Starter master page:

```
<div class="customLogo">
 <SharePoint:SPLinkButton runat="server" NavigateUrl="~sitecollection/">
  <SharePoint:SiteLogoImage LogoImageUrl="/Style Library/Waffles/logo.png"
   AlternateText="Back to Home" ToolTip="Back to Home" runat="server"/>
 </SharePoint:SPLinkButton>
</div>
```

8. Replace the static search HTML with the `PlaceHolderSearchArea` content placeholder and the `SmallSearchInputBox` delegate control:

```
<div class="customSearch">
 <asp:ContentPlaceHolder id="PlaceHolderSearchArea" runat="server">
  <SharePoint:DelegateControl runat="server" ControlId="SmallSearchInputBox"
   Version="4"/>
 </asp:ContentPlaceHolder>
</div>
```

9. Because the `customHead` `<div>` should not show in the dialogs in SharePoint 2010, add the `s4-notdlg` CSS class:

```
<div class="customHead customPagePadding s4-notdlg">
```

10. Replace the static top navigation with the SharePoint Global Navigation control and the corresponding data source:

```
<div class="customTopNavHolder">
 <PublishingNavigation:PortalSiteMapDataSource
  ID="topSiteMap"
  runat="server"
  EnableViewState="false"
  SiteMapProvider="GlobalNavigation"
  StartFromCurrentNode="true"
  StartingNodeOffset="0"
```

```
    ShowStartingNode="false"
    TrimNonCurrentTypes="Heading"/>

  <SharePoint:AspMenu
   ID="TopNavigationMenuV4"
   EncodeTitle="false"
   Runat="server"
   EnableViewState="false"
   DataSourceID="topSiteMap"
   AccessKey="<%$Resources:wss,navigation_accesskey%>"
   UseSimpleRendering="true"
   UseSeparateCss="false"
   Orientation="Horizontal"
   StaticDisplayLevels="1"
   MaximumDynamicDisplayLevels="1"
   SkipLinkText=""
   CssClass="s4-tn">
  </SharePoint:AspMenu>
</div>
```

11. Because the `customNav` `<div>` should not show in the dialogs in SharePoint 2010, add the `s4-notdlg` CSS class:

```
<div class="customNav customPagePadding s4-notdlg">
```

12. Add the default SharePoint 2010 status bar `<div>` tags between the `customNav` closing `</div>` and the `customBody` `<div>`:

```
</div>

<div class="s4-notdlg">
 <div id="s4-statusbarcontainer">
  <div id="pageStatusBar" class="s4-status-s1"></div>
 </div>
</div>

<div class="customMain">
```

13. Remove all the content in the `customBody` `<div>`. This will be replaced with body content from the Starter master page. For this step, remove everything after `<div class="customBody">` and before the `customClear` `<div>` that is two lines above the `customFooter` `<div>`.

14. In the now mostly empty `customBody` `<div>`, add the entire `s4-leftpanel` `<div>` from the Starter master page:

```
<div class="customBody">
 <div id="s4-leftpanel" class="s4-notdlg">
  <asp:ContentPlaceHolder id="PlaceHolderLeftNavBar" runat="server">
   <PublishingNavigation:PortalSiteMapDataSource
    ID="SiteMapDS"
    runat="server"
    EnableViewState="false"
    SiteMapProvider="CurrentNavigation"
```

```
        StartFromCurrentNode="true"
        StartingNodeOffset="0"
        ShowStartingNode="false"
        TrimNonCurrentTypes="Heading"/>

  <SharePoint:AspMenu
   ID="CurrentNav"
   EncodeTitle="false"
   runat="server"
   EnableViewState="false"
   DataSourceID="SiteMapDS"
   UseSeparateCSS="false"
   UseSimpleRendering="true"
   Orientation="Vertical"
   StaticDisplayLevels="2"
   MaximumDynamicDisplayLevels="0"
   CssClass="s4-ql"
   SkipLinkText="<%$Resources:cms,masterpages_skiplinktext%>"/>
  </asp:ContentPlaceHolder>

  <asp:ContentPlaceHolder id="PlaceHolderLeftActions" runat ="server"/>
 </div>
```

15. The previous step added the default starter left navigation; but for the Randy's Waffles
site, the main pages of the site will not show left navigation. Only the pages that need left
navigation will show it, such as some of the Site Settings pages. Remove the contents of the
`PlaceHolderLeftNavBar` content placeholder and replace them with the following code that
will hide the left navigation by default:

```
<asp:ContentPlaceHolder id="PlaceHolderLeftNavBar" runat="server">
 <style type="text/css">
 #s4-leftpanel {
  display: none;
 }
 .s4-ca {
  margin-left:0px;
 }
 .customBody {
  padding:20px 40px 40px;
  width: 878px;
 }
 </style>
</asp:ContentPlaceHolder>
```

16. Now you will add the main body `<div>` from the Starter master page. After the `s4-leftpanel`
closing `</div>`, add the Starter master page `s4-ca` `<div>` and all of its contents:

```
  <asp:ContentPlaceHolder id="PlaceHolderLeftActions" runat ="server"/>
 </div>

<div class="s4-ca">
 <div class="s4-notdlg">
  <SharePoint:DelegateControl ControlId="GlobalSiteLink3-mini"
   Scope="Farm" runat="server"/>
```

```
    </div>

    <div class="s4-notdlg">
     <asp:ContentPlaceHolder id="PlaceHolderPageTitleInTitleArea" runat="server" />
    </div>

    <asp:ContentPlaceHolder id="PlaceHolderPageDescription" runat="server" />

    <div>
     <asp:ContentPlaceHolder id="PlaceHolderMain" runat="server"/>
    </div>
   </div>

   <div class="customClear"></div>
  </div>
```

17. Along with adding all the standard body content, the previous step added the social I Like It and Tags and Notes controls, which are not needed in the Randy's Waffles branding. Remove the following code from the `s4-ca` `<div>`:

```
<div class="s4-notdlg">
  <SharePoint:DelegateControl ControlId="GlobalSiteLink3-mini"
   Scope="Farm" runat="server"/>
</div>
```

18. Because both the `customFooter` `<div>` and the `customBottom` `<div>` should not show in the dialogs in SharePoint 2010, add the `s4-notdlg` CSS class:

```
<div class="customFooter customPagePadding s4-notdlg">
...
<div class="customBottom s4-notdlg"></div>
```

19. Move the developer dashboard code up from the Starter master page code to right after the `customBottom` closing `</div>`:

```
<div class="customBottom s4-notdlg"></div>

<div id="DeveloperDashboard" class="ms-developerdashboard">
 <SharePoint:DeveloperDashboard runat="server"/>
</div>

</div>
```

20. Remove any of the remaining Starter master page code that is located after the developer dashboard closing `</div>` but before the three closing `</div>`s and the `PlaceHolderFormDigest`. Be sure to leave all the remaining code that is below `PlaceHolderFormDigest`, until the end of the page.

After you have performed these steps, the Randy's Waffles master page is complete. You should check it in, publish it as a major version, and approve it before other users will be able to see the changes.

Unfortunately, just having the master page completed isn't enough; you also need to make some changes to the custom CSS. Figure 8-18 shows the current state of the branding.

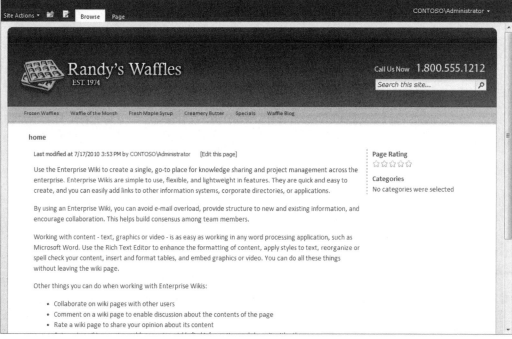

FIGURE 8-18

Adjusting the CSS for SharePoint

Earlier, in the section "Adding HTML Branding Assets," you added the existing images and CSS to the Style Library. Now you will make changes to that CSS because SharePoint needs some specific styling above and beyond what was created for the HTML mockup. Because the design is using a Strict DOCTYPE, the case of the CSS selectors must match precisely with the corresponding elements in the master page HTML. As you are adding the CSS, be careful to ensure that the cases of the CSS selectors are consistent with the code listings. The following steps walk you through the changes to `style.css`. (As before, any changed code is in bold.)

1. From the Site Objects menu, click All Files ⇨ Style Library ⇨ Waffles, right-click style.css, and then select Check Out.

2. The link style needs to be updated to include a few SharePoint-specific link selectors. The updated list of selectors will add the color and text decoration to links with more specific identifiers, including visited links and links in Web Parts:

```
a, a:link, a:visited, .ms-WPBody a:visited, .ms-WPBody a:link {
    color: #f77d1c;
    text-decoration: none;
}
```

3. A few top navigation styles from the HTML mockup can be removed because they will have specific SharePoint styles added later. Remove all the following lines of CSS:

```
.customTopNavItem {
 float:left;
 font-size:1.5em;
 height:17px;
 padding:7px 10px 5px;
 border-left: 1px solid transparent;
 border-right: 1px solid transparent;
}
.customTopNavItem a {
 color: #292929;
}
.customTopNavItem a:hover {
 text-decoration:none;
}
.customTopNavItem:hover {
 background-color: #ffebc8;
 border-color: #e5ad45;
}
.customTopNavItem:hover a {
 color: #292929;
}
```

4. You need to change the customBody CSS to remove the line height, set the width, and change the padding. Because the home page will have vastly different body styling from standard pages, these styles will be updated on the specific page layouts. Also, because this branding will be used throughout SharePoint, including application pages and lists, overflow will be set to auto. This allows very wide pages to scroll inside the branding, rather than exceed the width of the branding and show over the background.

```
.customBody {
 background-image: url(subpage_bg.gif);
 background-color:white;
 background-repeat: repeat-x;
 min-height: 420px;
 font-size:120%;
 padding: 20px 20px 40px;
 width: 918px;
 overflow:auto;
 border-color:#bbbbbb;
 border-style:solid;
 border-width:0 1px;
}
```

5. Because the banner on the home page will be created at the page level with a Web Part, add some style to change the link color. (This will make more sense in the next chapter when you create the actual home page content.)

```
.customBannerText {
 float:left;
 line-height:27px;
```

```
color: #eef0f0;
font-size: 248%;
}

/* override banner text color inside of a Web Part */
.ms-WPBody a.customBannerText {
color: #EEF0F0;
}
```

6. Several styles need to be added to the search area, including hiding the out-of-the-box search button and adding a stylized button:

```
/* hide search button */
.customSearch .ms-sbgo img {
display: none;
}

/* fancy search button */
.customSearch .ms-sbgo a {
display: block;
height:20px;
width:62px;
background:transparent url('seach_go.gif') no-repeat scroll left top;
margin: 0px;
padding: 0px;
position: relative;
top: 0px;
}
```

7. Several styles need to be added to handle the top navigation elements, including hiding the out-of-the-box arrows, the item style, hover state, selected item style, the dynamic fly-out holder, and the fly-out item and hover state:

```
/* arrow for flyouts */
.menu-horizontal a.dynamic-children span.additional-background,
.menu-horizontal span.dynamic-children span.additional-background {
padding-right:0px;
background-image:none;
}

/* item style */
.s4-tn li.static > .menu-item {
color:#292929;
white-space:nowrap;
border:0px none transparent;
background-color:transparent;
height:17px;
padding:7px 10px 5px;
display:inline-block;
vertical-align:middle;
font-size:1.5em;
border-left: 1px solid transparent;
```

```
  border-right: 1px solid transparent;
}

/* item style hover */
.s4-tn li.static > a:hover {
 background-color: #ffebc8;
 border-color: #e5ad45;
 color: #292929;
 text-decoration: none;
}

/* selected style */
.s4-tn li.static > .selected {
 background-color: #ffebc8;
 border-color: #e5ad45;
 color: #292929;
}

/* flyout holder */
.s4-tn ul.dynamic {
 background-color:#F09100;
 border:0px none;
 padding-top:1px;
}

/* flyout item */
.s4-tn li.dynamic > .menu-item {
 display:block;
 white-space:nowrap;
 font-weight:normal;
 background-color: #ffebc8;
 background-repeat: repeat-x;
 border: 1px solid #F09100;
 border-top: 0px;
 color: #292929;
 line-height: 1.2em;
 font-size:1.5em;
}

/* flyout item hover */
.s4-tn li.dynamic > a:hover {
 font-weight:normal;
 text-decoration:none;
 background-color: white;
 color: #292929;
}
```

8. Lastly, several SharePoint-specific CSS styles need to be added. Each of these style rules begins with a comment that describes its specific usage. The first few are the styles that were removed from the `<head>` section of the Starter master page:

```
/* hide body scrolling (SharePoint will handle) */
body {
 height:100%;
```

```css
  overflow:hidden;
  width:100%;
}

/* popout breadcrumb menu needs background color for firefox */
.s4-breadcrumb-menu {
  background:#F2F2F2;
}

/* body area  */
.s4-ca {
  margin-left:165px;
}

/* fix scrolling on list pages */
#s4-bodyContainer {
  position: relative;
}

/* fix the font on some ootb menus */
.propertysheet, .ms-authoringcontrols {
  font-family: Verdana,Arial,sans-serif;
  line-height: normal;
}

/* fix the font on forms like the survey */
.ms-ltviewselectormenuheader .ms-viewselector a,
.ms-ltviewselectormenuheader .ms-viewselectorhover a,
.ms-formlabel {
  font-family: calibri, arial, sans-serif;
}

/* hide the hover state for teh ribbon links */
#s4-ribbonrow a:hover {
  text-decoration: none;
}

/* fix ribbon line height */
#s4-ribbonrow {
  line-height: normal;
}

/* make the ribbon color match the branding*/
body #s4-ribboncont {
  background-color: #313031;
}

/* make Site Settings links look normal */
.ms-linksection-level1 ul li a {
  font-weight:normal;
}

/* make the site actions colors match the branding */
.ms-siteactionsmenuinner  {
```

```
    background:url("/_layouts/images/bgximg.png") repeat-x scroll 0 -467px #313031;
    border-color:#313031;
    }

/* fix margins when dialog is up */
.ms-dialog .customPageWidth, .ms-dialog .customBody {
    margin-left:0 !important;
    margin-right:0 !important;
    min-height:0 !important;
    min-width:0 !important;
    width:auto !important;
    height:auto !important;
    background-color: white !important;
    background-image: none !important;
    padding: 0px !important;
    overflow:inherit;
    }

/* dialog bg */
.ms-dialog body {
    background-color: white;
    background-image: none;
    }

/* fix dialog padding */
.ms-dialog .s4-wpcell-plain {
    padding: 4px;
    }

/* fix field edit mode width problems */
.ms-formfieldvaluecontainer {
    overflow:hidden;
    }

/* fix the blog font size */
.ms-PostBody {
    font-size: 100%;
    }
```

With all these styles added to your custom CSS, branding for the Randy's Waffles master page is complete. The CSS file needs to be checked in and published as a major version before anyone can see the changes. Remember that because the Style Library doesn't have a publishing workflow enabled, you won't have to approve it. Figure 8-19 shows the finished master page.

Of course, the inside parts of the page still don't look like the HTML mockup. These areas will be handled by the custom page layouts, which you learn about in the next chapter.

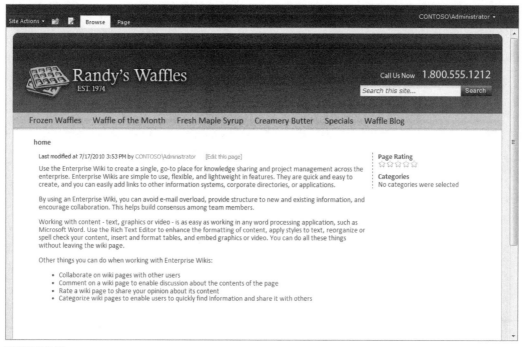

FIGURE 8-19

SUMMARY

This chapter focused on providing you with a good understanding of how master pages work, not only in SharePoint 2010 but also in traditional ASP.NET applications. You learned how SharePoint requires specific content placeholders to function properly, and you looked at how they are used in both the out-of-the-box master pages and the Starter master pages. Not only was a Starter master page customization explained, but an HTML mockup was converted into a functioning custom master page. Armed with this knowledge, you should be able to effectively customize Starter master pages to create your own custom branded master pages.

The next chapter describes how page layouts work in SharePoint Server 2010, and walks you through the process of creating page layouts that can be used with the Randy's Waffles master page you created in this chapter.

Page Layouts

➤ An overview of how page layouts work in SharePoint Server publishing sites

➤ Using page layouts to style publishing pages

➤ How page layouts are related to content types and site columns

➤ Creating custom content types to use with page layouts

➤ Creating both simple and complex custom page layouts

Page layouts, first introduced with Microsoft Office SharePoint Server 2007 (MOSS), enable publishing sites to have another level of templating beyond just master pages. Page layouts are critical to web content management because they enable content authors to create pages with specific editable fields and pre-defined HTML for content arrangement. Because page layouts work hand-in-hand with master pages, designers and developers should have a strong understanding of both to fully appreciate how page layouts are used in SharePoint.

In many ways, page layouts have changed only in minor ways for SharePoint 2010; however, the topic is still critical for understanding the power of SharePoint publishing. This chapter focuses on providing a deep understanding of how page layouts work and how you can create your own page layouts for use in SharePoint 2010. To follow along with the examples in the chapter, you will need to have SharePoint Server 2010; SharePoint Foundation does not include the capability to use page layouts. At the end of the chapter, you will work through an example that creates the page layouts required for Randy's Waffles, the public-facing Internet website that was started earlier in the book.

UNDERSTANDING PAGE LAYOUTS

Although traditional SharePoint sites are very good at enabling teams to collaborate and share many types of documents with ease, large organizations often need to share information in a more traditional web page–based format. This concept is even more important when SharePoint Server publishing is used for content that is available to public-facing Internet websites. In such scenarios, content authors expect to be able to create web pages easily themselves, without intervention from designers and developers or even their own company's IT department. The SharePoint Server Publishing Feature enables content authors to accomplish all this from the comfort of their own browser. When a content author creates a publishing page in SharePoint server, the page derives much of its look and feel, as well as its editable fields, from a page layout.

You can tell whether a page is a publishing page by the URL; all publishing pages are located in a document library known as Pages, so by default their URLs always contain /Pages/. In fact, every publishing page is using a page layout, even if one wasn't selected upon its creation.

The easiest way to create a page layout is to use SharePoint Designer 2010, but you can also create page layouts with the SharePoint Web user interface, and edit and upload their code from any text editor. You will learn more about both of these techniques later in this chapter. After you have created a page layout and subsequently published and approved it in a SharePoint Server site, content authors can then create pages that are based on the page layout.

Master Pages and Page Layouts

Master pages are closely associated with page layouts, because all pages in SharePoint, including those based on page layouts, have a master page applied to them. *Master pages*, along with providing much of the general SharePoint functionality, provide a unified design to all of the page layouts. *Page layouts* use field controls to define a specific look and define editable data for various types of pages. For example, you might have one page layout that is an article page and another that is a welcome page, yet they both can utilize the same master page design. Figure 9-1 shows how page layouts and master pages are used by SharePoint Server to render a page to the end user.

Another reason why master pages and page layouts are directly related has to do with content placeholders. Content placeholders were discussed in the previous chapter in greater detail, but for a quick refresher, remember that master pages define areas, or content placeholders, into which pages can inject content affecting the general layout of the master page. Much like content pages, page layouts also refer to these placeholders via the ASP:Content tags.

> *Be cautious when creating custom content placeholders for your master page and page layout. If the master page is later switched to one that doesn't contain matching placeholders, an error will be displayed.*

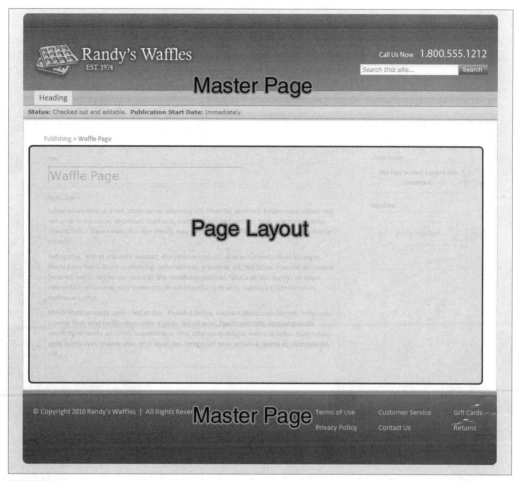

FIGURE 9-1

Applying Page Layouts to Content

Before getting too deep into the topic of how page layouts work behind the scenes, it would be helpful to first try them out using the out-of-the-box page layouts. Be sure that you have a publishing site created for the examples in this chapter. There is a brief description of how to create a publishing site in Chapter 5.

1. Authenticate on your SharePoint 2010 publishing site, and then click Site Actions ➪ New page.

Figure 9-2 shows the New Page dialog. You can see that unlike SharePoint 2007, you only need to enter a page name to create a page.

The examples in this chapter are based on the Enterprise Wiki site template. To create a publishing site, you can use the Enterprise Wiki site template, the Publishing Portal site template, or you can simply activate the publishing features manually for your SharePoint Server site. If you don't use the Enterprise Wiki template, some of the steps may differ in the examples. For example, Enterprise Wiki pages can just be edited and then saved and closed, and all users will be able to see the changes. Other publishing sites may require you to publish the changes first. You can achieve this simply from the ribbon by clicking the Publish tab and then clicking the Publish button. Also, if the publishing approval workflow is enabled, you will need to approve the changes before users will be able to see them

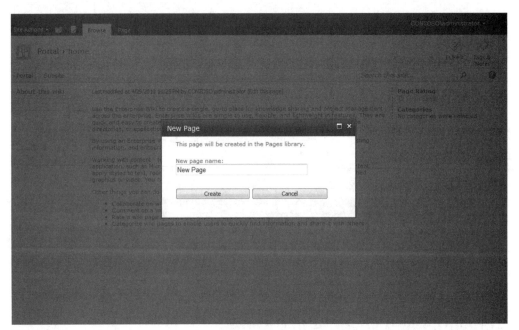

FIGURE 9-2

2. You can enter whatever name you would like, but you should probably pick a name that accurately describes the page you are creating. In this case, you can simply name the page **Demo Page**, and then click Create.

After a bit of processing, a new page is opened in edit mode. Notice that you didn't have to select a page layout; this is because SharePoint 2010 uses a default page layout for new pages.

3. Enter whatever information you'd like, and then click Save & Close.

If you want to change the page layout, the process is quite simple in SharePoint 2010. First, edit the page again and then from the ribbon, click Page ➪ Page Layout, and you are presented with a list of available page layouts (see Figure 9-3).

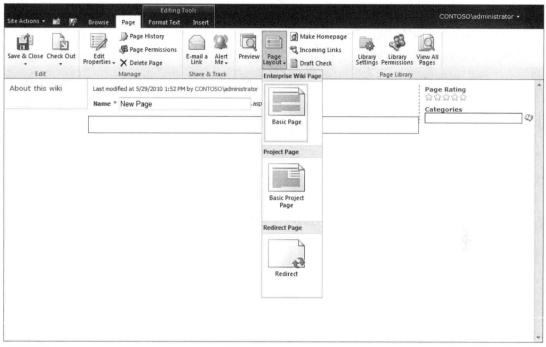

FIGURE 9-3

You will learn more about the out-of-the-box page layout later in the chapter, but for now, you can select any of the available page layouts and it will be applied to the page. This is also a new feature for SharePoint 2010. In SharePoint 2007, there were more steps to this process. Note that, by default, Enterprise Wiki sites offer only a limited number of page layouts. The following section shows you how to change this.

Out-of-the-Box Page Layouts

SharePoint Server 2010 publishing sites come with several pre-built page layouts that you can use right away when working with pages. You can view all the available layouts from the Site Settings menu by clicking Page Layouts and site templates under Look and Feel. Then scroll down to the Page Layouts section.

The available page layouts are grouped into categories according to the content type on which they are based. This is the same text that appears in parentheses before each page layout name in this menu. You will learn more about how page layouts and content types are related later in this chapter.

The following page layouts are included by default:

➤ (Article Page) Body only

➤ (Article Page) Image on left

➤ (Article Page) Image on right

➤ (Article Page) Summary links

➤ (Enterprise Wiki Page) Basic Page

➤ (Project Page) Basic Project Page

➤ (Redirect Page) Redirect

➤ (Welcome Page) Advanced Search

➤ (Welcome Page) Blank Web Part page

➤ (Welcome Page) People search results

➤ (Welcome Page) Search box

➤ (Welcome Page) Search results

➤ (Welcome Page) Site directory home

➤ (Welcome Page) Splash

➤ (Welcome Page) Summary Links

➤ (Welcome Page) Table of Contents

You can control which page layouts are available to content authors from this menu. For example, you could allow them to use any page layout or constrain them to selecting from only certain page layouts. Depending on the site template that was used when creating your publishing site, this may be set to allow only certain page layouts. In a moment, you will see an example of what the page layout selection looks like when this option is set to "Pages in this site can use any layout."

Shown in Figure 9-4 is another important option found on this screen. New Page Default Settings enables you to control which page layout is used when creating new pages.

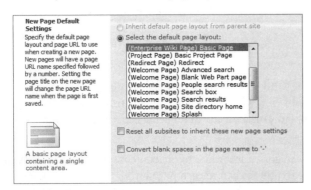

FIGURE 9-4

Recall from the previous section that when you created a new page, you didn't have to choose a page layout; that's because this option was set to use one by default.

To allow all the page layouts to be available for use, change the Page Layouts section to "Pages in this site can use any layout," and click OK. Now, if you go back to the page you created in the previous section or create a new page, you will notice many more options in the Page Layout drop-down in the ribbon (see Figure 9-5).

Page Layouts and the Master Page Gallery

Page layouts are always created at the top level of a SharePoint Server site collection. They are added to the Master Page Gallery, and as such they live among the site's master pages. Just like master pages, you can access them either from SharePoint Designer or directly from the SharePoint Web user interface. To access the Master Page Gallery from the SharePoint Web user interface, browse to the top level of your SharePoint site and click Site Actions ⇨ Site Settings, and under Galleries click Master pages and page layouts. This gallery shows a list of all the master pages and page layouts available to your site collection.

The Master Page Gallery is also where you can create new page layouts using just the SharePoint Web user interface:

1. From the ribbon, click Documents ⇨ New Document ⇨ Page Layout.

    This brings up the New Page Layout menu.

2. Select Publishing Content Types for the Content Type Group, and select Page from the Content Type Name.

3. Give your new page layout a URL Name, Title, and Description, and then click OK.

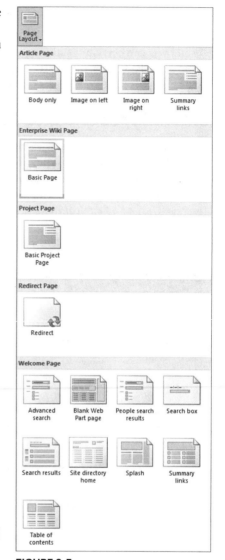

FIGURE 9-5

 You can differentiate the page layouts from the master pages in the Master Page Gallery by their file extension. All master pages have a file extension of `.master`, *whereas all page layouts have the standard ASP.NET file extension of* `.ASPX`.

This creates a bare-bones page layout and places it in the Master Page Gallery. To download the existing page layout, click the filename. Then, from the ribbon, click Documents ⇨ Download a Copy. From there, you can make changes using whatever text-editing program you like. Then, to upload a new version, from the ribbon click Documents ⇨ Upload Document. Be sure to also publish and approve the file before trying to use it; both options can be found in the Documents tab of the ribbon.

While you can certainly make page layouts using the Web user interface, the process is a lot easier from SharePoint Designer 2010. Later in this chapter you will look at adding page layouts to SharePoint from SharePoint Designer.

Content Types and Site Columns

Designers and developers often find content types confusing when it comes to page layouts in SharePoint. While content types are certainly used for many other things in SharePoint, such as lists, they are critical to the creation of page layouts as well. One particularly tricky concept to understand with page layouts is that they are always based on exactly one content type, which in turn is made up of *site columns*.

If you look at a publishing page in edit mode, you will see several editable field controls. Figure 9-6 shows a number of editable field controls on a page.

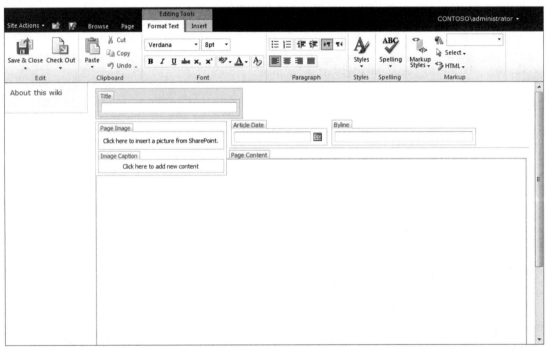

FIGURE 9-6

These editable fields are defined by which site columns are available in the underlying content type. To put it another way, editable field controls have their data stored in the site columns that define them. You will see an example of creating a custom page layout later in this chapter, but for now it's useful to understand that when you create a custom page layout, you first select the content type on which it is based. From there you can select from the available site columns, both those in the content type itself and any that are inherited from its parent content type, "Page." Figure 9-7 shows a diagram of this relationship; note that you don't have to use all of the available site columns when creating a page layout.

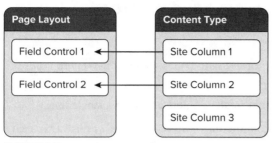

FIGURE 9-7

To gain a better understanding of how all these concepts are related, the out-of-the-box page layout "Image on left" can be analyzed. This page layout is based on the Article Page content type. The content type has a Publishing HTML site column named Page Content. The Image on left page layout has an editable field control in it called Page Content, which is directly related to the site column. In turn, any page that uses the Image on left page layout, when edited can have Page Content information entered and saved.

In SharePoint 2010, pages can have their page layouts switched on-the-fly from the ribbon interface, as you saw earlier. If the page is switched to a page layout based on a content type that doesn't have the same site columns, those field controls will disappear from the page itself, but any content that was saved in them will be stored for later use.

Out-of-the-Box Content Types for Page Layouts

When creating your own page layouts, you can base them on any of the out-of-the-box content types. As mentioned earlier, they are all based on the publishing content type of Page (or another content type that itself is based on the Page content type); therefore, all page layouts include several standard site columns, including title, comments, start/end dates, contact info, and audience info. Here is a breakdown of the available content types, including the information they can store beyond the typical page information:

➤ **Article Page** — Used for creating news articles and other generic pages. Along with the normal page information, this content type can store images, image captions, summary links, a byline, and article date.

➤ **Enterprise Wiki Page** — Used for the Enterprise Wiki pages. Along with the normal page information, it can store ratings and wiki categories.

➤ **Project Page** — Based on the Enterprise Wiki Page content type, this contains all the same site columns but also stores project-specific information such as a web page link and a task status option field. While the name may seem to indicate it, this content type is not related to Microsoft Project Server. This is simply a content type that includes project information.

➤ **Redirect Page** — Used only for creating pages that automatically redirect to other pages. It's generally not very useful for creating new page layouts. Along with the normal page information, it can store a redirect URL.

➤ **Welcome Page** — Frequently used as a home page or landing page. Along with the normal page information, it can store a page image and two summary links fields.

Site Columns for Page Layouts

Several out-of-the-box site columns are available for use with your own custom content types, including the following:

➤ **Single line of text** — Columns that contain small amounts of text in a single line.

➤ **Multiple lines of text** — Columns that contain one or more sentences of plain text, rich text (including bold, italics, text alignment, and hyperlinks), or enhanced rich text (including everything from rich text as well as pictures, tables, and hyperlinks).

➤ **Choice (menu to choose from)** — Columns that contain information based on a list of options.

➤ **Number (1, 1.0, 100)** — Columns that contain a numerical value.

➤ **Currency ($, ¥, €)** — Columns that contain a monetary value.

➤ **Date and Time** — Columns that contain calendar or time-of-day information.

➤ **Lookup (information already on this site)** — Columns that make it easy for you to select and display information that's already stored on a site.

➤ **Yes/No (check box)** — Columns that contain true- or false-based data.

➤ **Person or Group** — Columns that contain user names or SharePoint groups.

➤ **Hyperlink or Picture** — Columns that contain a hyperlink to a web page or display an image from the Web.

➤ **Calculated (calculation based on other columns)** — Columns that display information based on the result of a formula. The formula can use information from other lists and columns, dates, or numbers.

➤ **Full HTML content with formatting and constraints for publishing** — Columns that contain rich HTML content for publishing pages. Content and formatting constraints may be applied to the column.

➤ **Image with formatting and constraints for publishing** — Columns that contain links to images defined in the item properties. Each column displays an image, and optional formatting and constraints may be applied to it.

➤ **Hyperlink with formatting and constraints for publishing** — Columns that contain hyperlinks. Link formatting and constraints may apply.

➤ **Summary Links data** — Columns that contain summary links for a page. Summary links include a title, description, image, and URL, and are used on publishing pages to present grouped links by using a set of shared styles.

➤ **Rich media data for publishing** — (New for SharePoint Server 2010) Columns that contain rich media, such as video and audio.

➤ **Managed Metadata** — (New for SharePoint Server 2010) Columns containing terms that can be selected from specific managed metadata term sets.

As you can see, many different types of data can be stored in site columns. Every site column that is added to a content type ultimately can become an editable field control that is available to the page layouts that are based on it. Although content types provide a powerful way of defining data for use in a site, this power would be severely limited if SharePoint forced you to create a new content type for every page layout. Fortunately, content types that are created or are available in SharePoint can be used in as many page layouts as you like. This enables you to create a content type that is displayed in several ways via different page layouts in a SharePoint site.

Both content types and most site columns can be created either with the SharePoint Web user interface or with SharePoint Designer. Later in this chapter you will create your own page layouts based on an existing content type, as well as a page layout based on your own custom content type and custom site column.

 Unfortunately, only site columns that are based on SharePoint Foundation 2010 features, such as the Choice site column, can be created with SharePoint Designer 2010. Site columns that are specific to publishing, such as Publishing HTML, Publishing Image, Publishing Hyperlink, Summary Links, Media Field, and Managed Metadata, must use the traditional method of creating site columns — with the SharePoint Web user interface. To create one of these site columns, authenticate to your SharePoint Server, and then click Site Actions ⇨ Site Settings ⇨ Site Columns ⇨ Create. Once created, the site columns work similarly to the site columns that can be created with SharePoint Designer.

Page Layout Structure

To gain a better understanding of how page layouts are structured, take a look at the following code from a simple page layout:

```
<%@ Page language="C#"
Inherits="Microsoft.SharePoint.Publishing.PublishingLayoutPage,
Microsoft.SharePoint.Publishing, Version=14.0.0.0,
Culture=neutral,PublicKeyToken=71e9bce111e9429c"
meta:webpartpageexpansion="full" meta:progid="SharePoint.WebPartPage.Document" %>

<%@ Register Tagprefix="SharePointWebControls"
Namespace="Microsoft.SharePoint.WebControls" Assembly="Microsoft.SharePoint,
Version=14.0.0.0, Culture=neutral, PublicKeyToken=71e9bce111e9429c" %>

<%@ Register Tagprefix="WebPartPages" Namespace="Microsoft.SharePoint.WebPartPages"
Assembly="Microsoft.SharePoint, Version=14.0.0.0, Culture=neutral,
```

```
PublicKeyToken=71e9bce111e9429c" %>

<%@ Register Tagprefix="PublishingWebControls"
Namespace="Microsoft.SharePoint.Publishing.WebControls"
Assembly="Microsoft.SharePoint.Publishing, Version=14.0.0.0, Culture=neutral,
PublicKeyToken=71e9bce111e9429c" %>

<%@ Register Tagprefix="PublishingNavigation"
Namespace="Microsoft.SharePoint.Publishing.Navigation"
Assembly="Microsoft.SharePoint.Publishing,
Version=14.0.0.0, Culture=neutral, PublicKeyToken=71e9bce111e9429c" %>

<asp:Content ContentPlaceholderID="PlaceHolderMain" runat="server">
<WebPartPages:SPProxyWebPartManager runat="server"
id="spproxywebpartmanager"></WebPartPages:SPProxyWebPartManager>

<h1><SharePointWebControls:TextField FieldName="Title" runat="server"/></h1>

<PublishingWebControls:RichHtmlField FieldName="PublishingPageContent" runat="server"/>

 <WebPartPages:WebPartZone id="BottomZone" runat="server" title="Bottom
Zone"></WebPartPages:WebPartZone>
</asp:Content>
```

Page layouts begin with the @ Page directive that defines what language they are written in, as well as a setting that causes them to inherit the SharePoint Publishing code. Note that unlike content pages, no specific master page is declared for page layouts. SharePoint knows to apply whatever Site master page is currently set for the site.

After the page directive, several controls are registered. These enable the page layout to utilize the necessary SharePoint functionality whenever needed. After the register statements, all other page layout content must be placed inside of <asp:Content> tags known as *content controls*. Each content control corresponds to specific content placeholders in the master page, identified by the ContentPlaceHolderID. Any content entered into the content control will override anything that was inside the corresponding content placeholder in the master page. If anything is placed outside of the content controls, SharePoint will throw an error.

In this example, the PlaceHolderMain content control starts with a SPProxyWebPartManager that is added automatically whenever a Web Part zone is used. Next is a text field control for the page title, surrounded by an <h1> HTML tag, and another rich HTML field control for storing the main page content. Lastly, there is a Web Part zone that enables content authors to add as many Web Parts as they like to the bottom of the page. When a publishing page is created that is based on this particular page layout, content authors will be limited to adding only the title, the page content, and Web Parts to the page.

Types of Content in Page Layouts

As stated earlier, all content that will be added to page layouts must be added to content controls. These content controls can contain the following types of content:

➤ **Text/HTML/CSS/ASP.NET controls** — All types of standard page content can be added to content controls in a page layout. Any content that you add to a content control will appear on all pages created from the page layout. HTML is often used in content controls to lay out the other types of content listed below. For example, a content control can contain HTML `div` tags to arrange the various field controls and Web Parts. HTML and CSS can also be used to apply internal style sheets for overriding CSS that was previously applied by the master page or the out-of-the-box SharePoint CSS. Styles applied at this level will apply only to the pages that use the particular page layout.

➤ **Field controls** — Field controls are editable containers that enable content authors to add content to the page. They are created from the site columns that have been added specifically by a designer to the page layout. SharePoint automatically stores a history of all the content entered into field controls.

➤ **Web Parts** — A Web Part is a modular unit of functionality that serves as another means of displaying site information to end users. Some Web Parts aggregate data from various areas of a SharePoint website, whereas other Web Parts are used to enter content such as rich HTML. An important consideration when working with Web Parts is that their data is not version controlled as field controls are. If storing previous versions of content is important to you, Web Parts would not be an appropriate content storage mechanism for your page layout. It is also worth noting that a Web Part placed directly on a page layout (not in a Web Part zone) is specifically limited in its usefulness. Web Parts that are placed directly on page layouts are not editable by content authors from their browser, and their content will persist across every page that is created from the page layout. Chapter 10 covers Web Parts in more detail.

➤ **Web Part zones** — A Web Part zone is a type of container that allows content authors to configure and arrange Web Parts either horizontally or vertically directly from their web browser. They make it possible to add any number of configurable Web Parts directly to a SharePoint page. Web Parts that are placed in Web Part zones can contain unique content from page to page; thus, editing a Web Part in a Web Part zone on one page will not affect the same Web Part on a different page. Web Part zones cannot be added to master pages; they can only be added to content pages or page layouts.

 Unlike in SharePoint 2007, Web Part zones in SharePoint 2010 are not the only place where content authors can place and configure Web Parts. In SharePoint 2010, content authors can place Web Parts anywhere within wiki page content areas and in publishing HTML field controls. This is a powerful new feature, but it may also require special training for content authors, who are no longer constrained to using only Web Part zones that a designer has pre-defined.

All these concepts come together when SharePoint Server displays a web page to an end user. The master page creates the outer page design and brings in a lot of the out-of-the-box SharePoint functionality; it is then merged with the page layout, which defines the inner page design and visually organizes the Web Parts and field controls. The field controls, in turn, are defined by the underlying content type and site columns. To the end user, this all appears simply as a SharePoint web page, but to you, as the designer, these separate moving parts represent areas you can customize.

CREATING PAGE LAYOUTS

Although the existing page layouts are certainly very useful, the real fun starts when you create your own custom page layout. The following sections describe how to create a simple page layout with SharePoint Designer 2010, as well as how to create a custom content type with custom site columns for use in creating another custom page layout.

> *When editing page layouts in SharePoint Designer 2010, you need to edit them in Advanced mode. If you try to edit a page layout in Normal mode (sometimes known as Safe mode) SharePoint Designer 2010 will warn you that there aren't any editable regions in Normal mode, and it will offer to edit the file in Advanced mode. In Normal mode, the entire file is highlighted in yellow, indicating that it cannot be edited.*

Creating a Simple Page Layout with SharePoint Designer

The following steps walk you through creating a very simple page layout with SharePoint Designer 2010 and applying it to a SharePoint Server 2010 publishing site:

1. Open your SharePoint Server site in SharePoint Designer 2010.

2. From the Site Objects menu on the left side, click Page Layouts.

3. From the ribbon, click New Page Layout.

4. From the New dialog box, leave Content Type Group set to Page Layout Content Types; for Content Type Name, select Article Page; enter a URL Name of **DemoLayout.aspx**; enter a Title of **Demo Page Layout**; and then click OK (see Figure 9-8).

   SharePoint Designer will create a basic page layout and open it.

5. Select the Toolbox pane on the right, scroll down to the bottom, and expand the section named SharePoint Controls.

   If the Toolbox pane is not shown, click View from the ribbon and then Task Panes ⇨ Toolbox.

6. Expand Page Fields and Content Fields. Page Fields shows all the site columns that were inherited from the parent content type. Content Fields shows all the site columns that were added to the actual content type from which the page layout was created (see Figure 9-9).

7. Drag the Page Content site column from the Content Fields into the `PlaceHolderMain`. If you switch to Code view, it should look like Figure 9-10.

   This adds the Page Content field control to the page layout and enables content authors to add content to the page layout.

8. Click Ctrl+S to save the page layout.

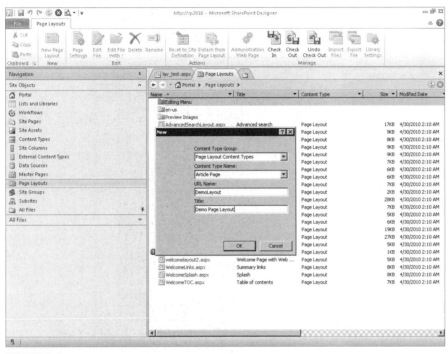

FIGURE 9-8

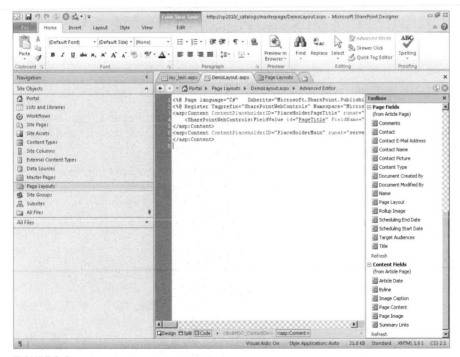

FIGURE 9-9

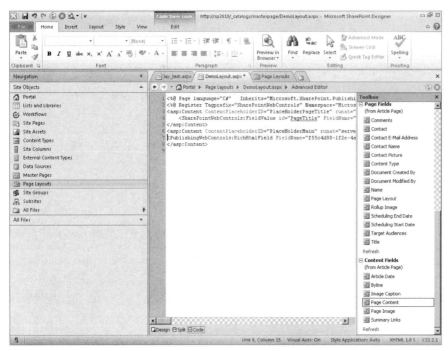

FIGURE 9-10

Even though the page layout is created, you still need to check it in and approve it before content authors can use it. The following steps describe how to do this.

1. Click back on the Page Layouts item in the Site Objects menu, and then click the icon for `DemoLayout.aspx`.

2. From the ribbon, click Check In and select Publish a major version and click OK.

3. SharePoint will indicate that "This document requires content approval. Do you want to view or modify its approval status?" Click Yes. This will open a web browser and show a view of the Master Page Gallery sorted by Approval Status.

4. Click the arrow to the right of DemoLayout, select Approve/Reject, and then from the Approve/Reject dialog, click Approved and then OK (see Figure 9-11).

Finally, you can test the new page layout by creating a page and switching its layout to the newly created page layout:

1. Click Site Actions ⇨ New Page.

2. Give the page a name, and then click Create.

3. Select the new page layout from the ribbon by clicking Page ⇨ Page Layout ⇨ Demo Page Layout.

4. Because this is a very simple page layout, only the Page Content field is editable. Edit the content and click Save & Close (see Figure 9-12).

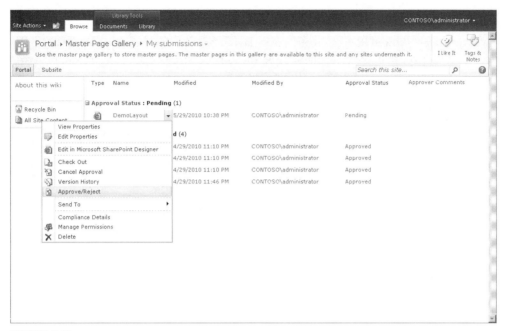

FIGURE 9-11

FIGURE 9-12

If you make further changes to the page layout, all pages based on the page layout will be updated.

Creating a Custom Content Type for Page Layouts

The previous example showed how to create a page layout based on an existing content type. If you want more field controls than those available from the out-of-the-box content types, simply create a new content type and add whatever site columns you want.

The following steps illustrate how to use SharePoint Designer 2010 to create a custom content type that inherits from the Article Page content type, add a custom Choice site column, and then use that content type to create a page layout. This page layout will allow pages to be created with the typical Article Page field controls, as well as provide a custom Choice field for tracking low, medium, or high priority.

1. Open your SharePoint Server site in SharePoint Designer 2010.

2. From the Site Objects menu on the left side, click Site Columns.

3. To create a new Choice column, from the ribbon, click New Column ➪ Choice (see Figure 9-13).

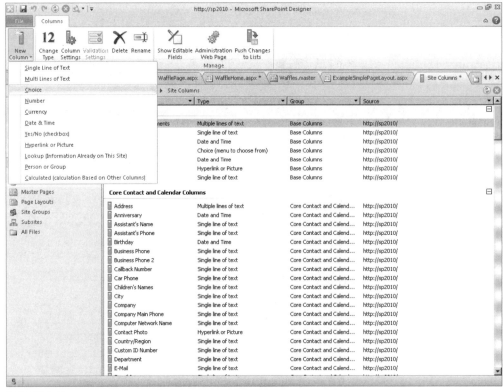

FIGURE 9-13

4. Name the Site Column as **Demo Priority**, select Custom Columns from the Existing group select box, and then click OK.

5. In the Column Editor dialog, enter a description (this is optional, but can be helpful when looking through the large list of site columns later), enter the available choices (**Low,** **Medium,** and **High**) on separate lines, enter the default value Medium, leave Display set to Drop-down menu, uncheck Allow blank values (see Figure 9-14), and then click OK.

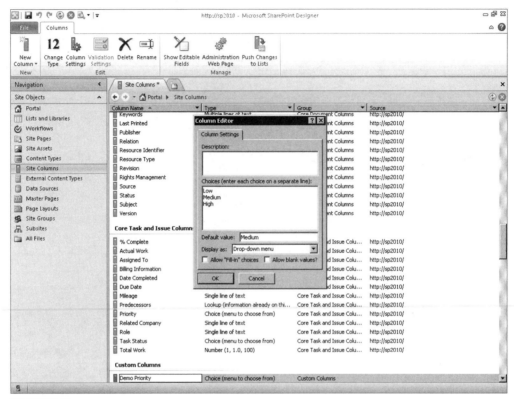

FIGURE 9-14

6. Click the disk icon in the top-left corner of SharePoint Designer to save the site column.

7. From the Site Objects menu on the left side, click Content Types.

8. From the ribbon, click Content Type, which is in the New tab group.

9. For the Name, enter **Demo Content Type.** For the Select parent content type from drop-down, choose Page Layout Content Types. For the Select parent content type drop-down, select Article Page and for the Existing group drop-down, select Page Layout Content Types, and then click OK.

All content types that are going to be used for creating page layouts need to have a parent content type of either the Page content type or another content type that already has Page set as its parent. In this case, Article Page fits the criteria because it is based on the Page content type. If you don't want to inherit from an existing content type, you select a parent content type from Publishing Content Types and select Page for the content type.

10. Select the newly created Demo Content Type, which is located under Page Layout Content Types in the main window, and then from the ribbon, click Edit Columns, and then Add Existing Site Column (see Figure 9-15).

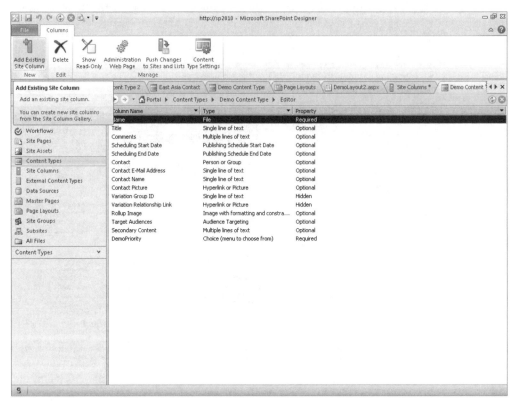

FIGURE 9-15

11. Scroll down to Custom Columns, select Demo Priority, and then click OK (see Figure 9-16).

12. Click the disk icon in the top-left corner of SharePoint Designer to save the content type.

Now that the content type is saved, you can follow the same steps to create a page layout based on it. Be sure to select the Demo Content Type when creating the new page layout. In addition, be sure to drag in the new field control Demo Priority from the Content Fields section of the Toolbox to the PlaceHolderMain. Before saving, checking-in and approving the new page layout, you can even add some layout or formatting by adding HTML around Page Content and Demo Priority. As long as you place the HTML inside the PlaceHolderMain, all of it will show within the rendered page.

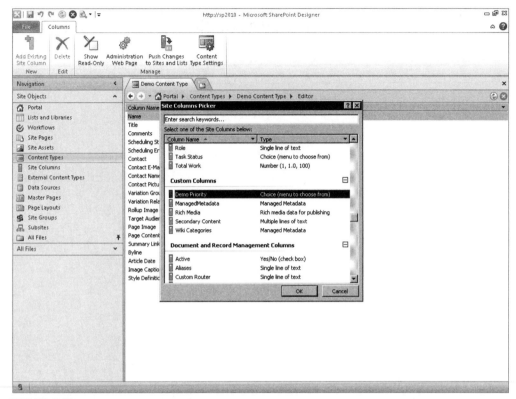

FIGURE 9-16

The following code snippet shows an example of what the `PlaceHolderMain` for the new page layout could look like:

```
<asp:Content ContentPlaceholderID="PlaceHolderMain" runat="server">
 <div style="padding:8px;">
  <p>Priority: <SharePointWebControls:DropDownChoiceField DisableInputFieldLabel="true"
FieldName="7c6b57f7-70f1-43b9-a495-fde0b32470a7"
runat="server"></SharePointWebControls:DropDownChoiceField></p>

  <PublishingWebControls:RichHtmlField FieldName="f55c4d88-1f2e-4ad9-aaa8-819af4ee7ee8"
runat="server"></PublishingWebControls:RichHtmlField>
 </div>
</asp:Content>
```

Figure 9-17 shows a page based on the page layout in Edit mode.

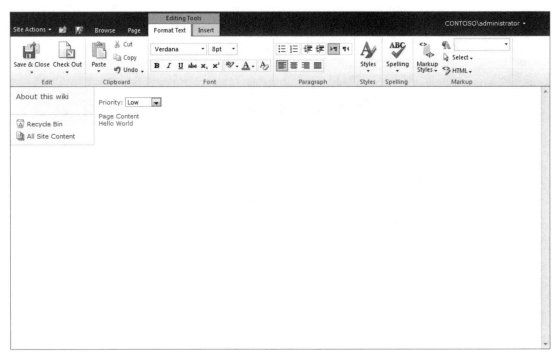

FIGURE 9-17

The next section describes how to create more branding-intensive page layouts, which will be based on out-of-the-box content types but include HTML for layout as well as Web Part zones. These page layouts will complement the Randy's Waffles master page branding that was added in the previous chapter.

Internet Site Page Layout Examples

Recall from the previous chapter that the Randy's Waffles branding was only half completed. The master page is branding the outer shell of the design, but the page level was left showing the out-of-the-box Enterprise Wiki home page (see Figure 9-18).

In the next two sections you will complete the Randy's Waffles branding. The examples will rely on the master page and related images and CSS from the Randy's Waffles example in the previous chapter. You can download the completed branding assets for the master page from the downloads for Chapter 8, but without having gone through that example, you may find the following examples difficult to understand.

Two page layouts are involved in the Randy's Waffles branding: a subpage page layout and a home-page page layout. The home-page page layout is used primarily to avoid having a second master page for just the top level of the website. By using a specific page layout for that level, you can avoid complexity; page layouts involve far less code than a second master page would involve. Because the subpage layout represents a more typical page layout and would most likely be used on far more pages, we'll start with that example.

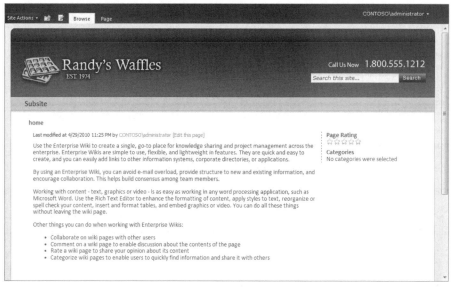

FIGURE 9-18

Creating the Subpage Page Layout

As shown in Figure 9-19, the original HTML mockup for the subpage had the appearance of an article.

FIGURE 9-19

This example is based on the Article Page content type and leverages the out-of-the-box site columns that are included with it.

 You can find the files used to create this example, as well as the final code with the downloads for the book, at www.wrox.com.

1. Open your SharePoint Server site in SharePoint Designer 2010.

2. From the Site Objects menu on the left side, click Page Layouts.

3. From the ribbon, click New Page Layout.

4. In the New dialog box, leave Content Type Group set to Page Layout Content Types. For Content Type Name, select Article Page; enter a URL Name of **WafflePage** (SharePoint will add the .ASPX extension for you when the page layout is created); enter a Title of **Waffle Page**; and then click OK.

SharePoint Designer will create a basic page layout and open it.

5. Switch to Code view by clicking Code at the bottom of the main window.

With the almost empty page layout opened in Code view, you can start adding HTML from the HTML mockup that was created in Chapter 3. (The files are available with the downloads for this chapter.)

6. Open sub.html and copy the contents of `<div class="customBody">`, which includes customBreadcrumbs, customBodyLeft, and customBodyRight. (You can omit the customClear div because that was included in the master page created in Chapter 8). Paste all this code into the new page layout after `<asp:Content ContentPlaceholderID="PlaceHolderMain" runat="server">`.

The PlaceHolderMain should now look similar to this:

```
<asp:Content ContentPlaceholderID="PlaceHolderMain" runat="server">
 <div class="customBreadcrumbs">
  <a href="#">Site Name</a> &gt; Page Title
 </div>

 <div class="customBodyLeft">
  <h1>Frozen Waffles</h1>

  <p>Lorem ipsum dolor...</p>
 </div>

 <div class="customBodyRight">
  <div class="customBodyImage">
   <img src="waffle_photo.jpg" alt="Frozen Waffle Stack" />
  </div>
  <a href="#" class="customOrderNow" title="Order Now"></a>
 </div>
</asp:Content>
```

In the next few steps, you will replace portions of this code with field controls and Web Parts. This will change static text and HTML into content that can be edited by content authors.

7. Replace the contents of customBreadcrumbs with an <asp:SiteMapPath> control:

```
<div class="customBreadcrumbs">
 <asp:SiteMapPath runat="server"/>
</div>
```

This control will display a traditional breadcrumb trail like the one used in SharePoint 2007 or the NightandDay master page in SharePoint 2010. It builds the breadcrumb using the default site map data provider that is defined in the web.config file on the web server. Site map data providers are what ASP.NET uses to store site map infrastructure data to be used in various navigation elements.

8. Replace the Frozen Waffles that is inside the <h1> tags with the Title field control. You can do this by deleting Frozen Waffles and then dragging Title from the Page Fields section of the Toolbox on the right.

```
<h1><SharePointWebControls:TextField
FieldName="fa564e0f-0c70-4ab9-b863-0177e6ddd247"
 runat="server"></SharePointWebControls:TextField></h1>
```

9. Replace the <p> tags containing the Greeked Lorem Ipsum text with the Page Content field control. You can just delete the <p> tags and then drag Page Content from the Content Fields section of the Toolbox.

```
<div class="customBodyLeft">
<h1><SharePointWebControls:TextField
FieldName="fa564e0f-0c70-4ab9-b863-0177e6ddd247"
runat="server"></SharePointWebControls:TextField></h1>

<PublishingWebControls:RichHtmlField
FieldName="f55c4d88-1f2e-4ad9-aaa8-819af4ee7ee8"
runat="server"></PublishingWebControls:RichHtmlField>
</div>
```

10. Replace the waffle_photo <img> tag with the Page Image field control. Delete the entire <img> tag and drag in the Page Image from the Content Fields section of the Toolbox.

```
<div class="customBodyImage">
 <PublishingWebControls:RichImageField
FieldName="3de94b06-4120-41a5-b907-88773e493458"
runat="server"></PublishingWebControls:RichImageField>
</div>
```

For the Order Now button, content authors will need some flexibility to add an HTML button and maybe a link or some JavaScript. A Web Part enables that sort of flexibility. To allow content authors to add a Web Part to the page, you can use either a publishing HTML field or a Web Part zone. Rather than add a publishing HTML site column to the content type, a Web Part zone is probably less complicated.

11. Delete the `<a href>` and then add a Web Part zone. SharePoint Designer needs to be in Design view or Split view for adding Web Part zones, so switch to the Split view by clicking Split at the bottom of the main window. Then, from the ribbon, click Insert ⇨ Web Part Zone. You can switch back to Code view when you are done.

Notice that adding a Web Part zone not only adds a `<WebPartPages:WebPartZone>` control where your cursor was placed, but also adds a `<WebPartPages:SPProxyWebPartManager>` control to the top of the `PlaceHolderMain`. The `SPProxyWebPartManager` only needs to be added to the page once to handle multiple Web Part zones. If you want, you can change the title of `<WebPartPages:WebPartZone>` from "Zone 1" to something more meaningful like "Right Zone." For editing purposes, this can be helpful if you need to add more than one Web Part zone to a page layout. You can also change the default ID that is applied to the Web Part zone. This ID is generated automatically to be uniquely different from any other IDs in the page layout. IDs cannot start with numbers, and they must not contain spaces or special characters. Also, if you change the ID, be sure you don't accidently replicate another ID that is already on the page.

This completes the changes to `PlaceHolderMain`. Now turn your attention to the `PlaceHolderPageTitle` content placeholder. In the Randy's Waffles master page, this placeholder is located inside the `<title>` HTML tag for the page. Anything placed inside this placeholder will override the contents of the `<title>` tag for the page. Because the website is a public-facing Internet site, some branding would be nice here. By adding "Randy's Waffles" before the Page Title field control, every page that uses this page layout will have that text before the actual name of the page in the HTML title that shows in web browsers.

12. Add the text **Randy's Waffles -** before the `<SharePointWebControls:FieldValue>` in the `PlaceHolderPageTitle`:

```
<asp:Content ContentPlaceholderID="PlaceHolderPageTitle" runat="server">
Randy's Waffles - <SharePointWebControls:FieldValue id="PageTitle"
FieldName="Title" runat="server"/>
</asp:Content>
```

13. The page layout is almost done. The last step is to introduce a style that controls the line height for pages created from this page layout. This CSS isn't placed in the main style sheet because you don't want this line height to apply to all the out-of-the-box SharePoint pages, only the ones that will be used on the pages about Randy's Waffles. To do this, you need to add an `<asp:Content>` control that points to the `PlaceHolderAdditionalPageHead` content placeholder in the master page. This placeholder is located at the bottom of the `<head>` section of the master page, so any content placed in the `<asp:Content>` will be loaded after all the other master page CSS. Add the following code to the page layout, outside of any existing `<asp:Content>` control:

```
<asp:Content ContentPlaceholderID="PlaceHolderAdditionalPageHead"
runat="server">
 <style type="text/css">
  .customBody {
   line-height:150%;
```

```
    }
    </style>
</asp:Content>
```

14. This completes the subpage page layout. Now you can save and publish the page layout and try it out from within the SharePoint Web user interface. To save the page, click the little disk icon at the top of the page in SharePoint Designer.

Although the page layout has been physically created, you still need to check it in and approve it before content authors can use it:

1. Click back on the Page Layouts item in the Site Objects menu, find `WafflePage.aspx`, and click its icon.

2. From the ribbon, click Check In, select Publish a major version, and then click OK.

3. SharePoint notifies you that "This document requires content approval. Do you want to view or modify its approval status?" Click Yes. This opens a web browser to a view of the Master Page Gallery, sorted by Approval Status.

4. Click the arrow to the right of WafflePage, and then select Approve/Reject. In the Approve/Reject dialog, click Approved and then OK.

With the page layout checked in and approved, you can utilize it to create the subpage for Randy's Waffles by following these steps:

1. Click Site Actions ⇨ New Page.

2. Name the page **Sub Page**, and then click Create.

3. SharePoint creates a new page, and the new page layout can be selected from the ribbon by clicking Page ⇨ Page Layout ⇨ Waffle Page.

Figure 9-20 shows the new page layout in edit mode. All that's left to do is add some content to the page.

4. Enter a title and some page content. For the Page Image, you can insert a picture from SharePoint and select `/Style Library/Waffles/waffle_photo.jpg`.

This photo is available with the rest of the branding images for Randy's Waffles that were added to the Style Library in Chapter 8.

5. For the Web Part, click the Add a Web Part button, select Media and Content ⇨ Content Editor, and then click Add. Click the link labeled "Click here to Add New Content," and then from the ribbon, click Format Text ⇨ HTML ⇨ Edit HTML Source and add the following code:

```
<a title="Order Now" class="customOrderNow" href="#"></a>
```

6. Turn off the Web Part chrome. With the Web Part selected, from the ribbon, click Web Part Tools ⇨ Options ⇨ Web Part Properties. In the panel that appears on the right, expand Appearance and change Chrome Type to None, and then click OK.

Figure 9-21 shows the Web Part properties panel.

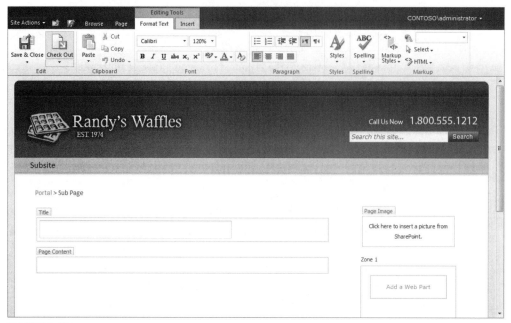

FIGURE 9-20

FIGURE 9-21

7. When you are satisfied with how the page looks, click the disk icon at the top of the page to save and close it. Remember from the earlier note that you may need to publish and approve the file before users will see it.

Figure 9-22 shows the finished Randy's Waffles page.

FIGURE 9-22

 You may notice that your new page does not automatically show in the SharePoint global navigation. By default, publishing site navigation is set to show only sites. You can change this easily by clicking Site Actions ⇨ Site Settings, and under Look and Feel, clicking Navigation. You can adjust the global navigation to show subsites, pages, or both.

Creating the Home-Page Page Layout

For this example, you will be creating the Randy's Waffles home-page page layout. Figure 9-23 shows the HTML mockup look and feel for the home page.

FIGURE 9-23

Unlike the previous example, this page layout will be based on the Welcome Page content type. There is no reason why it couldn't use the Article Page content type as well, but because it's more of a landing page, Welcome Page is probably a more appropriate starting point.

1. Ensure that your site is still open in SharePoint Designer.

2. From the Site Objects menu on the left side, click Page Layouts.

3. From the ribbon, click New Page Layout.

4. In the New dialog box, leave Content Type Group set to Page Layout Content Types; for Content Type Name, select Welcome Page; enter a URL Name of **WaffleHome.aspx**; enter a Title of **Waffle Home Page**; and then click OK.

SharePoint Designer will create a basic page layout and open it.

5. Switch to Code view by clicking Code at the bottom of the main window.

With the almost empty page layout opened in Code view, you can start adding HTML from the HTML mockup created in Chapter 3 (the files are available with the downloads for this chapter).

6. Open `index.html` and copy the contents of `<div class="customBody">`. (You can omit the `.customClear` div because that was included in the master page created in Chapter 8.) Paste all this code into the new page layout after `<asp:Content ContentPlaceholderID="PlaceHolderMain" runat="server">`. The `PlaceHolderMain` should now look like this:

```
<asp:Content ContentPlaceholderID="PlaceHolderMain" runat="server">
<div class="customBanner">
        <a href="#" class="customBannerText">Join Our Waffle of the Month Club</a>
        <a href="#" class="customBannerButton" title="Join Our Waffle of the Month
Club"></a>
  </div>
  <div class="customClear"></div>

  <div class="customGapBeforePod"></div>
  <div class="customClear"></div>

  <div class="customPodHolder">
      <div class="customPod">
      <div class="customPodHeader">Fresh Maple Syrup</div>
      <p>Lorem ipsum...</p>
       <a href="#">More Info</a>
        </div>
        <div class="customPod">
      <div class="customPodHeader">Fresh Maple Syrup</div>
      <p>Lorem ipsum...</p>
      <a href="#">More Info</a>
         </div>
         <div class="customPod">
      <div class="customPodHeader">Fresh Maple Syrup</div>
      <a href="#">20 Frozen Waffles for $20.00</a>
      <p>Lorem ipsum...</p>
      <br/>
      <a href="#">3000 Frozen Waffles for $60.00</a>
      <p>Lorem ipsum...</p>
         </div>
  </div>
  </asp:Content>
```

In the next few steps, you will replace portions of this code with field controls and Web Parts. On a home page like this, it can be tricky to determine what should be publishing

HTML field controls and what should be Web Parts. Keep in mind that Web Parts do not store history; but also consider that if you want to add field controls, you need to create a new content type and add a site column. Adding site columns to the out-of-the-box content types is not typically recommended. For the Randy's Waffles home page, the top graphical area will be a Web Part zone and the bottom text columns will be one large publishing HTML field control.

7. Start by replacing the banner area with a Web Part zone. Remove all the content between `<div class="customBanner">` and the matching `</div>`. Temporarily switch to the Split view by clicking the Split button at the bottom of the main window. Then, from the ribbon, click Insert ⇨ Web Part Zone. You can switch back to Code view when you are done.

As before, note that adding a Web Part zone not only adds a `<WebPartPages:WebPartZone>` control where your cursor was placed, but also a `<WebPartPages:SPProxyWebPartManager>` control to the top of `PlaceHolderMain`. Change the title of `<WebPartPages:WebPartZone>` from "Zone 1" to something more meaningful, such as "Banner Zone."

8. Replace the "pod" area with a publishing HTML field control. Remove all the content between `<div class="customPodHolder">` and the matching `</div>`, and then drag Page Content from the Content Fields section of the Toolbox.

```
<div class="customPodHolder">
<PublishingWebControls:RichHtmlField
FieldName="f55c4d88-1f2e-4ad9-aaa8-819af4ee7ee8"
runat="server">
</PublishingWebControls:RichHtmlField>
</div>
```

This will allow content authors to add HTML for the three columns that were shown in the HTML mockup. Now, as in the previous example, you can add some branding to the `PlaceHolderPageTitle`.

9. Add the text Randy's Waffles before the `<SharePointWebControls:FieldValue>` in the `PlaceHolderPageTitle`:

```
<asp:Content ContentPlaceholderID="PlaceHolderPageTitle" runat="server">
Randy's Waffles - <SharePointWebControls:FieldValue id="PageTitle"
FieldName="Title"  runat="server"/>
</asp:Content>
```

Again, like the previous example, some styles should only be applied to pages created from this page layout.

10. Add the following code to the page layout outside of any existing `<asp:Content>` control:

```
<asp:Content ContentPlaceholderID="PlaceHolderAdditionalPageHead"
runat="server">
<style type="text/css">
  .customBody {
  background-image:url(/style%20library/Waffles/hero.jpg);
  background-repeat:no-repeat;
  font-size:110%;
  padding:0 20px !important;
  width: 918px !important;
```

```
    }
    .s4-ca {
     background-color: transparent;
    }
    #s4-titlerow {
     display: none;
    }
   </style>
  </asp:Content>
```

This CSS code takes care of a number of things that are specific to the home page:

➤ It changes the `.customBody` background to include the large waffle photo and changes some padding and width to ensure that the image is shown edge to edge instead of having padding as normal content would. Note that the URL for the image may need to change if you are using this branding in a subsite collection.

➤ The `!important` properties are set on the padding and width styles because they need to override styles that appear later in the master page.

➤ The background color of `.s4-ca` is changed from white to transparent to ensure that the waffle photo shows through.

➤ The `#s4-titlerow` is hidden; this is where normal pages would show titles and descriptions, but for the home page you don't need any of that.

11. Click the little disk icon at the top of the page in SharePoint Designer to save the page.

Like the previous examples, even though the page layout has been created, you still need to check it in and approve it before content authors can use it:

1. Click back on the Page Layouts item in the Site Objects menu, find `WaffleHome.aspx`, and click its icon.

2. From the ribbon, click Check In, select Publish a major version, and then click OK.

3. SharePoint notifies you that "This document requires content approval. Do you want to view or modify its approval status?" Click Yes. This opens a browser window to a view of the Master Page Gallery, sorted by Approval Status.

4. Click the arrow to the right of WaffleHome, select Approve/Reject, and then from the Approve/Reject dialog box, click Approved and then OK.

Now that the page layout is available for use, it can be selected as one of the available page layouts. Unlike the previous example, instead of making a new page, you will change the existing home page page layout and then add the Randy's Waffles content to make it complete:

1. Navigate to the home page and click Site Actions ➪ Edit Page. From the ribbon, click Page ➪ Page Layout ➪ Waffle Home Page.

The new page layout is loaded with the existing content of the page. Next you will update the page content to look more like the Randy's Waffles home page.

2. In the Banner Zone, click the Add a Web Part button, select Media and Content ⇨ Content Editor, and then click Add. Click the link labeled Click here to Add New Content; and from the ribbon, click Format Text ⇨ HTML ⇨ Edit HTML Source, and add the following code:

```
<a class="customBannerText" href="#">Join Our Waffle of the Month Club</a> <a
title="Join Our Waffle of the Month Club" class="customBannerButton"
href="#"></a>
```

3. Turn off the Web Part chrome. With the Web Part selected, from the ribbon, click Web Part Tools ⇨ Options ⇨ Web Part Properties. In the panel that appears on the left, expand Appearance, change Chrome Type to None, and then click OK.

With the banner set up, the next task is to change the body content.

4. Scroll down to Page Content, select all the existing content, and delete it. From the ribbon, click Format Text ⇨ HTML ⇨ Edit HTML Source. The HTML for this area can be copied directly from the customPodHolder <div> from the HTML mockup. Paste the following HTML into the box, and then click OK:

```
<div class="customPod">
 <div class="customPodHeader">Fresh Maple Syrup</div>
 <p>Lorem ipsum...</p>
  <a href="#">More Info</a>
</div>
<div class="customPod">
 <div class="customPodHeader">Fresh Maple Syrup</div>
 <p>Lorem ipsum...</p>
 <a href="#">More Info</a>
</div>
<div class="customPod">
 <div class="customPodHeader">Fresh Maple Syrup</div>
 <a href="#">20 Frozen Waffles for $20.00</a>
 <p>Lorem ipsum...</p>
 <br/>
 <a href="#">3000 Frozen Waffles for $60.00</a>
 <p>Lorem ipsum...</p>
</div>
```

You can modify the Lorem ipsum text, replacing it with something longer or more meaningful, but for the purposes of this example, the full text would take up too much space in the code snippet.

5. When you are satisfied with the page, click the disk icon at the top of the page to save and close it. Remember from the earlier note that you may need to publish and approve the file before users will see the changes.

Figure 9-24 shows the finished Randy's Waffles home page.

FIGURE 9-24

SUMMARY

In the world of SharePoint branding, the master page often seems to take center stage; but when you begin to understand SharePoint's publishing capabilities, it becomes obvious that page layouts are a worthy co-star. In this chapter, you have learned about the close relationship between master pages, content placeholders, and page layouts. You have also learned that page layouts are not only responsible for the inner design of a SharePoint page, but also control the layout of the editable field controls and Web Parts. You also have seen how page layouts are based on a content type that dictates the types of data that can be stored via the use of site columns.

By walking through the hands-on examples, you have created your own page layout with field controls and Web Parts, as well as your own custom content type and site columns. You should now have a healthy appreciation for page layouts and their influence on web content management in SharePoint 2010.

10

Web Parts and XSLT

WHAT'S IN THIS CHAPTER?

➤ An overview of what Web Parts are and how they are used in SharePoint

➤ How to use the Content Editor Web Part to add CSS and JavaScript to a page

➤ How XSL is used to style XML data

➤ How to use the XML Viewer Web Part to leverage XML and XSL in SharePoint 2010

➤ How to use the XSLT List View Web Part

➤ How to use the Content Query Web Part

The previous chapter introduced Web Parts and how to use them to create great looking pages. This is certainly a great use for Web Parts, but there are many more uses for them in SharePoint. This chapter dives a bit deeper by describing examples of how to create dynamic content on your site by using some out-of-the-box Web Parts in SharePoint 2010.

Many of the out-of-the-box SharePoint Web Parts utilize XML (Extensible Markup Language) to bring data out of SharePoint for displaying on the screen. However, XML alone would be pretty terrible to look at, since it's meant to be read by computers, not humans. This is why XSL (Extensible Stylesheet Language) and XSLT (Extensible Stylesheet Language Translations) were created: to provide a simple mechanism for applying stylistic changes to XML, often to translate it from raw data into human-readable formats such as HTML. SharePoint leverages XML and XSL heavily in Web Parts to allow designers and developers to customize the appearance of data. Also, note that the terms XSLT and XSL are often used interchangeably; however, XSLT is actually a subset of XSL. You will learn more about how both work later in this chapter.

WHAT ARE WEB PARTS?

You may recall from the previous chapter that a Web Part is a modular unit of functionality that serves as another means of displaying site information to end users. Web Parts can take many forms, from list and site page aggregation to rich HTML content. Unlike field controls, Web Parts data and content is not versioned as changes are made. Also, in the previous chapter you learned about how Web Parts in SharePoint 2010 can be placed directly inside rich HTML areas in wiki pages and publishing pages, or they can be placed in Web Part zones that have been defined on pages or page layouts.

Types of Web Parts in SharePoint

There are three easily segmented types of Web Parts:

➤ **Out-of-the-box** — Out-of-the-box Web Parts are included with your version of SharePoint.

➤ **Custom Web Parts** — Custom Web Parts are simply those that your team develops on its own. Typically, these are .NET projects that are deployed to the SharePoint site to be used in whatever way you see fit. Because these Web Parts typically are written in Visual Studio using the .NET Framework, anything you can do there, you can do in a Web Part. This makes Web Parts a very powerful feature of any SharePoint deployment.

➤ **Third-party Web Parts** — Third-party Web Parts are pre-packaged custom Web Parts that have been created by some company that you can use in your site, most often for a fee. An example of a third-party Web Part is the Group Email Web Part from Bamboo Solutions, which enables you to send an e-mail to all users in a SharePoint site. This is a really cool feature that isn't included out-of-the-box but that Bamboo Solutions has created to enhance your own SharePoint administration.

Adding a Web Part to a Page

To get an idea of what a Web Part is, take a look at Figure 10-1. This shows a typical team site in edit mode. This page has one List View Web Part, displaying a view of the Shared Documents library.

To add a Web Part to this page, simply click anywhere in the rich HTML content area, and then click Insert ⇨ Web Part from the ribbon. The ribbon will expand to show a list of categories and available Web Parts (see Figure 10-2).

You can select from the list and then add the Web Part to the page by clicking Add. With the Web Part added to the page (in this case, an Image Viewer Web Part), you can easily adjust its properties. Click the Web Part, and then click Web Part Tools ⇨ Options ⇨ Web Part Properties from the ribbon (see Figure 10-3); alternatively, you could click the small downward facing arrow at the upper-right of the Web Part.

Figure 10-4 shows the Web Part properties menu for the Image Viewer Web Part.

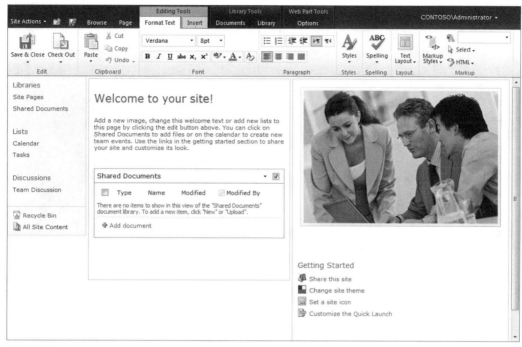

FIGURE 10-1

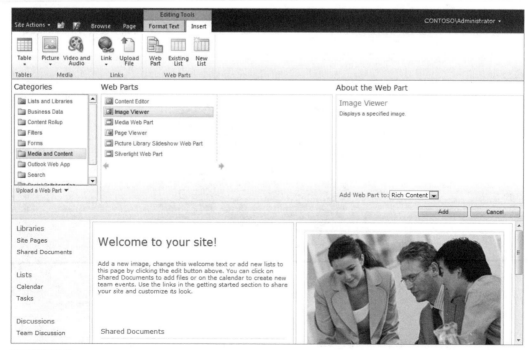

FIGURE 10-2

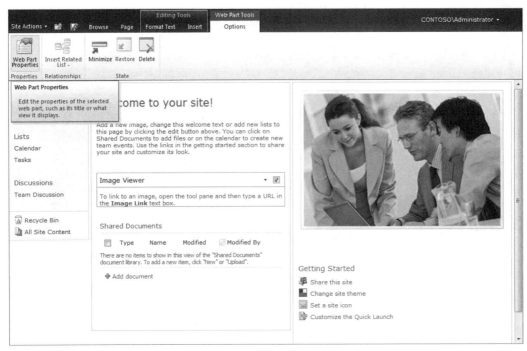

FIGURE 10-3

FIGURE 10-4

This shows the power of Web Parts: Content authors can add them throughout a SharePoint site to leverage many different types of functionality that isn't available in other areas of SharePoint. Next, you will take a look at how the Content Editor Web Part can be used to add different types of content to your SharePoint site.

USING THE CONTENT EDITOR WEB PART

One of the most commonly used Web Parts for SharePoint branding is the Content Editor Web Part (CEWP). The CEWP is interesting because it not only allows you to add rich HTML content to a page, it also allows you to place CSS and other script source code, such as JavaScript or Flash, on a page. This is very useful because while standard rich HTML fields in SharePoint allow you to enter source as well, SharePoint typically strips out all scripting code from them as the page is saved. This is best illustrated by some examples.

Adding CSS to a CEWP to Hide the Quick Launch Menu

In the following example, you will learn how to add CSS to hide the Quick Launch menu on a single page (a very common request in SharePoint). For this example, you can use a basic SharePoint 2010 team site:

1. Edit the page by clicking Site Actions ⇨ Edit Page.

2. Place your cursor in the main content area, and then click Insert ⇨ Web Part from the ribbon.

3. From Categories, select Media and Content, and from Web Parts, select Content Editor, and then click Add (See Figure 10-5).

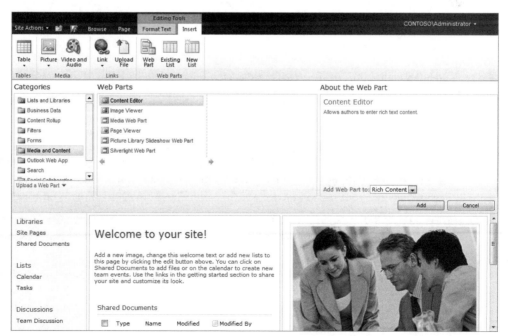

FIGURE 10-5

If you are used to how the Content Editor Web Part worked in SharePoint 2007, you will notice that it behaves a little differently in SharePoint 2010.

4. To start adding content to the Web Part, click the little arrow on the right side of the Web Part, and then select Edit Web Part (see Figure 10-6). This will open the Web Part tool pane on the right side of the page.

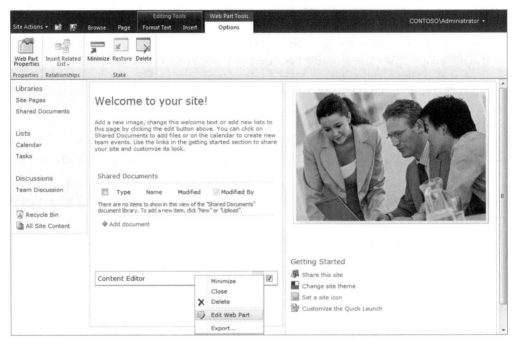

FIGURE 10-6

In SharePoint 2007, the first two options would have been Rich Text Editor and Source Editor. Notice in Figure 10-7 that neither of these options is showing in the new CEWP tool pane.

Don't worry, though; you can still edit content in the CEWP in SharePoint 2010. To just edit the content of the Web Part (like the Rich Text Editor button would have done in SharePoint 2007), simply click in the middle of the Web Part where it says "Click here to add new content." From there, you can edit the content just like any other rich HTML area in SharePoint 2010, by using the ribbon. In the next step, you will see that this is also where you would add your own HTML code (like the SharePoint 2007 Source Editor button).

5. If you haven't done so already, click the link in the Web Part that says "Click here to add new content," and then from the ribbon click Format Text ➪ HTML ➪ Edit HTML Source (See Figure 10-8).

Notice that you also have an option to Convert to XHTML. This can be useful for content authors who are proficient with HTML but are not skilled at creating XHTML-compliant code. Pressing this button will convert anything entered into the HTML source to valid XHTML code.

FIGURE 10-7

FIGURE 10-8

6. After clicking Edit HTML Source, you are presented with a dialog for entering HTML source code. For this example, you will be hiding the Quick Launch menu on the left side of the page. Enter the following CSS code into the box, and then press OK:

```
<style type="text/css">
  body #s4-leftpanel { display: none; }
  .s4-ca { margin-left: 0px; }
</style>
```

This code will hide the HTML that holds the Quick Launch menu and will reset the main content area margin to not reserve space for the Quick Launch. After pressing OK, you will most likely will see a notification that says "Warning: The HTML source you entered might have been modified." This message can be confusing; it indicates that SharePoint might change the code that was entered to protect the content author from entering something invalid. However, it's worth noting that this message shows regardless of whether the code has been changed.

You will notice immediately that the Quick Launch has been hidden, but you will probably want to hide the Content Editor Web Part so that users don't see it on the page.

7. From the tool pane on the right, expand Appearance, change Chrome Type to None, and then click OK. Don't worry, you will still be able to see the Web Part when the page is in edit mode.

8. From the ribbon, click Save & Close to save the page.

You can see in Figure 10-9 that the Quick Launch menu has been hidden on just this page, thanks to the CSS you entered into the Content Editor Web Part.

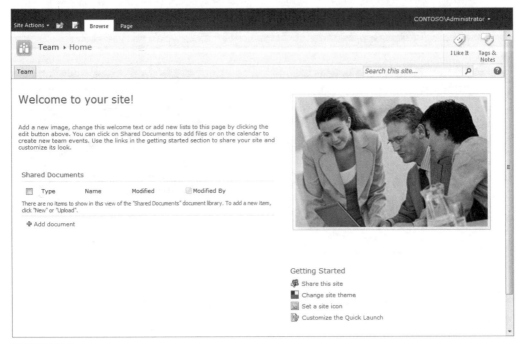

FIGURE 10-9

The previous example was fairly simple, but what if you want to add more complex JavaScript or Flash to the page? While you could add this code directly from the Edit HTML Source button, like you did before, there are some subtle annoyances that can occur in SharePoint 2010 when entering script code. One such problem is if you are using a JavaScript `document.write()` command to add content to the page. SharePoint gets confused and adds a duplicate entry every time the page is saved.

One way to get around these issues is to upload the script source to a document library, and then simply link to the script from a CEWP. For example, to add the current date to the page, you could use some simple, pre-built JavaScript like the following code that was found at `cgiscript.net`:

```
<script language="JavaScript">
// ***********************************************
// AUTHOR: WWW.CGISCRIPT.NET, LLC
// URL: http://www.cgiscript.net
// Use the script, just leave this message intact.
// Download your FREE CGI/Perl Scripts today!
// ( http://www.cgiscript.net/scripts.htm )
// ***********************************************
        var now = new Date();
        var days = new Array(
          'Sunday','Monday','Tuesday',
          'Wednesday','Thursday','Friday','Saturday');
        var months = new Array(
          'January','February','March','April','May',
          'June','July','August','September','October',
          'November','December');
        var date = ((now.getDate()<10) ? "0" : "")+ now.getDate();
        function fourdigits(number)      {
          return (number < 1000) ? number + 1900 : number;}
      today =   days[now.getDay()] + ", " +
        months[now.getMonth()] + " " +
        date + ", " +
          (fourdigits(now.getYear()));
      document.write(today);
</script>
```

In the following example you will upload this code to the Site Assets document library and then link to it from a CEWP. The code is available with the downloads for this chapter.

1. Save the JavaScript current date code to your local file system as `date.js`.

2. From the home page of your team site, click Site Actions ➪ View All Site Content, and then click the Site Assets link.

3. Click the Add document link in the middle of the page. From the Upload Document dialog, click the Browse button, and then select date.js from your file system, and click OK.

   With the file uploaded to the Site Assets folder, you can now link to it from a Content Editor Web Part.

4. Navigate back to the home page of your team site and click Site Actions ➪ Edit Page.

5. Place your cursor in the main content area and from the ribbon click Insert ➪ Web Part.

6. From Categories, select Media and Content, and from Web Parts, select Content Editor, and then click Add.

7. Like in the previous example, click the little arrow on the right side of the Web Part and select Edit Web Part.

   This time, instead of entering the HTML source directly, you will link to the uploaded JavaScript file.

8. From the Web Part tool pane on the right, for Content Link, enter the path to the newly uploaded `date.js` file. If your SharePoint site collection is at the root of your web application, the reference will be `/SiteAssets/date.js`.

9. Again, it's probably a good idea to hide the Web Part chrome. From the tool pane on the right, expand Appearance and change Chrome Type to None, and then click OK.

10. Click Save & Close from the ribbon to save the page.

You can see in Figure 10-10 that JavaScript adds the current date to this page.

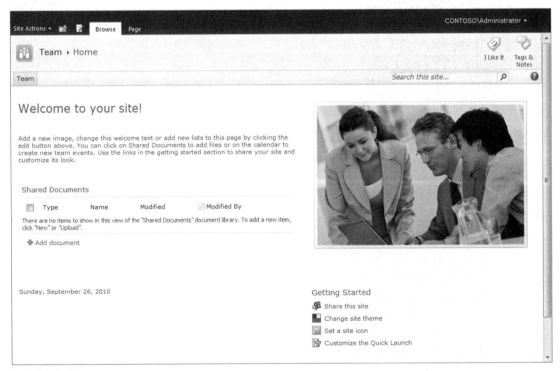

FIGURE 10-10

The CEWP can be useful for adding all sorts of content, even content that isn't normally allowed in rich HTML areas (like JavaScript and Flash code). This is because SharePoint is less strict with the CEWP then it is with other rich HTML areas. Just remember that if the CEWP is available to content authors, they, too, can place script code on the page. Some guidance or governance may be needed to ensure content authors use this power responsibly. In the next section, you will learn about how XSL works, and later you will work with more SharePoint Web Parts that leverage XSL for their styling.

A BRIEF XSL PRIMER

The Extensible Stylesheet Language (XSL) is the basis for styling XML output in web applications. It would be easy to draw parallels between what it does and what you saw CSS does for HTML output in Chapter 7. In CSS, you create rules for how certain HTML elements appear in the rendered HTML output within the clients' browser. XSL does essentially the same thing for XML output.

One main difference, though, is that there are a finite number of elements that you can style within CSS. That is, you can only apply rules to the number of supported elements within the HTML language. You can get to those elements in different ways (classes, IDs, selectors, etc.), but you can only apply rules to those elements.

In XML, there aren't any elements that are defined. Anything can be an element. Consider the following `quiz.xml` file, which is available with the downloads for this chapter:

```
<?xml version="1.0" encoding="utf-8" ?>
<quiz>
  <question>
    <questionID>1</questionID>
    <displayQuestion type="choice">Which platform is SharePoint built
      on?</displayQuestion>
    <answers>
      <answer>PhP</answer>
      <answer>ColdFusion</answer>
      <answer>ASP.NET</answer>
      <answer>J2EE</answer>
    </answers>
  </question>
  <question>
    <questionID>2</questionID>
    <displayQuestion type="choice">What assets do SharePoint branders typically
      modify?</displayQuestion>
    <answers>
      <answer>CSS Rules</answer>
      <answer>Master Pages</answer>
      <answer>Page Layouts</answer>
      <answer>Images</answer>
      <answer>All of the above</answer>
    </answers>
  </question>
</quiz>
```

 This XML file will be used in several examples in the first half of this chapter. To follow along with the examples, you should have this file saved to a location on your computer that can be browsed with Internet Explorer.

There is neither a `<table>` tag nor a `<html>` tag. The "tags" in an XML file are node names contrived by the author of the XML document. These could literally be anything.

Furthermore, this is just one example. If you had a separate XML file that was used for a different purpose, there would pretty much be no nodes that matched up. So, XML needs its own styling mechanism so that it displays in a browser something that is useful, easy to read, and consistent with the branding of your site — in other words, not like Figure 10-11 (which is how the above code would look in your browser without any styling).

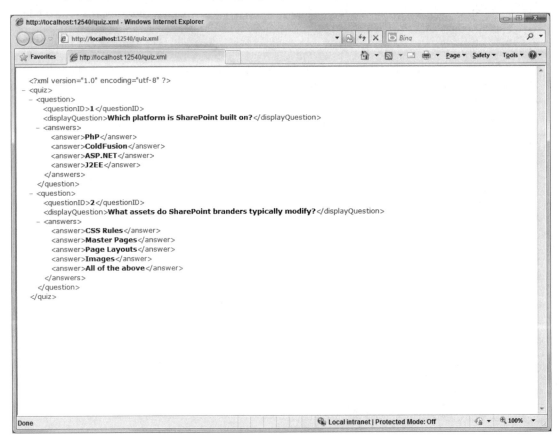

FIGURE 10-11

If a user were presented with that, it wouldn't mean very much. However, with XSL, the page could look more like Figure 10-12.

Figure 10-12 is much easier to understand than Figure 10-11. This is what XSL does; it makes XML readable to the typical web user. With this example in mind, it should be obvious that XSL is just the way to style XML data into a format your customers can understand. XSL is to XML what CSS is to HTML. You will learn how to add this XSL file later in the chapter.

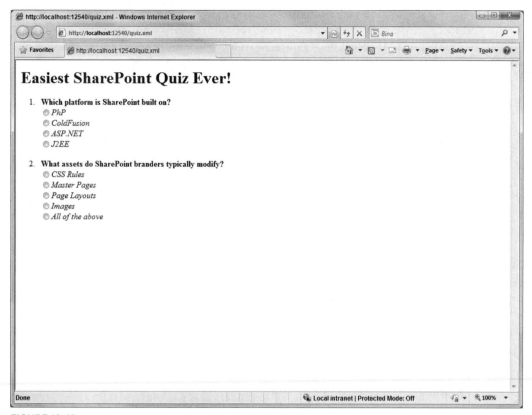

FIGURE 10-12

When discussing XSL, there are three concepts that you need to be familiar with:

➤ **XSL Transformations (XSLT)** — The language for displaying your XML data in XHTML format

➤ **XPath** — The language for navigating through your XML data

➤ **XSL Formatting Objects (XSL-FO)** — A language for styling XML for printed or paged media; not typically used with SharePoint

The XPath language tells your browser how to read your XML document. If you want to read each "question" node and then dive into each "answer" subnode, you do this through XPath. This is simply a way for the XSL to understand the architecture of your XML data.

Beyond that, there is the transformation and formatting of your XML data. The transformation is saying that, for each "question" node in our example, we want it to be an ordered list item and then each "answer" child node to be a radio button item. This is done through XSLT.

Finally, there is the styling of the XHTML rendering of your XML data. For example, you want each answer to be in italics. If this XML were going to be used for printed media, XSL-FO could be used to style the data. Because this XML is intended to be shown on the web, XSLT is the better choice for applying style.

It is important to understand that all this will overlap and, like most things in web application development, there are different ways to accomplish the same task. For example, in your XSLT, since you are creating HTML elements to represent your XML data, you can easily slip your style rules into the HTML element.

To see how this works, we will modify quiz.xml and add an XSL stylesheet. The first step is to add a reference to a new XSLT stylesheet in your XML document, as shown in bold in the following code:

```
<?xml version="1.0" encoding="utf-8" ?>
<?xml-stylesheet type="text/xsl" href="quiz.xsl"?>
<quiz>
    << content removed for brevity >>
</quiz>
```

With this change in place, be sure to save the file. This new line simply tells your browser to look at a file called quiz.xsl and apply its rules to the XML data before rendering it to the user. This is just like adding a CSS style sheet reference to the head element of your HTML document.

Now you need to create your XSL document, quiz.xsl, in the same location on your computer as quiz.xml. Since XML and XSL are not compiled languages, you can write your code in whichever text editor you like. Certainly programs like Visual Studio and SharePoint Designer offer benefits like IntelliSense and color coding to help read and create your code much more efficiently, but something as simple as Notepad will work.

With that in mind, create a file called quiz.xsl and add the following lines to it:

```
<xsl:stylesheet version="1.0" xmlns:xsl="http://www.w3.org/1999/XSL/Transform">
</xsl:stylesheet>
```

This creates the actual style sheet that will be used for your XML document. Next, you need to tell your XSL document what to read, which means you need to add some XPath language, which you can see in bold in the following code:

```
<xsl:stylesheet version="1.0" xmlns:xsl="http://www.w3.org/1999/XSL/Transform">
  <xsl:template match="/">
    <html>
      <body>
        <h1>Easiest SharePoint Quiz Ever!</h1>
        <ol>
        </ol>
      </body>
    </html>
  </xsl:template>
</xsl:stylesheet>
```

The first line of the new text tells the parser to begin at the root node of the XML document (the / is the expression used to select the root node). As shown in the following table, there are several expressions in XPath that you can use when trying to select nodes. You will learn more about these expressions later in the chapter.

EXPRESSION	DESCRIPTION	EXAMPLE
[name of the node]	Selects all child nodes of the named node.	quiz selects all the child nodes of the quiz element in the XML document.
/	Selects from the root node.	/ starts from the root of the XML document. /quiz selects the quiz root element. quiz/question selects all question elements that are children of the quiz node.
//	Selects nodes in the XML document regardless of where they are in the document.	//question selects all question elements in the XML document, regardless of where they are located.
.	Selects the current node.	. selects the current node.
..	Selects the parent node.	.. at the question level would select quiz.
@	Selects attributes.	//displayQuestion/@type selects the attribute type from displayQuestion.

So far, the XSL template is saying, start with the root node and, before doing anything else, add some static HTML text to make the results more readable for the user. That is why you see the HTML elements and the h1 element. This is just static text that will get displayed on every XML document that uses this XSL style sheet.

Once the basic rendering is set up for your XML page, you will want to iterate through all question nodes and format them in a way that is readable to most users. Fortunately, there is an XSL element that is built to do exactly that: for-each. You can see the <xsl:for-each> element in use in the new text added to the XSL spreadsheet (highlighted in bold):

```
<xsl:stylesheet version="1.0" xmlns:xsl="http://www.w3.org/1999/XSL/Transform">
  <xsl:template match="/">
    <html>
      <body>
        <h1>Easiest SharePoint Quiz Ever!</h1>
        <ol>
          <xsl:for-each select="quiz/question">
            <li>
              <strong>
                <xsl:value-of select="displayQuestion"/>
              </strong>
              <br/>
            </li>
            <br/>
          </xsl:for-each>
        </ol>
      </body>
    </html>
  </xsl:template>
</xsl:stylesheet>
```

Notice that the `for-each` element is using an XPath expression for the `select` attribute. In this expression (`quiz/question`), the parser is going to take all question nodes that are children of the quiz node. Knowing the format of the XML document being parsed, you could have just as easily used `//question` for this attribute, as follows:

```
<xsl:for-each select="//question">
```

This would have selected all question nodes, regardless of where they reside.

You will also notice another XSL element has been used in this example: `value-of`. This element, as the name implies, displays the value of the node selected by the XPath expression in the `select` attribute. So, with the XPath expression of simply `displayQuestion`, the `value-of` element will just show the value of the `displayQuestion` node in the question element.

The last thing that needs to be done is iterate through the answers and display them as radio buttons. To do this, add the bolded text in the following code:

```
<xsl:stylesheet version="1.0" xmlns:xsl="http://www.w3.org/1999/XSL/Transform">
  <xsl:template match="/">
    <html>
      <body>
        <h1>Easiest SharePoint Quiz Ever!</h1>
        <ol>
          <xsl:for-each select="quiz/question">
            <li>
              <strong>
                <xsl:value-of select="displayQuestion"/>
              </strong>
              <br/>
              <xsl:for-each select="answers/answer">
                <span style="font-style: italic;">
                  <input type="radio">
                    <xsl:attribute name="name">
                      <xsl:value-of select="../../questionID"/>
                    </xsl:attribute>
                    <xsl:value-of select="."/>
                  </input>
                </span>
                <br/>
              </xsl:for-each>
            </li>
            <br/>
          </xsl:for-each>
        </ol>
      </body>
    </html>
  </xsl:template>
</xsl:stylesheet>
```

Although most of this will be a review of what you have done to this point, a couple of interesting things are worth pointing out. The first is all the styling going on. In this example, the entire answer list item is in italics because of the following line:

```
<span style="font-style: italic;">
```

Since you are already providing HTML elements as part of the rendering process for this XML document, you can easily include a `<span>` element and provide whatever styling you want through CSS rules in the style attribute of the `<span>` element. For many web developers, this is probably the easiest way to get the style they want applied to their XML document.

The other thing that is interesting to note is how the radio button lists are defined:

```
<input type="radio">
  <xsl:attribute name="name">
    <xsl:value-of select="../../questionID"/>
  </xsl:attribute>
  <xsl:value-of select="."/>
</input>
```

Of particular note is the part highlighted in bold. The first thing that is interesting is that this code is setting a particular attribute for the radio input element. In this case, it is programmatically setting the name attribute of the radio HTML element. Why is this necessary? If you don't set the name attribute, all radio elements will be selectable (meaning you could select all answers on all questions). To make the answers act in a manner consistent with a quiz, you need each answer group for each question to allow only one answer. To do this, you need to create a radio button listing (or grouping) so that each question has a group of radio buttons that are mutually exclusive. Set the name attribute of all radio button elements for a single question to something unique for that question. So, all answers for question #1 might have a name attribute of q1, while all answers for question #2 would have something like q2 for its name attribute. This will allow the answers to be a single-select option for each question.

To do this, you need to have a unique identifier for each set of answers. In this example (based on the XML file from the beginning of the chapter), there is a node on the parent (at the same level as displayQuestion) called questionID. The basic tree for this is as follows:

quiz ⇨ question (includes questionID) ⇨ answers ⇨ answer

Since this code is running at the "answer" level, to get to the questionID level, you have to navigate back up two levels. Using XPath, you can do this through the following expression:

```
../../questionID
```

This code is also setting the value of the radio button with the following line:

```
<xsl:value-of select="."/>
```

This is using the " . " expression to select the value of the current node.

At this point, your XSL style sheet is complete and should resemble the following:

```
<xsl:stylesheet version="1.0" xmlns:xsl="http://www.w3.org/1999/XSL/Transform">
  <xsl:template match="/">
    <html>
      <body>
        <h1>Easiest SharePoint Quiz Ever!</h1>
        <ol>
          <xsl:for-each select="quiz/question">
            <li>
```

```
          <strong>
            <xsl:value-of select="displayQuestion"/>
          </strong>
          <br/>
          <xsl:for-each select="answers/answer">
            <span style="font-style: italic;">
              <input type="radio">
                <xsl:attribute name="name">
                  <xsl:value-of select="../../questionID"/>
                </xsl:attribute>
                <xsl:value-of select="."/>
              </input>
            </span>
            <br/>
          </xsl:for-each>
        </li>
        <br/>
      </xsl:for-each>
    </ol>
  </body>
</html>
    </xsl:template>
  </xsl:stylesheet>
```

Save these changes and reload the `quiz.xml` in your browser; it should look like Figure 10-12. Obviously, you would need to do some more work on this to make it function like a quiz (make it into a web form and post the results to some page that could consume it and do whatever you wanted with the quiz results), but this should give you a good idea of how to understand the basics of XSL.

And with this primer complete, you are ready to start seeing how to apply XSL to style Web Parts in SharePoint 2010.

If you would like to learn more about XSL, you should consider picking up the following books:

➤ *Beginning XSLT and XPath: Transforming XML Documents and Data* (Wrox)

➤ *XSLT 2.0 and XPath 2.0 Programmer's Reference, 4th Edition* (Wrox)

Additionally, you might find the following websites useful:

➤ *The W3C Recommendation for XSL Transformations (XSLT):* `www.w3.org/TR/xslt`

➤ *w3schools XSL Tutorial:* `www.w3schools.com/xsl/xsl_languages.asp`

➤ *w3schools XSLT Tutorial:* `www.w3schools.com/xsl/xsl_intro.asp`

➤ *w3schools XPath Tutorial:* `www.w3schools.com/xpath/default.asp`

➤ *w3schools XSL-FO Tutorial:* `www.w3schools.com/xslfo/xslfo_intro.asp`

USING THE XML VIEWER WEB PART

This section describes a basic example of how you can use XML and XSL in SharePoint 2010 by providing a short demonstration of the XML Viewer Web Part. This Web Part enables you to provide XML data and to have an XSL style sheet be displayed directly in your SharePoint 2010 portal. There are several options for configuring this, which you will see as this section progresses.

For this example, you can use any type of SharePoint 2010 page, but the screenshots will show a simple team site.

1. Begin by editing the page by clicking Site Actions ➪ Edit Page or by clicking the small Edit button on the top-left of the page.

2. Next, place your cursor somewhere in one of the editable content areas. Wherever the cursor is placed is where the Web Part will appear. To add a new Web Part to the page, click Insert ➪ Web Part from the ribbon.

3. From the Web Parts menu, in the Categories list, click Content Rollup. Select XML Viewer from the Web Parts list, and then click Add. This adds the empty XML Viewer Web Part to the page (see Figure 10-13).

FIGURE 10-13

4. Click the "open the tool page" hyperlink so that you can begin adding your XML data and XSL stylesheet. When you click the link, you will see the tool pane, as shown in Figure 10-14.

FIGURE 10-14

For this example, the XML settings shown in Figure 10-14 are the only ones you need to adjust. Just by looking at the options presented, you can probably tell there are different ways to get the data into the Web Part. For both the XML data and the XSL style sheet, you can choose to manually enter the static data or link to an external source.

The ability to add a URL to an XML link opens a world of opportunity in just a few clicks. While it is certainly okay to enter in the static data manually here or even to link to a static XML or XSL document, another option might not be intuitive by looking at this screen. If you are comfortable working with the .NET Framework (or something similar), you can create a web page that retrieves current line-of-business data from your data repository and presents it as valid XML data that you can present on your main page. For example, you could have all your business data stored in a SQL Server 2008 database. You could create a page that queries your database and serves its results in XML format with an XML content type. That way, your data is always current and provides a cheap and easy way to get line-of-business data reported directly to your site. The XML link can even tie directly into other types of valid XML data on the web, such as RSS feeds.

However, for this example, it's sufficient to just show how to enter the data manually. For this step, you can use the XML data from the previous section. Remember that this XML is available with the downloads for this chapter:

```
<?xml version="1.0" encoding="utf-8" ?>
<quiz>
  <question>
    <questionID>1</questionID>
```

```
        <displayQuestion type="choice">Which platform is SharePoint
built on?</displayQuestion>
        <answers>
          <answer>PhP</answer>
          <answer>ColdFusion</answer>
          <answer>ASP.NET</answer>
          <answer>J2EE</answer>
        </answers>
      </question>
      <question>
        <questionID>2</questionID>
        <displayQuestion type="choice">What assets do SharePoint branders
typically modify?</displayQuestion>
        <answers>
          <answer>CSS Rules</answer>
          <answer>Master Pages</answer>
          <answer>Page Layouts</answer>
          <answer>Images</answer>
          <answer>All of the above</answer>
        </answers>
      </question>
    </quiz>
```

Notice that you will be starting with the basic XML data without a reference to an XSL file. The Web Part will create the relationship for you, so it wouldn't make sense to add one here.

5. Click the XML Editor button on the tool pane shown in Figure 10-14. This will present the Text Editor dialog. Simply paste in the XML data and click OK to close the editor.

Now, for the XSL data, you will use the final XSL style sheet from the previous section, which is also available for download:

```
<xsl:stylesheet version="1.0" xmlns:xsl="http://www.w3.org/1999/XSL/Transform">
  <xsl:template match="/">
    <html>
      <body>
        <h1>Easiest SharePoint Quiz Ever!</h1>
        <ol>
          <xsl:for-each select="quiz/question">
            <li>
              <strong>
                <xsl:value-of select="displayQuestion"/>
              </strong>
              <br/>
              <xsl:for-each select="answers/answer">
                <span style="font-style: italic;">
                  <input type="radio">
                    <xsl:attribute name="name">
                      <xsl:value-of select="../../questionID"/>
                    </xsl:attribute>
                    <xsl:value-of select="."/>
                  </input>
                </span>
                <br/>
              </xsl:for-each>
```

```
            </li>
            <br/>
          </xsl:for-each>
        </ol>
      </body>
    </html>
  </xsl:template>
</xsl:stylesheet>
```

6.   From the tool pane shown in Figure 10-14, press the XSL Editor button to launch another Text Editor dialog. Paste the XSL code into the box, and then press the OK button to close the Text Editor.

7.   You now have all the information you need for this Web Part, which means you can press the OK button in the tool pane to apply these changes and close the tool pane. Your SharePoint page should now resemble Figure 10-15.

FIGURE 10-15

You can see that the XML data is now included in your SharePoint page and that it is styled according to the rules you have created in your XSL style sheet.

8.   The last step is to save the page. You can do this from the ribbon by clicking Page ➪ Save & Close, or by clicking the small Save & Close icon at the upper-left of the ribbon.

Although this is a fairly simple example, it is fitting because this is a fairly simple Web Part. As long as you have valid XML data and a valid XSL style sheet, you simply have to add the information to the Web Part, and you are done. And there is no real difference between including the data statically using the text editors included in the tool pane or linking to an external data source. So, while this Web Part is powerful on its own, the ease of configuring it makes it an even more impressive tool to include in your branding efforts.

USING THE XSLT LIST VIEW WEB PART

You may remember XSLT List View Web Parts (or XLV for short) from Chapter 4, but they are worth discussing in the context of Web Parts, especially because XLVs can be styled using XSL. The XSLT List View Web Part combines the flexibility of the Data View Web Part (DVWP) with the ease of use of the List View Web Part. If you aren't familiar with the DVWP, it was often used in SharePoint 2007 to show information from SharePoint lists and libraries in a very custom way. It was possible to apply filtering, sorting, grouping, conditional formatting, as well as customize the look and feel and rendering behavior of the Web Part. The problem was that any changes that were made to it, including very basic changes, needed to be done through SPD.

The List View Web Part in SharePoint 2007 was fairly basic. If you've seen a view in the previous version, you've seen the LVWP. There wasn't too much customization that was easily possible without making complex modifications to the CAML used to render the view. But unlike the DVWP, it was easy to make changes through the SharePoint user interface.

The XSLT List View Web Part in SharePoint 2010 has views that are based on XSLT, which makes it possible to add filtering and conditional formatting. The big difference is that if you have a list that has several items in it, you can create a custom view with conditional formatting, filtering, and sorting, but you can still change back to a standard view. This ability to change between standard looking views and views with customized behavior is a big change with SharePoint 2010.

In the following example you will learn how to edit the XSL for an XLV in SharePoint Designer 2010. It's worth noting that you can change the display of XLVs in SharePoint Designer without diving into editing XSL directly. The example in Chapter 4 describes how you can use the SharePoint Designer UI to make conditional changes to the XLV display. In the following example, however, the focus will be on editing the actual XSL, not on the capabilities of SPD.

For this example, you should create a new page using the SharePoint web user interface. The screenshots for this section are based on a team site.

1. Open your SharePoint 2010 site, navigate to your new page, and add the Links Web Part (located in the Lists and Libraries Category) to your main page.

If you don't remember how to add Web Parts to your site, review the preceding "Using the XML Viewer Web Part" section. When you finish adding the Web Part, your home page should resemble Figure 10-16.

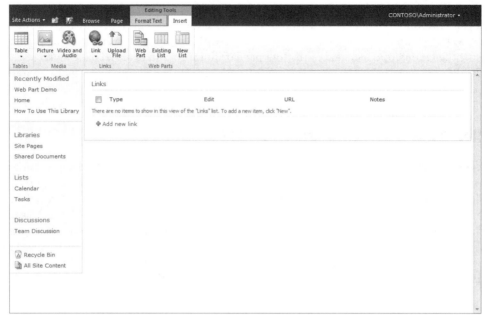

FIGURE 10-16

2. Add a few links just so that you have something to style in the next steps. You can do this by clicking the "Add new link" hyperlink at the bottom of the Web Part. After adding your links, be sure to save the page.

You will notice that clicking any of the links opens the link in the same window/tab of your browser. There isn't a property of this list that will tell the hyperlink to open in a new window. Since all List View Web Parts are now XML data styled by XSL rules, you can go into the code of the Web Part and modify the rendering behavior of the list to add this simple change, as described in the following step.

3. Open SharePoint Designer 2010, and then open your new page for editing. (If you unfamiliar with SharePoint Designer 2010, refer to Chapter 4). The page you created most likely will be in the Site Pages library. From the navigation panel on the left side of SPD, click Site Pages to open the gallery, and then right-click on your page and select Edit in Advanced Mode. When the page is open, if you are looking at the Split view in the editing pane, you should see your Web Part, as shown in Figure 10-17. If you are not viewing the page in Split view, choose the Split option at the bottom.

If you scroll through the Code view, you will notice that the basic definition of the Web Part is stored in XML format, as shown in the following code snippet. If you don't see this right away, it might be easier to search. Just remember that your view name will be unique to your environment:

```
<XmlDefinition>
    <View Name="{1A560587-790A-4240-A2F7-5BCA92E50E51}" MobileView="TRUE"
    Type="HTML" Hidden="TRUE" OrderedView="TRUE" DisplayName=""
    Url="/SitePages/LVWP.aspx" Level="1" BaseViewID="1" ContentTypeID="0x"
```

```
        ImageUrl="/_layouts/images/links.png">
            <Query>
                <OrderBy>
                    <FieldRef Name="Order" Ascending="TRUE"/>
                </OrderBy>
            </Query>
            <ViewFields>
                <FieldRef Name="DocIcon"/>
                <FieldRef Name="Edit"/>
                <FieldRef Name="URLwMenu"/>
                <FieldRef Name="Comments"/>
            </ViewFields>
            <RowLimit Paged="TRUE">30</RowLimit>
            <Toolbar Type="Standard"/>
        </View>
    </XmlDefinition>
```

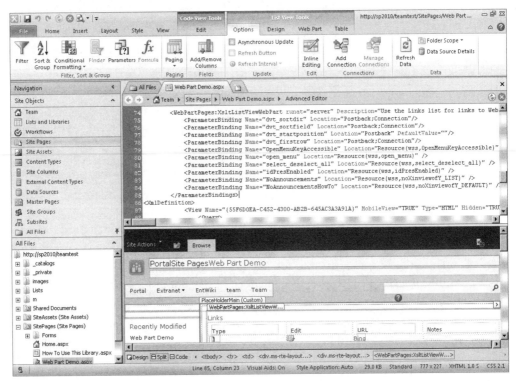

FIGURE 10-17

At this point, there are no visible XSLT rules that you can modify. However, the page *is* getting styled using XSLT rules included on the server. And, with SharePoint Designer, you can actually take a snapshot of those rules, put a local copy of them as a part of the Web Part, and then edit them directly. This enables you to have custom rendering for this specific Web Part without necessarily affecting other instances of the same Web Part, as described in the following steps.

4. While still in SharePoint Designer 2010, place your cursor on the Links List View Web Part (in either the Code or Design pane), and then click the Design tab of the List View Tools section of the ribbon, as shown in Figure 10-18.

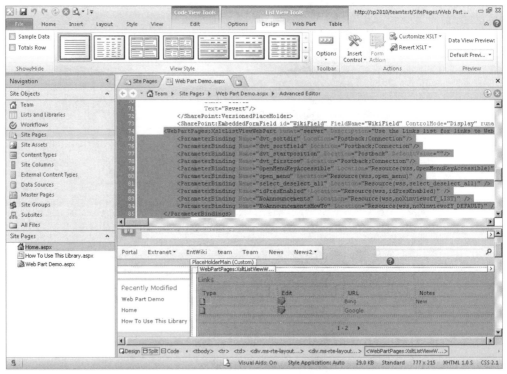

FIGURE 10-18

5. In the Actions section of the ribbon, you should see a Customize XSLT drop-down with the options Customize Entire View and Customize Item. Select the Customize Entire View (because you want to affect each item in the list, not just a single item).

   You may not notice anything initially, but look again at the Code pane. Before you implemented this change, your page was probably a few hundred lines. However, now that you have modified the XSLT directly on this page, your line count is probably more than 2000. By adding the XSLT rules directly to your page, the amount of code in the page significantly increased.

6. While still in the Split view of the editor window, click any of the links in your List View Web Part displayed in the Design pane. This should take you near the section of the XSLT code that is rendering out this column. It is a little tricky to read, so if you don't see it right away, hitting Ctrl+F and doing a quick search for the first link can be helpful. The code we are looking for looks like this:

```
<a onfocus="OnLink(this)" href="{$url}">
    <xsl:choose>
        <xsl:when test="$desc=''">
```

```
            <xsl:value-of disable-output-escaping="no" select="$url" />
        </xsl:when>
        <xsl:otherwise>
            <xsl:value-of select="$desc" />
        </xsl:otherwise>
    </xsl:choose>
</a>
```

7.   To implement the change for this example, you need only to modify the first line of this code to change the `href` to go nowhere and add a JavaScript `onclick` event, which will open the link in a new browser window:

```
<a onfocus="OnLink(this)" href="javascript:void();"
onclick="window.open('{$url}');">
```

8.   Remember to save the file before viewing it in your browser. After you save the file, some server warnings will pop up, namely one that warns that you will customize the page and another that says the server may remove unsafe content. Select Yes for both of them.

You'll notice that when you go back to your page in your browser, it will look exactly as it did before you modified any XSLT. After all, you simply modified a property of the rendered hyperlink. As such, nothing will be visibly different when you reload the page with your new changes. However, if you click any of the hyperlinks in your list, they will now open in a new window.

This was a simple example to show how you can change the behavior of the List View Web Part by editing the XSL. Although this example was very basic, more significant changes can also be applied by editing the XSL, such as controlling the look and feel as well as how the Web Part itself renders in the browser. For example, you could have just as easily added a CSS class property to the hyperlink, which would point to CSS rules you have created in a custom style sheet. Or you could have changed the entire layout of the Web Part by removing the columns and changing it to an HTML list. If you are comfortable with XSLT, you now have a powerful mechanism for branding the List View Web Parts in your site collection.

It is also worth pointing out that, even while you are changing the rendering behavior through XSLT rule changes, this doesn't affect what you can do with the list in the browser. In other words, you can still add and remove columns or items in the list. The List View Web Part still has the same functionality it had before you changed anything; now it just renders the way you want it to.

CREATING A CONTENT ROLLUP WITH THE CONTENT QUERY WEB PART

The Content Query Web Part (CQWP), included in SharePoint Server publishing sites, enables you to query other content throughout the current site collection and display it in very customizable ways. This allows you to create highly configurable content rollups that can surface content from other areas of a SharePoint site so that readers can easily consume related content.

If you are used to how the CQWP worked in SharePoint 2007, there are some powerful new features that are worth learning about. And because it is so powerful and easy to style, the CQWP can be a useful tool for any SharePoint brander. In the following example, you will learn how to create a CQWP that rolls up news articles from a subsite, as well as how to use some of the new SharePoint 2010 features to filter and even style the results.

Configuring the Query and Sorting in the CQWP

To follow along with this example, you should start with a SharePoint Server publishing site. (An Enterprise Wiki was used for the screenshots in this section). If you need a refresher on creating a publishing site, refer to the beginning of Chapter 5.

1. Because you will be rolling up news article pages, you should create a new subsite to hold those pages. For simplicity, use the Publishing site template to create a site called **News**.

2. In the News subsite, create at least two new pages. For each of them change the page layout to Image on left. If you don't see Image on left as a page layout option, you can add it from Site Settings ➪ Page Layouts and site templates, as described in Chapter 9. Also, for each page be sure to enter content for the Page Image, Article Date, Byline, and Page Content (see Figure 10-19).

FIGURE 10-19

After saving each page, make sure that you publish and approve them. Refer to Chapter 9 if you need more information on creating pages or changing page layouts.

If you forget to publish and approve the article pages, they will not show up in the Content Query Web Part rollup.

3. Navigate back to the top level site and edit the page with Site Actions ➪ Edit Page. Place your cursor in the main content area, and then click Insert ➪ Web Part from the ribbon. From Categories, select Content Rollup, and from Web Parts, select Content Query, and then click Add (see Figure 10-20).

FIGURE 10-20

4. When the page refreshes, in the new CQWP, click the link to open the tool pane.

The Web Part tool pane will open on the right side of the screen. Expand the Query section and you will see options to "Show items from all sites in this site collection," Show items from the following site and all subsites," and to "Show items from the following list" (see Figure 10-21).

5. Select "Show items from the following site and all subsites," and then click Browse.

6. From the Select Site dialog, click your newly created News site, and then click OK (see Figure 10-22).

FIGURE 10-21

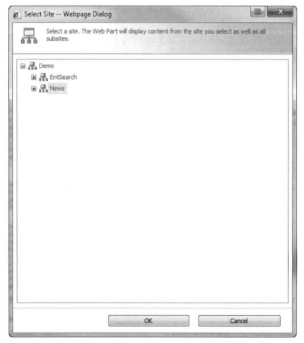

FIGURE 10-22

7. Make sure Show items from this list type is set to Pages Library because we are rolling up publishing pages. Then, from the Content Type section, for "Show items of this content type group," select Page Layout Content Types, and for "Show items of this content type," select Article Page.

This will limit the results of the rollup to only showing the news articles, not any other type of page in the site (see Figure 10-23).

FIGURE 10-23

8. Click Apply from the bottom of the tool pane. You should see that the News articles are being rolled up to the Web Part. They are currently being sorted by the order in which they were published.

9. To change the sort order, expand the Presentation section of the tools pane. For this example, you can ignore the "Group items by" option and focus on setting "Sort items by" to Scheduling Start Date (see Figure 10-24). When you have the sorting set up properly, click Apply at the bottom of the tool pane.

Scheduling Start Date is the actual name of the Article Date field that you entered on each page. By sorting by this field, you change the order of the items just by changing the Article Date field on the page. Figure 10-25 shows the updated Web Part. Notice that articles are sorting properly by date.

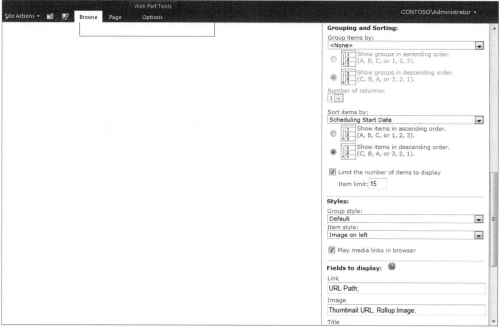

FIGURE 10-24

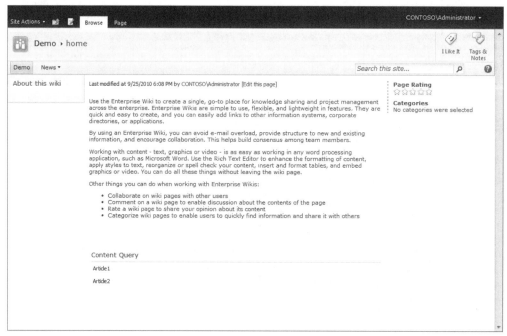

FIGURE 10-25

In this section of the tools pane, you can also change the order of the sorting from ascending or descending, and you can also use "Limit the number of items" to show only a certain number of items in the rollup. The latter of those settings can be particularly useful if you are rolling up long articles and need to reduce the amount of space they take up on the page.

Working with Fields to Display in the CQWP

Up until now, the rollup display has been quite minimal, just showing the article title. Next, you will look at some of the ways you can style the display of these items.

1. From the tool pane in the Presentation group, you will see the Styles section. This includes the Group style and Item style drop-downs. These include pre-built XSL styles that can be selected for displaying the items in different ways. Shortly you will learn how to add your own XSL selection to this list, but for now keep the Group style set to Default and the Item style set to Image on left.

The next section, Fields to Display, is new for SharePoint 2010 and provides a lot of flexibility for the CQWP. In SharePoint 2007, if you wanted to display many out-of-the-box and any custom fields in a CQWP, you needed to export the Web Part and edit the XML to update something called `CommonViewFields`. This was tedious and extremely confusing. In SharePoint 2010, the Fields to Display section handles this for you. When an item style is selected, SharePoint looks through the corresponding XSL and determines which values are being displayed and provides a text box in the Fields to Display section for each of them. You can enter as many field names as you'd like for each box (separated by semicolons), and behind the scenes SharePoint will try display the first corresponding field that is not empty. At first glance, this option may be confusing, but after trying it out, it should make a lot more sense.

2. From the Fields to Display section, you will see that SharePoint is displaying a few options for the Image on left item style. Figure 10-26 shows the default settings; notably, Image is set to Thumbnail URL; Rollup Image; and Description is set to Comments;.

3. Neither of these corresponds to fields that were filled out on your news articles, but if you change these values to fields that were used, the Web Part will display them. For the Image box, add Page Image; and for the Description, add Page Content; (see Figure 10-27).

These are the display names for the fields on your article page layouts.

4. Click Apply, and you should see that the Web Part shows the image and page content, as shown in Figure 10-28.

If you look closely at Figure 10-28, you will notice that the page content is actually showing HTML markup as well as content. You can create your own XSL styles and control the display of the CQWP to not only fix this, but you can also add any style that you can imagine. In the next example, you will use SharePoint Designer to easily change the XSL associated with the CQWP.

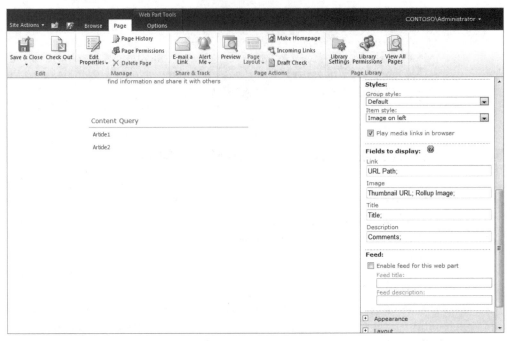

FIGURE 10-26

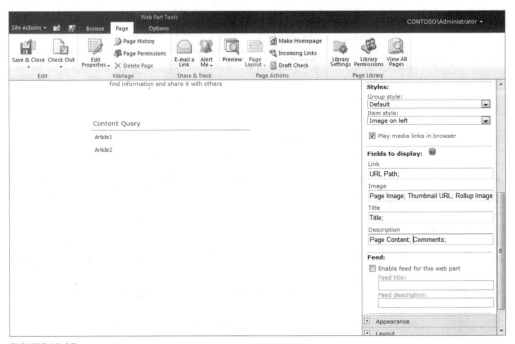

FIGURE 10-27

FIGURE 10-28

Working with XSL and the CQWP

1. Open your top-level site in SharePoint Designer, and from the Site Objects pane, click All Files and navigate to Style Library ➪ XSL Style Sheets (See Figure 10-29).

    This directory contains XSL style sheets that are used by various Web Parts in SharePoint. The ones that are used by the CQWP are as follows:

    ➤ `ContentQueryMain.xsl` — The parent style sheet that the CQWP uses to do a lot of processing and call in other style sheets

    ➤ `Header.xsl` — Styles that are applied for group headings in the CQWP

    ➤ `ItemStyle.xsl` — Styles that are applied for each item in the CQWP

In this example, you are customizing the existing `ItemStyle.xsl` file. If you are worried about the implications of customization, you can create your own item style XSL style sheet and set up the Content Query Web Part to load it automatically. To learn more about this, check out Liam Cleary's blog post "SharePoint 2010 – Content Query Web Part Continued," at www.helloitsliam.com/Lists/ Posts/Post.aspx?ID=225.

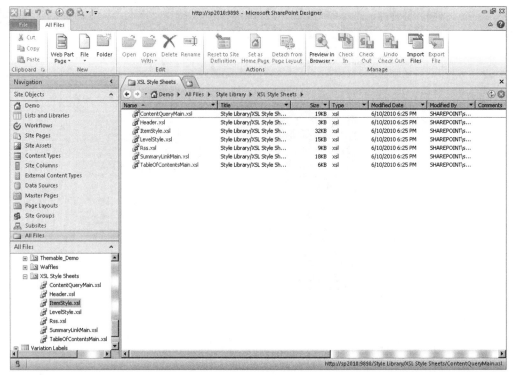

FIGURE 10-29

2. Open and check out `ItemStyle.xsl` for editing.

The code of this file is interesting. It is similar to the other XSL style sheets you have seen earlier in this chapter, but consider that it is being called by `ContentQueryMain.xsl` for each item that is being rolled up by the CQWP. The file consists of many `<xsl:template>` entries that correspond to the item styles that show in the Web Part tool pane. For this example, you will be copying the default template and making adjustments.

3. Select and copy the entire Default template from

`<xsl:template name="Default" match="*" mode="itemstyle">` to `</xsl:template>`, and paste it to the bottom of the file just before the closing `</xsl:stylesheet>`.

4. Replace the first line of the template with the following code. (The bolded areas are what will be changing.)

```
<xsl:template name="WaffleStyle" match="Row[@Style='WaffleStyle']"
mode="itemstyle">
```

This is how the template name is designated in the Item Style drop-down in the Web Part tool pane. Note that `name` and `match` should refer to the same text. Next, you will be making a few changes to the XSL to enhance the display of the items in the CQWP.

5. Start by changing the `<img>` tag to include an inline style that sets the height of the image to 100px. This will ensure that each image is approximately the same size, no matter how big the original page image was.

6. Find the line that looks like `<img class="image" src="{$SafeImageUrl}" title="{@ImageUrlAltText}">` and add an inline style to it, as follows:

```
<img class="image" src="{$SafeImageUrl}" title="{@ImageUrlAltText}"
    style="height: 100px;">
```

Next, because the text of each item could be fairly lengthy, it might be a good idea to truncate the text after a certain amount of characters. This will help control the size of the CQWP on the page by displaying only a teaser of the article page text.

7. Find the line that looks like `<xsl:value-of select="@Description" />`, and change the `select` value from `@Description` to `substring(@Description, 1, 255)`. This will truncate the description after 255 characters have been displayed. Change the line to this:

```
<xsl:value-of select="substring(@Description, 1, 255)" />
```

8. To remove the HTML markup from the item display, change the previous line to include `disable-output-escaping="yes"`. This will allow the HTML of the page content to display properly instead of showing the actual markup. The new line will look like this:

```
<xsl:value-of select="substring(@Description, 1, 255)"
    disable-output-escaping="yes" />
```

9. Save `ItemStyle.xsl` in SharePoint Designer, click Yes for the Site Definition Page Warning (see the preceding Note about customization for more information), and then right-click the filename and select Check In and Publish a major version.

10. Go back to your browser, refresh the page, and make sure the page is in edit mode. By refreshing the page, you will ensure that the Web Part tool pane has loaded your new XSL entry. Then under Presentation and Styles, change Item style to WaffleStyle and click Apply. Figure 10-30 shows the Item style setting.

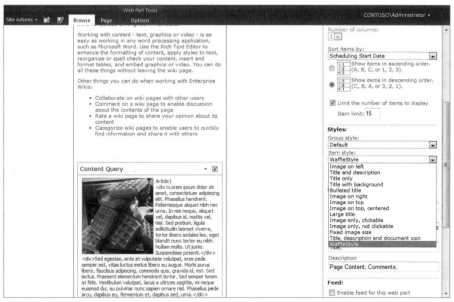

FIGURE 10-30

You can see from Figure 10-31 that the page image is now smaller, the page content is not showing HTML markup, and the page content is truncating after the first 255 characters.

FIGURE 10-31

Although this is a fairly simple change, you can see that by changing the XSL for the CQWP, you can make it look like whatever you want.

> *In the previous example, you truncated the page content after 255 characters, but the method for doing so was quite simple. For a more robust solution to showing preview text, including the ability to strip out HTML and to not truncate in the middle of words, check out Waldek Mastykarz's blog post at* `http://blog.mastykarz.nl/` `generating-short-description-content-query-web-part/`.

Using Filters with the Content Query Web Part

In SharePoint 2010, the CQWP filtering options have been enhanced to include filtering by `PageFieldValue` (content on the page) and by `PageQueryString` (URL query strings). `PageFieldValue` can be useful for filtering by a category or metadata fields on the page that contains the CQWP. For this example, you will be using `PageQueryString` to filter what is shown in the CQWP by query strings appended to the URL.

1. From the Web Part tool pane, in the Query section under Additional Filters, select `Byline` and `contains` for "Show items when," and then in the empty text box, enter **[PageQueryString: BylineFilter]**, and then click OK at the bottom of the tool pane. Figure 10-32 shows the new filter settings.

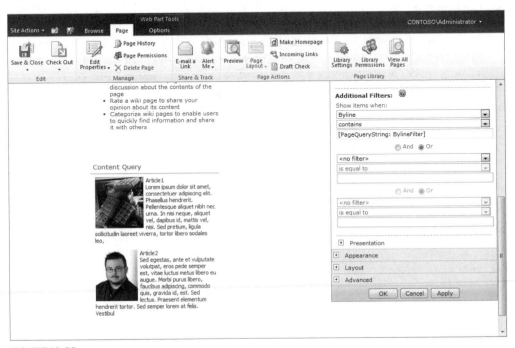

FIGURE 10-32

Notice that after you click OK in the tools pane, the CQWP now shows no items. Don't be alarmed; the CQWP is now looking for `BylineFilter=` in the URL to filter out any items that do not have that value in the Byline field.

2. To test the filtering, save the page and then append some values to the URL, as follows:

```
http://SHAREPOINTSITE/Pages/home.aspx?BylineFilter=Waffles
```

If you choose a `BylineFilter` value that is included in one of your article page bylines, when the page refreshes, the CQWP will filter out all the other items and show only the ones that have that value in the byline of the page. If you didn't enter Waffles into any of the bylines, you may need to navigate to one of your article pages and refresh your memory for what you entered for the byline and change the `ByLineFilter` value.

This can be a very useful feature for reusing rollups for multiple types of content. You could have a page of HTML links with different query strings all pointing to the same CQWP page and see different results for each.

The CQWP enables you to disseminate information from other sites in your site collection with the same look and feel and functionality. After configuring it, you can even export the CQWP to other sites so that the configuration can be reused. This provides a powerful mechanism for content authors to roll up information in many different ways, simply by configuring a Web Part in their browser without having to write code or complex queries.

SUMMARY

Much of the content in SharePoint 2010, particularly with Web Parts, is now based on XML and is styled through XSLT. To be able to style these Web Parts, you must have at least a basic understanding of how XSL works and how you can use it to force your content to render in a way that is consistent with the overall style you have created for your site.

Beyond that, a huge part of branding any SharePoint site (or any website for that matter) is ensuring that content is consistent, readable, and useful. Understanding how to use Web Parts such as the Content Query Web Part gives you a great amount of power to create solutions that achieve this standard.

If you don't understand Web Parts and how they can be used in your SharePoint sites, you are going to have a tough time taking a cool site and filling it with the content needed to make the site useful. And if you don't understand XSL and XSLT, you will have an even tougher time making those Web Parts match the overall look and feel of your SharePoint site.

11

Deploying Branding in SharePoint

WHAT'S IN THIS CHAPTER?

➤ Introduction to branding deployment in SharePoint

➤ Customized and uncustomized files

➤ Options for deploying SharePoint branding assets

➤ Creating a SharePoint solution and feature

➤ Deployment recommendations

Most of the chapters throughout this book have discussed the processes involved in planning and creating your SharePoint branding. This chapter discusses the final piece of the design process: deployment. In other words, this chapter covers your options for putting your design into production. By understanding the pros and cons of each option, you can better understand what approach would be best for your specific project.

If you are already familiar with the concept of SharePoint branding deployment you may be thinking to yourself, "Isn't this a developer topic?" In some cases, it most definitely is a developer topic, whereas in other cases developer involvement may not be needed at all. However, because designers often play a key role in the SharePoint branding process, it is crucial that you be familiar with the options for branding deployment. That way, you can cooperate with developers or server administrators if necessary to work through the details of deploying your SharePoint branding assets. In some cases, you might even be the person responsible for deploying the branding assets, in which case knowledge of the process is critical.

There have been significant improvements to the tools used to deploy custom branding to SharePoint 2010, making the process easier than ever before. This chapter discusses the various options and approaches available for deploying branding files to SharePoint 2010 and helps you to understand the decision points along the way so that you can make the right choice for your project.

INTRODUCTION TO BRANDING DEPLOYMENT IN SHAREPOINT

When the earliest versions of SharePoint were released around 1999, the product was designed to be a web-based document management tool that facilitated collaboration across an organization. Each subsequent version of the product has made it easier to customize the UI. As discussed earlier in the book, the tool of choice for customizing the SharePoint UI used to be Microsoft FrontPage. However, when trying to upgrade from SharePoint 2003 to SharePoint 2007, SharePoint administrators realized that the customizations made to SharePoint by FrontPage caused a big headache for them during the upgrade process.

SharePoint 2007 was the first version of the product that was specifically designed to allow a fully customizable UI. Previously, although it was possible to apply branding, the options were limited to using FrontPage or modifying the system CSS files. Most organizations opted to make changes using FrontPage, which resulted in customizing the files. At the time, that didn't seem like a big deal, but files that were customized by FrontPage couldn't be migrated to SharePoint 2007 with the customizations intact. In some cases, the files weren't able to be migrated at all and needed to be recreated. The issues caused by FrontPage customizations often caused migrations to take significant longer than originally expected. Therefore, it is no surprise that SharePoint administrators immediately became more involved with how branding files were being deployed to prevent this from happening in the future.

Beginning with SharePoint 2007, many better options were available for creating a custom branded SharePoint UI. Users were able to leverage custom master pages and page layouts and could make changes to CSS without having to modify system files. The tools to make those changes also improved with SharePoint Designer 2007, and there were better options for deploying branding; specifically, the ability to deploy files using SharePoint solutions and features was added, allowing files to be deployed in a safe and structured way. Although this functionality has generic sounding names, they are a key piece to the deployment process. SharePoint solutions and features will be discussed in more detail later in the chapter. The options for deploying SharePoint branding in SharePoint 2010 are very similar to the previous version, although the process has been somewhat streamlined due to the tools available — most notably, Visual Studio 2010.

Customized and Uncustomized Files

Although the terms *customized* and *uncustomized* are very generic sounding, customized and uncustomized files mean something very specific in the SharePoint vernacular. If you've been around SharePoint for a while, you might have heard the terms *ghosted* (uncustomized) and *unghosted* (customized) regarding files. Those terms have been deprecated, although you still may run across them in some of the code samples we'll be looking at later in the chapter.

Customized Files

A *customized file* is one whose source lives in the content database. A file can become customized if it is modified in any way either through the SharePoint user interface or by using SharePoint

Designer (SPD); with either option a version of the file is saved to the content database even if the file was originally uncustomized. Once a file has been customized, the source of the page is saved to the content database. When the customized page is rendered in the browser, the source is being pulled from the content database. Conversely, a file that is created using SPD or through the SharePoint user interface starts out as a customized file and cannot be reverted to an uncustomized state.

There are a couple things to clarify about how a file becomes customized. Simply editing content in the web browser does not customize the file. You could, however, customize a file by downloading and then uploading it again. A good example of this would be if you wanted to make a quick change to a master page and downloaded it from the Master Page Gallery and then uploaded the changed version. The same would be true for any other branding asset such as a page layout, CSS, or an image file.

As previously mentioned, it is also possible to customize files by editing them with SPD, although SharePoint 2010 makes this easier to control than previous versions. Chapter 2 discussed the new settings available in both Central Administration and at the Site Collection Administration level to help control whether customization by SPD is allowed. When customizations by SPD are turned off, users are only able to use the tool to edit the content areas of the page. If customization with SPD is enabled, users are prompted before saving files, warning them that their actions will cause the page to become customized.

If a file does become customized, it can be easily reset to an uncustomized state through the Site Settings menu in a site or by using SPD. Part of the reason why upgrading from SharePoint 2003 to 2007 was such a headache was because there wasn't an easy, out-of-the-box way to revert customized files back to an uncustomized state. The overall risk posed by customized files was far lower with SharePoint 2007 than with SharePoint 2003 because customizations can be easily reverted, and it is even lower with SharePoint 2010, but there are still plenty of reasons why many organizations choose to avoid them.

Aside from upgrading, why would you want to avoid customized files? There are a couple of reasons, the first being that one of the main goals for branding in SharePoint is to be able to enforce consistency of your design across all your sites. Customizing a file means that a unique version of the file is created that no longer inherits from the single version. For example, suppose that in your organization you had a master page that was used for every single department site. If someone in the Sales department customized the master page just for their site, it would no longer inherit from the standard master page and therefore changes made to the corporate master page wouldn't impact the Sales site. However, if your goal is to create a unique look for each site, then maybe it isn't a big deal if you create customized master pages all over the place. This example applies to more than just master pages, though; enforcing changes to any of your branding files, including CSS, page layouts, or others, could all potentially be impacted by customized files.

Another reason to avoid customized files is for performance. This doesn't mean that if you've got some customized files in your SharePoint site that your farm is going to slow to a snail's pace. This is more of an issue in situations where SharePoint is under a higher load with a large number of Requests Per Second (RPS), such as a public-facing Internet site or a large intranet. The reason for this is that customized files have additional overhead applied to them that uncustomized files don't have. If you happen to have an implementation that requires higher RPS, it will be more important to manage the number of customized files in SharePoint.

Uncustomized Files

It's probably fair to assume that most people reading this have created a site of some type in SharePoint. All the files used to create the out-of-the-box sites are *uncustomized*. This means that the source of the file lives on the file system, not in the content database. A pointer in the content database tells SharePoint to look for the source of the file on the server's file system. In this case, when the page is requested, SharePoint still looks to the content database but because the instance of the page does not include a source, the file is rendered from the file system.

Uncustomized files make it possible to have many copies of a file point to the same source — similar to how a template for a document works. For example, if you have many sites that use the same page layout, you could make modifications to a single file, and every place where the uncustomized page layout is used would be updated. This is very helpful from a design perspective because it enables you to make changes very easily.

You can deploy branding files to a SharePoint site in an uncustomized state by using a SharePoint *feature*, as discussed later in this chapter.

> *For more information on customized and uncustomized files, see Andrew Connell's MSDN article at* `http://msdn.microsoft.com/en-us/library/cc406685.aspx`. *Although the article was written for SharePoint 2007, the concepts still apply for SharePoint 2010.*

Options for Deploying SharePoint Branding Assets

As with any website, when a user types the URL of the SharePoint site into his or her browser, a combination of HTML, CSS, images, and other files are sent back to the user to render the site in the browser. SharePoint has its own file structure that dictates the options available regarding where the SharePoint-specific branding assets can be placed to properly render the web page to the user.

SharePoint Site

If you look at an out-of-the-box SharePoint site, you can get a good idea about where files need to be placed to deploy branding assets to a SharePoint site. This would mean placing master pages in the Master Page Gallery and other files such as CSS and images in the Style Library folder.

For sites with publishing enabled, a number of other document libraries are created where branding assets can be stored, such as the Pages library, Images, and Site Collection Images library.

Deploying custom branding assets to the SharePoint site is the recommended approach by Microsoft. More specifically, custom branding assets such as CSS, images, and custom scripts should be deployed within the Style Library. To prevent your custom files from getting confused with the out-of-the-box files already in the Style Library, it is recommended that all custom files be placed in a subfolder within the Style Library. The two exceptions to this recommendation are master pages and page layouts, of course, which must be deployed to the Master Page Gallery.

The Style Library is specifically recommended for sites with publishing enabled because it is accessible by all users who have access to any part of the site. This is important because the same branding assets are likely to be shared across all sites in a site collection, so if a user can't access where they were stored, the page will not render properly. For example, if for some reason a user has access to a subsite in a site collection but doesn't have access to the top-level site where the Style Library exists (and all the branding assets live), the pages can still render without issue.

Furthermore, the Style Library resides within the SharePoint site's file structure, which means they can be accessed readily through the web interface or SPD.

 If your goal is to deploy your branding assets to a SharePoint site, the approach that you use will determine whether the files you deploy are in a customized or uncustomized state. For example, if you simply want to manually upload files to your SharePoint site — either through the web interface in Site Settings or through SPD — then your files will be deployed in a customized state. However, if you want to deploy your files uncustomized, you need to use SharePoint features and solutions, which are discussed later in this chapter.

_layouts directory

Another option often considered is to deploy the files to SharePoint's `_layouts` virtual directory. On the server's file system this maps to the folder `C:\Program Files\Common Files\Microsoft Shared\Web Server Extensions\14\TEMPLATE\LAYOUTS`. Because each server should essentially be a mirror of the other in a multi-server deployment, with this option all the files live on the file system of each server in the farm. Additionally, all files deployed to this location are available to all SharePoint sites across the farm. This approach could be advantageous because files can be universally accessed from any site. This is actually how the SharePoint system files operate.

Although this is generally not the recommended approach for the majority of deployments, there are certainly situations in which deploying files to the `_layouts` directory would be appropriate. Before deciding on this approach it is important to evaluate the specific reasons why deploying to the SharePoint site would not meet your requirements. If it is determined that deploying to the `_layouts` directory is appropriate, be sure to create a subdirectory within the folder to segregate your custom files from the system files to avoid conflicts.

Deploying files to the `_layouts` directory poses some challenges. First, deploying files to this directory requires access to the file system of a server, which users in many organizations don't have. Second, the files need to be deployed to the file system of every web front-end server. This can be done manually (which is not recommended) or through the use of a SharePoint solution, which would have to be deployed by a farm administrator. In both cases, higher access is required than many users are typically granted. The reason for this is that deploying files directly to the file system of the server is obviously more risky. If this approach is to be used, it is strongly recommended that rigorous testing be performed to ensure that there is no negative impact to the server when the files are deployed.

DEPLOYING UNCUSTOMIZED FILES USING FEATURES AND SOLUTIONS

So far, this chapter has presented a high-level discussion about your various options for deploying files, as well as the impact of customized and uncustomized files. Obviously, deploying files in a customized fashion is pretty easy: You simply manually upload them through the SharePoint UI or with SPD. But what if you want to deploy your files in an uncustomized state — how would you do that?

Features

The primary mechanism used to provision uncustomized instances of files in SharePoint is called a *feature*. A feature enables a developer to deploy files and other site customizations or functionality to a site collection or individual site. Once activated, the feature deploys the files to SharePoint in an uncustomized state.

Although they have a generic-sounding name, features refer to something very specific in SharePoint. Every feature includes a `Feature.xml` file that provides basic information (title, description, scope of deployment, etc.), a unique ID, and the name and location for an assembly or one or more element manifest files. The element manifest file (called `elements.xml` by default in Visual Studio 2010) is what describes to SharePoint where to deploy the various files contained in the feature. When an assembly is referenced, it can be written to deploy files the same way that the element manifest would, except it requires compiled code instead of the Collaborative Application Markup Language (CAML) used by the element manifest file.

Solutions

By themselves, features enable you to deploy branding assets in an uncustomized state. However, the files related to the feature (`feature.xml`, element manifests, and the branding files to be deployed) ideally need a structured way to move files between servers. A SharePoint *solution* is a sealed cabinet (`.cab`) file with a `.wsp` extension. In fact, if you ever run across a solution file and want to take a peek at its contents, you can change the extension of the file to `.cab`, which enables you to open it and view its contents.

Features typically are used in conjunction with solutions. Although they are two distinct things, it is rare to use a feature without a solution, and vice versa. You can think of a solution as the delivery mechanism that gets the files to the SharePoint server. Once the files are on the server, the feature is what actually does the work to deploy the files to the site collection, individual site, or to whatever level the feature happens to be scoped at. From a branding perspective, the solution file would get the master page, page layouts, CSS, and other files to the server, and the feature (when activated) would place the files in the various libraries and folders.

Solutions help you organize files in a safe way to help ensure the reliability of the SharePoint servers. They provide a mechanism for moving files between server farms, such as between development and production environments. Additionally, solutions provide a way to simultaneously deploy files across multiple servers in the farm. Administrators can schedule the deployment of a solution during off hours to minimize its impact on the farm.

SharePoint 2010 offers two types of solutions:

> ➤ Farm solutions (also available with SharePoint 2007)
> ➤ Sandboxed solutions (new with SharePoint 2010)

Farm solutions, which are typically deployed by server administrators, are definitely a preferred approach to the alternative of manually deploying files to multiple servers. However, because farm solutions can deploy pretty much any type of file to the server, from an administrator's perspective it is a challenge to ensure that a farm solution won't negatively impact a SharePoint farm. Therefore, it is important to thoroughly test all deployed farm solutions.

From a branding perspective, farm solutions present a small challenge. Most custom branding files (such as master pages, page layouts, CSS, or images) are relatively harmless and easily deployed through the user interface or SPD; but if you are trying to avoid uncustomized files, what do you do? SharePoint 2010 provides a new type of solution, called a *sandboxed solution*, which can be uploaded and activated by site collection administrators so it no longer requires a farm administrator's intervention.

In a typical development environment, a sandbox is a safe place to run code because it won't impact other production areas. A sandbox is usually thought of as part of the development environment, but for SharePoint, sandboxed solutions can definitely be deployed in production. A sandboxed solution is a safe way to deploy files to a specific site collection on your SharePoint server. Farm administrators can actually validate and monitor a sandboxed solution, which enables them to define automated policies about what is allowed and not allowed in the sandbox. There are some limitations to the type of code that can be run in the sandbox, but in general these shouldn't prevent the deployment of most branding files.

 For more information on sandboxed solutions, see "Developing, Deploying, and Monitoring Sandboxed Solutions in SharePoint 2010," by Paul Stubbs (http://msdn.microsoft.com/en-us/magazine/ee335711.aspx).

Both farm solutions and sandboxed solutions are preferred ways to deploy your branding files, so which one should you choose? Sandboxed solutions provide an additional layer of protection that enables files to be deployed to the server while minimizing impact on the server. Farm administrators can provide additional validation to add yet another layer of protection. Finally, site collection administrators can upload the files directly to the site collection so that a farm administrator doesn't have to be directly involved. Ideally, sandboxed solutions should be the default way that you deploy your branding assets to SharePoint. Of course, some instances will require a farm solution, which is perfectly fine; but the rule of thumb should be to first try to deploy your branding files as a sandboxed solution.

 An additional benefit of using sandboxed solutions is that they provide an easy way to deploy your branding to SharePoint servers in the cloud, such as Microsoft Online.

DEPLOYMENT CONSIDERATIONS

Every SharePoint implementation presents new scenarios and challenges, so it is impossible to apply a one-size-fits-all approach to branding deployment. Depending on the size and scope of your project, as well as the skills and tools available, the deployment approach will vary. The following sections highlight a few of the key decision points to help you determine the correct approach for deploying your custom SharePoint branding.

Project Size

One of the most obvious considerations related to the deploying of branding assets is size of the project. Obviously, if you are working on a massive implementation that involves a highly customized design with a large number of files that need to be moved between different server environments, you would definitely want to consider an approach that involves solutions and features.

Conversely, many branding projects involve making relatively minor changes to a site that is viewed only by internal personnel. For these smaller branding projects, creating and maintaining the solution and feature isn't cost effective. In other words, you'd spend more time on the deployment itself than you did making the changes in the first place. For these types of scenarios, a manual deployment using SPD or by uploading files through the SharePoint UI makes the most sense.

Skill Set of the SharePoint Team

The ability to deploy files using SharePoint solutions and features requires more than a WYSIWYG editor. More specifically, it requires Visual Studio — ideally, Visual Studio 2010. Unlike project size, this decision point is far less cut-and-dried. Although the skill set of your team might initially limit your options for deployment, it shouldn't act as a roadblock. For example, maybe you are a pure web designer who has been tasked with creating a custom UI for your SharePoint site. After reading this book, you've been able to create an attractive design for your company's Internet site, but you've never opened Visual Studio in your life. Does this mean you should just punt and take the easy route? The answer is absolutely not. If you or someone on your team doesn't have the required skill set, then it is a great opportunity to learn. In other words, if your project calls for something more than simply deploying files through the user interface or SPD, it is important to account for the time to learn how to do it.

Maintainability

For many projects, much more effort is expended getting to the initial deployment than planning how changes will be applied after the site launches. For smaller implementations this isn't typically an issue because there are fewer moving parts; but in a large implementation you could have at least three environments, several site collections, and hundreds of sites. No matter what size your actual implementation is, for all except the smallest of implementations, making future changes will be far easier if you deploy files in an uncustomized state, similar to how Microsoft deploys the out-of-the-box files.

A typical SharePoint implementation can easily have several hundred sites or more. If all those sites, which could potentially exist in several site collections, need to have their custom UI updated with some new changes, as long as the files were initially applied as uncustomized, the process for updating them is fairly simple. Conversely, applying changes to all those files if they were customized on a site-by-site basis could be extremely tedious and time-consuming.

To apply changes to sites that have a UI that was created using uncustomized files, you first need to update the files, re-create your existing WSP file in Visual Studio 2010, and then upgrade the solution by redeploying the WSP to SharePoint. Because of the SharePoint integration with Visual Studio 2010, it is easy to apply changes to the SharePoint UI in a quick and efficient manner.

CREATING A SHAREPOINT SOLUTION AND FEATURE

This example uses Visual Studio 2010 to create a sandboxed solution in which we'll create a feature to deploy our custom branding files. The files for this exercise can be downloaded from the book's site at `wrox.com`.

Creating the Publishing Portal

The example described in this section deploys the files to the sample Internet site, which is based on the Publishing Portal site collection template. Although you can use an existing site, it would be best to create a new site collection to ensure that none of the files conflict.

1. To create the new site, open Central Administration, go to Application Management, and then click the link called Create site collection.

   Be sure that you've selected the correct web application. For this demo, we are using a new web application that doesn't yet have a site collection in order to better simulate how a typical Internet site would be deployed. Therefore, the URL will simply be the root of the web application. This example will use the URL `www.randyswaffles.com`.

2. Click the Publishing tab, and then select the Publishing Portal template for the site collection (see Figure 11-1).

3. Specify the primary site collection administrator, and then click OK.

Creating a New Solution in Visual Studio 2010

The first step in the deployment process is to create a new Visual Studio 2010 solution and a project. Unfortunately, the terminology is a little confusing here, because we are talking about a Visual Studio solution (`.sln` file) and a SharePoint solution (`.wsp` file). In this first example, we'll walk through the process to begin creating a Sandbox solution to deploy your branding files to a SharePoint site.

Once the site has been created, click the link to it. You should see an out-of-the-box-looking Publishing Portal with `nightandday.master` applied.

To create the SharePoint solution and feature, perform the following steps:

1. Open Visual Studio 2010 by clicking the Start button and then select All Programs ➪ Microsoft Visual Studio 2010 ➪ Microsoft Visual Studio 2010.

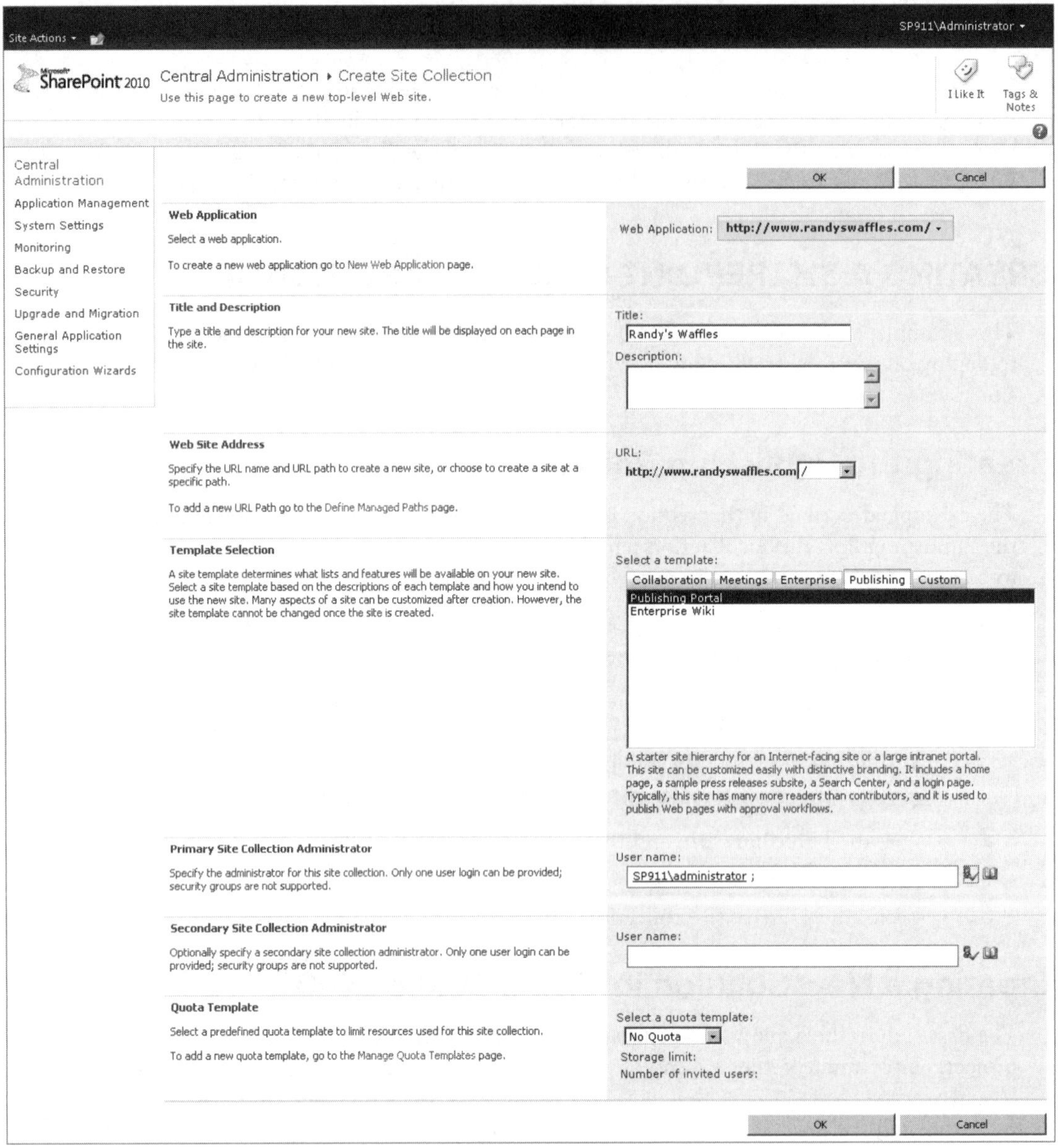

Site Actions ▾

Microsoft SharePoint 2010 Central Administration ▸ Create Site Collection
Use this page to create a new top-level Web site.

SP911\Administrator ▾

I Like It   Tags & Notes

Central Administration

Application Management
System Settings
Monitoring
Backup and Restore
Security
Upgrade and Migration
General Application Settings
Configuration Wizards

OK   Cancel

Web Application

Select a web application.

To create a new web application go to New Web Application page.

Web Application: **http://www.randyswaffles.com/** ▾

Title and Description

Type a title and description for your new site. The title will be displayed on each page in the site.

Title:
Randy's Waffles

Description:

Web Site Address

Specify the URL name and URL path to create a new site, or choose to create a site at a specific path.

To add a new URL Path go to the Define Managed Paths page.

URL:
http://www.randyswaffles.com / ▾

Template Selection

A site template determines what lists and features will be available on your new site. Select a site template based on the descriptions of each template and how you intend to use the new site. Many aspects of a site can be customized after creation. However, the site template cannot be changed once the site is created.

Select a template:

Collaboration | Meetings | Enterprise | Publishing | Custom

Publishing Portal
Enterprise Wiki

A starter site hierarchy for an Internet-facing site or a large intranet portal. This site can be customized easily with distinctive branding. It includes a home page, a sample press releases subsite, a Search Center, and a login page. Typically, this site has many more readers than contributors, and it is used to publish Web pages with approval workflows.

Primary Site Collection Administrator

Specify the administrator for this site collection. Only one user login can be provided; security groups are not supported.

User name:
SP911\administrator ;

Secondary Site Collection Administrator

Optionally specify a secondary site collection administrator. Only one user login can be provided; security groups are not supported.

User name:

Quota Template

Select a predefined quota template to limit resources used for this site collection.

To add a new quota template, go to the Manage Quota Templates page.

Select a quota template:
No Quota

Storage limit:
Number of invited users:

OK   Cancel

FIGURE 11-1

*You can create solutions and features without using Visual Studio 2010, but the process is made drastically simpler with the latest version. If you don't have Visual Studio 2010, try the WSPBuilder tool (*http://wspbuilder.codeplex.com/*).*

2. At the left side of the Start Page window, click New Project (see Figure 11-2). The New Project dialog will open (see Figure 11-3).

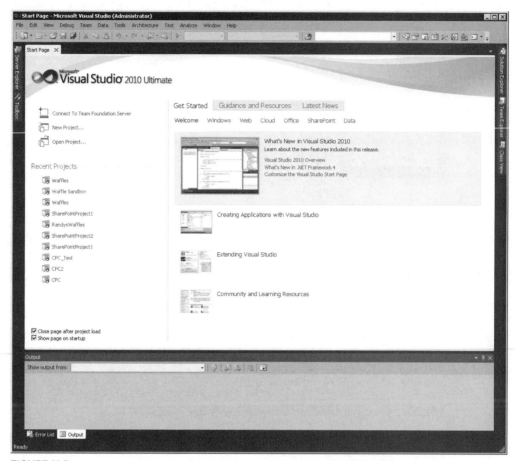

FIGURE 11-2

3. From the Installed Templates section of the left pane, expand the SharePoint section and select 2010 to display the various types of projects. You can choose either the templates under Visual Basic or the templates under C#. This example uses a template under the C# section.

Select Empty SharePoint Project and fill in the following values:

➤ **Name** — Waffles

➤ **Location** — c:\Projects

➤ **Solution Name** — Waffles

Leave the option checked to create a directory for solution, and click OK.

FIGURE 11-3

4.   The next screen, shown in Figure 11-4, prompts you for the site to use for debugging. The site you enter will also be the default location where the solution and feature are deployed. Enter the URL for the publishing portal you created at the beginning of this example. For this example, enter **http://www.randyswaffles.com**.

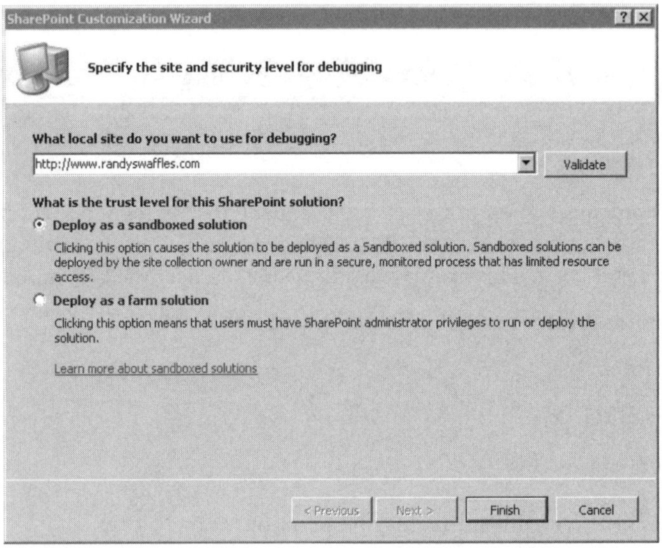

FIGURE 11-4

5. Choose the option for the type of SharePoint solution you'll be creating. For this example, choose a sandboxed solution (although a farm solution would work similarly); you can change the type of solution later, if necessary. Once you've selected the type of solution, click Finish.

Now your sandbox solution is created, but it doesn't really do anything. The next example will show how to add files to the Visual Studio 2010 and create a feature that will deploy to SharePoint.

Creating a Feature to Deploy a Master Page and Page Layouts

In this example, we'll create a feature that will deploy a custom master page and page layouts to the Master Page Gallery.

6. Once the project has been created, Visual Studio 2010 will display the empty project. From the Solution Explorer window, right-click the project name and select Add ➪ New Item. The Add New Item window will open, as shown in Figure 11-5.

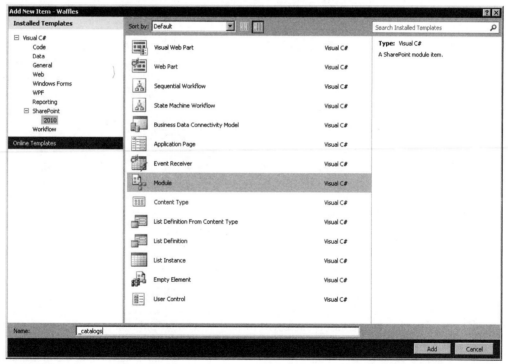

FIGURE 11-5

7. Select Module from the center section of the window, enter **_catalogs** in the Name field, and then click Add.

_catalogs is the location of the virtual folder where the Master Page Gallery lives. The goal is to match the structure of the virtual folders in your SharePoint site. A module is used to define a group of files that will be deployed by a feature to a specific location. In this case, all the files will be deployed to the Master Page Gallery. If you had other files that needed to be deployed to a different location, they'd require a separate module.

When the new module has been created, you'll notice that two files have been added to the module:

➤ Elements.xml is the element manifest file for the feature that will describe which files to deploy to SharePoint and where to deploy them.

➤ Sample.txt is just what it sounds like — a sample file — and it should be deleted to prevent any issues. Simply select Sample.txt and click the Delete key. Click OK to confirm that it is okay to delete the file.

8. Right-click the _catalogs module name in the Solution Explorer and select Add ➪ New folder and name it **masterpage**.

It is not necessary for the modules or folder names to match the SharePoint folder structure, but it does make it easier for others who may be new to SharePoint to understand what is happening in the project.

As you create the module and a folder, Visual Studio creates corresponding folders on the file system of the machine you are working on. In a real-world deployment, branding files are often created by a designer and then handed over to a developer to create the deployment, or at least the files are created on a specific site and then exported out of SharePoint before being added to Visual Studio to create a SharePoint solution. An easy way to give the custom SharePoint branding files you've created is to export them from SharePoint to a structure that mirrors where they are to be deployed, and then create a ZIP file. These files can then be moved into the same structure within the file structure created by Visual Studio. The branding files for this chapter have been extracted to a folder on the machine's file system, specifically c:\Waffle Branding Files.

9. Open the folder where the files have been extracted to, go to the _catalogs/masterpage folder, and move the contents to the c:\Projects\Waffles\Waffles_catalogs\masterpage folder.

10. After moving the files to the correct folder, you still need to import them into the Visual Studio project. To do that, click the Show All Files button (see Figure 11-6) and then select all the files in the _catalogs/masterpage folder by clicking the first file and holding down the Shift button while clicking on the last file. With all the files selected, right-click and choose the option Include In Project (see Figure 11-7).

After the files have been added to the project, notice that references to the files have been automatically added in the Elements.xml file. However, the schema that Visual Studio 2010 creates isn't what we need, so we'll need to make some changes manually. The reason for this is because although Visual Studio 2010 integrates with SharePoint, most of the integration is geared towards deploying files to SharePoint Foundation 2010. The schemas that are automatically created will not work for deploying branding assets.

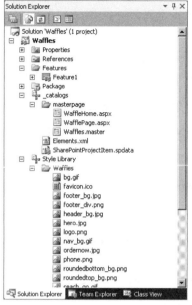

FIGURE 11-6

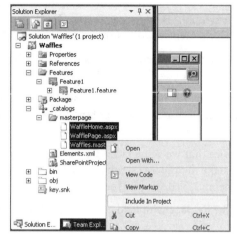

FIGURE 11-7

11. Change line 3 to read as follows:

```
<Module Name="_catalogs" Url="_catalogs/masterpage" Path="_catalogs/
masterpage">
```

12. On Line 4, highlight the following text:

```
<File Path="_catalogs\masterpage\
```

13. With the text highlighted, press Ctrl+F to open the Find and Replace dialog. Because the text is already highlighted, you don't have to paste it into the dialog. Click the Quick Replace button at the top, as we are going to make some changes (see Figure 11-8).

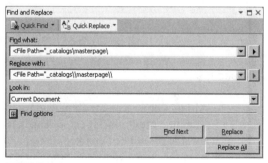

FIGURE 11-8

14. In the "Find what" box the string we highlighted is listed there. You'll notice that the string includes the \ character, which is also used by the Visual Studio search syntax as an escape character. In other words, when you use the \ character it allows you to find the characters used in wildcard notation, such as * and #. If you had a search string where you needed to perform a search that included one of those wildcard characters, you'd include the character immediately after a backslash *). In our case, we just want to be able to use the \ character, so we need to modify our search string to make sure the \ isn't escaped. To do this, we will need to modify the search string to the following:

```
<File Path="_catalogs\\masterpage\\
```

15. In the Replace with field, type **<File Url=".**

16. At the bottom of the Find dialog, press the + button to expand the Find options, if it isn't already expanded. (In Figure 11-9, the menu is expanded and a minus symbol replaces the plus symbol.) Be sure to check the Use box, and then select Wildcards from the drop-down. Click the Replace All button (refer to Figure 11-9). Three changes should have been made.

17. To complete the modifications to this file, highlight `Url="_catalogs/masterpage/WaffleHome.aspx" />` on Line 4, and then press Ctrl+F.

As before, the highlighted text should be displayed in the Find what box. Click the Quick Replace button and in the "Find what" field remove the filename and change it to read **Url="_catalogs/masterpage/*" />.**

Notice that we've replaced the actual filename with the * wildcard character. This helps to make the process significantly faster and enables you to avoid manually changing the `Elements.xml` file one line at a time.

18. In the Replace with field, enter **Type="GhostableInLibrary" />** (see Figure 11-10).

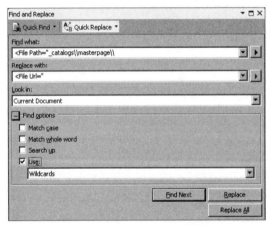

FIGURE 11-9

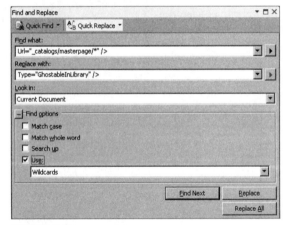

FIGURE 11-10

Although the `Type` attribute is optional, it is recommended that when you are deploying branding files to include `GhostableInLibrary`. This attribute lets SharePoint know that this file should be deployed in an uncustomized state. In fact, "ghosted" is the deprecated term for "uncustomized" (and "unghosted" is the deprecated term for "customized"). The official wording may have changed, but the old terms are still referenced, usually in code.

Again, in the Find options, make sure that Use Wildcards is selected and click the Replace All button. Once again, three changes should have been made. The result should look like this:

```xml
<?xml version="1.0" encoding="utf-8"?>
<Elements xmlns="http://schemas.microsoft.com/sharepoint/">
  <Module Name="_catalogs" Url="_catalogs/masterpage" Path="_catalogs/
masterpage">
      <File Url="WaffleHome.aspx" Type="GhostableInLibrary" />
```

```
              <File Url="Waffles.master" Type="GhostableInLibrary" />
              <File Url="WafflePage.aspx" Type="GhostableInLibrary" />
          </Module>
      </Elements>
```

This file should be all set, but we need to repeat this step for another module since we need to deploy more files to a different folder. The steps for creating the new module are basically identical to the previous steps, only different names are used.

> *Each module deploys files to a specific location in SharePoint. Because master pages and page layouts all deploy to the Master Page Gallery, they are added to the same module. We typically deploy images and CSS to a custom folder under the Style Library so that they have a separate module.*

Deploying Images and CSS

Deploying SharePoint branding files usually involves deploying files to at least two separate locations: the Master Page Gallery and a subfolder under the Style Library. The previous example showed how to create a feature and deploy files to the Master Page Gallery. This example will demonstrate how to add a second module to deploy files to a subfolder under the Style Library.

19. Right-click the project name and select Add ⇨ New Item.

20. From the Add New Item window, select Module. Name it **Style Library** and click Add. Once it has been created, you can delete the `Sample.txt` file, just as before.

21. Right-click the module and select Add ⇨ New folder and name it **Waffles**.

22. From the folder where the branding files have been extracted, move the files from the `Style Library\Waffles` folder to the corresponding folder in the Visual Studio file structure (`C:\ProjectsWaffles\Waffles\Style Library\Waffles`). There should be a total of 20 files.

23. Click the Show All Files button, select all the files in the folder, and then right-click and select Include In Project.

The references to the files should have been automatically added in the `Elements.xml`. As before, you need to edit the schema before it will deploy properly.

24. Start by changing line 3 to read as follows:

```
\<Module Name="Style Library" Url="Style Library/Waffles" Path="Style Library/
   Waffles">
```

25. On line 4, highlight the following text:

```
      <File Path="Style Library\Waffles\
```

Press Ctrl+F to bring up the Find and Replace dialog. Because the backspace (\ ) is an escape character, change the search sting to the following:

```
<File Path="Style Library\\Waffles\\
```

26. Click the Quick Replace button, and in the "Replace with" field, enter **<File Url=".**

Be sure to check the Use box and then select Wildcards from the drop-down. The completed screen should look like Figure 11-11.

27. Click the Replace All button. Twenty changes should have been made.

28. On line 4, highlight the following text:

```
Url="Style Library/Waffles/bg.gif" />
```

Press Ctrl+F to bring up the Find and Replace dialog.

29. Click the Quick Replace button and in the "Find what" field, change it to read **Url="Style Library/Waffles/*" />.**

30. In the "Replace with" field, enter **Type="GhostableInLibrary" />** (see Figure 11-12).

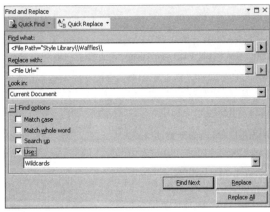

FIGURE 11-11

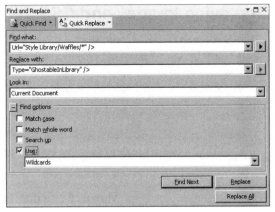

FIGURE 11-12

Make sure Use is checked and Wildcards is selected, and then click the Replace All button. Twenty changes should have been made. The result should look like this:

```
<?xml version="1.0" encoding="utf-8"?>
<Elements xmlns="http://schemas.microsoft.com/sharepoint/">
    <Module Name="Style Library" Url="Style Library/Waffles" Path="Style Library/
Waffles">
        <File Url="waffle_photo.jpg" Type="GhostableInLibrary" />
        <File Url="bg.gif" Type="GhostableInLibrary" />
        <File Url="favicon.ico" Type="GhostableInLibrary" />
        <File Url="footer_bg.jpg" Type="GhostableInLibrary" />
        <File Url="footer_div.png" Type="GhostableInLibrary" />
        <File Url="header_bg.jpg" Type="GhostableInLibrary" />
        <File Url="hero.jpg" Type="GhostableInLibrary" />
        <File Url="logo.png" Type="GhostableInLibrary" />
        <File Url="nav_bg.gif" Type="GhostableInLibrary" />
        <File Url="ordernow.jpg" Type="GhostableInLibrary" />
        <File Url="phone.png" Type="GhostableInLibrary" />
        <File Url="roundedbottom_bg.png" Type="GhostableInLibrary" />
```

```
            <File Url="roundedtop_bg.png" Type="GhostableInLibrary" />
            <File Url="seach_go.gif" Type="GhostableInLibrary" />
            <File Url="search_button.png" Type="GhostableInLibrary" />
            <File Url="searchbox.gif" Type="GhostableInLibrary" />
            <File Url="style.css" Type="GhostableInLibrary" />
            <File Url="subpage_bg.gif" Type="GhostableInLibrary" />
            <File Url="top_bg.gif" Type="GhostableInLibrary" />
            <File Url="top_bg.png" Type="GhostableInLibrary" />
        </Module>
    </Elements>
```

The feature is now complete and includes all the necessary modules to deploy the branding files. The next step in the process is to actually deploy the files to SharePoint.

Deploying the Solution

Even though the files should be ready to deploy now, before we move ahead, some housekeeping is required to make this a little cleaner.

31. Along the right side of Solution Explorer, double-click Feature1 under the Features folder to open the Feature Designer (see Figure 11-13). This is a GUI to control the various aspects of the feature you are about to deploy. First, change the Title of the feature to **Randys Waffles UI**. This will be the name of the feature that users see in SharePoint. Because there might be other features related to this website, we've made the distinction that this deploys the UI files.

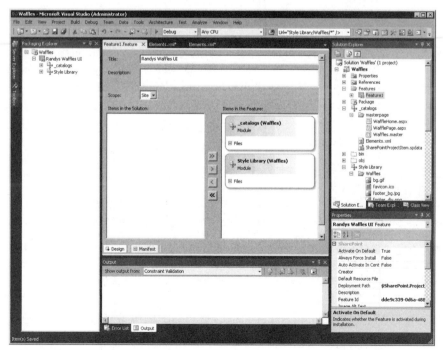

FIGURE 11-13

32. Change the scope of the feature to Site (refer to Figure 11-13). This is one of the areas where the terminology can be tricky, but Site actually refers to the site collection. (The option "Web" refers to an individual site.)

33. Right-click the project name and choose Deploy (see Figure 11-14).

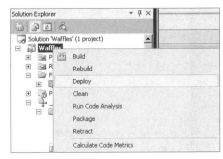

At the bottom of the screen, you should see the steps that are happening as Visual Studio 2010 deploys the solution and activates the feature for you. Your branding should now be successfully deployed!

FIGURE 11-14

 Don't panic if you get the following message when trying to deploy your Sandboxed solution: "Error occurred in deployment step 'Retract Solution': Cannot start service SPUserCodeV4 on [server]." To resolve this issue, make sure that the service Microsoft SharePoint Foundation Sandboxed Code Service is started in Central Administration. To get to the services in Central Administration, go to System Settings ⇨ Services on Server.

Testing the Solution

Although the files have deployed to the site, there's still a few steps remaining to apply the branding. The following steps walk you through the process of checking in your files and setting the master page and page layout so that you can verify that your solution deployed correctly.

34. Open the publishing portal you created in the web browser. Go to Site Actions ⇨ Site Settings and under the Look and Feel section click Master page. Select Waffles.master for the Site Master Page, and then click OK.

 If you are using a sandboxed solution you'll likely see a warning when you choose the master page. This is because sandboxed solutions deploy files to publishing sites in draft status. Until the files are published, users without adequate permissions to see draft files won't be able to access the site. You can use the Manage Content and Structure page under the Site Actions button to navigate to the folders to make the changes in bulk, rather than make the changes one by one.

35. When you browse back to the home page you should see that the new master page is applied; but you still need to switch to the custom page layout to complete the deployment. To apply the custom page layout for the home page, select Site Actions ⇨ Edit Page.

36. From the ribbon, select the Page tab, click the Page Layout button from the Page section, and then select WaffleHome.aspx (see Figure 11-15).

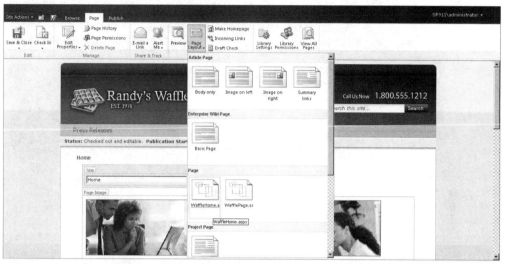

FIGURE 11-15

You should now be able to bask in the glory of your custom branded site. It looks perfect. Oh, wait. There's a character in the footer that didn't render properly (see Figure 11-16). This must be Murphy's Law! No problem; this is an easy fix.

FIGURE 11-16

It would have been easy enough to end this example here and have it work flawlessly. But in real world situations, minor changes always seem to be required once the files have been deployed.

Updating the Solution

Updating your files once you've deployed them is made much easier thanks to Visual Studio 2010. This example walks you through the process of making a very simple change and then deploying it to your SharePoint site.

37. Go back to Visual Studio, and then open `Waffles.master`. On line 465 you'll see the offending apostrophe character. Simply get rid of the one that's there and replace it with a normal one that you type in.

38. Right-click your project name in the Solution Explorer and click Deploy again. Refresh your home page in the browser and all should be right with the world again. Be sure to publish and approve the page, and the page should display as expected, as shown in Figure 11-17.

FIGURE 11-17

This example walked you through the process of deploying a sandboxed solution directly to a server. However, if you need to move your solution to another server or simply give it to someone else, that is also easy to do: Right-click the name of the project in the Solution Explorer and choose Package. Visual Studio 2010 will create a `.wsp` file in the Debug folder of the file structure it created for the project. In our example you could find the file at `C:\Projects\Waffles\Waffles\bin\Debug\Waffles.wsp`. Because this example was a sandboxed solution, a site collection administrator would be able to deploy from the Site Settings menu and then activate it. If you created a farm solution, you'd give the file to a farm administrator for them to deploy.

> *To change your solution to a farm solution, click the name of your project in the Solution Explorer in Visual Studio 2010. (In this example, you'd click Waffles.) In the bottom right, the properties window for the project will open. Simply change the value for Sandboxed Solution to False, as shown in Figure 11-18. You'll be prompted that changing this property will require you to have Farm administrator privileges to deploy. Press Yes to complete the change. You can convert back to a sandboxed solution by setting the value back to True.*

Although this example has quite a few steps, once you get the hang of it the whole process can be done relatively quickly. In addition, Visual Studio 2010, with its native SharePoint integration, makes the process significantly easier than previous versions.

THE SHAREPOINT UI DESIGNER'S ROLE IN THE DEPLOYMENT PROCESS

FIGURE 11-18

In many organizations, the role of SharePoint UI designer is played by someone who is also a farm administrator or possibly a developer. In other organizations the SharePoint UI designer role falls to the web designer. Regardless of the actual title on your business card, the deployment process for SharePoint branding files isn't just a one-person job. Suppose that your project team includes a SharePoint analyst, administrator, developer, and designer. In many organizations each of these people would put their heads down and never talk to one another. However, SharePoint is not only a tool that *enables* collaboration, but a tool that *requires* collaboration. In other words, all members of your project team need to work together to determine the best approach for deploying files — even branding files.

Many of you probably just rolled your eyes. What could branding possibly have to do with all members of the SharePoint team? Consider that the entire branding process begins with determining the project's requirements, which starts with the SharePoint analyst. Then those requirements are turned into a SharePoint design by the designer. The designer needs to determine where the files need to live on the server and ultimately how to get those files where they need to be. For smaller implementations this could mean just manually deploying the files in a customized state with SPD, but for larger implementations this would likely require a SharePoint solution and feature. In that case, the files are often handed off to a developer who creates the SharePoint solution, which is then deployed to the SharePoint server. The SharePoint administrator, who is responsible for keeping the servers running smoothly, then deploys the solution file or defines the policy regarding what is acceptable to be deployed as a sandboxed solution.

Clearly, the branding process and the deployment of those branding files go hand in hand. Whether directly or indirectly, everyone on the SharePoint team plays a role in the deployment process. Although smaller projects have a smaller team and the process involves fewer people, the decision points and the process remains the same.

If you wear all the hats on your SharePoint team it doesn't mean you can cut corners! It is still important to consider all the steps in the deployment process and ensure that you sufficiently test anything you deploy to a production server. Wearing all the hats gives you a lot of power, but be careful not to abuse it. Deploying branding files might seem relatively trivial, but it is often the small changes to servers that slip through the cracks and cause big problems.

RECOMMENDATIONS

The topic of how to deploy your branding files is complex. This chapter has discussed many of the different decision points related to branding deployment and how you can determine which approach will be best for your project. For starters, remember that master pages and page layouts need to be deployed to the Master Page Gallery, so the only decision is whether the files are customized or uncustomized.

Where you should put the rest of the files depends on the factors described earlier in the chapter. It is impossible to give prescriptive guidance that will work in every instance, but the following is a list of recommendations, in order of preference:

➤ **Deploy branding files to the SharePoint site with a sandboxed solution and feature** — This method provides the best combination of flexibility and security. Files are deployed in an uncustomized state to the SharePoint site, and this approach can also be used in multi-tenancy environments. Sandboxed solutions have tighter constraints regarding what types of files can be deployed, so there is significantly less risk in deploying files in this manner. They can even be deployed by site collection administrators, avoiding the involvement of the farm administrator.

Because sandboxed solutions are more limited in terms of the type of functionality that can be deployed, some situations may require a farm solution. In addition, sandboxed solutions are scoped to a single site collection, so when custom branding needs to be deployed across many site collections a farm solution might be a better approach.

➤ **Deploy branding files to the SharePoint site with a farm solution and feature** — This method was the recommended approach to deploy files in SharePoint 2007 and it remains a very good option for deploying branding files in SharePoint 2010. Although for many projects it is ideal to deploy files via a sandboxed solution, this approach is a close second. It provides the capability to deploy nearly any type of file because it allows files to deploy with full trust. However, the power to deploy files with full trust also makes this approach potentially more risky, so farm administrators should take extra steps to ensure that the solution will not negatively impact the farm's reliability.

In addition to the risk just described, negatives for this approach are that it can't be used in multi-tenancy scenarios and it requires a farm administrator to deploy. However, designers and developers who have worked with SharePoint 2007 might find this approach to be more familiar than sandboxed solutions.

➤ **Deploy branding files to the _layouts directory on the server, with the farm solution and feature** — Files deployed to the _layouts directory can be accessed by any user on any site on your SharePoint farm. In fact, this is the approach that Microsoft uses to deploy many of the branding files for SharePoint. Although this can be a huge benefit in some situations, the negative is that it requires you to deploy files to a folder on the SharePoint server where other system files live, which is inherently more risky. As described earlier, farm administrators should require additional validation to ensure that any files deployed with this approach won't cause any issues.

> ➤ **Deploy branding files to the SharePoint site using SPD or manually uploading through the user interface** — If you have a small project, a very short time frame, or you don't have a Visual Studio license, then this might be the best approach. All files, including the master pages, page layouts, and other branding-related files, are deployed as customized. However, it is relatively easy to deploy in this manner and is suitable in nearly all scenarios as long as you have the appropriate permissions.
>
> If you have a more complex project, need to move your branding files between environments easily, or generally need to deliver a high-performance branding implementation, then this approach is not recommended.

There are certainly other approaches to deploying your branding files that haven't been covered in this chapter. Most of these other approaches, such as custom site definitions, are very advanced topics. For more information on creating custom site definitions in SharePoint 2010, see Todd Baginski's blog post at `www.toddbaginski.com/blog/archive/2009/11/02/how-to-create-a-custom-site-definition-in-sharepoint-2010.aspx.aspx`.

SUMMARY

This chapter discussed the different decision points related to branding deployment, including where to deploy files, methods for deploying, and the difference between customized and uncustomized files. Each branding project presents its own unique set of requirements and challenges that need to be carefully considered with all members of your SharePoint team. It is important to talk about not only which approach will be optimal for the initial implementation, but also issues that might arise after implementation, including changes to the design and upgrades.

Visual Studio 2010 makes the deployment process for SharePoint branding significantly easier than it was in previous versions. Although not all projects require files to be deployed with SharePoint solutions and features, those that do can be done quickly.

There isn't a one-size-fits-all approach for deploying your branding files; each scenario is going to be different. However, by understanding the potential implications and risks of the approaches described in this chapter, you can make an informed decision.

PART IV
Other Branding Concepts

12

Page Editing and the Ribbon

WHAT'S IN THIS CHAPTER?

➤ Adding styles to the ribbon to help content authors create consistent content

➤ Adding your own buttons to the ribbon

➤ Using SharePoint dialogs to open new pages

➤ Working with the status bar and notification area

One of the most notable enhancements to the user interface (UI) of SharePoint 2010 is the addition of a ribbon directly inside the browser. The ribbon acts much the same way that it does in other Microsoft Office applications: It enables users to modify the settings and styles of the currently rendered page (among other things).

A part of any designer's role is to ensure that the content of a website fits the branding structure established for the entire site. Therefore, when a rich text editor is used in SharePoint, the fonts and colors should match the rest of the site. An easy way to do ad-hoc styling is by using the ribbon.

Furthermore, because the ribbon *is* part of the UI, you may be asked to enhance the ribbon to provide more of the functionality users need to perform their jobs. That's why it is important to at least understand the basics of how to add functionality to the ribbon and ensure that the functionality looks good and is consistent with the rest of the site.

This chapter will help you accomplish both of these goals by showing you how to use the ribbon to directly modify page content and enhance the ribbon to add the functionality needed by your users.

USING THE RIBBON TO CREATE CONSISTENT CONTENT

One of the primary concerns of any branding project is to ensure that everything, across all pages of a site, looks consistent. Most of this book focuses on things that are done at the code level or under the hood: Master pages, themes, and CSS control much of the look and feel of every page.

However, one thing that those tools do not necessarily control is the content components of each page. In Chapter 5, you learned about basic page editing using the ribbon. While this is certainly a powerful feature in SharePoint 2010, the edited content may or may not have the same look and feel as the rest of the site. This is because the edited page content, while inheriting whichever CSS rules have been applied to the applicable HTML elements, can still be styled in any way imaginable using the rich text editor.

How can brand consistency be enforced when SharePoint provides so many options for content authors to create anything they want? One option is that you could institute a policy that says content authors stick to very specific style guidelines as they create content. However, policy can be difficult to enforce as a site grows in size. The ribbon has a cool feature that can help you enforce specific styles; by adding CSS that the ribbon knows how to load, you can actually inject your own styles for content authors to always have at their disposal.

Adding Custom Styles to the Ribbon

SharePoint 2010 allows you to easily inject pre-built options into several of the areas of the Format Text tab in the ribbon. In this chapter, you will learn about adding styles to the following areas of the ribbon:

- ➤ Font Face
- ➤ Font Size
- ➤ Highlight Color
- ➤ Font Color
- ➤ Styles
- ➤ Markup Styles

Each of these items is described in Chapter 5, but you can refer to Figure 12-1 to see where each is located in the ribbon.

The following sections describe how to add styles for each of these areas. For each of them, you can add items simply by adding specific CSS classes to your SharePoint site. This can be done by adding a CSS file to the Style Library and applying it to SharePoint as either alternate CSS or from a master page, as follows:

```
<SharePoint:CssRegistration name="/Style Library/RichTextAdditions.css"
After="corev4.css" runat="server"/>
```

If you need a refresher on working with CSS and SharePoint, see Chapter 7.

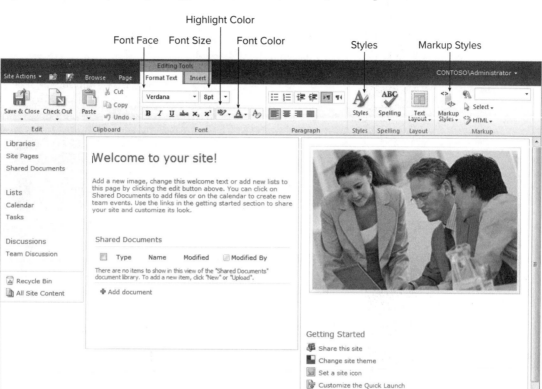

FIGURE 12-1

Font Face

If you add a style class that begins with `.ms-rteFontFace`, SharePoint 2010 will know to add a font to the font face drop-down in the ribbon. Note that like many of the following examples, font face requires a property called `-ms-name` that will define how the new font face will be labeled in the drop-down. Without the `-ms-name` property, the item will appear in the drop-down as a blank. The following is an example of how to add a font face to the ribbon:

```
.ms-rteFontFace-RandysFontFace {
    -ms-name:"Custom Comic Sans";
    font-family: 'Comic Sans MS';
}
```

In this example, an item will be added to the font face drop-down labeled "Custom Comic Sans," and, when it is clicked, the Comic Sans MS font will be applied to the selected text. Note that like all the other examples to follow, the name after `.ms-rteFontFace` is arbitrary but should be unique to your own CSS code. Figure 12-2 shows the new font face added to the drop-down.

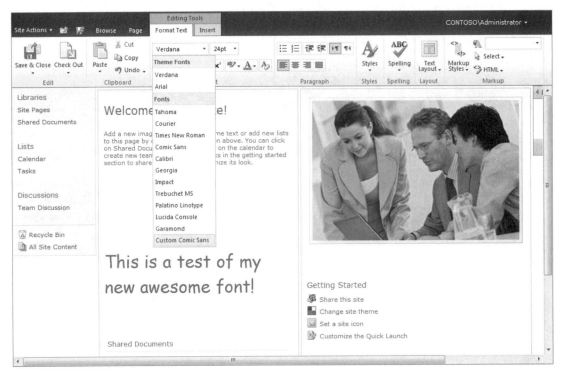

FIGURE 12-2

Font Size

By adding a style that begins with `.ms-rteFontSize`, SharePoint adds a font size to the font size drop-down. Note that unlike many of the other styles in this section, font size does not use the `-ms-name` property. Instead, it will simply show whatever value you set for the size. You can add any valid CSS font-size units (`pt`, `px`, `em`, etc.). The following example adds two font sizes to the ribbon:

```
.ms-rteFontSize-RandysFontSize {
  font-size: 500pt;
}
.ms-rteFontSize-RandysFontSize2 {
  font-size: 20em;
}
```

This example adds one font size of 500pt and another of 20em to the drop-down.

Highlight Color

Highlight color is the background color that shows behind text in SharePoint. If you add a style that begins with `.ms-rteBackColor`, SharePoint will add a highlight color to the drop-down in the ribbon. When the user hovers his or her mouse over the new color, the text that shows will be a combination of both the `-ms-color` property and the `-ms-name` property. If you want to keep the name simple, just set the `-ms-color` to the name of your new color and leave the `-ms-name` blank. The following is an example of adding a highlight color to the ribbon:

```
.ms-rteBackColor-RandysBackColor {
  background-color: purple;
  -ms-name: "";
  -ms-color:"CustomPurple";
}
```

In this example, the highlight color drop-down in the ribbon will have an added color that is named `CustomPurple` and displays the color purple behind the selected text.

Font Color

Font color is similar to highlight color, except it sets the color of the font rather than the background color. If you add a style that begins with `.ms-rteForeColor`, SharePoint adds a font color to the ribbon. The following example shows how to add a font color to the ribbon:

```
.ms-rteForeColor-RandysForeColor {
  color: lime;
  -ms-name: "";
  -ms-color:"CustomLime";
}
```

In this example, the font color drop-down will show a new color named `CustomLime` that sets the selected text to a lime color.

Markup Styles

Markup styles is an interesting item that adds both an HTML element and some style to a selected content. This requires two CSS classes for every one markup style that is added to the ribbon. The following example would add an item to the markup styles drop-down:

```
DIV.ms-rteElement-RandysElement {
  -ms-name:"My Custom Element";
}
.ms-rteElement-RandysElement {
  color:red;
}
```

When selected, it will add `<div>...</div>` around the selected content and then style that `<div>` with the second CSS class — in this case, setting the text color to red. Note that both classes are needed and must have matching names in order for the new markup style to work.

You can even make up your own HTML element and it will work; this example adds `<randy>...</randy>` around the selected text:

```
RANDY.ms-rteElement-RandysElement2 {
  -ms-name:"My Custom Element2";
}
.ms-rteElement-RandysElement2 {
  color:red;
}
```

This may not be useful for everyone, but maybe there are some edge cases for which creating your own HTML element would be beneficial.

Styles

Styles is similar to markup styles except without the added HTML markup. The following example adds a new style to the ribbon named `CustomStyle`:

```
.ms-rteStyle-RandysStyle {
  -ms-name:"CustomStyle";
  color: lime;
  font-size: 200pt;
}
```

When `CustomStyle` is clicked, the selected text will have the color lime and a font size of 200pt applied to it.

ADDING CUSTOM BUTTONS TO THE SHAREPOINT RIBBON

In the first section, we talked about adding styles to the ribbon to help enforce a consistent style throughout the SharePoint content. The ribbon provides a central place on every page that users can reference to make whatever changes they need to make. But the ribbon is also a good place to add buttons to perform custom functionality that might be required to solve specific business problems. In this section, we'll discuss extending the ribbon to provide other options to content authors to improve usability in your SharePoint site.

In many ways, this topic and those that follow through the rest of this chapter may dive deeper into code, perhaps outside of many designers' comfort zone. While it's not critical that you completely understand these topics, as a designer you may be asked to be involved with assisting developers or even be placed in charge of creating these types of customizations. At the very least, it's a good idea to understand how these customizations work so that you can make educated decisions as business requirements emerge that may necessitate them.

In this example, we'll walk through the steps to customize the ribbon by adding a button declaratively via XML:

1. Create a new solution in Visual Studio 2010 using the Empty SharePoint Project template and name it **Chapter12Example**.

2. When prompted, choose the SharePoint web application you want to use for testing and leave the Deploy as sandbox solution option selected. This will create a solution that should resemble Figure 12-3.

3. Right-click the Features node and choose Add Feature. Set the title of the feature to **WroxCH12** and save the changes. In the Solution Explorer, rename the Features parent node (e.g., Feature1) to **WroxCH12**.

    At this point, your project should look like Figure 12-4.

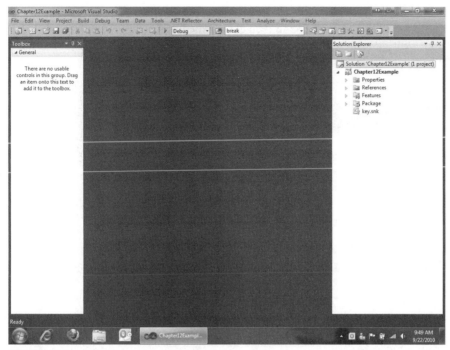

FIGURE 12-3

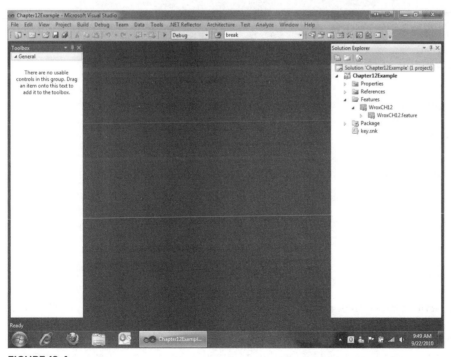

FIGURE 12-4

4. Now it's time to add an elements file to your solution. Right-click the project in the Solution Explorer, choose Add ⇨ New Item, and then choose the Empty Element template. Name your new elements file **RibbonItems,** as shown in Figure 12-5, and click the Add button, which will automatically add this item to the existing feature.

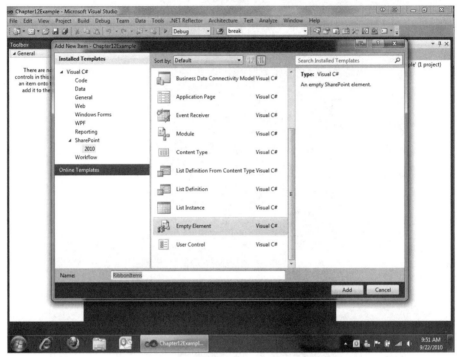

FIGURE 12-5

5. Double-click the RibbonItems element file from the Solution Explorer at the right to open the file, and then in the newly opened file, create a custom action by updating the file to look like the following code:

```xml
<?xml version="1.0" encoding="utf-8"?>
<Elements xmlns="http://schemas.microsoft.com/sharepoint/">
    <CustomAction
        Id="WroxRibbonControl"
        RegistrationType="List"
        RegistrationId="101"
        Location="CommandUI.Ribbon">
      ...
    </CustomAction>
</Elements>
```

Custom actions is a concept that has carried forward from previous versions of SharePoint. In SharePoint 2010, actions allow you to specify where a ribbon item will be displayed and who has rights to see that item. In this example, the button will display only for document libraries. This is achieved by specifying the `RegistrationType` (set to `List`) and `RegistrationId` (set to `101`) attributes.

For a list of the possible values for both RegistrationType *and* RegistrationId *and to learn more about custom actions, see* http://msdn.microsoft.com/en-us/library/ms460194.aspx.

The Id attribute simply needs to be a unique identifier for the custom action, and the Location attribute must be set to CommandUI.Ribbon (or one of it descendants) when specifying items for the ribbon.

6. To add the code that will actually add a new button to the ribbon, insert the following XML inside the custom action node that we started in step 5. Remove the . . . from the previous example and insert the following code before the </CustomAction>:

```
<CommandUIExtension>
    <CommandUIDefinitions>
        <CommandUIDefinition
            Location="Ribbon.Documents.New.Controls._children">
            <Button
                Id="NewUIRibbonControl.ShowWrox"
                Alt="Wrox.com"
                Sequence="1974"
                Command="ShowWrox"
                Image32by32="/_layouts/1033/images/GiveFeedback32.png"
                LabelText="Visit Wrox"
                TemplateAlias="o1"/>
        </CommandUIDefinition>
    </CommandUIDefinitions>
</CommandUIExtension>
```

The CommandUIExtension element is a container for both the CommandUIDefinitions and any associated handlers (CommandUIHandlers). The CommandUIDefinition element has a single attribute named Location that specifies where on the ribbon the button will be located. The Location attribute follows the general format of Ribbon.[Tab].[Group] .Controls._children. It is a dot-separated path that has Ribbon as its root and that ends with .Controls._children. This example will put the new button on all Document libraries, which is part of the Documents tab, under the New group (see Figure 12-6). This means that the Location attribute should be set to Ribbon.Documents.New.Controls._children.

With the Location identified, you can now tell the feature what to add to the ribbon and where to add it. Inside the CommandUIDefinition element, you can specify several different control types (a complete list is available at http://msdn.microsoft.com/en-us/library/ff458373.aspx), including the Button control. The button control has several attributes that can be used to control its style. In this example, the button is pretty basic and most of the attributes specified are self-explanatory. Two attributes worth noting are Command and TemplateAlias. The Command attribute tells the ribbon to which CommandUIHandler the Button is bound, and the TemplateAlias tells the ribbon what template to use for the Button. The TemplateAlias can specify a template that you have created or one of the out-of-the-box templates. In this example, you can use the out-of-the-box template o1, which displays the button with a large image.

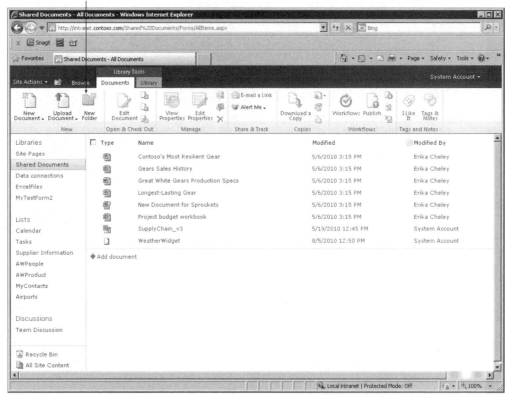

FIGURE 12-6

7. To make the button actually do something when it is clicked, add a `CommandUIHandler` to the element definition. The following XML shows the complete definition, including the XML from the previous steps (additions are in bold):

```xml
<?xml version="1.0" encoding="utf-8"?>
<Elements xmlns="http://schemas.microsoft.com/sharepoint/">
    <CustomAction
        Id="WroxRibbonControl"
        RegistrationType="List"
        RegistrationId="101"
        Location="CommandUI.Ribbon">
    <CommandUIExtension>
        <CommandUIDefinitions>
            <CommandUIDefinition
Location="Ribbon.Documents.New.Controls._children">
                <Button
                    Id="NewUIRibbonControl.ShowWrox"
                    Alt="Wrox.com"
                    Sequence="1974"
                    Command="ShowWrox"
Image32by32="/_layouts/1033/images/GiveFeedback32.png"
                    LabelText="Visit Wrox"
                    TemplateAlias="o1"/>
            </CommandUIDefinition>
```

```
            </CommandUIDefinitions>
          <CommandUIHandlers>
            <CommandUIHandler
               Command="ShowWrox"
CommandAction="javascript:window.open('http://www.wrox.com');" />
          </CommandUIHandlers>
        </CommandUIExtension>
      </CustomAction>
    </Elements>
```

This example illustrates the two required attributes: Command and CommandAction. Command is the name of the command and links to the Command attribute of the Button element in the CommandUIDefinition definition. CommandAction specifies script that will execute when the handler is invoked (i.e., when the button is clicked). In the example, the action is to simply open a new window that navigates to the Wrox website.

8. At this point, you are finished with all necessary changes and are ready to deploy the solution. Right-click the project in the Solution Explorer and choose Deploy.

9. To test your change, open a browser and navigate to the site to which the solution was deployed, and then navigate to a document library (if one does not exist you will need to create one) and choose the Documents tab in the ribbon. You should see an icon next to the New Folder button that says "Visit Wrox," similar to the image shown in Figure 12-7. Click the icon. A new browser should open and take you to the Wrox website.

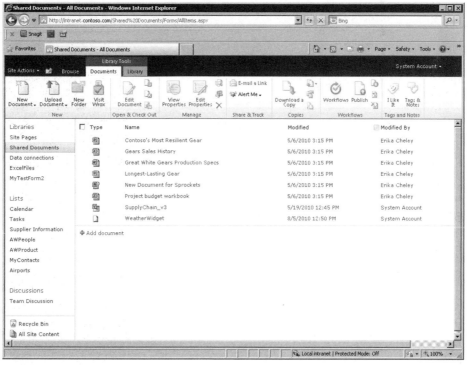

FIGURE 12-7

You have just created your first custom button for the new ribbon control in SharePoint 2010. Note that you should save this solution, as it will be used and enhanced throughout the remainder of this chapter.

OPENING PAGES IN DIALOGS

One of the nicer enhancements to the SharePoint 2010 UI is that most changes can be done without a page refresh. SharePoint employs a lot of Ajax and modal dialogs windows to help ensure that most changes you make on a page do not require an entire page refresh. You learned about SharePoint 2010 dialogs in Chapter 8; as a quick reminder, they are secondary windows that gain focus over the main window, and they must be interacted with or canceled before continuing. Dialog boxes in SharePoint 2010 can be dragged around within the browser window and even maximized to the full browser window size.

Fortunately, the modal dialogs are really easy to tap into when customizing your site. To see how this works, you will modify the example created earlier in the chapter to have the Wrox website open inside of a modal SharePoint 2010 dialog.

To get started, open the solution created earlier in the chapter (`Chapter12Example.sln`). Next, open the file named `Elements.xml` that is under the `RibbonItems` node and replace the `CommandUIHandler` node with the following:

```
<CommandUIHandler
    Command="ShowWrox"
    CommandAction="javascript:
        var options = {
            url: 'http://www.wrox.com',
            title: 'Wrox.com Website',
            allowMaximize: true,
            showClose: true,
            width: 800,
            height: 600
        };
        SP.UI.ModalDialog.showModalDialog(options);
        "
/>
```

Essentially, this change does two things. First, it creates a new `options` object with all the settings for the modal dialog interface. Second, it launches the modal dialog box using the `SP.UI.ModalDialog.showModalDialog()` method, which is a part of the SharePoint client API.

 For a full list of dialog options, review the SharePoint SDK

With the modified code in place, you can redeploy the solution. Simply right-click the project in Solution Explorer and select Deploy. Once the solution is deployed, you should see the `Wrox.com` website open when the button created in the previous section is clicked (see Figure 12-8).

FIGURE 12-8

WORKING WITH THE STATUS BAR AND NOTIFICATION AREA

SharePoint provides an easy way for you to give users feedback in the form of the status bar and the notification area, which enable you to provide immediate feedback to clients when certain criteria are met.

To see how this works, you can continue to modify the example created earlier in the chapter to learn how to use the status bar and notification area to give the user immediate feedback.

To get started, open the solution created earlier in the chapter (Chapter12Example.sln), and then open the file named Elements.xml (under the RibbonItems node). In this file, replace the CommandUIHandler node with the following code (additions are in bold):

```
<CommandUIHandler
    Command="ShowWrox"
    CommandAction="javascript:
        function demoCallback(dialogResult, returnValue)
        {
            SP.UI.Notify.addNotification('Thank you for visiting');
            var id = SP.UI.Status.addStatus('Wrox', 'Site Visited', true);
```

```
                    SP.UI.Status.setStatusPriColor(id, 'green');
                }
            var options = {
                url: 'http://www.wrox.com',
                title: 'Wrox.com Website',
                allowMaximize: true,
                showClose: true,
                width: 800,
                height: 600,
                dialogReturnValueCallback: demoCallback
            };
            SP.UI.ModalDialog.showModalDialog(options);
            "
    />
```

This new code adds a callback function (demoCallback) that will be called when the modal dialog is closed, which you can see with the new line added to the options object. The new function simply adds a notification, adds a new status, and then sets the status color. In this case, when a user closes the modal dialog box with the Wrox.com link in it, the status bar will turn green, indicating a status of "Site Visited" and displaying the message (or notification) "Thank you for visiting."

To see this change in action, simply redeploy the Chapter12Example.sln solution and then reload your document library in the browser. When you click the Visit Wrox button in the ribbon, the modal dialog will behave exactly as it did before. However, after you close the modal dialog, you will see your new status bar, as shown in Figure 12-9.

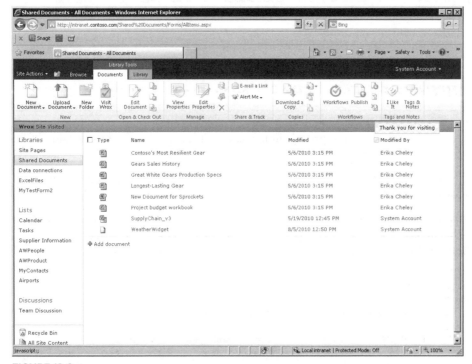

FIGURE 12-9

SUMMARY

The new SharePoint 2010 ribbon is a powerful tool that enables content editors to create custom styles. This means that you, as a designer, must ensure that users with sufficient permissions to make such changes are well versed in the style rules you are trying to enforce for your site. It is also important for you to understand how to add custom styles for content authors to use to create consistent content styling.

This chapter discussed the basics of editing page content using the ribbon, and then talked about how the user experience can be further customized. The ability to customize the ribbon and the dialog framework is an important way for site designers to be able to improve usability for users. Although this type of customization of the user experience often is performed by developers, the designers are ultimately the ones who define the overall user experience. Even if you are not directly involved in creating some of these customizations, it is important that you are part of the process.

13

The Client Object Model and jQuery

WHAT'S IN THIS CHAPTER?

➤ Objects supported by the Client Object Model

➤ Updating the site title using the Client Object Model

➤ Common list operations

➤ Using jQuery with SharePoint 2010

There are two basic approaches to accessing data programmatically in SharePoint. The first approach is to use the SharePoint API on the server. When you run code directly on the SharePoint server, the SharePoint API gives you complete control over all aspects of SharePoint and the data. If your application is not running on the server and needs to access the SharePoint data, you need to use the SharePoint web services. The web services offer similar functionality compared to the SharePoint API, although not every function is covered.

In SharePoint 2010, you have another option when programming against SharePoint data: the Client Object Model. The Client Object Model is a new approach to remotely programming against SharePoint data. Although using web services gives you broad coverage to SharePoint features, using the programming model and API is very different from using the server API. This makes it difficult for developers, as they need to learn two completely different programming models. Also, calling web services from JavaScript clients is complicated and requires a lot of manual XML creation and manipulation. The Client Object Model solves all these issues, making client-side programming easy and straightforward.

The Client Object Model is really three separate object models, one for the .NET CLR, one for Silverlight, and one for JavaScript. The .NET CLR version is used to create applications such as WinForms, Windows Presentation Foundation (WPF), and console applications, as well as PowerShell scripts. The Silverlight version works with both in-browser and out-of-browser Silverlight applications. The JavaScript version enables your Ajax and jQuery code to call back to SharePoint. You will read more about the Silverlight version in Chapter 14, "Silverlight and SharePoint Integration." We are not going to go into the .NET CLR version in this chapter, but as you will see in Chapter 14, once you learn how the Client Object Model works, you can easily program against any version. In this chapter, you will see how the Client Object Model works with JavaScript and jQuery to perform some common development tasks.

UNDERSTANDING THE CLIENT OBJECT MODEL

Understanding how the Client Object Model works will help you be more effective across all three versions. As shown in Figure 13-1, the Client Object Model fundamentally is a new Windows Communication Foundation (WCF) SharePoint service called `Client.svc` and three proxies: .NET CLR, Silverlight, and JavaScript. You program against the client proxies just as you do with any service. Calls to and from the server are sent in batches to increase network efficiency.

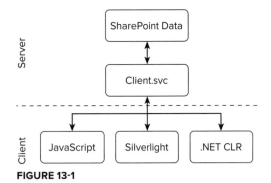

FIGURE 13-1

Objects Supported by the Client Object Model

One of the first questions that comes up when talking about the Client Object Model is, "What can you do with it?" Again, understanding how the Client Object Model works will help you appreciate its capabilities and limitations. The Client Object Model proxies are based on the `Microsoft.SharePoint .dll`. Right away this establishes what you can do to this API. The `Microsoft.SharePoint` API supports the most common objects, such as sites, webs, content types, lists, folders, navigations, and workflows. Obviously, this is not an exhaustive list. So, how do you find out if a particular object is supported in the Client Object Model? Fortunately, the help documentation for SharePoint 2010 is very good, and you can find the complete list on MSDN at `http://msdn.microsoft.com/en-us/library/ee544361.aspx`.

Another way to find out if a particular object is supported is to look at the attributes on the `Microsoft.SharePoint` API. Remember that the client proxies are created from the server API (`http://msdn.microsoft.com/en-us/library/microsoft.sharepoint.aspx`). The tool knows what to put in the client proxies by looking for the attribute named `ClientCallableTypeAttribute`. The Client Object Model does not require a reference to the server assemblies.

The `ClientCallableTypeAttribute` also specifies the name to call the object in the proxy. This brings up another important point about the Client Object Model. The names in the Client Object Model have been cleaned up a little by removing the "sp" from the beginning of most of the objects. But knowing how the Client Object Model is implemented enables you to look in the help documentation and see what the server object is and what the client object is called. For example, open the help page for the `SPSite` class, `http://msdn.microsoft.com/en-us/library/microsoft .sharepoint.spsite.aspx`. In the Syntax section at the top of the help topic, you can see the `ClientCallableTypeAttribute` and the name that it will be called in the proxy classes.

```
[ClientCallableTypeAttribute(
Name = "Site",
ServerTypeId = "{E1BB82E8-0D1E-4e52-B90C-684802AB4EF6}")]
[SubsetCallableTypeAttribute]
public class SPSite : IDisposable
```

At the heart of the Client Object Model is the `ClientContext` class, the object used to access the objects returned from the server and the queries sent to the server. The first step to programming the Client Object Model is to always get a reference to the current `ClientContext` using the static method on the `ClientContext` class, `SP.ClientContext.get_current()`. You will see how to use the `ClientContext` class in each of the examples throughout this chapter.

Although it is not possible to go into great depth about the entire Client Object Model API here, you should now have an understanding of how the Client Object Model works, and how to figure out what's in the client API, and how it maps to the server API. This was one of the goals of the SharePoint team: to make it easy for someone who already knows the server API to be productive quickly on the client API. Let's take a look at how to program with the Client Object Model in practice by walking through a few common scenarios.

The two main scenarios you will see are how to use the Client Object Model to read and write properties of the SharePoint site, and how to read and write data from the SharePoint List.

UPDATING THE SITE TITLE USING THE CLIENT OBJECT MODEL

One of the first examples to work with is to retrieve and update the site title. This is a very simple example, but it shows some of the basic patterns of using the Client Object Model.

1. Open Visual Studio and create a new empty SharePoint project called ClientOMProject.

2. Add a Visual Web Part project item to the project and name it **ChangeTitleWebPart**. Using a Visual Web Part will require this to be a farm solution.

3. Open the `ChangeTitleWebPart.ascx` page. Click the Design button at the bottom of the page to switch between Source view and Design view.

4. Add an HTML textbox and a button. Once in Design view, drag an Input (Text) control and an Input (Button) control from the HTML section of the Toolbox pane on the left.

5. Add the button click handler. Double-click on the button to create the JavaScript click event handler. Visual Studio will generate the following code for you.

```
<script language="javascript" type="text/javascript">
// <![CDATA[

    function Button1_onclick() {

    }

// ]]>
</script>

<p>
    <input id="Text1" style="width: 229px" type="text" /> 
    <input id="Button1" type="button" value="button"
      onclick="return Button1_onclick()" /></p>
```

6. Call the method to retrieve the site's title property. You need to use the Client Object Model to retrieve the site's title property, but you need to make sure the Client Object Model is loaded first. Add the following code inside your script tag to ensure the Client Object Model is ready before you use it.

```
ExecuteOrDelayUntilScriptLoaded(GetTitle, "sp.js");
```

7. Create the `GetTitle` method to retrieve the site's title property. In the previous step, you added code to call the `GetTitle` method when the Client Object Model was ready. Now you will implement the `GetTitle` method using the Client Object Model. Add the following code to retrieve the site's title property.

```
var site;
    var context;

    function GetTitle() {
        //Get the current client context
        context = SP.ClientContext.get_current();

        //Add the site to query queue
        site = context.get_web();
        context.load(site);

        //Run the query on the server
        context.executeQueryAsync(onQuerySucceeded, onQueryFailed);
    }
```

First you define the site and context variable to hold a reference for later. In the `GetTitle` function, you first get a reference to the current client context. This is the context that the page is running in, which in this example is `intranet.contoso.com`. The second step is to define which objects you want returned and load them onto the context's query queue using the load method. The last step is to execute the calls on the server. In Silverlight and

JavaScript this is an asynchronous call, so you will need to define a succeeded and failed callback handler.

8. Implement the failed callback handler. If your call to the server fails, the failed callback handler will fire. The callback provides some information to help you debug the problem such as the error message and call stack information. Add the following code to implement a failed callback handler that will display an alert box with the error message.

```
function onQueryFailed(sender, args) {
    alert('request failed ' + args.get_message() +
                '\n' + args.get_stackTrace());
}
```

9. Implement the succeeded callback handler. Add the following code to set the value of the textbox to the site's title property.

```
function onQuerySucceeded(sender, args) {
    document.getElementById("Text1").value = site.get_title();
}
```

10. Update the site's title on the button click event. Up to this point you have retrieved the Site's title, now you will add the ability to update the title. Add the following code to the button click handler.

```
function Button1_onclick() {
    //Update the Site's title property
    site.set_title(document.getElementById("Text1").value);
    site.update();

    //Add the site to query queue
    context.load(site);

    //Run the query on the server
    context. executeQueryAsync(onTitleUpdate, onQueryFailed);
}

function onTitleUpdate(sender, args) {

}
```

11. Press F5 to run the application. Once the site opens, you will need to add the `ChangeTitleWebPart` to the page. You should see something similar to Figure 13-2.

12. Refresh the page. You may have noticed that the title does not appear to update when you click the button. In fact, it does update but you will need to refresh the page to see the changes. Add the following code to refresh the page after the title is updated.

```
function onTitleUpdate(sender, args) {
    SP.UI.ModalDialog.RefreshPage(SP.UI.DialogResult.OK);
}
```

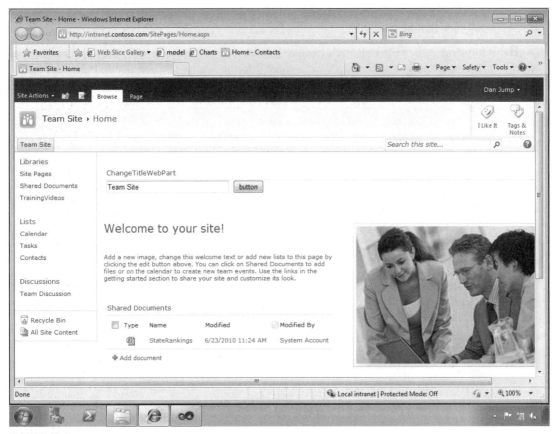

FIGURE 13-2

This code actually uses the new SharePoint dialog framework APIs to perform the page refresh.

Running the application now will display the site's title in the text box and then set the site's title when you click the button. After the title is updated, the page refreshes to show the new site title.

This is a very simple example, but it clearly demonstrates a code pattern for using the Client Object Model: Define the objects to retrieve, load them on the query queue, execute them on the server, and handle the callback. As you look at more complex examples in the next section, you will use this pattern over and over again.

COMMON LIST OPERATIONS

Now that you have a good understanding of the fundamentals, let's look at a few of the most common tasks you will use the Client Object Model for: reading and writing SharePoint list data. In this sample, you will add a Visual Web Part to the solution and add buttons to call the various operations. You also will see how to use a separate JavaScript file to contain most of the Client Object Model code to call SharePoint.

1. Add the following code to your Visual Web Part. This code will add five buttons for the different operations and some boilerplate code to call the functions. It also contains a reference to the external `ListOperations.js` file.

```
<script src="/SiteAssets/ListOperations.js" type="text/javascript"></script>

<script language="javascript" type="text/javascript">
// <![CDATA[

    function CreateButton_onclick() {
        CreateList();
    }

    function AddButton_onclick() {
        AddListItem();
    }

    function ReadButton_onclick() {
        ReadListItem();
    }

    function UpdateButton_onclick() {
        UpdateListItem();
    }

    function DeleteButton_onclick() {
        DeleteListItems();
    }

    // ]]>
</script>


<p><input id="CreateButton" type="button" value="Create List"
        style="width: 150px" onclick="CreateButton_onclick()" /></p>
<p><input id="AddButton" type="button" value="Add List Item"
        style="width: 150px" onclick="AddButton_onclick()" /></p>
<p><input id="ReadButton" type="button" value="Read List Item"
        style="width: 150px" onclick="return ReadButton_onclick()" /></p>
<p><input id="UpdateButton" type="button" value="Update List Item"
        style="width: 150px" onclick="return UpdateButton_onclick()" /></p>
<p><input id="DeleteButton" type="button" value="Delete List Item"
        style="width: 150px" onclick="return DeleteButton_onclick()" /></p>
```

2. Add a JavaScript file called `ListOperations.js` file to your Visual Web Part node. Set the deployment type property to Element File. And add a `Module` node to the elements file to deploy the `ListOperations.js` file to the Assets library. Deploying this to the Assets library will allow you to deploy this as a sandboxed solution to both on-premise SharePoint sites and to SharePoint online sites.

3. Add the following text to the `Elements.xml` file. You should need to add only the second `Module` node, as the first one was added by Visual Studio.

```xml
<?xml version="1.0" encoding="utf-8"?>
<Elements xmlns="http://schemas.microsoft.com/sharepoint/" >
  <Module Name="ListOperationsVisualWebPart" List="113" Url="_catalogs/wp">
    <File Path="ListOperationsVisualWebPart\ListOperationsVisualWebPart.webpart"
     Url="ListOperationsVisualWebPart.webpart" Type="GhostableInLibrary">
      <Property Name="Group" Value="Custom" />
    </File>
  </Module>
  <Module Name="jsFiles">
    <File Path="ListOperationsVisualWebPart\ListOperations.js"
     Url="SiteAssets/ListOperations.js" />
  </Module>
</Elements>
```

Now that you have the Visual Web Part complete, you should deploy it and verify that you can add the Web Part to the site and that the `ListOperations.js` file is in the `Assets` library. You should see something similar to Figure 13-3. Now you are ready to focus on the actual JavaScript.

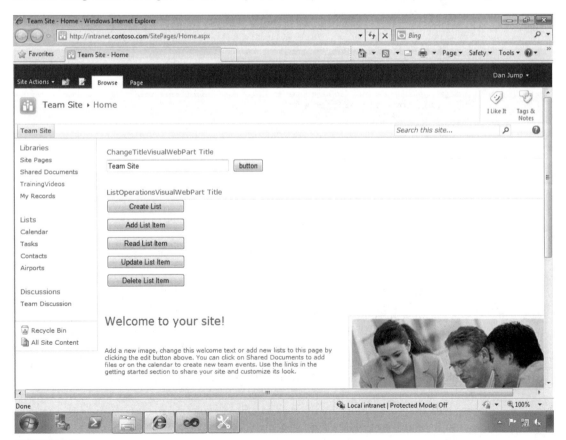

FIGURE 13-3

Creating Lists

There are many ways to create lists in SharePoint. But sometimes you may need to create them dynamically from the client. Using the Client Object Model makes this very easy and straight-forward. As you saw earlier, you need to get a reference to the ClientContext first. Next, you create a ListCreationInfo object to define the list and add it to the collection of lists in SharePoint. Finally, you define the actual field definitions for the columns of the list.

The most difficult part about creating a custom list is defining the fields. The fields are defined using Collaborative Markup Language (CAML). You can see all the values in the MSDN help page, at http://msdn.microsoft.com/en-us/library/ms948164.aspx. Add the following code to your ListOperations.js file. This code will create a list called Airports that has two fields: AirportName and AirportCode.

```
var site;
var context;

function CreateList() {
    var listTitle = "Airports";
    var listDescription = "List of Airports";

    //Get the current client context
    context = SP.ClientContext.get_current();

    var site = context.get_web();

    //Create a new list
    var listCreationInfo = new SP.ListCreationInformation();
    listCreationInfo.set_templateType(SP.ListTemplateType.genericList);
    listCreationInfo.set_title(listTitle);
    listCreationInfo.set_description(listDescription);
    listCreationInfo.set_quickLaunchOption(SP.QuickLaunchOptions.on);

    var airportList = site.get_lists().add(listCreationInfo);

    //Create the fields
    var airportNameField = airportList.get_fields().addFieldAsXml(
                '<Field DisplayName=\'AirportName\' Type=\'Text\' />', true,
                SP.AddFieldOptions.defaultValue);
    var airportCodeField = airportList.get_fields().addFieldAsXml(
                '<Field DisplayName=\'AirportCode\' Type=\'Text\' />', true,
                SP.AddFieldOptions.defaultValue);

    context.load(airportNameField);
    context.load(airportCodeField);

    context.executeQueryAsync(CreateListSucceeded, CreateListFailed);
}

function CreateListSucceeded() {
    alert('List created.');
}

function CreateListFailed(sender, args) {
    alert('Request failed. ' + args.get_message() + '\n' + args.get_stackTrace());
}
```

You can also create predefined lists, such as an announcements list, without the need to define any fields. You can also define other field types, such as numbers, date and time, and Boolean. You can find a complete list at `http://msdn.microsoft.com/en-us/library/ms948164.aspx`.

Adding List Items

Now that you have created a custom list, the next thing to do is to add new records to the list. To create a list item, first create a new list item using the `ListItemCreationInformation` object, and then add it to the list using the `addItem` method. Next, you set the values for all the fields in the list item using the `set_item` method. Finally, you call the update method on the list item to flag it for updating before calling `executeQueryAsync` to commit the changes on the server. Add the following code to the `ListOperations.js` file.

```
function AddListItem() {
    var listTitle = "Airports";

    //Get the current client context
    context = SP.ClientContext.get_current();
    var airportList = context.get_web().get_lists().getByTitle(listTitle);

    //Create a new record
    var listItemCreationInformation = new SP.ListItemCreationInformation();
    var listItem = airportList.addItem(listItemCreationInformation);

    //Set the values
    listItem.set_item('AirportName', 'Seattle/Tacoma');
    listItem.set_item('AirportCode', 'SEA');
    listItem.set_item('Title', 'SEATAC');

    listItem.update();
    context.load(listItem);

    context.executeQueryAsync(AddListItemSucceeded, AddListItemFailed);
}

function AddListItemSucceeded() {
    alert('List Item Added.');
}

function AddListItemFailed(sender, args) {
    alert('Request failed. ' + args.get_message() + '\n' + args.get_stackTrace());
}
```

Reading List Items

Reading lists follows the same pattern as other Client Object Model calls. First you get a reference to the client context and a reference to the list you want to read items from. In this case, you will read items from the Airports list that you created in the previous section. Next, you need to create a CAML query to specify which items you want returned.

You can learn more about CAML on MSDN at http://msdn.microsoft.com/
en-us/library/ms426449.aspx. *Building CAML queries can be fairly complicated. It is recommended that you use a CAML query builder to help you build
the correct query. A number of community CAML query tools are available on
CodePlex. You can find the one that works best for you by searching CodePlex,
at* www.codeplex.com/site/search?query=caml.

SharePoint provides a method, createAllItemsQuery, which returns a valid CAML string that
returns all items. If you look at the createAllItemsQuery method in SP.Debug.js or debug the
code, you will see the following CAML string that is returned:

```
<View Scope=\"RecursiveAll\">
    <Query></Query>
  </View>
```

After you specify the CAML query, you load the list items query on the context, and then execute
the query on the server asynchronously by calling executeQueryAsync.

Once the query returns from the server, in this case the ReadListItemsSucceeded method is called.
Iterate over the returned items by getting a reference to the enumerator and calling the moveNext
method in a while loop. On each iteration of the loop, you can get the current list item using the
get_current method of the item. Finally, once you have a reference to the item, you can call the
get_item method, passing in the string name of the field you want. Add the following code to the
ListOperations.js file to read the list items:

```
function ReadListItem() {
    var listTitle = "Airports";

    //Get the current client context
    context = SP.ClientContext.get_current();
    var airportList = context.get_web().get_lists().getByTitle(listTitle);

    var camlQuery = SP.CamlQuery.createAllItemsQuery();

    this.listItems = airportList.getItems(camlQuery);

    context.load(listItems);

    context.executeQueryAsync(ReadListItemSucceeded, ReadListItemFailed);
}

function ReadListItemSucceeded(sender, args) {
    var itemsString = '';
    var enumerator = listItems.getEnumerator();

    while (enumerator.moveNext()) {
        var listItem = enumerator.get_current();
```

```
            itemsString += 'AirportName: ' + listItem.get_item('AirportName') +
    ' AirportCode: ' + listItem.get_id().toString() + '\n';
        }

        alert(itemsString);
    }

    function ReadListItemFailed(sender, args) {
        alert('Request failed. ' + args.get_message() + '\n' + args.get_stackTrace());
    }
```

Updating List Items

Updating list items is very straightforward. First, get a reference to the current context, and then get a reference to the list item that you want to update. This can be done in a number of ways. For example, you could use a CAML query to find the correct record or to iterate over a number of records. This example gets a reference to the record by using the record ID. Once you have the item, you can call the set_item method, passing in the name of the field and the updated value. You need to call the update method on the item to flag that it is to be updated. Finally, call the executeQueryAsync method to perform the update on the server. Add the following code to the ListOperations.js file to update the first record in the Airports list.

```
    function UpdateListItem() {
        var listTitle = "Airports";

        //Get the current client context
        context = SP.ClientContext.get_current();
        var airportList = context.get_web().get_lists().getByTitle(listTitle);

        //Get the list item to update
        var listItem = airportList.getItemById(2);
        //Set the new property value
        listItem.set_item('AirportName', 'Seattle Tacoma Airport');
        listItem.update();

        context.executeQueryAsync(UpdateItemSucceeded, UpdateItemFailed);
    }

    function UpdateItemSucceeded() {
        alert('List Item Updated.');
    }

    function UpdateItemFailed(sender, args) {
        alert('Request failed. ' + args.get_message() + '\n' + args.get_stackTrace());
    }
```

As a brief aside, one of the problems is verifying that you have the correct item ID. In this case I have only one record but I used the ID of 2. This is because I previously created a record and deleted it. Then when I created the record again, SharePoint assigned it the next available ID, which was 2. This makes it difficult to get the correct ID during development. One easy technique is to use the List Service to view the list data as a REST request. SharePoint will return the data as an OData Atom feed in which you can verify the fields and the records, including the item IDs. For example, if you browse to the Airports list using the List Service path at `http://intranet.contoso.com/_vti_bin/listdata.svc/Airports`. You will see the following Atom feed:

```
<?xml version="1.0" encoding="utf-8" standalone="yes"?>
<feed xml:base="http://intranet.contoso.com/_vti_bin/listdata.svc/"
xmlns:d="http://schemas.microsoft.com/ado/2007/08/dataservices"
xmlns:m="http://schemas.microsoft.com/ado/2007/08/dataservices/metadata"
xmlns="http://www.w3.org/2005/Atom">
  <title type="text">Airports</title>
  <id>http://intranet.contoso.com/_vti_bin/listdata.svc/Airports/</id>
  <updated>2010-07-14T16:52:35Z</updated>
  <link rel="self" title="Airports" href="Airports" />
  <entry m:etag="W/&quot;2&quot;">
    <id>http://intranet.contoso.com/_vti_bin/listdata.svc/Airports(2)</id>
    <title type="text">SEATAC</title>
    <updated>2010-07-14T09:52:18-07:00</updated>
    <author>
      <name />
    </author>
    <link rel="edit" title="AirportsItem" href="Airports(2)" />
    <link rel="http://schemas.microsoft.com/ado/2007/08/dataservices/related/CreatedBy"
type="application/atom+xml;type=entry" title="CreatedBy" href="Airports(2)/CreatedBy" />
    <link
rel="http://schemas.microsoft.com/ado/2007/08/dataservices/related/ModifiedBy"
type="application/atom+xml;type=entry" title="ModifiedBy"
href="Airports(2)/ModifiedBy" />
    <link
rel="http://schemas.microsoft.com/ado/2007/08/dataservices/related/Attachments"
type="application/atom+xml;type=feed" title="Attachments"
href="Airports(2)/Attachments" />
    <category term="Microsoft.SharePoint.DataService.AirportsItem"
scheme="http://schemas.microsoft.com/ado/2007/08/dataservices/scheme" />
    <content type="application/xml">
      <m:properties>
        <d:ContentTypeID>0x010041919BD85A48CA4B95F735848786C29C</d:ContentTypeID>
        <d:Title>SEATAC</d:Title>
        <d:AirportName>Seattle Tacoma Airport</d:AirportName>
        <d:AirportCode>SEA</d:AirportCode>
        <d:Id m:type="Edm.Int32">2</d:Id>
        <d:ContentType>Item</d:ContentType>
        <d:Modified m:type="Edm.DateTime">2010-07-14T09:52:18</d:Modified>
        <d:Created m:type="Edm.DateTime">2010-07-11T22:09:54</d:Created>
        <d:CreatedById m:type="Edm.Int32">16</d:CreatedById>
        <d:ModifiedById m:type="Edm.Int32">16</d:ModifiedById>
        <d:Owshiddenversion m:type="Edm.Int32">2</d:Owshiddenversion>
        <d:Version>1.0</d:Version>
        <d:Path>/Lists/Airports</d:Path>
      </m:properties>
    </content>
  </entry>
</feed>
```

You can see the ID in a couple of places, first in the `href` attribute in the link node and again in the Id field under the properties node. This query actually returns all the records in the list. (In this case, there is only one record.) To drill down on to a specific record, you could use a path with the item ID in parentheses at the end, `http://intranet.contoso.com/_vti_bin/listdata.svc/Airports(2)`.

Deleting List Items

Deleting records using the Client Object Model is very similar to updating records. First, get a reference to the current context. Next, get a reference to the list item that you want to update. Again, in this example I will get a reference to the record by using the record ID. Once you have a reference to the list item, call the `deleteObject` method to mark the record for deletion. Then call `executeQueryAsync` to perform the deletion of the record on the server. Add the following code to the `ListOperation.js` file:

```
function DeleteListItems() {
    var listTitle = "Airports";

    //get the current client context
    context = SP.ClientContext.get_current();
    var airportList = context.get_web().get_lists().getByTitle(listTitle);

    //get the list item to delete
    var listItem = airportList.getItemById(2);
    //delete the list item
    listItem.deleteObject();

    context.executeQueryAsync(DeleteItemSucceeded, DeleteItemFailed);
}

function DeleteItemSucceeded() {
    alert('List Item Deleted.');
}

function DeleteItemFailed(sender, args) {
    alert('Request failed. ' + args.get_message() + '\n' + args.get_stackTrace());
}
```

You have seen some of the most common methods for operating with list data in SharePoint. Although this doesn't cover everything that you can do with the Client Object Model, you should have enough information to understand the basic pattern that is used in all the operations. With this basic information, you will be able to understand the reference documentation and samples in the SharePoint SDK and on MSDN.

The next section looks briefly at how you can combine the power of the Client Object Model with the flexibility of jQuery.

USING JQUERY WITH SHAREPOINT 2010

jQuery is an open source JavaScript library that helps you build rich, dynamic, client-side applications. The power in jQuery comes from its simplicity and powerful query syntax. One of jQuery's most powerful abilities is to quickly select various HTML DOM elements. Once you find the element or collection of elements, jQuery makes it easy to modify attributes and CSS for those elements. jQuery also supports extensibility through a rich plug-in model. In fact, a huge community of jQuery plug-ins is available. It is actually a core design point of jQuery to keep the core library small and provide most of the rich functionality via plug-ins.

Although it is not possible to cover all aspects of jQuery in this chapter, there is one very important jQuery API with which SharePoint developers and designers should become familiar: the Ajax library. You learned about calling SharePoint from the client using the Client Object Model earlier in this chapter, but the Client Object Model doesn't cover all SharePoint functionality. For example, Search is not covered by the Client Object Model and many others. The Client Object Model covers only APIs in the `Microsoft.SharePoint.dll`. This is where the jQuery Ajax library comes into play. Fortunately, SharePoint covers almost all its functionality with SOAP-based `.asmx` web services. The Ajax library makes it relatively easy to call these web services using jQuery from the client.

In this section, you will see how to call SharePoint web services using jQuery and dynamically display the results in a Content Editor Web Part (CEWP), without writing any server code.

Loading jQuery

You can download the jQuery library from `http://jquery.com`. The current version as of this writing is 1.4.2. The jQuery library is a single file called `jquery-1.4.2.js`. There are actually two versions of this file:

- ➤ `jquery-1.4.2.js` — A human-readable source version
- ➤ `jquery-1.4.2.min.js` — A minified and condensed version

I would recommend using the source version for development and the minified version in production. Download the `jquery-1.4.2.js` file and put it in somewhere on your SharePoint site. Create a `Scripts` folder under the `SiteAssets` library to hold your JavaScript files. The path would be `http://intranet.contoso.com/SiteAssets/Scripts/jquery-1.4.2.js`.

To add the jQuery library, use the following `script` tag on your page.

```
<script src="/SiteAssets/Scripts/jquery-1.4.2.js" type="text/javascript"></script>
```

Another option is to use the jQuery library hosted on Microsoft's content delivery network (CDN). The CDN geographically distributes the file around the world, making it faster for clients to download the file. With SharePoint on-premise installations, such as your intranet, this is not as important, but with SharePoint Online or SharePoint-based Internet sites, this will increase the perceived performance of your site. Add the following `script` tag to your page to use the Microsoft CDN to load the jQuery library:

```
<script src="http://ajax.microsoft.com/ajax/jquery/jquery-1.4.2.min.js"
type="text/javascript"></script>
```

Ajax Script Loader

One thing that you need to be concerned with when using jQuery is that the jQuery library is loaded only once. There are a number of ways that you could do this, but this section mentions three ways and the various caveats associated with each method.

The first method is to just include the `script` tags, like you saw previously, directly to the page or, even better, to the master page. You would need to ensure that no other components also add a reference to the jQuery library. Here, the term "components" refer to anything that may inject code when the page renders, such as Web Parts. This is an acceptable approach if you control the entire page, but many times this is not possible due to the modular nature of SharePoint development.

The next approach is to use the `ScriptLink` control. The `ScriptLink` control will ensure that the script is loaded only once and will also ensure that other dependencies have been loaded first. Add the following `ScriptLink` server-side tag to your page to load the jQuery library:

```
<SharePoint:ScriptLink ID="SPScriptLink"
    runat="server" Defer="false"
    Localizable="false" Name="jquery-1.4.2.js ">
</SharePoint:ScriptLink>
```

The `ScriptLink` control requires that you put the jQuery library file in the LAYOUTS directory, `C:\Program Files\Common Files\Microsoft Shared\Web Server Extensions\14\TEMPLATE\LAYOUTS`. This may not be possible if you have limited rights to the server, such as when you are creating sandboxed solutions. Also, even if the JavaScript library is in the LAYOUTS folder, the `ScriptLink` control is not allowed to run as a sandboxed solution. Therefore, I would not recommend this approach.

The third method, and the one that you should use, is to load jQuery using the Microsoft Ajax script loader, or another client-side script loader. One thing to be aware of is that the Microsoft ASP.NET Ajax library (`www.asp.net/ajaxLibrary`) is now included as part of the Ajax Control Toolkit (`http://ajaxcontroltoolkit.codeplex.com`). This means that the ASP.NET Ajax library was split into server controls, which are now in the Ajax Control Toolkit, and client code, which is now done using jQuery. So, most of the functionality that was provided is now done in jQuery or through a jQuery plug-in, except the script loader. The Ajax library script loader has not been released yet for jQuery, so you will need to use the existing `Start.js` script loader library until it is released.

Download the `Start.js` library to your Site Assets library's `Script` folder that you created earlier to hold your scripts. You can find the current script loader on Microsoft's CDN at `http://ajax.microsoft.com/ajax/beta/0910/Start.js`. You should also download the source version for development from `http://ajax.microsoft.com/ajax/beta/0910/Start.debug.js`. You could also load the `Start.js` library directly from the Microsoft CDN as well.

There are two steps to loading the jQuery library, or any of your custom JavaScript libraries. First, reference the script loader on your page using the following `script` tag:

```
<script src="/SiteAssets/Scripts/Start.debug.js" type="text/javascript"></script>
```

Or, if you are loading the library from the CDN, use the following `script` tag instead:

```
<script src="http://ajax.microsoft.com/ajax/beta/0911/Start.js"
type="text/javascript"></script>
```

The second step is to reference the jQuery library or your own libraries using the `Sys.loadScripts` method, which is part of the `Start.js` library. The `Sys.loadScripts` method takes an array of scripts to load and a callback function to call when they have been loaded. Add the follow code to load the jQuery library:

```
<script type="text/javascript">
    Sys.loadScripts(["/SiteAssets/Scripts/jquery-1.4.2.js "], function() {
        alert("jQuery Loaded");
    });
</script>
```

The Ajax Script Loader prevents the jQuery library from being loaded multiple times on the same page, even if you add many Web Parts that are using this code.

Calling SharePoint Web Services with jQuery

You have seen how to get SharePoint list data using the Client Object Model, but there are many types of SharePoint data that are not covered by the Client Object Model. The Client Object Model applies only to data in the `Microsoft.SharePoint.dll`, essentially functionality found in SharePoint Foundation only. To leverage other SharePoint data, such as profile data or search data, you will need to call the SharePoint web services. Calling these web services from the client using JavaScript has become much easier using the jQuery Ajax API. Let's first take a quick look at how to retrieve list data, in this case the Announcements list, using jQuery. You could do this using the Client Object Model, but this example should serve as a bridge from doing it with the Client Object Model to doing it with jQuery.

jQuery in the Content Editor Web Part

To keep things simple and demonstrate another technique for using JavaScript on your pages, you will use the Content Editor Web Part (CEWP) to display a list of announcements. This example does not require Visual Studio; everything can be done using only a web browser.

1. Start by adding a CEWP to the right column of your home page. You can find the CEWP in the Web Part gallery under the Media and Content category.

2. Put the Web Part into edit mode by selecting Edit Web Part from the Web Part's context menu. Click the link in the Web Part titled "Click here to add new content."

3. Next you want to actually edit the source HTML for the Web Part. Click the Editing Tools context-sensitive Format Text tab on the ribbon. In the Markup Ribbon group, select Edit HTML source from the HTML drop-down button. In the HTML source dialog, add the following code:

```
<!--Load the Script Loader-->
<script src="/SiteAssets/Scripts/Start.debug.js" type="text/javascript"></script>

<!-- Load jQuery library-->
<script type="text/javascript">

    Sys.loadScripts(["/SiteAssets/Scripts/jquery-1.4.2.js"], function() {
```

```
            GetAnnouncements();
        });
</script>


<script type="text/javascript">

    function GetAnnouncements() {

        var soapEnv = "<soap:Envelope
xmlns:soap='http://schemas.xmlsoap.org/soap/envelope/'> \
            <soap:Body> \
              <GetListItems xmlns='http://schemas.microsoft.com/sharepoint/soap/'> \
               <listName>Announcements</listName> \
               <viewFields> \
                <ViewFields> \
                   <FieldRef Name='Title' /> \
                   <FieldRef Name='Body' /> \
                   <FieldRef Name='Expires' /> \
                </ViewFields> \
               </viewFields> \
              </GetListItems> \
            </soap:Body> \
          </soap:Envelope>";

        jQuery.ajax({
            url: "/_vti_bin/lists.asmx",
            type: "POST",
            dataType: "xml",
            data: soapEnv,
            complete: GetListItemsComplete,
            contentType: "text/xml; charset=\"utf-8\""
        });
    }


    function GetListItemsComplete(xData, status) {
        jQuery(xData.responseXML).find("z\\:row").each(function () {
            $("<li>" + $(this).attr("ows_Title") + "</li>").appendTo("#Announcements");
        });
    }

</script>

<ul id="Announcements"></ul>
```

The GetAnnouncements function builds the SOAP message and then uses the jQuery.ajax API to
call the lists.asmx web service. The jQuery.ajax calls the GetListItemsCompleted callback
method when the web service returns. The GetListItemsComplete method parses the XML data
that returns from the lists.asmx web service. As it parses each record in the XML data, it appends
a list item to the Announcements list using the appendTo function.

There are two key pieces to calling various SharePoint web services. The first is to understand the exact SOAP XML required to call the service, and the second is to understand the returned XML data and how to parse it to extract the exact values required. Although these change between the various services, the code pattern is the same for all services. Unfortunately, discovering how to format the SOAP message can be a challenge. Although MSDN documents the methods, it does not tell you the exact SOAP format or which parameters are optional. One of the easiest ways to discover the syntax is to create a console application in Visual Studio that calls the web service you are interested in calling from JavaScript. Then use the web debugging tool Fiddler (`www.fiddler2.com`) to intercept and inspect the web service calls.

SUMMARY

In this chapter you have seen how the new Client Object Model makes accessing SharePoint data as easy on the client as it is on the server. The Client Object Model covers the `Microsoft` `.SharePoint.dll` API on the client through a proxy object model that closely mirrors the server object model. The Client Object Model offers a very efficient calling pattern that not only gives you control over when and how often you call the server but also gives you control over the amount of data that is returned.

You have learned how you can leverage the power of jQuery to access SharePoint web services using the `jQuery.Ajax` API. You have also seen a number of different approaches to loading the jQuery library and other custom libraries. In the end, jQuery and the Client Object Model are complementary techniques to bring all the power of SharePoint to the client to create very rich applications that can run in both on-premise and online scenarios.

These two techniques for accessing SharePoint data from the client will enable you to create dynamic branding solutions based on data in SharePoint.

14

Silverlight and SharePoint Integration

WHAT'S IN THIS CHAPTER?

➤ Understanding Silverlight features and tools

➤ Creating a Silverlight Web Part

➤ Accessing SharePoint data using the Client Object Model

➤ Extending Visual Studio to create Silverlight solutions

Silverlight delivers rich user experiences and the tools developers and designers need to rapidly create these experiences. Silverlight has had amazing penetration in the consumer space, with more than 500 million downloads and over 500,000 developers and designers (and more every day). As Silverlight reaches critical mass, many developers and designers are turning their Silverlight skills toward other platforms, such as SharePoint. I generally see two types of SharePoint developers: those who are new to Silverlight, and those who are new to SharePoint. So, this chapter delves somewhat deeper into programming than many of the other chapters, but designers are frequently asked to work with technologies like Silverlight because of the rich interactive user interfaces that they make available. Silverlight projects often involve designers and developers to ensure the application looks as nice as it performs. This chapter covers Silverlight as it pertains to SharePoint. To learn more about Silverlight development, check out Wrox's *Professional Silverlight 4*.

SILVERLIGHT FEATURES

Silverlight platform development is on a breathtaking pace, with a major new version delivered, on average, every 7 to 12 months. The Silverlight runtime works across multiple browsers and platforms. It also works both in the browser and out of the browser and on Windows

Phone 7 devices and other mobile devices. You can loosely think about Silverlight as a competitor to Adobe Flash. Let's briefly look at some of the major feature areas and how those features fit with SharePoint:

➤ **Media** — Silverlight's earliest renown was as a great platform for media. Silverlight supports video, such as h.264 standard. It also supports smooth streaming and video camera and microphone input. In this chapter, you will see how to leverage these features to deliver media in SharePoint.

➤ **Rich experiences** — Silverlight has a number of "rich experience" features, including copy and paste, drag and drop, and a fluid interface.

➤ **Business applications** — Although many Silverlight applications on the Internet are consumer-focused experiences, Silverlight has also been adding more features to make it a great platform for building business/SharePoint applications. These features include enhanced data binding, more forms controls, printing, the Managed Extensibility Framework, and internationalization support. Silverlight also supports dynamic theming, which enables Silverlight applications to look and feel like the SharePoint sites that host them.

➤ **Desktop applications** — Most people think about Silverlight running in the browser or in SharePoint (the latter being the case in this chapter), but Silverlight can be run out of the browser, on the user's desktop. When the application is running on the desktop, it can still connect to SharePoint data and runs in the same domain as its origin SharePoint site. When the application is running out of the browser, it gains additional features such as access to the local file system, the ability to call COM applications such as Office applications, notifications, and the ability to render HTML inside of the Silverlight application.

This is a most basic list of Silverlight features — just enough to give you an idea about what this platform makes available. You will use some of these features in the examples in this chapter. At this point, however, let's examine the tools that enable you to create these rich experiences.

SILVERLIGHT TOOLS

Silverlight development tools are split into two tools that work seamlessly together:

➤ **Expression Blend** — Expression Blend is part of the Expression Suite. Blend, shown in Figure 14-1, is a tool that *designers* will feel most comfortable with. It enables designers to create rich media and animated user experiences without writing code.

➤ **Visual Studio** — Visual Studio is the tool that *developers* will feel most comfortable with. Visual Studio enables developers to create rich Silverlight applications that contain code.

Both tools have code editors and visual designers, but Expression Blend has, by far, the best visual designer, and Visual Studio has, by far, the best code-editing tools.

Many developers who also design their applications use both tools interchangeably during the application development process. If a clear separation of duties exists between designers and developers, however, the two tools really shine, facilitating easier collaboration between designers and developers without requiring much knowledge about what the other is doing. In other words, the designer and developer are loosely coupled and can work independently of each other and can even work in parallel.

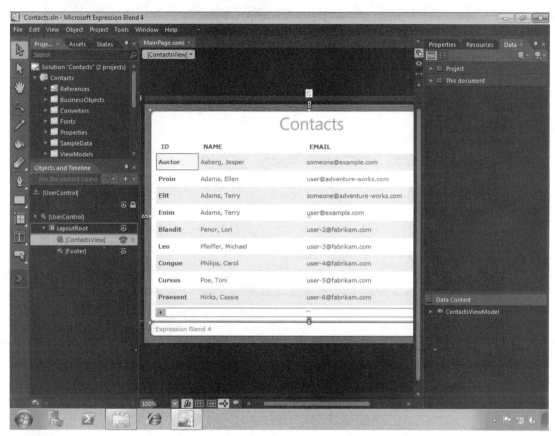

FIGURE 14-1

Out-of-the-Box

SharePoint has taken a big bet on Silverlight. This really speaks to the maturity of Silverlight. Microsoft is very conservative about the technologies they add to the Office and SharePoint platforms. But they saw the incredible value that Silverlight brings to the SharePoint developer. Not only do they support Silverlight in SharePoint, there are actually a number of places where SharePoint is built using Silverlight.

Let's look at a few examples of where Silverlight is used out-of-the-box in SharePoint. You'll most likely first encounter Silverlight in the Create dialog, where you can create new content in SharePoint (pages, lists, libraries, and sites). To open the Create dialog, click the Site Actions menu at the upper left of the site and then click More Options. Figure 14-2 shows a modal dialog open with the Silverlight-based page for adding new content.

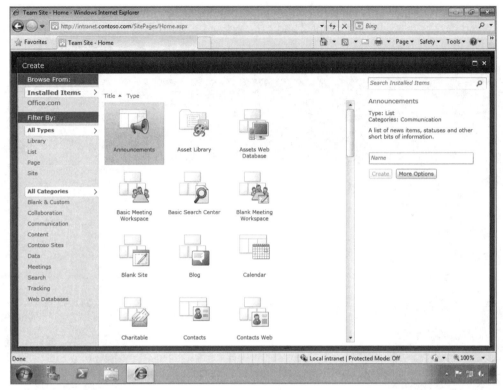

FIGURE 14-2

The Create dialog has animation effects for the icons as you navigate around the control and filter templates using the categories listed on the left side. This is a vastly better experience than you have without Silverlight. If you do not have Silverlight installed or enabled, you will default back to the old-style Create page, which is not as user friendly. Figure 14-3 shows the non-Silverlight Create page for comparison.

Another great example of an out-of-the-box Silverlight experience is on your personal My Site. Your personal My Site is your own private site on which you can store your own documents. Your My site also has a lot of profile information about you and your organization. Think of your personal My Site as a SharePoint version of your Facebook page. SharePoint ships with a Silverlight version of an Organization Browser. This very interesting control enables you to browse your organization both horizontally and vertically. Figure 14-4 shows an example of the Silverlight Organization Browser.

SharePoint has also made SharePoint a great platform for serving rich media. For example, they have a built-in Silverlight Media Web Part that you can easily add to any page to show videos. Silverlight is also used to quick preview media elements in asset libraries. The Silverlight media control is also interesting because you can change the skin simply by copying and modifying the `/Style Library/Media Player/ AlternateMediaPlayer.xaml` file. The media control even has a JavaScript API to do things such as play and stop the video. Figure 14-5 shows the media player and its associated context ribbon menu items.

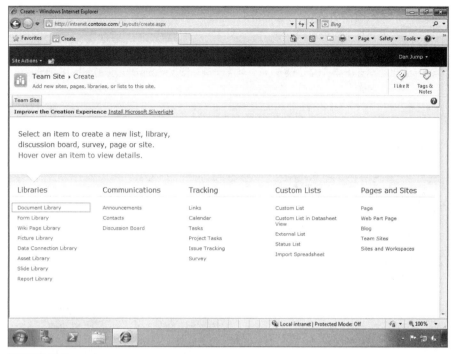

FIGURE 14-3

FIGURE 14-4

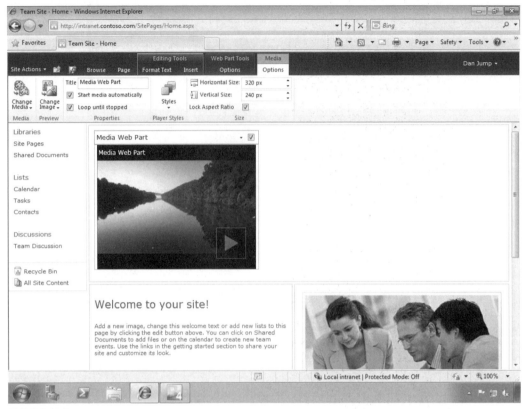

FIGURE 14-5

You will see Silverlight used in a number of other places as well (some are where you might not even realize). Even some of the new Office web applications use Silverlight to enhance the rendering and display of the Office documents.

All this integration is great for both SharePoint and Silverlight developers. You can assume that the integration of Silverlight in SharePoint will only increase in the future. Now that you know a little about Silverlight and where it is used in SharePoint, let's spend the rest of this chapter showing how to build your own Silverlight solutions in SharePoint.

Silverlight Web Part

SharePoint ships with a Silverlight Web Part, making it very easy for developers and power users to add Silverlight applications to SharePoint. You need to solve two basic problems when developing Silverlight applications for SharePoint: how to get the Silverlight application into SharePoint, and how to host the Silverlight application.

The first problem to solve is how do you get the Silverlight application into SharePoint. You can do so in a number of ways, as discussed in more detail in the next section. The easiest way is just to copy the Silverlight application to a SharePoint library. A simple Silverlight application consists of a single Zip file with the extension .xap. You can build these Silverlight applications yourself or you can download from various sites on the Internet or buy them from third-party developers. In this example, I downloaded a Weather application from the MSDN code gallery. You can download the source files from here: `http://code.msdn.microsoft.com/silverlightws/Release/ProjectReleases.aspx?ReleaseId=1660`. In fact, this was actually a Silverlight version 2 sample. I opened the solution in Expression Blend 4, and it upgraded the project to Silverlight version 4. The MSDN site also contains a prebuilt version of the `.xap` that you can use without any changes. Once you have the `.xap` file, follow these steps to upload the Silverlight application to the Shared Documents library on your site:

1. On the ribbon for the Shared Documents library, display the Documents tab, and then click Upload Document from the New group.

2. Browse to the Weather application's `.xap` file and click OK.

You now have the Silverlight application in SharePoint. The next problem to solve is how to host the Silverlight application. The most common way that developers add applications to SharePoint is using Web Parts. Web Parts in SharePoint allow developers to create "composite-able" units of functionality that power users can put together to make SharePoint sites and applications. SharePoint includes a Silverlight Web Part out-of-the-box. The Silverlight Web Part is as easy to use as setting the path to the Silverlight application. Let's go ahead and add the Silverlight Web Part to the home page of your site:

1. Put the page in edit mode by clicking Edit Page from the Site Actions menu in the upper left of your site.

2. Insert the Silverlight Web Part. Once the page is in edit mode, you will see the Editing Tools context ribbon tab. Display the Insert tab of the Editing Tools tab, and then click the Web Part button in the Web Parts group.

3. In the Categories section of the Insert Web Part gallery, select Media and Content. Then click Silverlight Web Part in the Web Parts list. Click Add to insert the Silverlight Web Part.

4. Enter the URL to the Silverlight application. When you click the Add button, you are prompted with a dialog to enter the URL to the Silverlight application. This is the path to the `.xap` file that you uploaded to the Shared Documents library. It should be something like `/Shared Documents/WeatherWidget.xap`.

5. Save the Page. Click the Save & Close button of the Edit group of the Page ribbon tab to save the page. You could also adjust other properties of the Web Part as well, such as the height and width, title, and others.

After you have added the Weather Silverlight application to the page, it will call out to the weather web service to retrieve the current weather conditions. Figure 14-6 shows an accurate and real weather forecast for Redmond, Washington.

The SharePoint team has done a good job of making it very easy for nondevelopers to add Silverlight functionality to any SharePoint site. But how do professional developers and designers add Silverlight applications using Visual Studio and Expression Blend? How do you follow proper application lifecycle management (ALM), such as source control. How do you follow SharePoint best practices, such as packing all SharePoint applications into SharePoint packages? In the next section, you will learn how to follow all these coding practices using Visual Studio and Expression Blend.

FIGURE 14-6

Visual Studio and Expression Blend

The biggest change for SharePoint 2010 is the availability of tools in Visual Studio 2010. SharePoint is a great platform now, with great tools to support it. In the past, you may have used a number of different tools and scripts to develop your SharePoint solutions, and most likely these were not Microsoft tools but community tools on sites such as CodePlex. All that has changed now. Now the SharePoint tools in Visual Studio are so good and extensible that you will rarely find occasion to develop outside of Visual Studio. That said, a few scenarios are not covered by the current release. The Visual Studio team knew that with the breadth of SharePoint they would not be able to cover everything right away. Taking this into account, they made it easy to extend the tools and add functionality. Later in this chapter, you will see some of the tools that my team has created to make Silverlight development even easier.

CREATING A SILVERLIGHT WEB PART

Earlier, you saw how easy it is to add a Silverlight application to the page using just the web browser, without writing any code. Now let's examine how to accomplish the same task using Visual Studio. Remember that you are trying to solve two problems. The first is how to get the

Silverlight .xap file deployed to SharePoint. The second is how to host the Silverlight application. Before delving into the details of how to do this, let's talk about the high-level process. For this solution, we will need two projects:

➤ **The Silverlight project** — This is just a standard Silverlight project and can be created with Visual Studio or Expression Blend.

➤ **The SharePoint project** — The SharePoint project will link to the Silverlight project and will deploy both the Silverlight application and the Web Part.

Adding a Silverlight Project

For this example, you are going to use one of the sample applications that ships with Expression Blend. Open Expression Blend and select the Contacts project from the Samples tab. Save a copy of the application under a new name by clicking Save Copy of Project under the File menu (in this case, **ContactsInSilverlight**). You should see something similar to Figure 14-7.

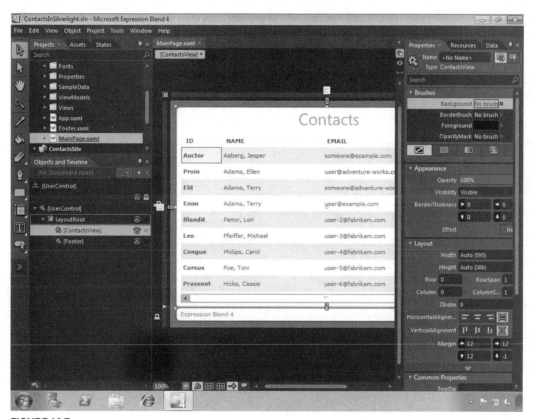

FIGURE 14-7

You can press F5 to compile and run the application. It is also a good practice to verify everything is working before moving on to the next step. You may get a warning that the application does not have a startup scene. This is because the sample contains projects: the Silverlight application and the web project that hosts the test page. To fix this error, click Startup from the right-click context menu of the `default.html` file in the web project. (Because you will be using SharePoint to host and test your Silverlight application, this test web project is not needed. You will delete the web project in the next section.) Figure 14-8 shows the application running in the test web server that Expression Blend creates.

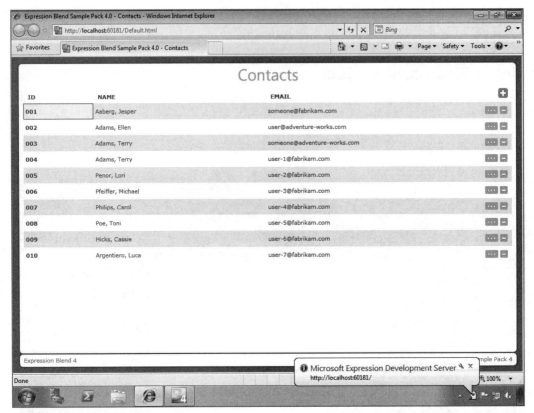

FIGURE 14-8

Next you add a SharePoint project to link to this Silverlight application.

Adding a SharePoint Project

Up to this point, you have not really done anything with SharePoint. But you can imagine that this is the step where you have been handed a Silverlight project from a designer, and now you must deploy the application to SharePoint and host the application in a Web Part. First you will add a SharePoint project to the solution:

1. Open the solution in Visual Studio. Right-click the solutions node in the Project tab panel in Expression Blend, and from the solution context menu, click Edit in Visual Studio.

Note that there are actually a couple of small bugs in the sample application that Visual Studio catches but Expression Blend does not. In the `ContactsViewSampleDataModel.xaml` file, there are actually two records with the `Name="Adams, Terry"`. To fix this, delete the `Contacts_ViewModels:ContactViewModel` node that this duplicate record is in or change the `Name` property to something unique. Also there is a missing assembly reference. Add a reference to `System.Windows.Controls.Data.Input`.

Figure 14-9 shows the Silverlight applications looks the same in the Visual Studio designer.

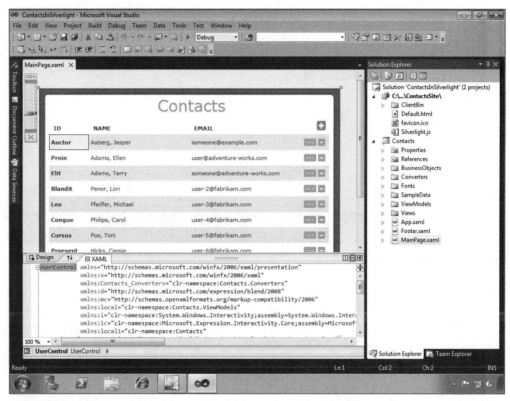

FIGURE 14-9

2. Delete the web project. You will be using SharePoint as the Silverlight host, so you will not need the web project that was included as part of the sample. Right-click the web project and click Remove. Click OK to verify.

3. Add a blank SharePoint project. Right-click the solution node in the Solution Explorer and click Add ➪ New ➪ Project from the context menu. Click the SharePoint node in the New Project dialog. Visual Studio ships with a number of SharePoint project templates. You can see the complete list in Figure 14-10. Name the project **ContactsSharePointProject**. Click OK to create the project.

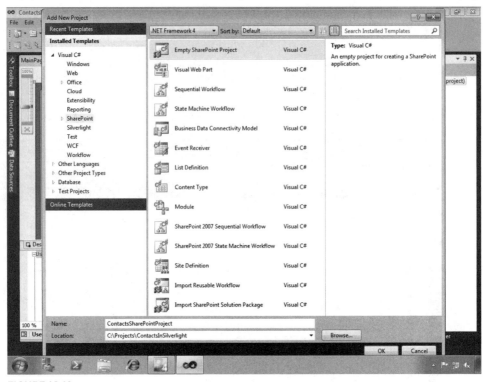

FIGURE 14-10

 SharePoint projects require Visual Studio to run with elevated permissions. If you are prompted, click Restart under different credentials to restart Visual Studio with administrator rights.

4. Specify the site and security level. When creating SharePoint projects, Visual Studio uses a wizard to set the URL to the SharePoint site and asks if this is a farm solution (full trust) or a sandboxed solution. Sandboxed solutions are the default. Silverlight applications can run in sandboxed solutions, and doing so is the best practice for deploying to SharePoint. Enter the site (in this case, use **http://intranet.contoso.com**). You should also click the Validate button to verify that the path is correct and everything is set up correctly on the SharePoint site. Click Finish to actually create the Empty SharePoint project.

Linking to the Silverlight Project

You now have a Visual Studio solution with two projects: SharePoint and Silverlight. The next task is to deploy the Silverlight application to SharePoint. The way that you deploy files to SharePoint is using modules. Let's go ahead and add a new module to deploy your Silverlight .xap file and a reference to the Silverlight project, so that when you build the SharePoint project, the Silverlight project will also build, and an updated copy of the Silverlight .xap file will be included in the SharePoint solution file, which is a .wsp file:

1. Add a new Module project item. Right-click the SharePoint project and choose Add ➪ New Item from the context menu. Visual Studio ships with 14 SharePoint 2010 project templates, as shown in Figure 14-11. Select Module and name it **SilverlightModule**. Click Add to create the module.

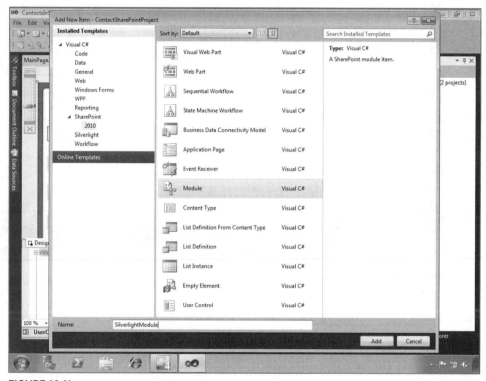

FIGURE 14-11

2. Delete the Sample.txt file. When you create a new module, Visual Studio creates a SharePoint project item that includes an Elements.xml file and a sample file called Sample.txt. You do not need this file, so you can delete it.

3. Add a reference to the Silverlight project. Normally when you add a reference to another project in Visual Studio, it adds a reference to the output of that project, which is typically the .dll. For Silverlight projects, however, you want a reference to the .xap file. View the Properties window of the SilverlightModule node in your project. You can add a reference to the Silverlight project by adding it to the Project Output References collection. Click the ellipse in the Project Output References property to set the reference. In the Project Output References dialog, click Add to a new reference, as shown in Figure 14-12. In the Project Name property, choose your Silverlight project from the drop-down list (in this case, Contacts). Set the Deployment Type property to Element File. Click OK to add the reference.

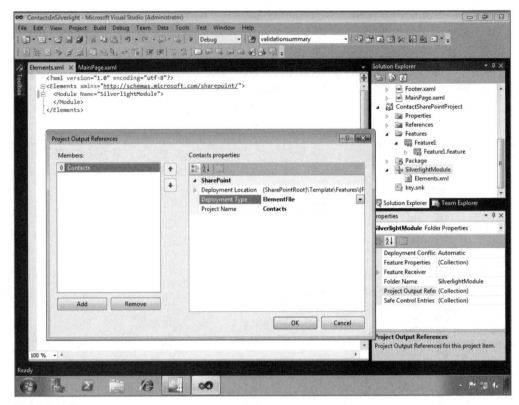

FIGURE 14-12

4. Set the deployment location. Now that you have referenced the Silverlight application, you need to specify where it will be deployed to within your SharePoint site. You specify this in the Elements.xml file. In the Elements.xml, the File node has two properties: Path and Url. The Path property is the relative reference to the file within the SharePoint package file, so normally you should not change this. The Url property is the path where the file should be deployed to on the SharePoint site. Set the Url to _catalogs/masterpage/ SilverlightModule/Contacts.xap. This will deploy the .xap file to the master page gallery library and create a folder called SilverlightModule:

```xml
<?xml version="1.0" encoding="utf-8"?>
<Elements xmlns="http://schemas.microsoft.com/sharepoint/">
  <Module Name="SilverlightModule">
  <File Path="SilverlightModule\Contacts.xap"
        Url="_catalogs/masterpage/SilverlightModule/Contacts.xap" />
  </Module>
</Elements>
```

Now you are ready to deploy your Silverlight application file to SharePoint. Set the SharePoint project as the startup project and press F5. SharePoint will build both projects, create the

SharePoint package file, deploy it to the sandboxed solution gallery, activate the solution, open the SharePoint site, and attach the debugger. Once the site opens, browse to the master page gallery at `http://intranet.contoso.com/_catalogs/masterpage`. You should see a folder called `SilverlightModule`. Open the `SilverlightModule` and verify that the `Contacts.xap` file is there. This step has been the programmatic equivalent of manually adding the `.xap` file to the Shared Documents library that you did earlier in this chapter. You could now go to the home page and manually add the Silverlight Web Part to display this application, but in the next section, you will learn how to automate this process in your Visual Studio solution.

Adding a Silverlight Web Part

You just completed the first step of deploying the Silverlight `.xap` file. Now you will complete the second step, which is to host the Silverlight application. There are a number of different approaches that you could take depending on your specific needs. You could just create a new page to host the Silverlight application just as you would in any ASP.NET website. The more common approach is to create a Web Part to host the application. This is what you are going to do in this sample. There are also a number of different ways to create the Web Part. You could create your own Web Part from scratch and add all the code to correctly render the Silverlight control within the Web Part. Although this gives you the most flexibility, it also requires the most work. What I think is a better approach and covers the most common scenarios is to leverage the existing built-in Silverlight Web Part provided by SharePoint. Let's add a Silverlight Web Part to your SharePoint project:

1. Add a Web Part. Although there are no specific project item templates out-of-the-box for a Silverlight Web Part, you can use the normal Web Part template as a starting point. Right-click the SharePoint project and click Add ➪ New Item from the context menu. Select Web Part (not the Visual Web Part) from the list of SharePoint 2010 project item templates. Name the Web Part **SilverlightWebpart**. Click Add to add the Web Part to the project.

2. Remove Custom Web Part. When you create a new Web Part, SharePoint adds a new SharePoint project item to your project that consists of three files. The first file is the `Elements.xml` file. This is used to define the location of the Web Part and the group name that it should be placed in. You will need this file, so don't delete it. The next two files are the actual Web Parts. Remember that a Web Part consists of two pieces: the actual code and an XML manifest file. Because you are going to use the built-in Silverlight Web Part, you can delete the code file: `SilverlightWebPart.cs`.

3. Add the Silverlight Web Part. You are going to use the Silverlight Web Part that ships with SharePoint so that the code side of the Web Part is already deployed. Replace the contents of the file `SilverlightWebpart.webpart` with the following:

```
<webParts>
  <webPart xmlns="http://schemas.microsoft.com/WebPart/v3">
    <metaData>
      <type name="Microsoft.SharePoint.WebPartPages.SilverlightWebPart,
          Microsoft.SharePoint, Version=14.0.0.0, Culture=neutral,
          PublicKeyToken=71e9bce111e9429c" />
      <importErrorMessage>
```

```
            Cannot import this Web Part.
        </importErrorMessage>
    </metaData>
    <data>
      <properties>
        <property name="HelpUrl" type="string" />
        <property name="AllowClose" type="bool">True</property>
        <property name="ExportMode" type="exportmode">All</property>
        <property name="Hidden" type="bool">False</property>
        <property name="AllowEdit" type="bool">True</property>
        <property name="Direction" type="direction">NotSet</property>
        <property name="TitleIconImageUrl" type="string" />
        <property name="AllowConnect" type="bool">True</property>
        <property name="HelpMode" type="helpmode">Modal</property>
        <property name="CustomProperties" type="string" null="true" />
        <property name="AllowHide" type="bool">True</property>
        <property name="Description" type="string">
          Contact Silverlight Web Part</property>
        <property name="CatalogIconImageUrl" type="string" />
        <property name="MinRuntimeVersion" type="string" null="true" />
        <property name="ApplicationXml" type="string" />
        <property name="AllowMinimize" type="bool">True</property>
        <property name="AllowZoneChange" type="bool">True</property>
        <property name="CustomInitParameters" type="string" null="true" />
        <property name="Height" type="unit">436px</property>
        <property name="ChromeType" type="chrometype">None</property>
        <property name="Width" type="unit">619px</property>
        <property name="Title" type="string">Contact Silverlight Demo</property>
        <property name="ChromeState" type="chromestate">Normal</property>
        <property name="TitleUrl" type="string" />
        <property name="Url" type="string">
          ~site/_catalogs/masterpage/SilverlightModule/Contacts.xap
        </property>
        <property name="WindowlessMode" type="bool">True</property>
      </properties>
    </data>
  </webPart>
</webParts>
```

The `.webpart` has two sections. The first section defines the code for the Web Part. In this case, it references the built in Silverlight Web Part in the `Microsoft.SharePoint.dll`. The second section defines all the properties supported by the Web Part. You need to change only a few. The most important is the `Url` that references the Silverlight `.xap` file. Set this to `~site/_catalogs/masterpage/SilverlightModule/Contacts.xap`. Note that this uses a special SharePoint variable called `~site` to refer to the current site that the Web Part is hosted in. The other properties that you should set are `Title`, `Description`, `Height`, and `Width`.

You now are done with your solution. It should look something like Figure 14-13. All that is left to do is deploy and test the solution.

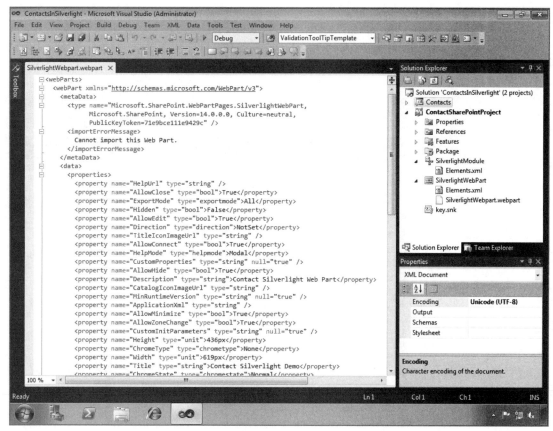

FIGURE 14-13

Deploying Silverlight to SharePoint

The solution you created is ready to deploy. Press F5 to deploy the SharePoint solution to the sand-boxed solution gallery. Doing so will deploy the Silverlight .xap file and the Silverlight Web Part. This solution does not contain a page to test the Web Part. To add a page manually, follow these steps:

1. When the site opens, create a new site page called **Contacts**.

2. With the page in Edit Mode, Click Insert ➪ Web Part from the Editing Tools tab on the ribbon.

3. In the Insert Web Parts panel, select Custom in the Categories column, click Contact Silverlight Demo, and then Click Add.

   You can see that your custom Silverlight Web Part shows up just like any other Web Part in the Web Part gallery. Unlike when you added the Silverlight Web Part earlier in this chapter, you are not prompted to enter a URL to the Silverlight application because you already defined it when you created the `.webpart` file.

4. Save the page to exit edit mode. Figure 14-14 shows your Silverlight application running in SharePoint.

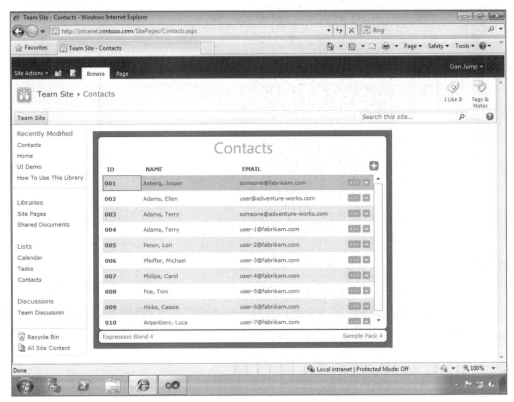

FIGURE 14-14

Now that you have everything working, let's take a quick look at how to debug these types of applications.

Debugging Silverlight Applications

Debugging Silverlight applications in SharePoint is actually very easy and straightforward. First, set your breakpoints in the Silverlight application just as you would do with any Visual Studio application. Then, enable Silverlight debugging in the SharePoint project. Right-click the SharePoint project and click Properties from the context menu. Display the SharePoint tab in the project Properties window. Now scroll down to enable Silverlight debugging (not Script debugging), as shown in Figure 14-15.

Press F5 to run the project. When the site opens, browse to the Contacts page you previously created. You will see that Visual Studio breaks on your breakpoint inside the Silverlight application, as expected.

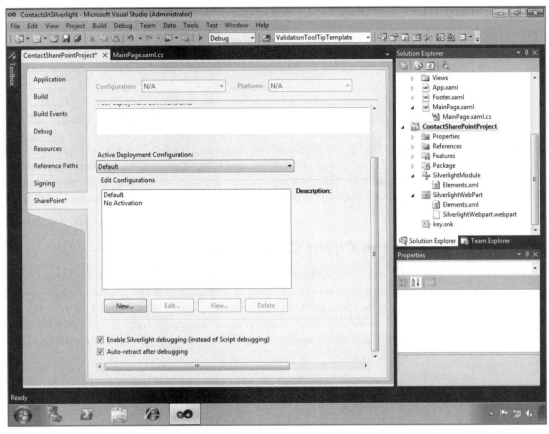

FIGURE 14-15

THE CLIENT OBJECT MODEL

Up to this point, you have learned how to create a SharePoint project to deploy your Silverlight applications. But SharePoint is just hosting the Silverlight application. The application is not really leveraging the SharePoint platform for things such as data. This is the real value of hosting Silverlight inside of SharePoint: leveraging all the data and services that make up the SharePoint platform. You learned in Chapter 13 how to call the Client Object Model using JavaScript; now you will learn how to leverage the Client Object Model from Silverlight.

In this section, you learn how to hook up your Contacts application to real SharePoint data using the Client Object Model. The Client Object Model is a new API for SharePoint that enables client applications to efficiently and easily program against the SharePoint server. There are three versions of the Client Object Model: EcmaScript, .NET CLR, and Silverlight. They all are very consistent; after learning one, you should be able to program them all. Although it is beyond the scope of this chapter to teach you everything about the Client Object Model, I will show you how to get started and pull data from SharePoint.

Referencing the Client Object Model

The Silverlight Client Object Model is contained in the following two assemblies:

➤ `Microsoft.SharePoint.Client.Silverlight.dll`

➤ `Microsoft.SharePoint.Client.Silverlight.Runtime.dll`.

Add a reference to these assemblies in your Silverlight project using the standard Visual Studio Add Reference dialog. They are located in the `C:\Program Files\Common Files\Microsoft Shared\ Web Server Extensions\14\TEMPLATE\LAYOUTS\ClientBin` folder. These will be added to you Silverlight `.xap` file. This is not the best practice because it increases the size of your applications and increases the download times. These files are relatively small, 407 KB total. It is not a huge hit, but every little bit helps. Later, you will see how to decouple these from your solution and dynamically load them at runtime.

Reading Lists with the Client Object Model

The Contacts application uses the Sample Data features of Expression Blend and Visual Studio to render data into the designer while you are creating the application. It also switches when running to pull data from a different location. In this case, the data is hard-coded into the application. You can see this switch in the `ContactsViewModel` constructor. This code checks to see whether the app is running in a design tool. If it is not, you want to load the real data, not the sample data (which is defined in the XAML for the page):

```
if(!DesignerProperties.IsInDesignTool)
{
        this.PopulateContacts();
}
```

For this application, you can replace the `PopulateContacts` method with your own implementation. In this case, we will actually get the data from SharePoint using the Client Object Model:

1. Add a `using` statement for the Client Object Model. Edit the `ContactsViewModel.cs` file and add this code to the top of the page:

   ```
   using Microsoft.SharePoint.Client;
   ```

2. Add class variables. The Silverlight Client Object Model is an asynchronous API. You will need to define a couple of variables to track references across method calls. Add the following variables to the `ContactsViewModel` class:

   ```
   public class ContactsViewModel : INotifyPropertyChanged
   {
     ClientContext ctx;
     ListItemCollection contactsListItems;
   ...
   ```

3. Get the list data from SharePoint. In the `PopulateContacts` method of the class, you need to get a reference to the current client context. Then you need to specify which list you want returned and which items in the list you want returned. And finally you need to load the

query on the client context and execute it on the SharePoint server. The `ExecuteQueryAsync` method executes all the queries that have been loaded onto the client context asynchronously. Once the SharePoint server is finished, it calls back on one of the two callback methods passed depending on whether the request succeeded or failed. Add the follow code to the `ContactsViewModel.cs` file to get the list data from SharePoint:

```
private void PopulateContacts()
{
    //Get Data from SharePoint using the Client Object Model

    //Get a reference to the current client context
    ctx = ClientContext.Current;

    //Specify the List and Listitems to return
    List contactsList = ctx.Web.Lists.GetByTitle("Contacts");
    contactsListItems =
        contactsList.GetItems(CamlQuery.CreateAllItemsQuery());

    //Add query to context and execute it on the server
    ctx.Load(contactsListItems);
    ctx.ExecuteQueryAsync(ContactsLoaded, ContactsLoadedFail);
}
```

Figure 14-16 shows what the Contacts list looks like in SharePoint. This is just a normal SharePoint list that I created using sample data from the AdventureWorks database.

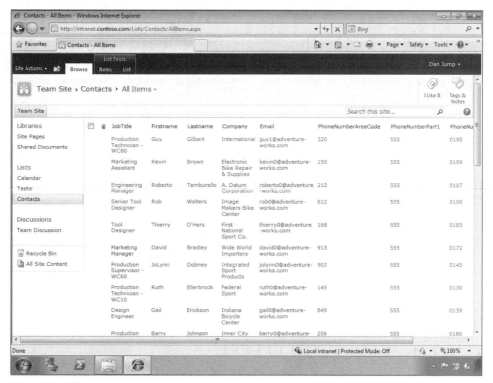

FIGURE 14-16

4. Handle the failed callback. In the `ExecuteQueryAsync` method, one of the parameters is the failed callback method. In this example, you will implement a handler that doesn't actually do anything. I normally use this during development as a place to set a breakpoint, but in a production application you would want to take the appropriate action, such as writing to the event log. The callback contains a `ClientRequestFailedEventArgs` parameter. This contains details about the error (for example, error code, error details, the error message, and even stack trace information). Add the following code to the `ContactsViewModel.cs` to handle the failed callback:

```
void ContactsLoadedFail(object sender,
ClientRequestFailedEventArgs args)
{
    string error = args.Message;
}
```

5. Load the Contacts collection. In the succeeded callback method, you can iterate through the `contactsListItems` collection, which was populated when you executed the query on the server. For this example, you are creating new `ContactViewModel` objects and adding them to the Contacts collection. Most of the code in this is just mapping and formatting the values returned from SharePoint into values expected by the application's object model. I also formatted some of the data to match the format of the sample data (for example, padding the Id field with leading zeros). Also because my sample Contacts list in SharePoint didn't have all the fields used in the sample application, I concatenated different fields together using `string.Format` and even had to use a regular expression to strip out special characters from the company names. The last important thing to talk about with this code is about threading. Silverlight executes the calls to SharePoint on a background thread. Therefore, if you want to do something to the UI, such as update the contacts, you must do this on the UI thread. To get back on the UI thread, you need to wrap your code in a `Dispatcher.BeginInvoke` method. Everything inside of the `BeginInvoke` will run on the UI thread:

```
void ContactsLoaded(object sender, ClientRequestSucceededEventArgs args)
{
    foreach (ListItem ci in contactsListItems)
    {
        ContactViewModel cvm = new ContactViewModel();
        cvm.Id = ci.Id.ToString("D3"); //pad with leading zeros
        cvm.Name = string.Format("{0}, {1}",
            ci.FieldValues["Lastname"].ToString(),
            ci.FieldValues["Title"].ToString());
        cvm.Email = ci.FieldValues["Email"].ToString();
        cvm.Phone.Number = string.Format("{0}-{1}-{2}",
            ci.FieldValues["PhoneNumberAreaCode"].ToString(),
            ci.FieldValues["PhoneNumberPart1"].ToString(),
            ci.FieldValues["PhoneNumberPart2"].ToString());
        //need to strip out non alphanumeric chars for validation
        Regex regEx = new Regex("\\W|[0-9]");

        cvm.Blog.Address = string.Format("http://blogs.{0}.com/{1}{2}",
            regEx.Replace(ci.FieldValues["Company"].ToString(),""),
            ci.FieldValues["Title"].ToString(),
            ci.FieldValues["Lastname"].ToString());
        cvm.Website.Address = string.Format("http://www.{0}.com",
```

```
            regEx.Replace(ci.FieldValues["Company"].ToString(),""));

    //call back on the UI thread
    System.Windows.Deployment.Current.Dispatcher.BeginInvoke(() =>
    {
        Contacts.Add(cvm);
    });
}
```

That is all the code required to connect your application to live SharePoint list data. Press F5 to run the application. When the site opens, browse to the Contacts page that you created earlier. There is no need to change anything on the page. SharePoint will load the page using the new version of the Silverlight application that you just built. This is very convenient while developing because you need to set up the page in SharePoint only once and can then focus on the Silverlight code. You should now see the list data in your application as shown in Figure 14-17.

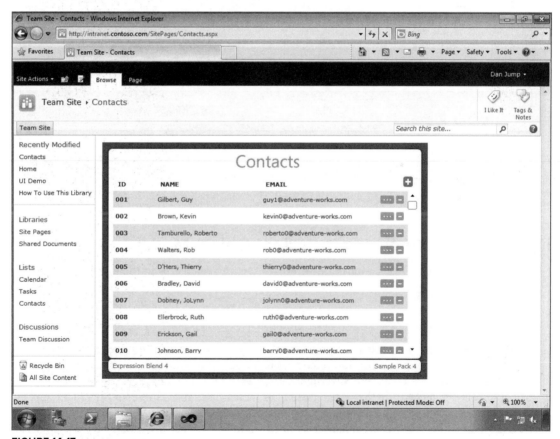

FIGURE 14-17

This example also has a details page, which you can see when you click the ellipse for any given record (see Figure 14-18).

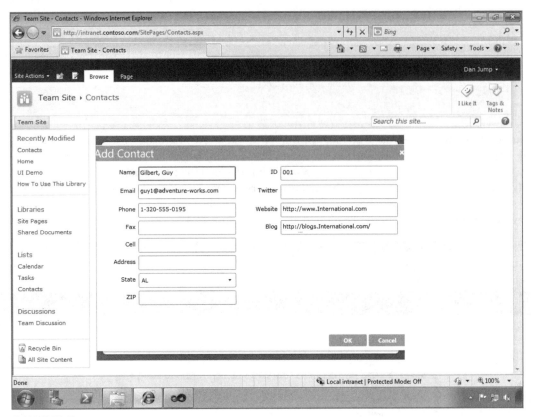

FIGURE 14-18

Dynamically Referencing the Client Object Model

The SharePoint Client Object Model for Silverlight requires references to the following assemblies:

➤ `Microsoft.SharePoint.Client.Silverlight.dll`

➤ `Microsoft.SharePoint.Client.Silverlight.Runtime.dll`

Earlier in the chapter, you added a reference to these assemblies using the standard Visual Studio Add Reference dialog. When you add references in Visual Studio, the referenced assemblies are, by default, copied and packaged into Silverlight `.xap` files. This is not a best practice for the Silverlight Client Object Model because the added assemblies increase the size of all your Silverlight applications by 407KB. There are also maintenance issues. What happens if or when Microsoft updates these files? How do you plan to update the embedded files? Another benefit is that the browser will cache this `.xap` file just as it would any other file based on the cache policies that are set. Therefore, the `.xap` file will be stored in the browser's cache location and subject to the user's actions, meaning if the user clears the browser cache, the `.xap` will be downloaded again on the next request. The best practice is to dynamically load the assemblies at runtime. Doing so solves all the problems associated with embedding them in your `.xap` files.

In addition to the `Microsoft.SharePoint.Client.Silverlight.dll` and `Microsoft` `.SharePoint.Client.Silverlight.Runtime.dll` files, SharePoint ships with a prebuilt `.xap` called `Microsoft.SharePoint.Client.xap`. This `.xap` file is located in the same folder as the other Silverlight Client Object Model files: `C:\Program Files\Common Files\Microsoft Shared\Web Server Extensions\14\TEMPLATE\LAYOUTS\ClientBin`. The `Microsoft.SharePoint.Client` `.xap` contains copies of the `Microsoft.SharePoint.Client.Silverlight.dll` and `Microsoft` `.SharePoint.Client.Silverlight.Runtime.dll` files. You need to add only a small amount of code to your Silverlight applications to dynamically load this application at runtime. Let's look at what is needed to convert your Silverlight Contacts application from using the statically referenced Client Object Model to the dynamic one:

1. Stop Visual Studio from embedding the Client Object Model assemblies. In the Solution Explorer, expand the References node and click the `Microsoft.SharePoint.Client` `.Silverlight` node. In the Properties window, change the Copy Local property to False. Do this also for the `Microsoft.SharePoint.Client.Silverlight.Runtime` node. This will stop Visual Studio from adding these files to your `.xap` package file. You still need to have a reference to these files for design-time support, such as IntelliSense, and compile support.

2. Call a method to load assemblies at runtime. You could actually optimize this step based on your application needs, but at some point before you use them, you must load the assemblies from the SharePoint server. In this example, you will replace the direct call to `PopulateContacts` with the call to load the Silverlight Client Object Model, first passing in the callback to the `PopulateContacts` method. Change the code in the `ContactsViewModel` constructor to look like the following code:

```
if (!DesignerProperties.IsInDesignTool)
{
    //PopulateContacts();
    LoadClientOM loadClientOM =
    new LoadClientOM(delegate() { PopulateContacts(); });
}
```

3. Create a class to dynamically load the Silverlight Client Object Model. You need to create a class called `LoadClientOM`. Right-click the Silverlight project and choose Add ➪ Class and name the class **LoadClientOM.cs**. This class will be responsible for dynamically loading the Client Object Model. This code is generic and can be used in any of your Silverlight applications unchanged. You might consider refactoring this into a separate reusable assembly. To keep the example as simple as possible, just add a class file to your project. Add the following code to the `LoadClientOM.cs` file you just created:

```
using System;
using System.Net;
using System.Windows;
using System.Windows.Controls;
using System.Windows.Documents;
using System.Windows.Ink;
using System.Windows.Input;
using System.Windows.Media;
using System.Windows.Media.Animation;
using System.Windows.Shapes;
using System.IO;
using System.Reflection;
```

```
using System.Windows.Resources;

namespace Contacts
{
    public class LoadClientOM
    {
        private Action action;

        public LoadClientOM(Action action)
        {
            this.action = action;
            WebClient client = new WebClient();
            client.OpenReadCompleted +=
            new OpenReadCompletedEventHandler(ReadCompleted);
            client.OpenReadAsync
            (new Uri("/_layouts/clientbin/Microsoft.SharePoint.Client.xap",
UriKind.Relative));
        }

        void ReadCompleted(object sender, OpenReadCompletedEventArgs e)
        {
            Stream assemblyStream;
            AssemblyPart assemblyPart;

            assemblyStream = Application.GetResourceStream(new
StreamResourceInfo(e.Result, "application/binary"),
new Uri("Microsoft.SharePoint.Client.Silverlight.Runtime.dll",
UriKind.Relative)).Stream;
            assemblyPart = new AssemblyPart();
            Assembly b = assemblyPart.Load(assemblyStream);

            assemblyStream = Application.GetResourceStream(new
StreamResourceInfo(e.Result, "application/binary"),
new Uri("Microsoft.SharePoint.Client.Silverlight.dll", UriKind.Relative)).Stream;
            assemblyPart = new AssemblyPart();
            Assembly a = assemblyPart.Load(assemblyStream);

            //Call back on the passed delegate
            if (action != null)
            {
                action();
            }
        }
    }
}
```

The `LoadClientOM` constructor takes one parameter, the callback method to call after the assemblies have been loaded. Next, the constructor uses the `WebClient` class to download the `Microsoft.SharePoint.Client.xap` asynchronously from the `clientbin` folder of the current site where the Silverlight application is running. Once the download is complete, the `ReadCompleted` method is called. The `ReadCompleted` method extracts and loads the assemblies from the Silverlight .xap package file. After the assemblies have been loaded, the callback action delete is called if specified. In this example, the callback method is the `PopulateContacts` method.

That is all you need to convert the application to dynamically load the Silverlight Client Object Model. You can run the project and see that the application does not look any different.

SHAREPOINT 2010 EXTENSIBILITY PROJECTS

You have seen how to integrate and build a Silverlight Web Part for SharePoint from beginning to end. Although doing so involves a number of steps, once you do it a couple of times and get your head around it, it's not too bad. But it would be better if there were an actual Silverlight project template to build a Silverlight Web Part. Fortunately, Visual Studio is highly extensible, making it easy to build in functionality that may be missing. That is exactly what my team has done; we built a few new extensibility features into Visual Studio, including a Silverlight Web Part. You can download the SharePoint 2010 Extensibility Project from MSDN Code Gallery at `http://code.msdn.microsoft.com/vsixforsp`. The project contains three templates: Silverlight and Sharepoint project template, Sharepoint ribbon project template, and OBA Deployment project template. You should look at the other templates, as well, but for now the one you should download is the Silverlight and SharePoint project template.

Installing the Visual Studio Extension

Install the Silverlight Web Part Visual Studio project template by running the Silverlight Web Part `.vsix` file you downloaded from the MSDN Code Gallery. After installing the Silverlight extension, you can verify its installation by clicking Tools ⇨ Extension Manager from the main menu in Visual Studio. You can also disable or remove the extension from the Extension Manager dialog, as shown in Figure 14-19.

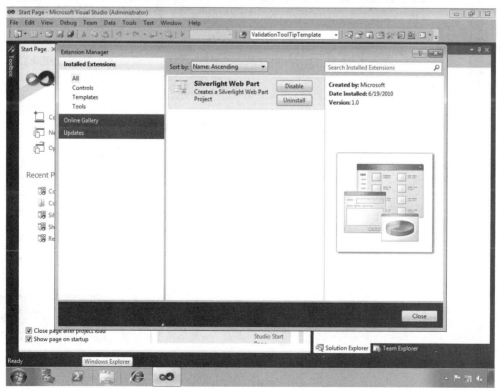

FIGURE 14-19

Creating a Silverlight Web Part Using a Visual Studio Extension Project

Once you have the Silverlight Web Part extension installed, creating a new Silverlight Web Part is as easy as creating any other Visual Studio project:

1. Open Visual Studio and open the New Project dialog. Select the SharePoint-2010 node on the left. Scroll down and select the Silverlight Web Part template. This is a new project template that was added when you installed the extensibility project. Click OK to start the New Project Wizard.

2. The first page of the New Project Wizard looks just like any SharePoint New Project Wizard. You must enter the path for the SharePoint server. In this case, enter **http://intranet.contoso. com** and click Next.

3. Enter information about the project. On this page, you enter the name to give to the Silverlight project and the title and description of the Web Part. You also specify where to deploy the Silverlight `.xap` file. In this example, I chose the Site Assets library as the deployment location, as shown in Figure 14-20. Enter the wizard values and click Finish to generate the project files.

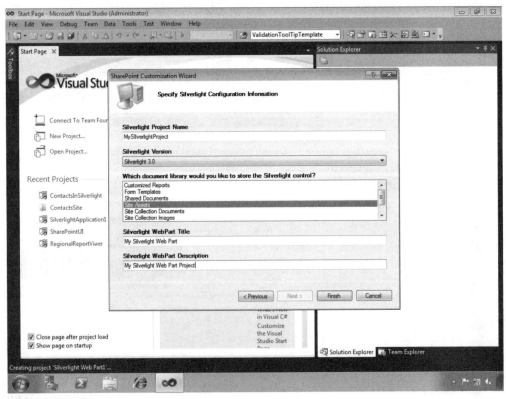

FIGURE 14-20

When the wizard completes, it creates a solution with two projects, just like you did manually earlier in the chapter. Although it is beyond the scope of this chapter to go into detail about the implementation, there are a few things to point out. First, note that this Silverlight Web Part generates the Silverlight control from scratch and does not use the built-in Silverlight Web Part. So, examining the generated code is a good learning tool for creating more advanced Silverlight Web Parts. Second, the Silverlight project that the wizard generates contains code that uses the Silverlight Client Object Model to create a list of all the SharePoint lists. To enable this sample code, open the MainPage .xaml.cs file, press Ctrl+A to select all the code, and click the Uncomment button on the toolbar (or press Ctrl+K,U). The project is ready to run. Press F5 to run the project. Once the site opens, put the page in edit mode and insert a new Web Part. By default, the Web Part will be under the Custom category on the Web Part gallery dialog. Save the page and you will see a Silverlight application listing all the SharePoint lists with an item count, as shown in Figure 14-21.

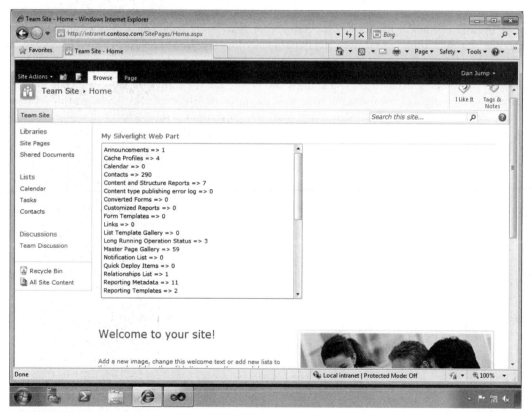

FIGURE 14-21

The Silverlight VSIX extensibility project is a great learning tool for beginners to get up to speed quickly with building Silverlight applications for SharePoint. It also is a great tool for experts to rapidly develop Silverlight applications.

SUMMARY

This chapter described how to build a simple Silverlight Web Part for SharePoint and how to access SharePoint data using the Client Object Model. It's important to remember that with Silverlight development on SharePoint, you are solving two fundamental problems: how to get the Silverlight application into SharePoint, and how to host and display the Silverlight application. You saw that there are a number of ways to solve the first problem, from simply copying the .xap file to a document library to having it completely automated as part of your solution. You also learned that there are a few ways to host Silverlight applications in SharePoint, from using the built-in Silverlight Web Part to completely building your own Silverlight Web Part. You also saw an example of how Visual Studio can be extended to make completing complex tasks easier, such as creating Silverlight solutions.

A third problem to solve is how to interact with SharePoint and SharePoint data. You learned how to use the SharePoint Client Object Model to access SharePoint data. You also saw how you could optimize your Silverlight applications by dynamically loading the SharePoint Client Object Model.

There is so much to learn about SharePoint and Silverlight development, and this chapter covered only the most basic aspects to get you started and pointed in the right direction. With the incredibly fast pace of Silverlight innovations and the rapid adoption of Silverlight across the world, coupled with the power and depth of the SharePoint platform, Silverlight is the perfect technology for building rich collaborative business applications for the enterprise and the Internet.

INDEX